A note about the cover

Is everything *really* an argument? Seeing the images on the cover might make you wonder. The protests from the Arab Spring of 2011, for example, instantly call to mind the very public unrest across Egypt and the Middle East. But what does an image of a beauty pageant tiara say about a person who covets one? How does a smartphone argue for or against the ways that technology is shaping how we communicate with one another? The "99%" sign from an Occupy movement protest, familiar to many who have followed recent political debate, invites you to think about how policy conversations take place, as well as about how demographic information and self-identification shape the American public. And as for the hybrid car and its plug, what's your best call? A plea for us to be more responsible energy consumers? Imposed limits on the freedom that automobiles have afforded us? What's your take?

everything's an argument

Sixth Edition

EVERYTHING'S AN argument

Andrea A. Lunsford
STANFORD UNIVERSITY

John J. Ruszkiewicz
UNIVERSITY OF TEXAS AT AUSTIN

BEDFORD / ST. MARTIN'S
Boston ◆ New York

For Bedford/St. Martin's

Senior Developmental Editor: Adam Whitehurst
Senior Production Editor: Ryan Sullivan
Senior Production Supervisor: Dennis Conroy
Executive Marketing Manager: Molly Parke
Editorial Assistant: Nicholas McCarthy
Copy Editor: Steven Patterson
Indexer: Melanie Belkin
Photo Researcher: Julie Tesser
Permissions Manager: Kalina K. Ingham
Art Director: Lucy Krikorian
Text Design: Anna Palchik and Graphic World Inc.
Cover Design: Billy Boardman
Cover Photos: (top to bottom) © Mohammed Huwais/AFP/Getty Images; © Bernhard Lang/Getty Images; © Karen Bleier/AFP/Getty Images; © Fry Design Ltd/Getty Images; © The Image Bank/Getty Images
Composition: Graphic World Inc.
Printing and Binding: RR Donnelley and Sons

President, Bedford/St. Martin's: Denise B. Wydra
Presidents, Macmillan Higher Education: Joan E. Feinberg and Tom Scotty
Editor in Chief: Karen S. Henry
Director of Development: Erica T. Appel
Director of Marketing: Karen R. Soeltz
Production Director: Susan W. Brown
Associate Production Director: Elise S. Kaiser
Managing Editor: Shuli Traub

For information, write: Bedford/St. Martin's, 75 Arlington Street, Boston, MA 02116   (617-399-4000)

ISBN 978-1-4576-0606-9

Acknowledgments

Acknowledgments and copyrights appear at the back of the book on pages 487–91, which constitute an extension of the copyright page. It is a violation of the law to reproduce these selections by any means whatsoever without the written permission of the copyright holder.

PREFACE

When the first edition of *Everything's an Argument* appeared more than a decade ago, college writing courses that focused on critical reasoning and persuasion were typically second-semester or optional upper-division offerings. Today, influenced by a growing concern that students in college should know how to analyze and make effective arguments, and, perhaps, by the success of *Everything's an Argument* itself, even introductory college writing classes have now adopted the core tenets of this book, summed up by the purposefully controversial title of the text. First, language provides the most powerful means of understanding the world and of using that understanding to help shape lives. Second, arguments seldom if ever have only two sides; rather, they present a dizzying array of perspectives, often with as many "takes" on a subject as there are arguers. As a result, arguments are always in response to other arguments, part of an ongoing conversation that builds throughout our lives. Understanding arguments, then, calls for carefully considering a full range of perspectives and strategies before coming to judgment and joining the conversation. Finally, and most important, all language and symbols are in some way argumentative, pointing in a direction and asking for yet another response, whether it be understanding, identification, or persuasion.

In each previous edition, we have described *Everything's an Argument* as a labor of love for us, and it remains so. Our affection for the book derives in part from knowing that it helps students to make ethical judgments in a world where that ability grows ever more essential. But we have also enjoyed tracking the evolution of argument in our culture and responding to the needs of writers. *Everything's an Argument* first appeared just as new media and technologies were reshaping the ways persuasive writing could be framed and shared. We tried to help writers work creatively in these new environments. Today, students (and instructors) at all levels find themselves overwhelmed by the sheer number of sources technology makes available for their projects; predictably, they want guidance on identifying, evaluating, integrating, and documenting sources for academic projects. Anticipating that need in our previous edition, we offered a chapter on "Academic Arguments." Now, a wholly refreshed version of that material anchors an important six-chapter section on "Research and Arguments," providing writers with an innovative and in-depth guide to serious academic writing. Beginning with a clear explanation of what academic writing actually looks like, the new section illustrates what successful writers do when they build arguments from source materials. And because students read and write in more digital formats than ever, this edition features integrated e-Pages selections available online. These multimodal selections extend the breadth of the examples in *Everything's an Argument* to include videos, speeches, audio slideshows, an interactive infographic, and more.

In another significant improvement, we have restructured the chapters in Part 2, "Writing Arguments," to offer more clearly sequenced advice for preparing specific types of arguments. Exercises appear throughout these chapters precisely where they are needed (instead of all at the end) to reinforce the concepts under discussion. The chapters also now include a section of specific writing "projects," most of them new to this edition.

Throughout the text, and especially in the chapter "Structuring Arguments," we have given added attention not only to Rogerian rhetoric but to Invitational rhetoric as well, understanding that the need for arguments based on the kind of careful listening and mutual respect that can bring people together has never been greater than it is today. In addition, we've added a discussion of *kairos*, seizing the timely and opportune moment in any argument, in Chapter 1.

So as our audience has grown and culture has made new demands on writers' expectations, our approach has evolved. But we haven't altered our basic approach and attitude. A best-seller in its field since its debut, *Everything's an Argument* apparently strikes a chord with students and instructors who expect a book on argument to be candid, balanced, and attuned to everyday events. They also have come to expect a stylish and visually striking presentation of issues and concepts. To that end, we have reframed our chapters to deliver their materials more methodically and efficiently, yet in language that we hope is just as welcoming and readable as ever. We use more lists and charts to highlight or summarize key points, but also have made an effort to reduce textual interruptions.

As in previous editions, we offer many fresh arguments, provocative visual images, and multimodal selections to illuminate the ways we all use language to assert our presence in the world. We have tried to balance attention to the critical reading of arguments (*analysis*) with attention to the writing of arguments (*production*), demonstrating both activities with lively—and realistic—examples, on the principle that the best way to appreciate an argument may be to see it in action. Texts of every kind beckon for reactions, from a full reprint of a FactCheck .org study to a student's analysis of the "white lie," from a Netflix screenshot to a novel defense of Wikipedia, from a film trailer that evaluates the media's portrayal of women to an international student's take on the way writing centers deal with international students. The new edition features twelve new full-length essays chosen for their topicality and usefulness as models of argument—on topics ranging from the threats posed by nuclear power to whether people who aren't attractive should receive government benefits to a rhetorical analysis of a David Brooks editorial. We have tried to keep the best and most popular materials from previous editions, but also to search for new examples and arguments—including visual and multimodal ones— that we believe capture the spirit of the times. As always, we want students to page through the book to find the next intriguing argument or to discover one of their own.

After all, our purpose in *Everything's an Argument* is to present argument as something we do almost from the moment we are born (in fact, an infant's first cry is as poignant a claim as we can imagine)—something as invaluable as good instincts and as worthy of careful attention and practice as any discipline. In pursuing this goal, we try to keep specialized terminology to a minimum. But we also see argument, and want students to regard it, as a craft both powerful and professional. So we have designed *Everything's an Argument* to be itself a case for civil persuasion, with a voice that aims to appeal to readers cordially but that doesn't hesitate to make demands on them when appropriate.

Here is a summary of the key features that continue to characterize *Everything's an Argument* and of the major new features in this edition:

Key Features

- An imaginative and winning approach, going beyond traditional pro/ con assumptions to show that argument is everywhere—in essays, music lyrics, news articles, scholarly writing, poems, advertisements, cartoons, posters, bumper stickers, billboards, Web sites, blogs, text messages, and other electronic environments.

- Student-friendly explanations in simple, everyday language, with many brief examples and a minimum of technical terminology.
- Fifteen full-length essays, including seven by student writers, that provide engaging models of extended verbal arguments in academic contexts over questions of fact, definition, evaluation, cause and effect, and proposals, as well as an extended model of rhetorical analysis.
- A handsome full-color design that brings the images in the text to life.
- Boxed discussions of "Cultural Contexts for Argument" that alert students to the fact that ways of arguing differ from culture to culture and make this book more useful to both native and non-native speakers of English.

New to This Edition

- A new six-chapter section on "Research and Arguments" that provides up-to-date advice for finding, evaluating, using, and documenting research materials in academic arguments. Additions to these chapters include:
  - A much-expanded section on exploring the Web for material, with advice on how to use advanced techniques to narrow and focus searches.
  - Detailed advice on synthesizing research materials and connecting ideas in sources.
  - A clear explanation of "patchwriting," and how to avoid it in research arguments.
- Nine new full-length arguments in Part 2—on topics ranging from playground safety to the magical appeal of the iPad—that provide engaging, topical new readings for students.
- Exercises sequenced and distributed throughout the genre chapters in Part 2, supported by new, separate writing project assignments.
- Chapters throughout the book revised to enhance clarity and readability, with new tables, charts, and lists.
- Attention to the goals of invitational argument, with projects that call for the strategies associated with this form of argument.

- A clear explanation of the ancient rhetorical principle of *kairos* and of how students can use it in their own writing.

- Regular attention in examples and readings to issues of technology and media.

- **e-Pages for *Everything's an Argument*.** Some aspects of argument are best experienced beyond the printed page. For instance, watching a film trailer on media representations of women demonstrates different strategies for appealing to audiences, and interacting with an infographic on food safety encourages new considerations for organizing evidence. To help extend what students read and learn in this book to the kinds of media they are most familiar with and excited by, we have added compelling multimodal selections to *Everything's an Argument*. For a complete list of e-Pages, see the book's table of contents. Instructors can also use the free tools accompanying the e-Pages to upload a syllabus, readings, and assignments to share with the class.

You and your students can access the e-Pages from a tab on the *Student Site for Everything's an Argument* at **bedfordstmartins.com /everythingsanargument/epages**. Students receive access automatically with the purchase of a new book. If the activation code printed on the inside front cover of the student edition does not work, it may be expired. Students can purchase access at the *Student Site*. Instructors receive access information in a separate email for all of the resources on the *Student Site*. You can also log in to request access information.

You Get More Digital Choices for *Everything's an Argument*

Everything's an Argument doesn't stop with a book. Online, you'll find both free and affordable premium resources to help students get even more out of the book and your course. You'll also find convenient instructor resources, such as downloadable sample syllabi, classroom activities, and even access to a nationwide community of teachers. To learn more about or order any of the products below, contact your Bedford/St. Martin's sales representative, email sales support (sales_support@bfwpub.com), or visit the Web site at **bedfordstmartins.com**.

e-Pages for *Everything's an Argument*

Connect conversations in *Everything's an Argument* to the Web with multimodal readings and questions that students can complete online. For a complete list of e-Pages, see the book's table of contents. For access, visit **bedfordstmartins.com/everythingsanargument/epages**. Note: Students receive access to e-Pages automatically with the purchase of a new book.

Student Site for Everything's an Argument
bedfordstmartins.com/everythingsanargument

Send students to free and open resources, choose flexible premium resources to supplement your print text, or upgrade to an expanding collection of innovative digital content.

Free and open resources for *Everything's an Argument* provide students with easy-to-access reference materials, visual tutorials, and support for working with sources.

- five free videos of real writers from VideoCentral

- three free tutorials from *ix visual exercises* by Cheryl Ball and Kristin Arola

- *Bedford Bibliographer,* a tool for collecting source information and making a bibliography in the MLA, APA, and Chicago styles

VideoCentral is a growing collection of videos for the writing class that captures real-world, academic, and student writers talking about how and why they write. VideoCentral can be packaged with *Everything's an Argument* for free. An activation code is required. To order VideoCentral packaged with the print book, use ISBN 978-1-4576-4301-9.

Re:Writing Plus gathers all of Bedford/St. Martin's premium digital content for composition into one online collection. It includes hundreds of model documents, the first ever peer-review game, and VideoCentral. *Re:Writing Plus* can be purchased separately or packaged with the print book at a significant discount. An activation code is required. To order *Re:Writing Plus* packaged with the print book, use ISBN 978-1-4576-4299-9.

i-series

Add more value to your text by choosing one of the following tutorial series, free when packaged with *Everything's an Argument*. This popular series presents multimedia tutorials in a flexible format—because there are things you can't do in a book. To learn more about package options or any of the products below, contact your Bedford/St. Martin's sales representative or visit **bedfordstmartins.com**.

ix visualizing composition 2.0 (available online) helps students put into practice key rhetorical and visual concepts. To order *ix visualizing composition* packaged with the print book, use ISBN 978-1-4576-4302-6.

i•claim 2.0: *visualizing argument* (available online) offers a new way to see argument—with six multimodal tutorials, an illustrated glossary, more than fifty multimedia arguments, and integrated gradebook reporting. To order i•*claim: visualizing argument* packaged with the print book, use ISBN 978-1-4576-4321-7.

i•cite: *visualizing sources* (available online as part of *Re:Writing Plus*) brings research to life through an animated introduction, four tutorials, and hands-on source practice. To order i•*cite: visualizing sources* packaged with the print book, use ISBN 978-1-4576-4304-0.

Bedford e-Book to Go for *Everything's an Argument*

Students can purchase *Everything's an Argument* in downloadable e-book formats for computers, tablets, and e-readers. For more details, visit **bedfordstmartins.com/ebooks**.

Instructor Resources

You have a lot to do in your course. Bedford/St. Martin's wants to make it easy for you to find the support you need—and to get it quickly.

Instructor's Notes for Everything's an Argument is available both in print and a PDF format that can be downloaded from **bedfordstmartins.com /everythingsanargument/catalog**. *Instructor's Notes* includes chapter overviews, teaching tips, and possible responses and discussion points for the Respond prompts. To order the print version of the book, use ISBN 978-1-4576-0926-8.

TeachingCentral (bedfordstmartins.com/teachingcentral) offers the entire list of Bedford/St. Martin's print and online professional resources in one place. You'll find landmark reference works, sourcebooks on pedagogical issues, award-winning collections, and practical advice for the classroom—all free for instructors.

Bedford Bits (**bedfordbits.com**) collects creative ideas for teaching a range of composition topics in an easily searchable blog. A community of teachers—leading scholars, authors, and editors—discuss revision, research, grammar and style, technology, peer review, and much more. Take, use, adapt, and pass the ideas around. Then, come back to the site to comment or share your own suggestions.

Bedford Coursepacks allow you to easily integrate our most popular content into your own course management systems. For details, visit **bedfordstmartins.com/coursepacks**.

Acknowledgments

We owe a debt of gratitude to many people for making *Everything's an Argument* possible. Our first thanks must go to the thousands of students we have taught in our writing courses over nearly four decades, particularly first-year students at the Ohio State University, Stanford University, and the University of Texas at Austin. Almost every chapter in this book has been informed by a classroom encounter with a student whose shrewd observation or perceptive question sent an ambitious lesson plan spiraling to the ground. (Anyone who has tried to teach claims and warrants on the fly to skeptical first-year students will surely appreciate why we have qualified our claims in the Toulmin chapter so carefully.) But students have also provided the motive for writing this book. More than ever, they need to know how to read and write arguments effectively if they are to secure a place in a world growing ever smaller and more rhetorically challenging.

We are grateful to our editors at Bedford/St. Martin's who contributed their talents to our book, beginning with Joan Feinberg, who has enthusiastically supported the project and provided us with the resources and feedback needed to keep us on track, and continuing with Denise Wydra, who has maintained this invaluable support. With this edition we welcome a new editor, Adam Whitehurst, to *Everything's an Argument*. He brought new energy to the project and exactly the fresh perspective we needed to decide upon and then execute the improvements, big and small, you will find throughout the sixth edition. We especially appreciate his help in identifying new readings and images and pointing out problems in those we might have relied on for too long.

We are similarly grateful to others at Bedford/St. Martin's who contributed their talents to our book: Shuli Traub, managing editor; Ryan Sullivan, senior project editor; Dennis Conroy, senior production supervisor; Lucy Krikorian, art director; Molly Parke, executive marketing manager; Julie Tesser, art researcher; Margaret Gorenstein, permissions editor; Steven Patterson, copyeditor; and Nicholas McCarthy, editorial assistant.

We'd also like to thank the astute instructors and students who reviewed the fifth edition: Timothy Bang, St. Cloud State University; Duncan Barlow, University of North Florida; Victoria Barrett, Ball State University; Joy Cooney, Dixie State College of Utah; Donna Elliott, Tulsa Community College; Rebekah Fitzsimmons, University of Florida; Laura Gray-Rosendale, Northern Arizona University; Jeffrey Gross, University of Kentucky; Tina Hultgren, Kishwaukee College; Dawnelle Jager, SUNY Environmental Science and Forestry; David Lawrimore, University of Florida; Shanon Lawson, Pikes Peak Community College; Jacki Lyon, Xavier University; Sean McDougle, University of Tennessee–Knoxville; Andrew McFadyen-Ketchum, Pepperdine University; Gina Merys, Creighton University; Maureen Newey, Cal State University–East Bay; Kirk Perry, Portland Community College; Zach Petrea, Heartland Community College; Samantha Ruckman, Arizona State University; Gregory Schneider, Old Dominion University; Cara Snider, West Virginia University; Worth Weller, Indiana University–Purdue University Ft. Wayne; Sean Wheaton, Clark College; and Darcy Zabel, Friends University.

Thanks, too, to John Kinkade, who once again has prepared the instructor's notes for this sixth edition. Finally, we are grateful to the students whose fine argumentative essays appear in our chapters: Rachel Kolb, Claire Liu, Taylor Pearson, Jennifer Pier, Sayoh Mansaray, Jack Chung, Lia Hardin, Sean Kamperman, Manasi Deshpande, Max Cougar Oswald, and Brian Riady. We hope that *Everything's an Argument* responds to what students and instructors have said they want and need. And we hope readers of this text will let us know how we've done: please share your opinions and suggestions with us at bedfordst martins.com/everythingsanargument.

Andrea A. Lunsford
John J. Ruszkiewicz

CONTENTS

 For readings that go beyond the printed page, see
bedfordstmartins.com/everythingsanargument/epages.

bedfordstmartins.com/everythingsanargument/epages

Part 2:
Writing Arguments   121

 bedfordstmartins.com/everythingsanargument/epages

bedfordstmartins.com/everythingsanargument/epages

10. Evaluations 214

bedfordstmartins.com/everythingsanargument/epages

bedfordstmartins.com/everythingsanargument/epages

Part 3:
Style and Presentation
in Arguments   307

bedfordstmartins.com/everythingsanargument/epages

Part 4:
Research and Arguments 365

16. Academic Arguments 367

17. Finding Evidence 395

bedfordstmartins.com/everythingsanargument/epages

e-Pages

Jennifer Siebel Newsom, *Trailer for* Miss Representation 🄴

New York Times (with photos by Jim Wilson), *An Education, Over the Border and Under the Radar* 🄴

🄴 bedfordstmartins.com/everythingsanargument/epages

everything's an argument

PART 1

READING AND UNDERSTANDING arguments

Everything Is an Argument

On Friday, June 17, 2011, women in Saudi Arabia took to their cars, defying the law forbidding women to drive and making a defiant argument with their own bodies. Some women were arrested; others eventually relinquished the wheel to husbands or male relatives, but the statement had been made, stirring up a barrage of news coverage and images like the ones above, each of which makes an argument that women should have the freedom to drive.

The "women driving day" in Saudi Arabia was related, in part, to what has been called the "Arab Spring" of 2011. The uprisings began much earlier in the year, after a street vendor in Tunisia, Mohamed Bouazizi, set himself on fire in protest of a government that would not allow him to eke out even the most modest living. Bouazizi's horrifying death inspired others to bring down President Zine el-Abidine Ben Ali.

In late January 2011, huge crowds gathered in Cairo's Tahrir Square, making arguments that eventually forced the ouster of President Hosni Mubarak. Throughout several weeks, protesters tweeted and texted

Mohamed Bouazizi

messages and images to tell the world what was happening, like these two sent on January 25 and January 27:

> TravellerWMo-ha-med
> Police throws rocks @ demonstrtrs while we raised our arms.
> We're unarmed, they're in full gear. We are strong, they're weak.
> #25jan#Egypt
> 25 January 2011 16:27:33

> PackafyPakinanAhmed
> after 2 days of protesting, tear gas Is like fresh air, rubber
> bullets are like raindrops, sticks r like thai massage....
> 27 January 2011 02:03:02

Tweets, blog postings, and images all offered arguments for freedom from repressive regimes, arguments that found voice in music as well. The events in Cairo, for example, inspired the rap "#Jan25," by Omar Offendum, Freeway the Narcicyst, Amir Sulaiman, and Ayah, which went viral on YouTube:

> I heard them say the revolution won't be televised
> Al Jazeera proved them wrong
> Twitter has them paralyzed
> 80 million strong
> And ain't no longer gonna be terrorized
> Organized, mobilized, vocalized . . .

These examples demonstrate one fact of contemporary life in the digital age: anyone, anywhere, with access to a smart phone, can mount an argument that can circle the globe in seconds. The revolutionary arguments advanced in the Middle East were enabled in essential ways by social networking and digital tools increasingly available to all.

We've chosen particularly dramatic examples of arguments (on Twitter, on blogs, on YouTube, on the Web) to open this chapter as a way of introducing our claim that arguments are all around us, in every medium, in every genre, in everything we do. There may be an argument on the T-shirt you put on in the morning, in the sports column you read on the bus, in the prayers you utter before an exam, in the off-the-cuff political remarks of a teacher lecturing, in the assurances of a health center nurse that, "This won't hurt one bit."

The clothes you wear, the foods you eat, and the groups you join make nuanced, sometimes unspoken arguments about who you are and what you value. So an argument can be any text — written, spoken, aural, or visual — that expresses a point of view. In fact, some theorists claim that language is inherently persuasive. When you say, "Hi, how's it going?" in one sense you're arguing that your hello deserves a response. Even humor makes an argument when it causes readers to recognize — through bursts of laughter or just a faint smile — how things are and how they might be different.

More obvious as arguments are those that make a direct claim based on or drawn from evidence. Such writing often moves readers to recognize problems and to consider solutions. Persuasion of this kind is usually easy to recognize:

> [W]omen unhappy in their marriages often enter full-time employment as an escape. But although a woman's entrance into the workplace does tend to increase the stability of her marriage, it does not increase her happiness.
>
> —The Popular Research Institute, Penn State University

> We will become a society of a million pictures without much memory, a society that looks forward every second to an immediate replication of what it has just done, but one that does not sustain the difficult labor of transmitting culture from one generation to the next.
>
> —Christine Rosen, "The Image Culture"

RESPOND ●

Can an argument really be any text that expresses a point of view? What kinds of arguments—if any—might be made by the following items?

a Boston Red Sox cap

a Livestrong bracelet

the "explicit lyrics" label on a best-selling rock CD

the health warning on a package of cigarettes

a belated birthday card

a Rolex watch

Why We Make Arguments

In the politically divided and entertainment-driven culture of the United States today, the word "argument" may well call up primarily negative images: the angry face or shaking fist of a politician or news "opinion-ator" who wants to drown out other voices and win at all costs. This is a view of argument we want to explore and challenge in this book. In fact, there are many other ways to argue, including the **invitational arguments** described by researchers Sonja Foss, Cindy Griffin, and Josina Makau. Such arguments are interested in inviting others to join in mutual exploration based on respect. In addition to invitational argument, another kind of argument, called **Rogerian argument** (after psychotherapist Carl Rogers), approaches audiences in nonthreatening ways, finding common ground and establishing trust among those who disagree about issues. Writers who take a Rogerian approach try to see where the other person is coming from, looking for "both/and" or "win/win" solutions whenever possible. (For more on Rogerian strategies, see Chapter 7.)

We have many reasons to argue, then, and not all of them are about winning. In addition to convincing and persuading others, we use arguments to inform, to explore, to make decisions, and even to meditate or pray.

RESPOND ●

What are your reasons for making arguments? Keep notes for two days about every single argument you make, using our broad definition to guide you. Then identify your reasons: How many times did you aim to persuade? To convince? To inform or explain? To explore? To decide? To meditate?

The risks of Rogerian argument

"You say it's a win–win, but what if you're
wrong–wrong and it all goes bad–bad?"

Some arguments, of course, *are* aimed at winning, especially those related to politics, business, and law. Two candidates for office, for example, vie for a majority of votes; the makers of one soft drink try to outsell their competitors by appealing to public tastes; and two lawyers try to outwit each other in pleading to a judge and jury. In your college writing, you may also be called on to make an argument that appeals to a "judge" and "jury" (your instructor and classmates). You might, for instance, argue that peer-to-peer music and film file sharing is legal because of the established legal precedent of fair use. In doing so, you may need to defeat your unseen opponents—those who regard such file sharing as theft.

When you argue to win, you are often trying to convince or persuade someone. So what's the difference between these two reasons for arguing? Arguments to convince lead audiences toward conviction, toward agreeing that a claim is true or reasonable or that an action is desirable. Arguments to persuade aim to move others from conviction to *action*. These and other purposes or goals of argument are worth considering in a little more detail, remembering that academic arguments often combine purposes.

Arguments to Convince

Many reports, white papers, and academic articles typically aim to convince rather than persuade their audiences. In a report on the safety record of nuclear plants for a college course, you would likely present evidence to convince general audiences (including an instructor and fellow students) that the issue merited their attention and concern. Even then, the presence of those who might disagree always needs to be considered. In the following passage, controversial political scientist Charles Murray uses intelligence quotient (IQ) correlations to raise questions about higher education that many readers of the *Wall Street Journal*, where his article appeared, may find troubling:

> There is no magic point at which a genuine college-level education becomes an option, but anything below an IQ of 110 is problematic. If you want to do well, you should have an IQ of 115 or higher. Put another way, it makes sense for only about 15% of the population, 25% if one stretches it, to get a college education.
> —Charles Murray, "What's Wrong with Vocational School?"

Murray uses numbers to draw a seemingly objective conclusion about who should attend college, hoping to convince some readers to consider his point. But he's also arguing against those—perhaps a majority of his audience—who prefer to believe that higher education should be encouraged for all.

MOORE MADNESS

Often an image offers an argument intended to convince. On page 8, a cartoonist offers a criticism of well-known activist filmmaker Michael Moore to convince readers that Moore embodies the very qualities he condemns in others.

Arguments to Persuade

In many situations, writers want not only to convince audiences but to move them to action, whether that involves buying a product, voting for a candidate, or supporting a policy. Advertisements, political blogs, YouTube videos, and newspaper editorials use all the devices of rhetoric to motivate action or produce change. Here Daniel Ben-Ami drives home his argument at the end of an essay on the London-based Web site *Spiked* examining "Why people hate fat Americans":

> By focusing on fat Americans the critics of consumption are saying, implicitly at least, that people should consume less. They are arguing for a world in which Americans become more like those who live in the poorer countries of the world. . . . Yet implementing such a viewpoint is a super-size mistake. Our aspiration for the world should be to give the poor the advantages of affluence enjoyed by those in the

Student protests such as this one could be considered arguments to persuade.

West. Living standards in countries such as Ethiopia and Niger should be, at the very least, as high as those in America today. In that sense we should all aim to be fat Americans.

In this passage, Ben-Ami dramatizes his point by balance and repetition in the structure of his sentences, by reminders in the final paragraph of poverty in Ethiopia and Niger, and by a final ironic call for others to grow as fat as Americans. With these rhetorical moves, he pushes from analysis toward action, which is typical of most persuasive writing.

In your college writing, you can use these same techniques to get your points across and to urge action. You may also use images to help you persuade, perhaps in a college essay arguing that politicians should address the rising costs of attending college.

Arguments to Inform

Often, writers argue to inform others, to give information, much like a bumper sticker that simply provides an organization's name and Web address:

R & L's House of Ribs:
www.R&L.com

A visual argument to inform in Key West, Florida

In fact, a first step in selling anything is to tell customers it exists. The classic poster announcing the first *Batman* film in 1989 carried the iconic image and only two words: "June 23." Many student writers use Twitter to make arguments that inform: a student we know sends weekly Tweets that tell her followers what new Korean film she has seen most recently so that they can check it out for themselves.

Arguments to Explore

Many important issues today call for arguments to explore them. If there's an "opponent" in such a situation at all (often there is not), it's likely the status quo or a current trend that, for one reason or another, is puzzling. In trying to sort through the extraordinary complexities of the 2011 budget debate, philosophy professor Gary Gutting shows how two distinguished economists—John Taylor and Paul Krugman—draw completely different conclusions from the exact same sets of facts. Exploring how such a thing could occur led Gutting to the conclusion that the two economists were arguing from the same sets of facts, all right, but that they did not have *all* the facts possible; those missing or unknown facts allowed them to fill in the blanks as they could, thus leading them to different conclusions.

Exploratory arguments can also be personal, such as Zora Neale Hurston's ironic exploration of racism and of her own identity in "How It Feels to Be Colored Me." If you keep a journal or blog, you have no doubt found yourself making arguments to explore issues near and dear to you. Perhaps the essential argument in any such piece is the writer's assertion that a problem exists—and that the writer or reader needs to understand it and respond constructively to it if possible.

Arguments to Make Decisions

Closely allied to exploratory arguments are arguments that aim to make good, sound decisions, whether about cutting budgets or choosing a career. For college students, choosing a major is a momentous decision, and one way to go about making that decision is to argue your way through several alternatives. By the time you've explored the pros and cons of each alternative, you should be a little closer to a good decision.

Arguments to make decisions occur all the time in the public arena as well. In the summer of 2011, the British tabloid *News of the World* was found to have hacked into the voice messages of a young murder victim as well as relatives of military personnel killed in Afghanistan and Iraq.

Sometimes decisions are not so easy to make.

Dana Summers-Tribune Media Services

These revelations forced Rupert Murdoch, owner of the tabloid (as well as of the much larger News Corporation), and his top advisers to argue their way to a decision, which was to close down *News of the World*. In commenting on Murdoch's decision, the *New York Times* reported that:

Former British Deputy Prime Minister Lord Prescot signs on in support of an inquiry into the *News of the World* phone hacking scandal.

The move to close *The News of the World* was seen by media analysts as a potentially shrewd decision: jettisoning a troubled newspaper in order to preserve the more lucrative broadcasting deal and possibly expand the company's other British tabloid, *The Sun*, to publish seven days a week.

Murdoch's decision (which ultimately fell through) was hotly debated on all sides throughout Britain, a debate that led others to decide to call for a full public inquiry into phone hacking by the British media, and even by the government.

Arguments to Meditate or Pray

Sometimes arguments can take the form of prayer or intense meditations on a theme. In such cases, the writer or speaker is most often hoping to transform something in himself/herself or to reach peace of mind. If you know a familiar prayer or mantra, think for a moment of what it "argues" for and how it uses quiet meditation to accomplish that goal. Such meditations don't have to be formal prayers, however. Look, for example, at an excerpt from Michael Lassell's poem "How to Watch Your Brother Die." This poem, which evokes the confusing emotions of a man during the death of his gay brother, uses meditative language that allows readers to understand the speaker and to meditate on life and death themselves:

> Feel how it feels to hold a man in your arms whose arms are used to holding men.
> Offer God anything to bring your brother back.
> Know you have nothing God could possibly want.
> Curse God, but do not abandon Him.
> —Michael Lassell, "How to Watch Your Brother Die"

Another sort of meditative argument can be found in the stained-glass windows of churches and other public buildings. Dazzled by a spectacle of light, people pause to consider a window's message longer than they might if the same idea were conveyed on paper.

The Tree of Jesse window in France's Chartres Cathedral

Occasions for Argument

In an ancient textbook of **rhetoric** (the art of persuasion), the philosopher Aristotle provides an elegant scheme for classifying occasions for argument based on time—past, future, and present. But remember that all classifications overlap to a certain extent, so don't be surprised when arguments about the past have implications for the future or when those about the future bear on the present day.

Arguments about the Past

Debates about what has happened in the past, or **forensic arguments**, are common in business, government, and academia. The contentious nature of some forensic arguments is evident in this excerpt from a letter to the editor of the *Atlantic Monthly*:

Occasions for Argument

	Past	*Future*	*Present*
What is it called?	Forensic	Deliberative	Epideictic
What are its concerns?	What happened in the past?	What should be done in the future?	Who or what deserves praise or blame?
What does it look like?	Court decisions, legal briefs, legislative hearings, investigative reports, academic studies	White papers, proposals, bills, regulations, mandates	Eulogies, graduation speeches, inaugural addresses, roasts

Robert Bryce's article on the U.S. military's gas consumption in Iraq ("Gas Pains," May *Atlantic*) is factually inaccurate, tactically misguided, and a classic case of a red herring.

—Captain David J. Morris

In replying to this letter, the author of the article, Robert Bryce, disputes Morris's statements, introducing more evidence in support of his original claim.

Forensic arguments rely on evidence and testimony to re-create what can be known about events that have already occurred as well as on precedents (past actions or decisions that influence present policies or decisions) and on analyses of causes and effects. When a housekeeper for a New York hotel accused French politician Dominique Strauss-Kahn of sexual assault, the case depended on exactly what had happened in the past: the prosecution's job was to show beyond a reasonable doubt that sexual assault had occurred while the defense was to offer a different version of the past events. Evidence (including DNA evidence) and testimony will be key constituents in these arguments about the past.

Or consider the ongoing arguments over Christopher Columbus's "discovery" of America: Are his expeditions cause for celebration or unhappy chapters in human history? Or some of both? As these examples suggest, arguments about history are often forensic.

Arguments about the Future

Debates about what will or should happen in the future—**deliberative arguments**—often establish policies for the future: *Should two people of the same sex be allowed to marry?* and *Should the U.S. Treasury Department bail out failing banks and businesses in times of economic chaos?* are examples of questions that deliberative bodies such as legislatures, congresses, or parliaments answer by making laws or establishing policies.

But arguments about the future can also be speculative, advancing by means of projections and reasoned guesses, as shown in this passage from an essay by *Wired* editor Kevin Kelly, who has argued for several years that "we are headed toward screen ubiquity":

As portable screens become more powerful, lighter, and larger, they will be used to view more. . . . Hold an electronic tablet up as you walk along a street, and it will show an annotated overlay of the real street ahead—where the clean restrooms are, which stores sell your favorite items, where your friends are hanging out. Computer chips are so small, and screens so thin and cheap, that in the next 40 years semi-transparent eyeglasses will apply an informational layer to reality. . . . In this way screens will enable us to "read" everything, not just text. Last year alone, five quintillion transistors were embedded into objects other than computers. Very soon most manufactured items, from shoes to cans of soup, will contain a small sliver of dim intelligence, and screens will be the tool we use to interact with this transistorized information.

—Kevin Kelly, "Reading in a Whole New Way"

Arguments about the Present

Arguments about the present—**epideictic** or **ceremonial arguments**—are usually about contemporary values, that is, widely held beliefs and assumptions that are debated within a society. Often heard at public occasions, they include inaugural addresses, sermons, eulogies, graduation speeches, and civic remarks of all kinds. President Ronald Reagan was a master of ceremonial discourse, and he was particularly adept at defining the core values of the American way of life:

Ours was the first revolution in the history of mankind that truly reversed the course of government, and with three little words: "We the people." "We the people" tell the government what to do, it doesn't tell us. "We the people" are the driver, the government is the car. And we decide where it should go, and by what route, and how fast.

—Ronald Reagan, "Farewell Address"

More typical than Reagan's impassioned address are values arguments that explore contemporary culture, praising what's admirable and blaming what's not. In the following argument, student Latisha Chisholm looks at rap after Tupac Shakur:

With the death of Tupac, not only did one of the most intriguing rap rivalries of all time die, but the motivation for rapping seems to have changed. Where money had always been a plus, now it is obviously more important than wanting to express the hardships of Black communities. With current rappers, the positive power that came from the desire to represent Black people is lost. One of the biggest rappers now got his big break while talking about sneakers. Others announce retirement without really having done much for the soul or for Black people's morale. I equate new rappers to NFL players that don't love

Are rappers since Tupac—like Jay-Z—only in it for the money? Many epideictic arguments either praise or blame contemporary culture.

the game anymore. They're only in it for the money. . . . It looks like the voice of a people has lost its heart.

—Latisha Chisholm, "Has Rap Lost Its Soul?"

As in many ceremonial arguments, Chisholm here reinforces common values such as representing one's community honorably and fairly.

RESPOND●

In a recent magazine, newspaper, or blog, find three editorials—one that makes a forensic argument, one a deliberative argument, and one a ceremonial argument. Analyze the arguments by asking these questions: Who is arguing? What purposes are the writers trying to achieve? To whom are they directing their arguments? Then decide whether the arguments' purposes have been achieved and how you know.

Kinds of Argument

Yet another way of categorizing arguments is to consider their status or stasis—that is, the *kinds of issues they address*. This system, called **stasis theory**, was used in ancient Greek and Roman civilizations to define questions designed to help examine legal cases. The questions were posed in sequence because each depended on the question(s) preceding it. Together, the questions helped determine the point of contention in an argument. A modern version of those questions might look like the following:

- Did something happen?
- What is its nature?
- What is its quality or cause?
- What actions should be taken?

Each stasis question explores a different aspect of a problem and uses different evidence or techniques to reach conclusions. You can use these questions to explore the aspects of any topic you're considering. We use the stasis issues to define key types of argument in Part 2.

Did Something Happen? Arguments of Fact

An **argument of fact** usually involves a statement that can be proved or disproved with specific evidence or testimony. For example, the question of pollution of the oceans—is it really occurring?—might seem relatively easy to settle. Either scientific data prove that the oceans are being polluted as a result of human activity, or they don't. But to settle the matter, writers and readers need to ask a number of other questions about the "facts."

- Where did the facts come from?
- Are they reliable?
- Is there a problem with the facts?
- Where did the problem begin and what caused it? (For more on arguments based on facts, see Chapter 4.)

What Is the Nature of the Thing? Arguments of Definition

One of the most hotly debated issues in American life today involves a question of definition: is a human fetus a human being? If one argues that it is, then a second issue of definition arises: is abortion murder? As

Mark Cadena and Stuart Hata in San Francisco's City Hall after their wedding on November 3, 2008, the day before a California ballot referendum ended several months of legalized marriage ceremonies between same-sex couples in the state. The debate over this issue involves arguments of fact (Does a "civil union" or "domestic partnership" provide the same benefits as a "marriage"?) as well as more basic arguments of definition (Are these forms of legal recognition the same thing? Must "marriage" involve two people of the opposite sex?).

you can see, issues of definition can have mighty consequences, and decades of debate may nonetheless leave the matter unresolved.

Bob Costas used an important definitional distinction to eulogize Mickey Mantle, a great New York Yankee baseball player who had many human faults:

> In the last year, Mickey Mantle, always so hard upon himself, finally came to accept and appreciate the distinction between a role

model and a hero. The first he often was not, the second he always will be.

—Bob Costas, "Eulogy for Mickey Mantle"

But **arguments of definition** can be less weighty than these, though still hotly contested: Is playing video games a sport? Is Batman a tragic figure? Is Mitt Romney a conservative or a moderate? (For more about arguments of definition, see Chapter 9.)

What Is the Quality or Cause of the Thing? Arguments of Evaluation

Arguments of evaluation present criteria and then measure individual people, ideas, or things against those standards. For instance, writer Molly Ivins praises Barbara Jordan by making explicit the qualities and achievements that make someone a "great spirit":

> Barbara Jordan, whose name was so often preceded by the words "the first black woman to . . ." that they seemed like a permanent title, died Wednesday in Austin. A great spirit is gone. The first black woman to serve in the Texas Senate, the first black woman in Congress (she and Yvonne Brathwaite Burke of California were both elected in 1972, but Jordan had no Republican opposition), the first black elected to Congress from the South since Reconstruction, the first black woman to sit on major corporate boards, and so on. Were it not for the disease that slowly crippled her, she probably would have been the first black woman on the Supreme Court—it is known that Jimmy Carter had her on his short list.
> —Molly Ivins, "Barbara Jordan: A Great Spirit"

In examining a circumstance or situation, we are often led to wonder what accounts for it: *how did Barbara Jordan achieve what she did, or what happened as a result of her work?* We want to know what shaped the situation she grew up in, what causes led to her development into a "great spirit." (For more about arguments of evaluation, see Chapter 10; for causal arguments, see Chapter 11.)

What Actions Should Be Taken? Proposal Arguments

Proposal arguments present an issue or problem so vividly that readers say *What can we do?* For example, in developing an argument about rising tuition at your college, you might use all the prior stasis questions to

Barbara Jordan addressing fellow members of Congress in 1978

study the issue and establish how much and for what reasons tuition is rising. But the final question—*What actions should be taken?*—will be the most important, since it will lead you to develop proposals for action. In examining a nationwide move to eliminate remedial education in four-year colleges, John Cloud offers a moderate proposal to address the problem:

> Students age twenty-two and over account for 43 percent of those in remedial classrooms, according to the National Center for Developmental Education. [. . . But] 55 percent of those needing remediation must take just one course. Is it too much to ask them to pay extra for that class or take it at a community college?
>
> —John Cloud, "Who's Ready for College?"

For more about proposal arguments, see Chapter 12.

STASIS QUESTIONS AT WORK

Suppose you have an opportunity to speak at a student conference on the issue of global warming. You are tentatively in favor of strengthening industrial pollution standards aimed at reducing global warming trends. But to learn more about the issue, you use the stasis questions to get started.

- **Did something happen?** Does global warming exist? *No*, say many in the oil and gas industry; at best, evidence for global warming is inconclusive. *Yes*, say most scientists and governments; global warming is real and has reached serious proportions. To come to your conclusion, you'll weigh the facts carefully and identify problems with opposing arguments.

- **What is the nature of the thing?** Skeptics define global warming as naturally occurring events; most scientists base definitions on human causes. You look at each definition carefully: *How do the definitions foster the goals of each group? What's at stake for each group in defining it that way?*

- **What is the quality or cause of the thing?** Exploring the differing assessments of damage done by climate change leads you to ask who will gain from such analysis: *Do oil executives want to protect their investments? Do scientists want government money for grants? Where does evidence for the dangers of global warming come from? Who benefits if the dangers are accepted as real and present, and who loses?*

- **What actions should be taken?** If global warming is occurring naturally or causing little harm, then arguably *nothing* needs or can be done. But if it is caused mainly by human activity and dangers, action is definitely called for (although not everyone may agree on what such action should be). As you investigate the proposals being made and the reasons behind them, you come closer to developing your own argument.

Audiences for Arguments

Exploring stasis questions will help you to think about the audience(s) you are addressing, from the flesh-and-blood person sitting across a desk when you negotiate a student loan, to your "friends" on social media, to the "ideal" person you imagine for what you are writing.

Readers and writers in context

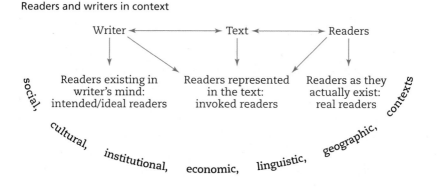

The figure at the top of this page shows just how many dimensions an audience can have as writers and readers negotiate their relationship to a verbal or visual text.

As authors of this book, we are thinking about students like you: you are our intended readers. Though we don't know you personally, we see you in our minds, for we *intend* to write for you. In the same way, the editors of *Rego: The Latino College Magazine* had a clear sense of whom they wanted to reach with their publication. They even offered a graphic to define their audience precisely, identifying it as "the Latino collegiate, postcollegiate, and college-bound demographic."

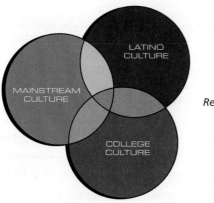

Rego defines its audience.

So texts, whether oral, written, or *digital*, have **intended audiences**, those the writer wants to address. But they also have **invoked readers**, those represented in the text itself. (The covers of *Rego*, for example, invoked an audience through representations in the text—of hip Latinos and Latinas.)

In addition to intended and invoked readers, arguments will also have "real" readers who may not be among those a writer originally imagines. You may post something on the Web, for instance, and find that it is read by people you did not address or invoke at all! In the same way, you may read email not sent to you but rather forwarded (sometimes unwittingly) from someone else. As a writer, you want to think carefully about these real readers and to take care with what you post online.

Considering Contexts

No consideration of audiences can be complete without understanding that reading always takes place in a series of contexts that move outward, from the most immediate situation (the specific circumstance in which the reading occurs) to broader environments (including local and community or institutional contexts like school or church, as well as cultural and linguistic contexts).

When reporter Louise Story of the *New York Times* wrote a front-page story saying that many women attending prestigious colleges planned to abandon their professional careers when they had children, she provoked very different responses from various audiences, depending on their contexts. Jack Schafer of Slate.com, for example, found the story full of evasive qualifying terms, such as *many* and *seems*, that made its claims meaningless:

> While bogus, "Many Women at Elite Colleges Set Career Path to Motherhood" isn't false: It can't be false because it never says anything sturdy enough to be tested. So, how did it get to Page One? Is there a *New York Times* conspiracy afoot to drive feminists crazy and persuade young women that their place is in the home?
> —Jack Schafer, "Weasel-Words Rip My Flesh!"

Faculty members at the schools Story examined put the piece in a different context, that of professional women in general. Quoted in a *BU Today* article, Deborah Belle, a professor of psychology at Boston University, found it sadly emblematic of the dilemma professional women still face:

> I think the thing that resonates so badly with me about the *New York Times* article is that the onus is always on the woman, and that's not where it should be. . . . Of course there are superheroes who can do it all, but that's not the point. The point is that none of us should be forced to be in these positions.
> —Deborah Belle, qtd. in "The Do-It-All Dilemma"

And female students themselves—from a different generation than their professors—placed the story in their own contexts. Here's Alana Steinhardt from that same *BU Today* article, bringing personal values to bear on the controversy:

> Why have kids if you can't see them grow up, and be there for the experience? . . . At BU, I'm preparing myself to be a more well-rounded person. That doesn't necessarily mean I have to work.

As you compose arguments of your own, you need to think carefully about the contexts that surround your readers—and to place your topic in its context as well.

CULTURAL CONTEXTS FOR ARGUMENT

Considering What's "Normal"

If you want to communicate effectively with people across cultures, then learn about the traditions in those cultures and examine the norms guiding your own behavior:

- Explore your assumptions! Most of us regard our ways of thinking as "normal" or "right." Such assumptions guide our judgments about what works in persuasive situations. But just because it may seem natural to speak bluntly in arguments, consider that others may find such aggression startling or even alarming.

- Remember: ways of arguing differ widely across cultures. Pay attention to how people from groups or cultures other than your own argue, and be sensitive to different paths of thinking you'll encounter as well as to differences in language.

- Don't assume that all people share your cultural values, ethical principles, or political assumptions. People across the world have different ways of defining *family*, *work*, or *happiness*. As you present arguments to them, consider that they may be content with their different ways of organizing their lives and societies.

- Respect the differences among individuals *within* a given group. Don't expect that every member of a community behaves—or argues—in the same way or shares the same beliefs. Avoid thinking, for instance, that there is a single Asian, African, or Hispanic culture or that Europeans are any less diverse or more predictable than Americans or Canadians in their thinking. In other words, be skeptical of stereotypes.

Appealing to Audiences

Aristotle identified three time-tested ways writers can appeal to audiences, and he labeled them *pathos*, *ethos*, and *logos*—appeals that are as effective today as they were in Aristotle's time, though we usually think of them in slightly different terms.

Emotional Appeals: Pathos

Emotional appeals, or **pathos**, generate emotions (fear, pity, love, anger, jealousy) that the writer hopes will lead the audience to accept a claim. Here is a plea from Doctors without Borders that uses pathos to urge us to contribute to their cause:

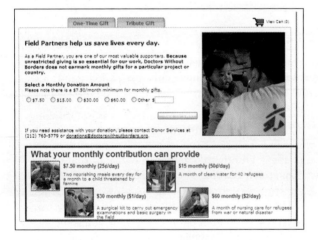

Concrete and descriptive language paints pictures in readers' minds as well, making an emotional appeal that can create a bond between writer and readers. (For more about emotional appeals, see Chapter 2.)

Ethical Appeals: Ethos

When writers or speakers come across as trustworthy, audiences are likely to listen to and accept their arguments. That trustworthiness (along with fairness and respect) is a mark of **ethos**, or credibility. Showing that you know what you are talking about exerts an ethical appeal, as does emphasizing that you share values with and respect your audience. Visuals can also make strong ethical appeals: think how flags, logos, or even badges convey credibility and authority, as in this Doctors without Borders symbol:

MEDECINS SANS FRONTIERES
DOCTORS WITHOUT BORDERS

For more about ethical appeals, see Chapter 3.

Logical Appeals: Logos

Appeals to logic, or **logos**, are often given prominence and authority in U.S. culture: "Just the facts, ma'am," a famous early TV detective on *Drag-net* used to say. Indeed, audiences respond well to the use of reasons and evidence—to the presentation of facts, statistics, credible testimony, cogent examples, or even a narrative or story that embodies a sound reason in support of an argument. (For more about logical appeals, see Chapter 4.)

Kairos: Seizing the Opportune Moment in Arguments

In Greek mythology, Kairos—the youngest son of Zeus—was the god of opportunity. In images, he is most often depicted as running, and his most unusual characteristic is a shock of hair on his forehead. As Kairos dashes by, you have a chance to seize that lock of hair, thereby seizing the opportune moment; once he passes you by, however, you have missed that chance.

Considering your rhetorical situation calls on you to think hard about **kairos**, that is, about the suitable time and place for making an argument and the most opportune ways to make it. Being aware of kairos means being able to understand and take advantage of shifting circumstances and to choose the best (most timely) proofs and evidence for that particular place, situation, and audience.

The effectiveness of many arguments depends on whether or not they are timely. For example, in 2010 Congressional Republicans took advantage of Americans' fears of rising national debt to argue for their agenda to make broad cuts to the federal budget. The timing of their message resonated with the American public, and in the next election they trounced

Democrats, taking control of the House of Representatives (and nearly the Senate as well). By 2011, however, long periods of high unemployment had become Americans' number one concern, and talk of cuts to federal and state budgets lost some of its political clout because such arguments were no longer timely.

In another example, a student was interested in why the tennis match between Billie Jean King and Bobby Riggs (dubbed "The Battle of the Sexes") caused such a sensation: her research led her to identify several key elements that came together in 1973 to create the perfect opportune — or kairotic — moment for a woman to take on a man in tennis, and win.

In your own arguments, thinking about kairos is important early on as you study the context or conversation surrounding your topic and look for opportune moments to get your own point of view into that conversation. It's also important to think about kairos when you analyze your arguments: how can you frame your claims and evidence to resonate with your audience?

RESPOND•

What common experiences, if any, do the following objects, brand names, and symbols evoke, and for what audiences in particular? What sorts of appeals do they make: to pathos, ethos, or logos?

> a USDA organic label
>
> the golden arches
>
> the Sean John label as seen on its Web site
>
> a can of Coca-Cola
>
> Sleeping Beauty's castle on the Disney logo
>
> Oprah Winfrey
>
> the Vietnam Veterans Memorial
>
> Ground Zero at the World Trade Center site
>
> an AIDS ribbon

Summing Up Argument: Rhetorical Situations

Thinking about arguments, their contexts, audiences, and appeals brings us to another helpful concept: that of the **rhetorical situation**, a shorthand phrase for the entire set of relationships depicted in the following triangular diagram:

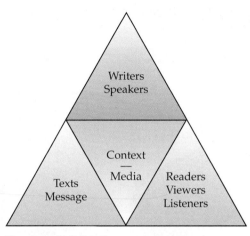

The rhetorical situation

Remember, though, that rhetorical situations are *dynamic*, with all elements affecting one another: for example, a change in audience could affect your handling of the topic and the appeals you use. *Thinking rhetorically* means keeping all these elements in mind, and doing so might even lead you to challenge the title of this text: is everything an argument?

RESPOND•

Take a look at the bumper sticker below, and then analyze it. What is its purpose? What kind of argument is it? Which of the stasis questions does it most appropriately respond to? To what audiences does it appeal? What appeals does it make and how?

2
Arguments Based on Emotion: Pathos

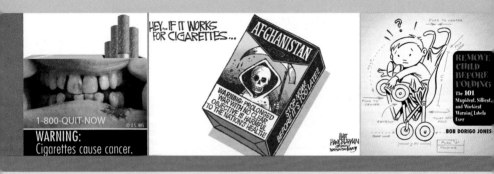

Emotional appeals (*appeals to pathos*) are powerful tools for influencing what people think and believe. We all make decisions—even including the most important ones—based on our feelings. That's what the Food and Drug Administration hoped to capitalize on when it introduced nine new warning labels for cigarettes, one of which you see above. One look at the stained, rotting teeth and the lip sore may arouse emotions of fear strong enough to convince people not to smoke.

Editorial cartoonist for *Newsday* Walt Handelsman borrows the emotional strategy of cigarette warning labels to stir up opposition to continuing conflict in Afghanistan. His imaginary "package" (shown above) evokes fear through an iconic image (Death with his sickle) and stirs political anger via an explicit alert: "Prolonged war with no clear objective is harmful to the nation's health!" Yet such labels lead Bob Dorigo Jones, an opponent of lawsuit abuse, in an entirely different direction, publishing a book entitled *Remove Child before Folding: The 101 Stupidest, Silliest, and Wackiest Warning Labels Ever*. His intention is to make us laugh and thereby, perhaps, to question or even doubt the effectiveness of such scary warnings.

The kinds of arguments packed into these three images all appeal to emotion, and modern science has shown us that we often make decisions based on just such appeals. So when you hear that formal or academic arguments should rely solely on facts, remember that facts alone often won't carry the day, even for a worthy cause. The civil rights struggle for gay marriage in the last few years provides a particularly good example of a movement that persuaded people equally by means of the reasonableness and the passion of its claims. Like many debates, the one over gay marriage provoked high emotions on every side, emotions that sometimes led more to divisiveness than progress toward solutions.

Of course, we don't have to look hard for less noble campaigns that are fueled with emotions such as hatred, envy, and greed, campaigns that drive wedges between groups, making them fearful or hateful. For that reason alone, writers should not use emotional appeals casually. (For more about emotional fallacies, see p. 75.)

Reading Critically for Pathos

Late on the night of May 1, 2011, the White House blog carried this post: "Tonight, President Obama addressed the Nation to announce that the United States has killed Osama bin Laden, the leader of al Qaeda." Earlier

President Obama addresses the nation. You can see this speech in e-Pages at **bedfordstmartins.com/everythingsanargument/epages**.

that evening, the president had appeared on TV to deliver that brief address, setting off a barrage of texts, tweets, and YouTube postings as the United States recalled the devastating attacks of September 11, 2001. Ten years later, the president could finally tell the American people that the mastermind of that attack was dead.

The president's address to the nation was very brief—under ten minutes. As he spoke directly to the American people, some fifty-six million people tuned in: the *Huffington Post* announced that some four thousand tweets per second were sent during the nine and a half minutes of the speech. Clearly, the remarks stirred powerful emotions, as in this passage whose concrete and descriptive language brought back vivid memories:

> The images of 9/11 are seared into our national memory. . . . And yet we know that the worst images are those that were unseen to the world. The empty seat at the dinner table. Children who were forced to grow up without their mother or their father. Parents who would never know the feeling of their child's embrace. Nearly three thousand citizens taken from us, leaving a gaping hole in our hearts.

Yet as analysts pointed out, the president's speech was also measured. As President George W. Bush had done before him, Obama was careful to say that the United States is not and never has been at war with Islam—but with terrorism. Rather, he simply announced that "a small team of Americans . . . killed Osama bin Laden and took custody of his body." Rather than celebrating or gloating, the president spoke with calm control about American values:

> So Americans understand the costs of war. Yet as a country, we will never tolerate our security being threatened, nor stand idly by when our people have been killed. We will be relentless in defense of our citizens and our friends and allies. We will be true to the values that make us who we are. And on nights like this one, we can say to those families who have lost loved ones to al Qaeda's terror: Justice has been done.
>
> —from whitehouse.gov/blog

Note that last sentence: "Justice has been done." Using the passive voice puts the emphasis on justice, leaving out who or what had brought that justice. That is just one way in which this passage is understated and calm. Note also the use of words that signal resolve: "we will never tolerate . . . nor stand idly by." We will be "relentless in defense" and "true to the values." Here the president appeals to emotions that he says "make us who we are."

Reactions to the announcement of Osama bin Laden's death

Outside the White House, stronger emotions were on display as crowds celebrated with chants of "USA, USA, USA."

RESPOND●

Working with a classmate, make a list of reasons why speakers in highly charged situations like this one (the president speaking on the death of Osama bin Laden) would need to use emotional appeals cautiously, even sparingly. What consequences might heightened emotional appeals lead to? What is at stake for the speaker in such situations, in terms of credibility and ethos?

Using Emotions to Build Bridges

You may sometimes want to use emotions to connect with readers to assure them that you understand their experiences or, to use President Bill Clinton's famous line, "feel their pain." Such a bridge is especially important when you're writing about matters that readers regard as sensitive. Before they'll trust you, they'll want assurances that you understand the issues in depth. If you strike the right emotional note, you'll establish an important connection. That's what Apple founder Steve Jobs does in a 2005 commencement address in which he tells the audience that he doesn't have a fancy speech, just three stories from his life:

> My second story is about love and loss. I was lucky. I found what I loved to do early in life. Woz [Steve Wozniak] and I started Apple in my parents' garage when I was twenty. We worked hard and in ten years, Apple had grown from just the two of us in a garage into a $2 billion company with over four thousand employees. We'd just released our finest creation, the Macintosh, a year earlier, and I'd just turned thirty, and then I got fired. How can you get fired from a company you started? Well, as Apple grew, we hired someone who I thought was very talented to run the company with me, and for the first year or so, things went well. But then our visions of the future began to diverge, and eventually we had a falling out. When we did, our board of directors sided with him, and so at thirty, I was out, and very publicly out. . . .
>
> I didn't see it then, but it turned out that getting fired from Apple was the best thing that could have ever happened to me. The heaviness of being successful was replaced by the lightness of being a beginner again, less sure about everything. It freed me to enter one of the most creative periods in my life. During the next five years I started a company named NeXT, another company named Pixar and fell in love with an amazing woman who would become my wife. Pixar went on to create the world's first computer-animated feature film, *Toy Story*, and is now the most successful animation studio in the world.
>
> —Steve Jobs, "You've Got to Find What You Love, Jobs Says"

In no obvious way is Jobs's recollection a formal argument. But it prepares his audience to accept the advice he'll give later in his speech, at least partly because he's speaking from meaningful personal experiences.

A more obvious way to build an emotional tie is simply to help readers identify with your experiences. If, like Georgina Kleege, you were blind and wanted to argue for more sensible attitudes toward blind people, you might ask readers in the first paragraph of your argument to confront their prejudices. Here Kleege, a writer and college instructor, makes an emotional point by telling a story:

> I tell the class, "I am legally blind." There is a pause, a collective intake of breath. I feel them look away uncertainly and then look back. After all, I just said I couldn't see. Or did I? I had managed to get there on my own—no cane, no dog, none of the usual trappings of blindness. Eyeing me askance now, they might detect that my gaze is not quite

focused. . . . They watch me glance down, or towards the door where someone's coming in late. I'm just like anyone else.

—Georgina Kleege, "Call It Blindness"

Given the way she narrates the first day of class, readers are as likely to identify with the students as with Kleege, imagining themselves sitting in a classroom, facing a sightless instructor, confronting their own prejudices about the blind. Kleege wants to put them on edge emotionally.

Let's consider another rhetorical situation: how do you win over an audience when the logical claims that you're making are likely to go against what many in the audience believe? Once again, a slightly risky appeal to emotions on a personal level may work. That's the tack that Michael Pollan takes in bringing readers to consider that "the great moral struggle of our time will be for the rights of animals." In introducing his lengthy exploratory argument, Pollan uses personal experience to appeal to his audience:

The first time I opened Peter Singer's *Animal Liberation*, I was dining alone at the Palm, trying to enjoy a rib-eye steak cooked medium-rare. If this sounds like a good recipe for cognitive dissonance (if not

A visual version of Michael Pollan's rhetorical situation

© The New Yorker Collection 1992 Robert Mankoff from cartoonbank.com. All rights reserved.

indigestion), that was sort of the idea. Preposterous as it might seem to supporters of animal rights, what I was doing was tantamount to reading *Uncle Tom's Cabin* on a plantation in the Deep South in 1852.
—Michael Pollan, "An Animal's Place"

In creating a vivid image of his first encounter with Singer's book, Pollan's opening builds a bridge between himself as a person trying to enter into the animal rights debate in a fair and open-minded, if still skeptical, way and readers who might be passionate about either side of this argument.

Using Emotions to Sustain an Argument

You can also use emotional appeals to make logical claims stronger or more memorable. That is the way that photographs and other images add power to arguments. In a TV attack ad, the scowling black-and-white photograph of a political opponent may do as much damage as the claim that he bought his home on the cheap from a financier convicted of fraud. Or the attractive skier in a spot for lip balm may make us yearn for brisk, snowy winter days. The technique is tricky, however. Lay on too much emotion—especially those like outrage, pity, or shame, which make people uncomfortable—and you may offend the very audiences you hoped to convince.

But sometimes a strong emotion such as anger adds energy to a passage, as it does when writer Stuart Taylor and history professor K. C. Johnson react in outrage when Mike Nifong, a prosecutor charged with deliberately lying about evidence in an emotionally charged rape case at Duke University, received only a twenty-four-hour sentence for his misconduct. In an op-ed in the *Washington Post*, the authors review the wider dimensions of the biased prosecution and turn their ire especially on faculty who were too eager to pillory three white student athletes at Duke for an alleged crime against a minority woman that subsequent investigations proved never occurred. As you read the following excerpt, notice how the authors' use of emotional language might lead some readers to share their anger and others to resent it:

To be sure, it was natural to assume at first that Nifong had a case. Why else would he confidently declare the players guilty? But many academics and journalists continued to presume guilt months after massive evidence of innocence poured into the public record. Indeed, some professors persisted in attacks even after the three defendants were declared innocent in April by North Carolina Attorney General Roy Cooper—an almost unheard-of event.

Brushing aside concern with "the 'truth' . . . about the incident," as one put it, these faculty ideologues just changed their indictments from rape to drunkenness (hardly a rarity in college); exploiting poor black women (the players had expected white and Hispanic strippers); and being born white, male and prosperous.

This shameful conduct was rooted in a broader trend toward subordinating facts and evidence to faith-based ideological posturing. Worse, the ascendant ideology, especially in academia, is an obsession with the fantasy that oppression of minorities and women by "privileged" white men remains rampant in America. Its crude stereotyping of white men, especially athletes, resembles old-fashioned racism and sexism.

—Stuart Taylor and K. C. Johnson, "Guilty in the Duke Case"

In using language this way, writers can generate emotions by presenting arguments in their starkest terms, stripped of qualifications or subtleties. Readers or listeners are confronted with core issues or important choices and asked to consider the consequences.

A sign posted outside the house where the party at the center of the Duke rape case occurred urges prosecutor Mike Nifong to apologize.

It's difficult to gauge how much emotion will work in a given argument. Some issues—such as racism, rape, abortion, and gun control—provoke strong feelings and, as a result, are often argued on emotional terms. But even issues that seem deadly dull—such as funding for Medicare and Social Security—can be argued passionately when proposed changes in these programs are set in human terms: cut benefits and Grandma will have to eat cat food; don't cut benefits and Social Security will surely go broke, leaving nothing for later generations of seniors. Both alternatives might scare people into paying enough attention to take political action.

Using Humor

Humor has always played an important role in argument, sometimes as the sugar that makes the medicine go down. You can slip humor into an argument to put readers at ease, thereby making them more open to a proposal you have to offer. It's hard to say no when you're laughing. Humor also makes otherwise sober people suspend their judgment and even their prejudices, perhaps because the surprise and naughtiness of wit are combustive: they provoke laughter or smiles, not reflection. That may be why TV shows like *South Park* and *Modern Family* became popular with mainstream audiences, despite their sometimes controversial subjects. Similarly, it's possible to make a point through humor that might not work in more sober writing. Although there were many arguments for and against the repeal of the military's Don't Ask, Don't Tell policy in the fall of 2011, the satirical newspaper *The Onion* printed an article in which it simultaneously celebrated and bemoaned an unconsidered consequence of allowing gay men and women to serve openly, namely gay troops' new vulnerability to being publicly broken up with by their significant others back home:

> Hailed as a monumental step toward equality by gay rights activists, hundreds of Dear John letters reportedly began reaching newly outed troops overseas this week, notifying soldiers for the first time ever that their same-sex partners back home were leaving them and starting a new life with someone else.
>
> According to Pentagon observers, the torrent of brusque, callous letters—which followed Tuesday's repeal of the Don't Ask, Don't Tell policy—has left romantically betrayed homosexuals in every branch of the service grappling with feelings of rejection and despair, a momentous milestone in U.S. military history.

"For too long, gays and lesbians in the armed forces were barred from receiving such letters, leaving them woefully unaware that the person they once called their soul mate had been cheating on them throughout their deployment," said Clarence Navarro of the Human Rights Campaign, an LGBT advocacy group. "But now all troops, regardless of their sexual orientation, are free to have their entire lives ripped out from underneath them in a single short note." "This is a great day for homosexuals," Navarro added. "Even those who now have nothing to return home to."

—*The Onion*, "First-Ever Gay 'Dear John' Letters
Begin Reaching U.S. Troops Overseas"

Our laughter testifies to what many people in favor of the repeal had argued all along: that the repeal of Don't Ask, Don't Tell would show that gay troops were just like anyone else in our military, right down to having their hearts broken in a callous manner.

A writer or speaker can use humor to deal with especially sensitive issues. For example, sports commentator Bob Costas, given the honor of eulogizing the great baseball player Mickey Mantle, couldn't ignore problems in Mantle's life. So he argues for Mantle's greatness by admitting the man's weaknesses indirectly through humor:

It brings to mind a story Mickey liked to tell on himself and maybe some of you have heard it. He pictured himself at the pearly gates, met by St. Peter, who shook his head and said, "Mick, we checked the record. We know some of what went on. Sorry, we can't let you in. But before you go, God wants to know if you'd sign these six dozen baseballs."

—Bob Costas, "Eulogy for Mickey Mantle"

Similarly, politicians use humor to admit problems or mistakes they couldn't acknowledge in any other way. Here, for example, is President George W. Bush at the 2004 Radio and TV Correspondents' Dinner discussing his much-mocked intellect:

Those stories about my intellectual capacity do get under my skin. You know, for a while I even thought my staff believed it. There on my schedule first thing every morning it said, "Intelligence briefing."

—George W. Bush

Not all humor is well-intentioned. In fact, among the most powerful forms of emotional argument is ridicule—humor aimed at a particular target. Eighteenth-century poet and critic Samuel Johnson was known for his stinging and humorous put-downs, such as this comment to an aspiring writer: "Your manuscript is both good and original, but the part that is good is not original and the part that is original is not good." Today, even bumper stickers can be vehicles for succinct arguments:

But ridicule is a two-edged sword that requires a deft hand to wield it. Humor that reflects bad taste discredits a writer completely, as does ridicule that misses its mark. Unless your target deserves assault and you can be very funny, it's usually better to steer clear of humor.

Using Arguments Based on Emotion

You don't want to play puppetmaster with people's emotions when you write arguments, but it's a good idea to spend some time early in your work thinking about how you want readers to feel as they consider your persuasive claims. For example, would readers of your editorial about campus traffic policies be more inclined to agree with you if you made them envy faculty privileges, or would arousing their sense of fairness work better? What emotional appeals might persuade meat eaters to consider a vegan diet—or vice versa? Would sketches of stage props on a Web site persuade people to buy a season ticket to the theater, or would you spark more interest by featuring pictures of costumed performers?

Consider, too, the effect that a story can have on readers. Writers and journalists routinely use what are called *human-interest stories* to give presence to issues or arguments. You can do the same, using a particular incident to evoke sympathy, understanding, outrage, or amusement. Take care, though, to tell an honest story.

RESPOND.

1. To what specific emotions do the following slogans, sales pitches, and maxims appeal?

    "Just do it." (ad for Nike)

    "Think different." (ad for Apple computers)

"Reach out and touch someone." (ad for AT&T)

"Yes we can!" (2008 presidential campaign slogan for Barack Obama)

"Country first." (2008 presidential campaign slogan for John McCain)

"By any means necessary." (rallying cry from Malcolm X)

"Have it your way." (slogan for Burger King)

"You can trust your car to the man who wears the star." (slogan for Texaco)

"It's everywhere you want to be." (slogan for Visa)

"Know what comes between me and my Calvins? Nothing!" (tag line for Calvin Klein jeans)

"Don't mess with Texas!" (anti-litter campaign slogan)

"Because you're worth it." (ad for L'Oréal)

2. Bring a magazine to class, and analyze the emotional appeals in as many full-page ads as you can. Then classify those ads by types of emotional appeal, and see whether you can connect the appeals to the subject or target audience of the magazine. Compare your results with those of your classmates, and discuss your findings. For instance, do the ads in news magazines like *Time* and *Newsweek* appeal to different emotions and desires from the ads in publications such as *Cosmopolitan*, *Spin*, *Sports Illustrated*, *Automobile*, and *National Geographic*?

3. How do arguments based on emotion work in different media? Are such arguments more or less effective in books, articles, television (both news and entertainment shows), films, brochures, magazines, email, Web sites, the theater, street protests, and so on? You might explore how a single medium handles emotional appeals or compare different media. For example, why do the comments pages of blogs seem to encourage angry outbursts? Are newspapers an emotionally colder source of information than television news programs? If so, why?

4. Spend some time looking for arguments that use ridicule or humor to make their point: check out your favorite Web sites; watch for bumper stickers, posters, or advertisements; and listen to popular song lyrics. Bring one or two examples to class, and be ready to explain how the humor makes an emotional appeal and whether it's effective.

3
Arguments Based on Character: Ethos

Whenever you read anything—whether it's a news article, an advertisement, a speech, or a text message—you no doubt subconsciously analyze the message for a sense of the character and credibility of the sender: *Does this reporter seem biased? Why should I be paying attention to this speaker?* Our culture teaches us to be skeptical of most messages that bombard us with slogans, and that skepticism is a crucial skill in reading and evaluating arguments.

The mottoes associated with various sources of global information aim to "brand" them by helping to establish their character, what ancient rhetors referred to as *ethos*. And sometimes, slogans like "Fair & Balanced," "All the News That's Fit to Print," or "Do No Harm" can be effective: at the very least, if a phrase is repeated often enough, it comes to sound natural and right. Maybe CNN is the most trusted name in news!

But establishing character usually takes more than repetition, as marketers of all kinds know. In the auto industry American companies like Ford or GM are trying to reinvent themselves as forward-looking producers of fuel-efficient cars like the Volt, and they have mounted huge campaigns aimed at convincing buyers that their ethos has changed — for the better. Other companies are challenging them: Toyota's third-generation Prius has developed a strong reputation, a "good character" among buyers; the Nissan Leaf—which describes itself as "100% electric. Zero gas. Zero tailpipe"—was named "world car of the year" at the New York International Auto Show as well as a "top safety pick" by the Institute for Highway Safety, thus building an ethos of clean energy and safety. Tata Motors, whose motto is "We care," offers the Nano, the world's cheapest car whose character, they say, can be described as "the people's car." All of these companies know that their success in sales will be directly linked to their ability to establish a convincing and powerful ethos for their products.

If corporations can establish an ethos for themselves and their products, consider how much character matters when we think about people, especially those in the public eye. We'll mention only two very different examples: actor Charlie Sheen and football star Tim Tebow. Despite film credits that include *Platoon* and *Young Guns*, Sheen earned a hard-drinking, womanizing "bad boy" ethos after the questionable behavior of the character he played on TV sitcom *Two and a Half Men*

Charlie Sheen

Tim Tebow

crossed catastrophically into his real life. And though Heisman Trophy–winner Tim Tebow won two NCAA football championships with the Florida Gators before moving into the National Football League, his fame and ethos owe almost as much to unequivocal displays of his Christian faith, signaled on-field by the kneeling gesture now known as Tebowing.

As is often the case, fame brings endorsements. Tebow's "good guy" ethos was on display controversially yet believably in a pro-life Super Bowl ad he made for the Christian group Focus on the Family in 2010. But the athlete is also on the payroll for Nike and for Jockey underwear—usually fully clothed in his ads. And Sheen? What corporation would want to associate its products with such a questionable, and some might say self-destructive, character? In 2012, automaker Fiat hired him to sell Americans on the "Abarth" performance version of its tiny 500 sedan. A TV spot shows him hurling the Abarth at top speed inside a mansion filled with beautiful women: "I love being under house arrest," Sheen muses. In this case, celebrity ethos matches the product perfectly—especially given Fiat's target audience of men.

So you can see why Aristotle treats ethos as a powerful argumentative appeal. Ethos creates quick and sometimes almost irresistible connections between audience and arguments. We observe people, groups, or institutions making and defending claims all the time and inevitably ask ourselves, *Should we pay attention to them? Can we trust them? Do we want to trust them?* Consider, though, that the same questions will be asked about you and your work, especially in academic settings.

In fact, whenever you write a paper or present an idea, you are sending signals about your character and reliability, whether you intend to or not. If your ideas are reasonable, your sources are reliable, and your language is appropriate to the project, you will suggest to academic readers that you're someone whose ideas *might* deserve attention. You can appreciate why even details like correct spelling, grammar, and mechanics will weigh in your favor. And though you might not think about it now, at some point you may need letters of recommendation from instructors or supervisors. How will they remember you? Often chiefly from the ethos you have established in your work. Think about it.

Understanding How Arguments Based on Character Work

Put simply, arguments based on character (ethos) depend on *trust*. We tend to accept arguments from those we trust, and we trust them (whether individuals, groups, or institutions) in good part because of their reputations. Three main elements—trustworthiness/credibility, authority, and unselfish or clear motives—add up to *ethos*.

To answer serious and important questions, we often turn to professionals (doctors, lawyers, engineers, teachers, pastors) or to experts (those with knowledge and experience) for wise and frank advice. Such people come with some already established ethos based on their backgrounds and their knowledge. Thus, appeals or arguments about character often turn on claims like these:

- A person (or group or institution) is or is not trustworthy or credible on this issue.

- A person (or group or institution) does or does not have the authority to speak to this issue.

- A person (or group or institution) does or does not have unselfish or clear motives for addressing this subject.

Establishing Trustworthiness and Credibility

Trustworthiness and credibility speak to a writer's honesty, respect for an audience and its values, and plain old likability. Sometimes a sense of humor can play an important role in getting an audience to listen to or "like" you. It's no accident that all but the most serious speeches begin with a joke or funny story: the humor puts listeners at ease and helps them identify with the speaker. When President Obama spoke at the White House Correspondents' Dinner on April 30, 2011, he was coming off escalating attacks by "birthers" claiming that he was not a citizen of the United States. Obama used the opening of his speech to address those claims—in a humorous way aimed at establishing his credibility: To the tune of "I Am a Real American" accompanied by iconic American images interrupted every few seconds by a pulsating copy of his birth certificate, the president opened his remarks with a broad smile, saying "My *fellow* Americans," to loud laughs and cheers. After offering the traditional Hawaiian greeting of "Mahalo," he went on to say that, this week,

> the State of Hawaii released my official long-form birth certificate. Hopefully, this puts all doubts to rest. But just in case there are any lingering questions, tonight I am prepared to go a step further. Tonight, for the first time, I am releasing my official birth *video.*

President Obama tells jokes at the White House Correspondents' Dinner

What followed was a clip from Disney's *The Lion King*, which brought down the house. The president had shown he had a sense of humor, one he could turn on himself, and doing so helped to build credibility: he was, in fact, a "real American." A little self-deprecation like this can endear writers or speakers to the toughest audiences. We'll often listen to people confident enough to make fun of themselves, because they seem clever and yet aware of their own limitations.

But humor alone can't establish credibility. Although a funny anecdote may help dispose an audience to listen to you, you will need to move quickly to make reasonable claims and then back them up with evidence. Showing your authority on a topic is itself a good way to build credibility.

You can also establish credibility by connecting your own beliefs to core principles that are well established and widely respected. This strategy is particularly effective when your position seems to be — at first glance, at least — a threat to traditional values. For example, when conservative author Andrew Sullivan argues in favor of legalizing same-sex marriages, he does so in language that echoes the themes of family-values conservatives:

> Legalizing gay marriage would offer homosexuals the same deal society now offers heterosexuals: general social approval and specific legal advantages in exchange for a deeper and harder-to-extract-yourself-from commitment to another human being. Like straight marriage, it would foster social cohesion, emotional security, and economic prudence. Since there's no reason gays should not be allowed to adopt or be foster parents, it could also help nurture children.
>
> —Andrew Sullivan, "Here Comes the Groom"

Yet another way to affirm your credibility as a writer is to use language that shows your respect for readers' intelligence. Citing trustworthy sources and acknowledging them properly prove, too, that you've done your homework (another sign of respect) and suggest that you know your subject. So does presenting ideas clearly and fairly. Details matter: helpful graphs, tables, charts, or illustrations may carry weight with readers, as will the visual attractiveness of your text, whether in print or digital form. Even correct spelling counts!

Writers who establish their credibility seem trustworthy. But sometimes, to be credible, you have to admit limitations, too, as the late biologist Lewis Thomas does as he ponders whether scientists have overstepped their boundaries in exploring the limits of DNA research:

> Should we stop short of learning some things, for fear of what we, or someone, will do with the knowledge? My own answer is a flat no, but I must confess that this is an intuitive response and I am neither inclined nor trained to reason my way through it.
> —Lewis Thomas, "The Hazards of Science"

As Thomas's comments show, a powerful way to build credibility is to acknowledge outright any exceptions, qualifications, or even weaknesses in your argument. For example, a Volkswagen ad from the 1970s with the headline "They said it couldn't be done. It couldn't," shows that pro basketball star Wilt Chamberlain, at seven feet, one inch, tall, just can't fit inside the Bug. This ad is one of a classic series in which

They said it couldn't be done.
It couldn't.

We tried. Lord knows we tried. But no amount of pivoting or faking could squeeze the Philadelphia 76ers' Wilt Chamberlain into the front seat of a Volkswagen.

So if you're 7'1" tall like Wilt, our car is not for you.

But maybe you're a mere 6'7". In that case, you'd be small enough to appreciate what a big thing we've made of the Volkswagen.

There's more headroom than you'd expect. (Over 37½" from seat to roof.)

And there's more legroom in front than you'd get in a limousine. Because the engine's tucked over the rear wheels where it's out of the way (and where it can give the most traction).

You can put 2 medium-sized suitcases up front (where the engine isn't), and 3 fair-sized kids in the back seat. And you can sleep an enormous infant in back of the back seat.

Actually, there's only one part of a VW that you can't put much into. The gas tank.

But you can get about 29 miles per gallon out of it.

Volkswagen pokes fun at itself and admits to limitations while also promoting the good points about its car. As a result, the company gains credibility in the bargain.

Making such concessions to objections that readers might raise sends a strong signal to the audience that you've looked critically at your own position and can therefore be trusted when you turn to arguing for its merits. Speaking to readers directly, using *I* or *you*, can also help you connect with them, as can using contractions and everyday or colloquial language. In a commencement address, for example, Oprah Winfrey argues that the graduates need to consider how they can best serve others. To build her case, she draws on her own experience — forthrightly noting some mistakes and problems that she has faced in trying to live a life of service:

> I started this school in Africa . . . where I'm trying to give South African girls a shot at a future like yours. And I spent five years making sure that school would be as beautiful as the students. . . . And yet, last fall, I was faced with a crisis. . . . I was told that one of the dorm matrons was suspected of sexual abuse.

Oprah Winfrey in South Africa

That was, as you can imagine, devastating news. First, I cried—
actually, I sobbed. . . . And the whole time I kept asking that question:
What is this here to teach me? And, as difficult as that experience has
been, I got a lot of lessons. I understand now the mistakes I made,
because I had been paying attention to all of the wrong things. I'd built
that school from the outside in, when what really mattered was the
inside out.

—Oprah Winfrey, Stanford University Commencement Address

In some situations, you may find that a more formal tone gives your
claims greater credibility. You'll be making such choices as you search
for the ethos that represents you best.

Claiming Authority

When you read or listen to an argument, you have every right to ask
about the writer's authority: *What does he know about the subject? What
experiences does she have that make her especially knowledgeable? Why should
I pay attention to this writer?*

When you offer an argument, you have to anticipate and be able to
answer questions like these, either directly or indirectly. Sometimes the
claim of authority will be bold and personal, as it is when writer and activist Terry Tempest Williams attacks those who poisoned the Utah deserts
with nuclear radiation. What gives her the right to speak on this subject?
Not scientific expertise, but gut-wrenching personal experience:

I belong to the Clan of One-Breasted Women. My mother, my grand-
mothers, and six aunts have all had mastectomies. Seven are dead.
The two who survive have just completed rounds of chemotherapy
and radiation.

I've had my own problems: two biopsies for breast cancer and a
small tumor between my ribs diagnosed as a "borderline malignancy."

—Terry Tempest Williams, "The Clan of One-Breasted Women"

We are willing to listen to Williams's claims because she has lived with
the nuclear peril she will deal with in the remainder of her essay.

Writers usually establish their authority in less striking ways. Attaching titles to their names, for example, subtly builds authority by saying
they hold medical or legal or engineering degrees, or some special certifi-
cation. Similarly, writers assert authority by mentioning their employers

and the number of years they've worked in a given field. As a reader, you'll likely pay more attention to an argument about global warming if it's offered by someone who identifies herself as a professor of atmospheric and oceanic science at the University of Wisconsin, than by your Uncle Sid, who sells tools. But you'll prefer your uncle to the professor when you need advice about a reliable rotary saw.

When your readers may be skeptical of both you and your claim, you may have to be even more specific about your credentials. That's exactly the strategy Richard Bernstein uses to establish his right to speak on the subject of "Asian culture." What gives a New York writer named Bernstein the authority to write about Asian peoples? Bernstein tells us in a sparkling example of an argument based on character:

> The Asian culture, as it happens, is something I know a bit about, having spent five years at Harvard striving for a Ph.D. in a joint program called History and East Asian Languages and, after that, living either as a student (for one year) or a journalist (six years) in China and Southeast Asia. At least I know enough to know there is no such thing as the "Asian culture."
>
> —Richard Bernstein, *Dictatorship of Virtue*

When you write for readers who trust you and your work, you may not have to make such an open claim to authority. But making this type of appeal is always an option.

Authority can also be conveyed through fairly small signals that readers may pick up almost subconsciously. On his blog, writer and media analyst Clay Shirky talks easily about a new teaching job. The italicized words indicate his confidence and authority:

> This fall, I'm joining NYU's journalism program, where, for the first time in a dozen years, I will teach undergraduates. . . . *I could tell* these students that when I was growing up, the only news I read was thrown into our front yard by a boy on a bicycle. They might find this interesting, but only in the way I found it interesting that my father had grown up without indoor plumbing. *What 19 year olds need to know* isn't how it was in Ye Olden Tymes of 1992; *they need to know what we've learned* about supporting the creation and dissemination of news between then and now. Contemplating what I should tell them, *there are only three things I'm sure of*: News has to be subsidized, and it has to be cheap, and it has to be free.
>
> —Clay Shirky, "Why We Need the New News Environment to Be Chaotic"

| CULTURAL CONTEXTS FOR ARGUMENT |

Ethos

In the United States, students are often asked to establish authority by drawing on personal experiences, by reporting on research they or others have conducted, and by taking a position for which they can offer strong evidence. But this expectation about student authority is by no means universal.

Some cultures regard student writers as novices who can most effectively make arguments by reflecting on what they've learned from their teachers and elders—those who hold the most important knowledge and, hence, authority. When you're arguing a point with people from cultures other than your own, ask questions like:

- Whom are you addressing, and what is your relationship with that person?

- What knowledge are you expected to have? Is it appropriate or expected for you to demonstrate that knowledge—and if so, how?

- What tone is appropriate? And remember: politeness is rarely, if ever, inappropriate.

Coming Clean about Motives

When people are trying to sell you something, it's important (and natural) to ask: *Whose interests are they serving? How will they profit from their proposal?* Such suspicions go to the heart of ethical arguments.

Here, for example, someone posting on the Web site Serious Eats, which is "focused on celebrating and sharing food enthusiasm" online, acknowledges—in a footnote—that his attention to Martha Stewart, her Web site, and a *Martha Stewart Living* cookbook may be influenced by his employment history:

> Martha Stewart* has been blipping up on the Serious Eats radar lately.
> First it was this astronaut meal she chose for her longtime Microsoft billionaire friend Charles Simonyi, "a gourmet space meal of duck breast confit and semolina cake with dried apricots." Talk about going above and beyond.

Then official word comes that marthastewart.com has relaunched with a fresh new look and new features. The site, which went live in its new form a few weeks before this announcement, is quite an improvement. It seems to load faster, information is easier to find, and the recipes are easier to read—although there are so many brands, magazines, and "omnimedia" on offer that the homepage is a little dizzying at first.

Full disclosure: I used to work at Martha Stewart Living *magazine.*
                                         —Adam Kuban, "Martha, Martha, Martha"

Especially in online venues like the one Kuban uses here, writers have to expect that readers will hold diverse views and will be quick to point out unmentioned affiliations as serious drawbacks to credibility. In fact, attacks on such loyalties are common in political circles, where it's almost a sport to assume the worst about an opponent's motives and associations.

But we all have connections and interests that represent the ties that bind us to other human beings. It makes sense that a woman might be concerned with women's issues or that investors might look out for their investments. So it can be good strategy to let your audiences know where your loyalties lie when such information does, in fact, shape your work.

Using Ethos in Your Own Writing

- Establish your credibility by connecting to your audience's values, showing respect for them, and establishing common ground where possible. How will you convince your audience you are trustworthy? What will you admit about your own limitations?

- Establish your authority by showing you have done your homework and know your topic well. How will you show that you know your topic well? What appropriate personal experience can you draw on?

- Examine your motives for writing. What, if anything, do you stand to gain from your argument? How can you explain those advantages to your audience?

RESPOND●

1. Consider the ethos of these public figures. Then describe one or two products that might benefit from their endorsements as well as several that would not.

   Cat Deeley—emcee of *So You Think You Can Dance*

   Margaret Cho—comedian

Johnny Depp—actor

Lady Gaga—singer and songwriter

Bill O'Reilly—TV news commentator

Marge Simpson—sensible wife and mother on *The Simpsons*

Jon Stewart—host of *The Daily Show* on Comedy Central

2. Opponents of Richard Nixon, the thirty-seventh president of the United States, once raised doubts about his integrity by asking a single ruinous question: *Would you buy a used car from this man?* Create your own version of the argument of character. Begin by choosing an intriguing or controversial person or group and finding an image online. Then download the image into a word-processing file. Create a caption for the photo that is modeled after the question asked about Nixon: *Would you give this woman your email password? Would you share a campsite with this couple? Would you eat lasagna that this guy fixed?* Finally, write a serious 300-word argument that explores the character flaws or strengths of your subject(s).

3. Take a close look at your Facebook page (or your page on any other social media site). What are some aspects of your character, true or not, that might be conveyed by the photos, videos, and messages you have posted online? Analyze the ethos or character you see projected there, using the advice in this chapter to guide your analysis.

4
Arguments Based on Facts and Reason: Logos

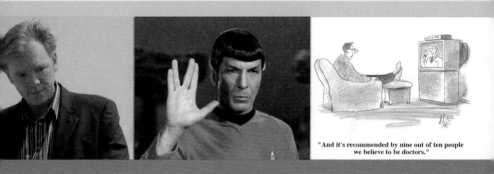

"And it's recommended by nine out of ten people we believe to be doctors."

These three images say a lot about the use and place of logic (*logos*) in Western, and particularly American, culture. The first shows David Caruso as Lt. Horatio Caine in the TV series *CSI: Miami,* in which crime lab investigators use science to determine the facts behind unsolved murder cases. The second refers to an even more popular TV (and film) series, *Star Trek,* whose Vulcan officer, Spock, reasons through logic alone; and the third is a cartoon spoofing a logical argument (nine out of ten prefer X) made so often that it has become something of a joke itself.

These images attest to the prominent place that logic holds: like the investigators on *CSI*, we continue to want access to the facts on the assumption that they will help us make the best arguments. We admire those whose logic is, like Spock's, impeccable, and we respond to implied arguments suggested when they begin, "Nine out of ten doctors recommend . . ." Those are odds that most accept, suggesting overwhelmingly that the next doctor will also agree with the prognosis. But these images also challenge or undercut our reliance on logic alone: Lt. Caine and Spock are characters drawn in broad and often parodic strokes; the "nine out of ten" cartoon directly spoofs such arguments. When the choice is between logic and emotion, however, most of us still say we respect *appeals to logos*—arguments based on facts, evidence, and reason (though we're inclined to test the facts against our feelings and against the ethos of those making the appeal).

Providing Hard Evidence

Aristotle helps us out in classifying arguments by distinguishing two kinds:

Artistic Proofs	Arguments the writer/ speaker creates	Constructed arguments	Appeals to reason; common sense
Inartistic Proofs	Arguments the writer/ speaker is given	Hard evidence	Facts, statistics, testimonies, witnesses, contracts, documents

We can see these different kinds of logical appeals at work in the most recent attempts of former vice president Al Gore to raise awareness and evoke action on global warming. On September 14, 2011, Gore launched a twenty-four-hour worldwide live-streamed event to introduce the new Climate Reality Project, beginning with a new thirty-minute multimedia presentation shown once an hour for twenty-four hours in every time zone across the globe. The project intends, according to its Web site, to bring

> the facts about the climate crisis into the mainstream and engage the public in conversation about how to solve it. We help citizens around the world reject the lies and take meaningful steps to bring about change.

The project, Gore claims, is guided by "one simple truth":

> The climate crisis is real and we know how to solve it.

Note the emphasis on "the facts about the climate crisis": Gore and his colleagues will have to rely on a lot of hard evidence and inartistic proof in asserting that the "climate crisis is real." In an essay in *Rolling Stone*, Gore summarized some of this evidence, saying that today

> the scientific consensus [for the reality of global warming] is even stronger. It has been endorsed by every National Academy of science of every major country on the planet, every major professional scientific society related to the study of global warming and 98 percent of

"Who Cares about Ice Bears?"

climate scientists throughout the world. In the latest and most author-itative study by three thousand of the very best scientific experts in the world, the evidence was judged "unequivocal."

Here Gore refers to testimony, statistics, and facts to carry his argument forward. But he also must rely on less "hard" evidence, as when he says:

> Determining what is real can be a challenge in our culture, but in order to make wise choices in the presence of such grave risks, we must use common sense and the rule of reason in coming to an agree-ment on what is true.

Common sense, Gore tells us, shows us that global warming has got to be true: just look around and see the evidence in the melting ice caps and the rising seas—and a lot more. Gore believes that this artistic ap-peal will go as far as the hard scientific evidence to convince readers to take action. (Seeing is believing, after all—or is it? See p. 59.) And action is what he's after. At the end of this long essay, he uses another bit of constructed reasoning to show that if everyday Americans make their position clear, the leaders will follow:

> Why do you think President Obama and Congress changed their game on "don't ask, don't tell"? It happened because enough Americans

delivered exactly that tough message to candidates who wanted their votes. When enough people care passionately enough to drive that message home on the climate crisis, politicians will look at their hole cards, and enough of them will change their game to make all the difference we need.

Will Gore and the Climate Reality Project convince global citizens that they are right about what is "true" about climate change? Not if other powerful voices can help it. A quick Google search for "global warming hoax" will take you to weekly updates providing countervailing studies and testimony. And Gore himself has been an often easy target for attack, especially after some leaked scientific email from Britain evoked charges that climate scientists were "doctoring" the facts, though independent critics eventually determined that the email wording was taken seriously out of context and that the email did not undermine the data on global climate change and its causes.

This cartoon suggests that changing the subject is a fallback strategy when the "facts" are inconvenient.

This ongoing controversy surrounding global warming is a good example of how difficult it can be to distinguish the good evidence from the slanted or fabricated kinds and to decide how to make sound decisions based on it.

IS SEEING BELIEVING?

Some of the debate over climate change centers on photographs, which may be telling "nothing but the truth"—or not. We have known for decades that all photographs in some way shape or interpret what they show, but in the age of Photoshop readers need to be even more careful about believing what they see, and writers need to be especially careful that the images they use are trustworthy. Whole books have been devoted to "digital fakery" and photographic manipulation, and examples are easy to find. In 2008, Iran was caught red-handed manipulating a photograph of missiles, as you see in the two photographs above: where did the fourth missile (in the right-hand photo) come from? So egregious was this example of manipulation that others like Boing Boing soon got into the act, inviting readers to join in by submitting their own manipulations of the original image on the left.

Today, when we can all slant discussions, cherry-pick examples, and alter images, writers need more than ever to be aware of the ethics of evidence, whether that evidence draws on facts, statistics, survey data, testimony and narratives, or commonsense reasoning.

RESPOND•

Discuss whether the following statements are examples of hard evidence or constructed arguments. Not all cases are clear-cut.

1. Drunk drivers are involved in more than 50 percent of traffic deaths.
2. DNA tests of skin found under the victim's fingernails suggest that the defendant was responsible for the assault.
3. A psychologist testified that teenage violence could not be blamed on video games.
4. An apple a day keeps the doctor away.
5. "The only thing we have to fear is fear itself."
6. Air bags ought to be removed from vehicles because they can kill young children and small-frame adults.

Facts

Gathering factual information and transmitting it faithfully practically define what we mean by professional journalism and scholarship. We'll even listen to people we don't agree with if their evidence is really good. Below, a reviewer for the conservative *National Review* praises William Julius Wilson, a liberal sociologist, because of how well he presents his case:

> In his eagerly awaited new book, Wilson argues that ghetto blacks are worse off than ever, victimized by a near-total loss of low-skill jobs in and around inner-city neighborhoods. In support of this thesis, he *musters mountains of data, plus excerpts from some of the thousands of surveys and face-to-face interviews that he and his research team conducted among inner-city Chicagoans.* It is a book that deserves a wide audience among thinking conservatives.
> —John J. Dilulio Jr., "When Decency Disappears" (emphasis added)

When your facts are compelling, they may stand on their own in a low-stakes argument, supported by little more than saying where they come from. Consider the power of phrases such as "reported by the *Wall Street Journal*," or "according to factcheck.org." Such sources gain credibility if they have reported facts accurately and reliably over time. Using such credible sources in an argument can also reflect positively on you.

But arguing with facts can also involve challenging even the most reputable sources if they lead to unfair or selective reporting. In recent years, bloggers and other online critics have enjoyed pointing out the biases or factual mistakes of "mainstream media" (MSM) outlets. These criticisms often deal not just with specific facts and coverage but with the overall way that an issue is presented or "framed." In the following highly rhetorical passage from liberal economist Paul Krugman's blog, he points out what, from his point of view, is a persistent tendency of the mainstream media to claim they are framing issues in "fair and balanced" ways by presenting two opposing sides as if they were equal:

> Watching our system deal with the debt ceiling crisis—a wholly self-inflicted crisis, which may nonetheless have disastrous consequences— it's increasingly obvious that what we're looking at is the destructive influence of a cult that has really poisoned our political system. . . . [T]he cult that I see as reflecting a true moral failure is the cult of balance, of centrism.
>
> Think about what's happening right now. We have a crisis in which the right is making insane demands, while the president and Democrats in Congress are bending over backward to be accommodating— offering plans that are all spending cuts and no taxes, plans that are far to the right of public opinion.
>
> So what do most news reports say? They portray it as a situation in which both sides are equally partisan, equally intransigent—because news reports always do that. And we have influential pundits calling out for a new centrist party, a new centrist president, to get us away from the evils of partisanship.
>
> The reality, of course, is that we already have a centrist president—actually a moderate conservative president. Once again, health reform—his only major change to government—was modeled on Republican plans, indeed plans coming from the Heritage Foundation. And everything else—including the wrongheaded emphasis on austerity in the face of high unemployment—is according to the conservative playbook.
>
> What all this means is that there is no penalty for extremism; no way for most voters, who get their information on the fly rather than doing careful study of the issues, to understand what's really going on.
>
> You have to ask, what would it take for these news organizations and pundits to actually break with the convention that both sides are equally at fault? This is the clearest, starkest situation one can imagine short of civil war. If this won't do it, nothing will.
>
> —Paul Krugman, "The Cult That Is Destroying America"

In an ideal world, good information—no matter where it comes from—would always drive out bad. But you already know that we don't live in an ideal world, so sometimes bad information gets repeated in an echo chamber that amplifies the errors.

Many media have no pretenses at all about being reputable. During the 2008 presidential campaign, the Internet blared statements proclaiming that Barack Obama was Muslim, even after dozens of sources, including many people with whom Obama had worshipped, testified to his Christianity. As a reader and researcher, you should look beyond headlines, bylines, reputations, and especially rumors that fly about the Internet. Scrutinize any facts you collect, and test their reliability before passing them on.

Statistics

You've probably heard the old saying that "There are three kinds of lies: lies, damned lies, and statistics," and, to be sure, it is possible to lie with numbers, even those that are accurate, because numbers rarely speak for themselves. They need to be interpreted by writers — and writers almost always have agendas that shape the interpretations.

Of course, just because they are often misused doesn't mean that statistics are meaningless, but it does suggest that you need to use them carefully and to remember that your interpretation of the statistics is very important. Consider an article from the *Atlantic* called "American Murder Mystery" by Hanna Rosin. The "mystery" Rosin writes about is the rise of crime in midsize American cities such as Memphis, Tennessee. The article raised a firestorm of response and criticism, including this analysis of statistical malfeasance from blogger Alan Salzberg:

> The primary statistical evidence given in the article of an association between crime and former Section 8 [housing project] residents, is a map that shows areas with high incidents of crime correspond to areas with a large number of people with Section 8 subsidies (i.e., former residents of housing projects). As convincing as this might sound, it has a fatal flaw: the map looks at total incidents rather than crime rate. This means that an area with ten thousand people and one hundred crimes (and one hundred Section 8 subsidy recipients) will look much worse than an area with one hundred people and one crime (and one Section 8 subsidy recipient). However, both areas have the same rate of crime, and, presumably, the same odds of being a victim of crime. Yet in Betts and Janikowski's analysis, the area with ten thousand people has a higher number of Section 8 subsidy recipients and higher crime, thus "proving" their theory of association.

When relying on statistics in your arguments, make sure you check and double-check them or get help in doing so: you don't want to be accused of using "fictitious data" based on "ludicrous assumptions"!

The text in the cartoon says it all.

"Now, keep in mind that these numbers are only as accurate as the fictitious data, ludicrous assumptions and wishful thinking they're based upon!"

© Original Artist. Reproduction rights obtainable from www.CartoonStock.com

RESPOND •

Statistical evidence becomes useful only when interpreted fairly and reasonably. Go to the *USA Today* Web site and look for the daily graph, chart, or table called the "USA Today snapshot." Pick a snapshot, and use the information in it to support three different claims, at least two of which make very different points. Share your claims with classmates. (The point is not to learn to use data dishonestly but to see firsthand how the same statistics can serve a variety of arguments.)

Surveys and Polls

When they verify the popularity of an idea or proposal, surveys and polls provide strong persuasive appeals because they come as close to expressing the will of the people as anything short of an election—the most decisive poll of all. However, surveys and polls can do much more than help politicians make decisions. They can also provide persuasive reasons for action or intervention. When surveys show, for example, that most American sixth-graders can't locate France or Wyoming on a map—not to mention Turkey or Afghanistan—that's an appeal for better instruction in geography. It always makes sense, however, to question poll numbers, especially when they support your own point of view. Ask who commissioned the poll, who is publishing its outcome, who was surveyed (and in what proportions), and what stakes these parties might have in its outcome.

Are we being too suspicious? No. In fact, this sort of scrutiny is exactly what you should anticipate from your readers whenever you do surveys to explore an issue. You should be confident that you've surveyed enough people to be accurate, that the people you chose for the study were representative of the selected population as a whole, and that you chose them randomly—not selecting those most likely to say what you hoped to hear.

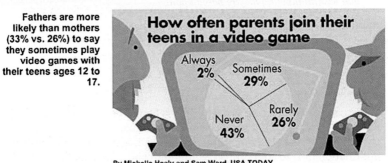

Fathers are more likely than mothers (33% vs. 26%) to say they sometimes play video games with their teens ages 12 to 17.

How often parents join their teens in a video game

Always 2%
Sometimes 29%
Never 43%
Rarely 26%

By Michelle Healy and Sam Ward, USA TODAY
Source: Pew Internet & American Life Project

USA Today is famous for the tables, pie charts, and graphs it creates to present statistics and poll results. What claims might the evidence in this graph support? How does the design of the item influence your reading of it?

On the other hand, as with other kinds of factual evidence, don't make the opposite mistake by discounting or ignoring polls whose findings are *not* what you had hoped for. In the following excerpts from a column in the *Dallas News*, conservative Rod Dreher forthrightly faces up to the results from a poll of registered Texas voters—results that he finds ominous for his Texas Republican Party:

> The full report, which will be released today, knocks the legs out from under two principles cherished by the party's grassroots: staunch social conservatism and hard-line immigration policies. At the state level, few voters care much about abortion, school prayer and other hot-button issues. Immigration is the only conservative stand-by that rates much mention—and by hitting it too hard, Republicans lose both the Hispanics and independents that make up what the pollster defines as the "Critical Middle." . . .
>
> This is not going to go down well with the activist core of the Texas GOP, especially people like me: a social conservative with firm views on illegal immigration. But reality has a way of focusing the mind, forcing one to realize that political parties are not dogma-driven churches, but coalitions that unavoidably shift over time.
>
> —Rod Dreher, "Poll's Shocking SOS for Texas GOP"

Dreher's frank acknowledgment of findings that did not please him also helps him to create a positive ethos as a trustworthy writer who follows the facts wherever they lead.

The meaning of polls and surveys is also affected by the way that questions are asked. Recent research has shown, for example, that questions about same-sex unions get differing responses according to how they are worded. When people are asked whether gay and lesbian couples should be eligible for the same inheritance and partner health benefits that heterosexual couples receive, a majority of those polled say yes—unless the word *marriage* appears in the question; then the responses are primarily negative. Remember, then, to be very careful in wording questions for any poll you conduct.

Finally, always keep in mind that the date of a poll may strongly affect the results—and their usefulness in an argument. In 2010, for example, nearly 50 percent of California voters supported building more nuclear power plants. Less than a year later, that percentage had dropped to 37 percent after the meltdown of Japanese nuclear power plants in the wake of the March 2011 earthquake and tsunami.

RESPOND •

Choose an important issue and design a series of questions to evoke a range of responses in a poll. Try to design a question that would make people strongly inclined to agree, another question that would lead them to oppose the same proposition, and a third that tries to be more neutral. Then try out your questions on your classmates.

Testimonies and Narratives

Writers can support their arguments with all kinds of human experience presented in the form of narrative or testimony, particularly if that experience is the writer's own. In courts, decisions often take into consideration detailed descriptions and narratives of exactly what occurred. Look at this reporter's account of a court case in which a panel of judges decided, based on the testimony presented, that a man had been sexually harassed by another man. The narrative, in this case, supplies the evidence:

> The Seventh Circuit, in a 1997 case known as *Doe v. City of Belleville,* drew a sweeping conclusion allowing for same-sex harassment cases of many kinds. . . . This case, for example, centered on teenage twin brothers working a summer job cutting grass in the city cemetery of Belleville, Ill. One boy wore an earring, which caused him no end of grief that particular summer — including a lot of menacing talk among his coworkers about sexually assaulting him in the woods and sending him "back to San Francisco." One of his harassers, identified in court documents as a large former marine, culminated a verbal campaign by backing the earring-wearer against a wall and grabbing him by the testicles to see "if he was a girl or a guy." The teenager had been "singled out for this abuse," the court ruled, "because the way in which he projected the sexual aspect of his personality" — meaning his gender — "did not conform to his coworkers' view of appropriate masculine behavior."
> — Margaret Talbot, "Men Behaving Badly"

Personal narratives can support a claim convincingly, especially if a writer has earned the trust of readers. In an essay arguing that people should pay very close attention to intuition, regarding it as important as more factual evidence, Suzanne Guillette uses personal narrative to good effect:

> It was late summer 2009: I was walking on a Long Island beach with my boyfriend Mark and some friends. When I saw Mark sit down next

to his friend Dana on a craggy rock, a sudden electric shock traveled straight up the center of my body. It was so visceral it made me stumble. And then my mind flashed to a recent dream I'd had of Dana sitting on Mark's lap as he rode a bike. *Don't be crazy,* I chided myself, turning to watch the surfers. *They're just friends.* But one night nine months later . . . Mark confessed that he and Dana had had an affair. . . . Each time I had a "flash," I realized that listening to it—or not—had consequences.

—Suzanne Guillette, "Learning to Listen"

This narrative introduction gives readers details to support the claim Guillette is making: we can make big mistakes if we ignore our intuitions. (For more on establishing credibility with readers, see Chapter 3.)

RESPOND●

Bring to class a full review of a recent film that you either enjoyed or did not enjoy. Using testimony from that review, write a brief argument to your classmates explaining why they should see that movie (or why they should avoid it), being sure to use evidence from the review fairly and reasonably. Then exchange arguments with a classmate, and decide whether the evidence in your peer's argument helps to change your opinion about the movie. What's convincing about the evidence? If it doesn't convince you, why not?

Using Reason and Common Sense

If you don't have "hard facts," you can support claims by using reason and common sense. The formal study of reasoning is called *logic*, and you probably recognize a famous example of deductive reasoning, called a syllogism:

All human beings are mortal.

Socrates is a human being.

Therefore, Socrates is mortal.

In valid syllogisms, the conclusion follows logically—and technically—from the premises that lead up to it. Many have criticized syllogistic reasoning for being limited, and others have poked fun at it, as in this cartoon:

Logic: another thing that penguins aren't very good at.

But few people use formal deductive reasoning to support claims. Even Aristotle recognized that most people argue perfectly well using informal rather than formal logic. To do so, they rely mostly on habits of mind and assumptions that they share with their readers or listeners.

In Chapter 7, we describe a system of informal logic that you may find useful in shaping credible arguments — **Toulmin argument**. Here, we briefly examine some ways that people use informal logic in their everyday lives. Once again, we begin with Aristotle, who used the term **enthymeme** to describe an ordinary kind of sentence that includes both a claim and a reason but depends on the audience's agreement with an assumption that is left implicit rather than spelled out. Enthymemes can be very persuasive when most people agree with the assumptions they rest on. The following sentences are all enthymemes:

We'd better cancel the picnic because it's going to rain.

Flat taxes are fair because they treat everyone the same.

I'll buy a PC instead of a Mac because it's cheaper.

NCAA football needs a playoff to crown a real national champion.

Sometimes enthymemes seem so obvious that readers don't realize that they're drawing inferences when they agree with them. Consider the first example:

> We'd better cancel the picnic because it's going to rain.

Let's expand the enthymeme a bit to say more of what the speaker may mean:

> We'd better cancel the picnic this afternoon because the weather bureau is predicting a 70 percent chance of rain for the remainder of the day.

Embedded in this brief argument are all sorts of assumptions and fragments of cultural information that are left implicit but that help to make it persuasive:

> Picnics are ordinarily held outdoors.
>
> When the weather is bad, it's best to cancel picnics.
>
> Rain is bad weather for picnics.
>
> A 70 percent chance of rain means that rain is more likely to occur than not.
>
> When rain is more likely to occur than not, it makes sense to cancel picnics.

For most people, the original statement carries all this information on its own; the enthymeme is a compressed argument, based on what audiences know and will accept.

But sometimes enthymemes aren't self-evident:

> Be wary of environmentalism because it's religion disguised as science.
>
> iPhones are undermining civil society by making us even more focused on ourselves.
>
> It's time to make all public toilets unisex because to do otherwise is discriminatory.

In these cases, you'll have to work much harder to defend both the claim and the implicit assumptions that it's based on by drawing out the inferences that seem self-evident in other enthymemes. And you'll likely also have to supply credible evidence. A simple declaration of fact won't suffice.

CULTURAL CONTEXTS FOR ARGUMENT

Logos

In the United States, student writers are expected to draw on "hard facts" and evidence as often as possible in supporting their claims: while ethical and emotional appeals are important, logical appeals tend to hold sway in academic writing. So statistics and facts speak volumes, as does reasoning based on time-honored values such as fairness and equity. In writing to global audiences, you need to remember that not all cultures value the same kinds of appeals. If you want to write to audiences across cultures, you need to know about the norms and values in those cultures. Chinese culture, for example, values authority and often indirect allusion over "facts" alone. Some African cultures value cooperation and community over individualism, and still other cultures value religious texts as providing compelling evidence. So think carefully about what you consider strong evidence, and pay attention to what counts as evidence to others. You can begin by asking yourself questions like:

- What evidence is most valued by your audience: Facts? Concrete examples? Firsthand experience? Religious or philosophical texts? Something else?
- Will analogies count as support? How about precedents?
- Will the testimony of experts count? If so, what kind of experts are valued most?

Providing Logical Structures for Argument

Some arguments depend on particular logical structures to make their points. In the following pages, we identify a few of these logical structures.

Degree

Arguments based on degree are so common that people barely notice them, nor do they pay much attention to how they work because they seem self-evident. Most audiences will readily accept that *more of a good thing* or *less of a bad thing* is good. In her novel *The Fountainhead*, Ayn Rand

A demonstrator at an immigrants' rights rally in New York City in 2007. Arguments based on values that are widely shared within a society—such as the idea of equal rights in American culture—have an automatic advantage with audiences.

asks: "If physical slavery is repulsive, how much more repulsive is the concept of servility of the spirit?" Most readers immediately comprehend the point Rand intends to make about slavery of the spirit because they already know that physical slavery is cruel and would reject any forms of slavery that were even crueler on the principle that *more of a bad thing is bad*. Rand still needs to offer evidence that "servility of the spirit" is, in fact, worse than bodily servitude, but she has begun with a logical structure readers can grasp. Here are other arguments that work similarly:

> If I can get a ten-year warranty on an inexpensive Kia, shouldn't I get the same or better warranty from a more expensive Lexus?
>
> The health benefits from using stem cells in research will surely outweigh the ethical risks.
>
> Better a conventional war now than a nuclear confrontation later.

Analogies

Analogies, typically complex or extended comparisons, explain one idea or concept by comparing it to something else.

Here, writer and founder of literacy project 826 Valencia, Dave Eggers, uses an analogy in arguing that we do not value teachers as much as we should:

> When we don't get the results we want in our military endeavors, we don't blame the soldiers. We don't say, "It's these lazy soldiers and their bloated benefits plans! That's why we haven't done better in Afghanistan!" No, if the results aren't there, we blame the planners. . . . No one contemplates blaming the men and women fighting every day in the trenches for little pay and scant recognition. And yet in education we do just that. When we don't like the way our students score on international standardized tests, we blame the teachers.
>
> —Dave Eggers and Ninive Calegari,
> "The High Cost of Low Teacher Salaries"

Precedent

Arguments from **precedent** and arguments of analogy both involve comparisons. Consider an assertion like this one, which uses a comparison as a precedent:

> If motorists in most other states can pump their own gas safely, surely the state of Oregon can trust its own drivers to be as capable. It's time for Oregon to permit self-service gas stations.

You could tease out several inferences from this claim to explain its reasonableness: people in Oregon are as capable as people in other states; people with equivalent capabilities can do the same thing; pumping gas is not hard, and so forth. But you don't have to because most readers get the argument simply because of the way it is put together.

Here is an excerpt from an extended argument by blogger Neil Warner, in which he argues that the "Arab Spring" of 2011 may not follow the same pattern as its historical precedents:

> ["Arab Spring"] is in many respects a fitting name, one that relates not only to the season in which the unrest really began but also captures perfectly the newfound optimism and youthful determination that seems to have embraced the region. Unfortunately, though, "Spring" as a term for popular movements does not have an encouraging history.
>
> The most comparable event with the same title is the so-called "Spring of the Nations" or "Springtime of the Peoples" of 1848–49. In one of the most stunning international events the world has ever witnessed, a wildfire of liberal revolution spread out across Europe following the

overthrow of the restored French monarchy in February of 1848. Traditional reactionary regimes fell like dominos and a sense of unity of purpose and hopefulness very comparable in some ways to 2011 in the Arab World embraced the populace, both working class and middle class, of Germany, Italy, the Austrian Empire, and elsewhere. An uprising in November 1848 even forced the Pope to flee Rome.

But by the end of 1849 it had all fizzled out, reactionary forces reassembled and the revolutionaries split, and the old order in Europe settled back down as if nothing had ever happened. . . .

With respect to the Arab world, we can already see the same pattern developing. After an initial panic following the overthrow of Mubarak, the Arab dictatorships of the region have consolidated themselves and clung on for dear life. . . .

—Neil Warner, "The Anatomy of a Spring"

You'll encounter additional kinds of logical structures as you create your own arguments. You'll find some of them in Chapter 5, "Fallacies of Argument," and still more in Chapter 7 on Toulmin argument.

5
Fallacies of Argument

PERSONAL ATTACK FALLACY

Can we let a shrimp like this run our great country?

The New Face Of Hitler

Vegetarians linked to higher brain power

AUSTRALIA'S elite high IQ group Mensa has mo[r]
than its fair share of vegetarians.

That might be more than coincidental, according [to]
new research which suggests that people who choose th[e]
vegetarian path are smarter than their carnivorous cou[n]
terparts.

The study, published in the *British Medical Journe*[l]
traced 8000 people from birth and found that those wh[o]

Do the arguments embedded in these three images look a little suspicious to you? Chances are, you recognize them as faulty reasoning of some kind. Such argumentative moves are called **fallacies**, arguments that are flawed by their very nature or structure. The first, a cartoon, represents a move familiar to all who follow political "attack" ads that focus on the character of the person (he's a shrimp!) rather than substance. The second, a protest image, uses scare tactics to compare the Obama administration to the Nazis; and the third, from a news article, illustrates false cause: high IQs could be caused by any number of things, but probably not vegetarianism alone!

Using fallacies can hurt everyone involved, including the person using them, because they make productive argument more difficult. They muck up the frank but civil conversations that people should be able to have, regardless of their differences. But fallacies can be powerful tools, so it's important that you can recognize and point them out in the works of others—and avoid them in your own writing. This chapter aims to help you meet these goals: here we'll introduce you to fallacies of argument classified according to the emotional, ethical, and logical appeals we've discussed earlier (see Chapters 2–4).

Fallacies of Emotional Argument

Emotional arguments can be powerful and suitable in many circumstances, and most writers use them frequently. However, writers who pull on their readers' heartstrings or raise their blood pressure too often can violate the good faith on which legitimate argument depends.

Scare Tactics

Politicians, advertisers, and public figures sometimes peddle their ideas by scaring people and exaggerating possible dangers well beyond their statistical likelihood. Such ploys work because it's easier to imagine something terrible happening than to appreciate its rarity.

Scare tactics can also be used to stampede legitimate fears into panic or prejudice. People who genuinely fear losing their jobs can be persuaded to fear that immigrants might work for less money. People who are living on fixed incomes can be convinced that minor changes to entitlement programs represent dire threats to their well-being. Such tactics have the effect of closing off thinking because people who are scared often act irrationally. Even well-intended fear campaigns—like those directed against the use of illegal drugs, smoking, or unprotected sex—can misfire if their warnings prove too shrill. People just stop listening.

Either-Or Choices

One way to simplify arguments and give them power is to reduce complicated issues to just two options, one obviously preferable to the other. Here is President Obama speaking to an Associated Press luncheon in 2012 and contrasting his vision of the country with what he wants listeners to believe is his opponents' view:

> Ask any company where they'd rather locate and hire workers—a country with crumbling roads and bridges, or one that's committed to high-speed Internet and high-speed railroads and high-tech research and development?

Obama is arguing that his economic policies will provide funds for exciting infrastructure developments whereas Republicans are so concerned with deficits that they are willing to allow the country to crumble, literally. A moment's thought, however, suggests that the choices here are too stark to reflect the complexity of the national economy. Yet, like most politicians, Obama can't seem to resist the power of this mode of argument.

Either-or choices can be well-intentioned strategies to get something accomplished. Parents use them all the time ("Eat your broccoli, or you won't get dessert"). But they become fallacious arguments when they reduce a complicated issue to excessively simple terms or when they're designed to obscure legitimate alternatives. For instance, to suggest that renewable power sources such as wind and solar represent the only long-term solution to our energy needs may have rhetorical power, but the choice is too easy and uncomplicated. Energy shortages can be fixed in any number of ways, *including* wind and solar power.

Slippery Slope

The **slippery slope** fallacy portrays today's tiny misstep as tomorrow's slide into disaster. Some arguments that aim at preventing dire consequences do not take the slippery slope approach (for example, the parent who corrects a child for misbehavior now is acting sensibly to prevent more serious problems as the child grows older). A slippery slope argument becomes wrongheaded when a writer exaggerates the likely consequences of an action, usually to frighten readers. As such, slippery slope arguments are also scare tactics. In recent years, the issue of same-sex marriage has evoked many slippery slope arguments:

> Anyone else bored to tears with the "slippery slope" arguments against gay marriage? Since few opponents of homosexual unions are brave enough to admit that gay weddings just freak them out, they hide behind the claim that it's an inexorable slide from legalizing gay marriage to having sex with penguins outside JC Penney's. The problem is it's virtually impossible to debate against a slippery slope.
>
> —Dahlia Lithwick, "Slippery Slop"

Ideas and actions do have consequences, but they aren't always as dire as writers fond of slippery slope tactics would have you believe.

Overly Sentimental Appeals

Overly **sentimental appeals** use tender emotions excessively to distract readers from facts. Often, such appeals are highly personal and individual and focus attention on heartwarming or heartwrenching situations that make readers feel guilty if they challenge an idea, a policy, or a proposal. Emotions become an impediment to civil discourse when they keep people from thinking clearly.

Such sentimental appeals are a major vehicle of television news, where tugging at viewers' heartstrings can mean high ratings. For example, when a camera documents the day-to-day sacrifices of parents who are trying to meet their mortgage payments and keep their kids in college in a tough economy, their on-screen struggles can represent the spirit of an entire class of people threatened by callous bankers. But while such individual stories stir genuine emotions, they seldom give a complete picture of a complex social or economic issue.

This image, taken from a gun control protest, is designed to elicit sympathy by causing the viewer to think about the dangers guns pose to innocent children and, thus, support the cause.

Bandwagon Appeals

Bandwagon appeals urge people to follow the same path everyone else is taking. Rather than think independently about where to go, it's often easier to get on board the bandwagon with everyone else.

Many American parents seem to have an innate ability to refute bandwagon appeals. When their kids whine, *Everyone else is going camping without chaperones,* the parents reply, *And if everyone else jumps off a cliff (or a railroad bridge or the Empire State Building), you will too?* The children groan—and then try a different line of argument.

Unfortunately, not all bandwagon approaches are so transparent. In recent decades, bandwagon issues have included the war on drugs, the nuclear freeze movement, the campaign against drunk driving, campaign finance reform, illegal immigration, the defense of marriage, and bailouts for banks and businesses. These issues are all too complex to permit the suspension of judgment that bandwagon tactics require.

Cartoonist Roz Chast's take on bandwagon appeals.

© The New Yorker Collection 1988 Roz Chast from cartoonbank.com. All rights reserved.

Fallacies of Ethical Argument

Because readers give their closest attention to authors they respect or trust, writers usually want to present themselves as honest, well-informed, likable, or sympathetic. But not all the devices that writers use to gain the attention and confidence of readers are admirable. (For more on appeals based on character, see Chapter 3.)

Appeals to False Authority

Many academic research papers find and reflect on the work of reputable authorities and introduce these authorities through direct quotations or citations as credible evidence. (For more on assessing the reliability of sources, see Chapter 18.) **False authority**, however, occurs when writers offer themselves or other authorities as sufficient warrant for believing a claim:

Claim	X is true because I say so.
Warrant	What I say must be true.
Claim	X is true because Y says so.
Warrant	What Y says must be true.

Though they are seldom stated so baldly, claims of authority drive many political campaigns. American pundits and politicians are fond of citing the U.S. Constitution and its Bill of Rights (Canadians have their Charter of Rights and Freedoms) as ultimate authorities, a reasonable practice when the documents are interpreted respectfully. However, the rights claimed sometimes aren't in the texts themselves or don't mean what the speakers think they do. And most constitutional matters are debatable—as volumes of court records prove. Likewise, religious believers often base arguments on books or traditions that wield great authority in a particular religious community. But the power of such texts is usually limited to that group and less capable of persuading others solely on the grounds of authority.

In short, you should pay serious attention to claims supported by respected authorities, such as the Centers for Disease Control, the National Science Foundation, or the *Globe and Mail*. But don't accept information simply because it is put forth by such offices and agencies. To quote a Russian proverb made famous by Ronald Reagan, "Trust, but verify."

Dogmatism

A writer who asserts or assumes that a particular position is the *only one* that is conceivably acceptable is expressing **dogmatism**, a fallacy of character that undermines the trust that must exist between those who make and listen to arguments. When people write dogmatically, they imply that no arguments are necessary: the truth is self-evident and needs no support.

Some arguments present claims so outrageous that they're unworthy of serious attention: attacks on the historical reality of the Holocaust fall into this category. But few subjects that can be defended with facts, testimony, and good reasons ought to be off the table in a free society. In general, whenever someone suggests that raising an issue for debate is totally unacceptable — whether on the grounds that it's racist, sexist, unpatriotic, blasphemous, insensitive, or offensive in some other way — you should be suspicious.

Ad Hominem Arguments

Ad hominem (Latin for "to the man") **arguments** attack the character of a person rather than the claims he or she makes: when you destroy the credibility of your opponents, you either destroy their ability to present reasonable appeals or distract from the successful arguments they may be offering. Here Christopher Hitchens questions whether former secretary of state Henry Kissinger should be appointed to head an important government commission:

> But can Congress and the media be expected to swallow the appointment of a proven coverup artist, a discredited historian, a busted liar, and a man who is wanted in many jurisdictions for the vilest of offenses?
>
> —Christopher Hitchens, "The Case against Henry Kissinger"

Ad hominem tactics like this turn arguments into two-sided affairs with good guys and bad guys, and that's unfortunate, since character often *does* matter in argument. People expect the proponent of peace to be civil, a secretary of the treasury to pay his taxes, and the champion of family values to be a faithful spouse. But it's fallacious to attack an idea by uncovering the foibles of its advocates or by attacking their motives, backgrounds, or unchangeable traits.

Stacking the Deck

Just as gamblers try to stack the deck by arranging cards so they are sure to win, writers **stack the deck** when they show only one side of the story—the one in their favor. In a Facebook forum on the documentary film *Super Size Me* (which followed a thirty-two-year-old man who ate three meals a day at McDonald's for thirty days with drastic health consequences), one student points out an example of stacking the deck:

> One of the fallacies was stacking the deck. Spurlock stated many facts and gave plenty of evidence of what can happen if you eat fast food in abundunce. Weight gain, decline in health, habit forming, and a toll on your daily life. But he failed to show what could happen if you ate the fast food and participated in daily exercise and took vitamins. The fallacy is that he does not show us both sides of what can happen. Possibly you could eat McDonalds for three meals a day for thirty days and if you engaged in daily exercise and took vitamins maybe your health would be just fine. But we were not ever shown that side of the experiment.
>
> —Heather Tew Alleman, on a Facebook forum

In the same way, reviewers have often been critical of Michael Moore's documentaries, like *Sicko,* that resolutely show only one side of the story (in this case, the evils of American health care). When you stack the deck, you take a big chance that your readers will react like Heather and decide not to trust you: that's one reason it's so important to show that you have considered alternatives in making any argument.

Fallacies of Logical Argument

You'll encounter a problem in any argument when the claims, warrants, or proofs in it are invalid, insufficient, or disconnected. In theory, such problems seem easy enough to spot, but in practice, they can be camouflaged by a skillful use of words or images. Indeed, logical fallacies pose a challenge to civil argument because they often seem reasonable and natural, especially when they appeal to people's self-interests. Whole industries (such as online psychics) depend on one or more of the logical fallacies for their existence. Political campaigns, too, rely on them in those ubiquitous fifteen-second TV spots.

Hasty Generalization

A **hasty generalization** is an inference drawn from insufficient evidence: because *my* Honda broke down, then *all* Hondas must be junk. It also forms the basis for most stereotypes about people or institutions: because *a few* people in a large group are observed to act in a certain way, *all* members of that group are inferred to behave similarly. The resulting conclusions are usually sweeping claims of little merit: *Women are bad drivers; men are slobs; English teachers are nitpicky; computer jocks are* . . . , and on and on.

To draw valid inferences, you must always have sufficient evidence (see Chapter 17) and you must qualify your claims appropriately. After all, people do need generalizations to make reasonable decisions in life. Such claims can be offered legitimately if placed in context and tagged

"Google must be anti-American because the company decorates its famous logo for occasions such as the anniversary of *Sputnik*, Earth Day, and Persian New Year but not Memorial Day in the United States." A hasty generalization? Check "doodles" at Google, and decide for yourself.

with appropriate qualifiers—*some, a few, many, most, occasionally, rarely, possibly, in some cases, under certain circumstances, in my limited experience.*

Faulty Causality

In Latin, this fallacy is known as *post hoc, ergo propter hoc*, which translates as "after this, therefore because of this"—the faulty assumption that because one event or action follows another, the first causes the second. Consider a lawsuit commented on in the *Wall Street Journal* in which a writer sued Coors (unsuccessfully), claiming that drinking copious amounts of the company's beer had kept him from writing a novel.

Some actions do produce reactions. Step on the brake pedal in your car, and you move hydraulic fluid that pushes calipers against disks to create friction that stops the vehicle. In other cases, however, a supposed connection between cause and effect turns out to be completely wrong. For example, doctors now believe that when an elderly person falls and breaks a hip or leg, the injury usually caused the fall rather than the other way around.

That's why overly simple causal claims should always be subject to scrutiny. In summer 2008, writer Nicholas Carr posed a simple causal question in a cover story for the *Atlantic*: "Is Google Making Us Stupid?" Carr essentially answered yes, arguing that "as we come to rely on computers to mediate our understanding of the world, it is our own intelligence that flattens" and that the more one is online the less he or she is able to concentrate or read deeply.

But others, like Jamais Cascio (senior fellow at the Institute for Ethics and Emerging Technologies) soon challenged that causal connection: rather than making us stupid, Cascio argues, Internet tools like Google will lead to the development of "fluid intelligence—the ability to find meaning in confusion and solve new problems, independent of acquired knowledge." The final word on this contentious causal relationship—the effects on the human brain caused by new technology—is still out, and will probably be available only after decades of intense research.

Begging the Question

Most teachers have heard some version of the following argument: *You can't give me a C in this course; I'm an A student.* A member of Congress accused of taking kickbacks can make much the same argument: *I can't be*

guilty of accepting such bribes; I'm an honest person. In both cases, the claim is made on grounds that can't be accepted as true because those grounds themselves are in question. How can the accused bribe taker defend herself on grounds of honesty when that honesty is in doubt? Looking at the arguments in Toulmin terms helps to see the fallacy:

Claim	**You can't give me a C in this course . . .**
Reason	**. . . because I'm an A student.**
Warrant	**An A student is someone who can't receive Cs.**

Claim	**Representative X can't be guilty of accepting bribes . . .**
Reason	**. . . because she's an honest person.**
Warrant	**An honest person cannot be guilty of accepting bribes.**

With the warrants stated, you can see why **begging the question** — assuming as true the very claim that's disputed — is a form of circular argument that goes nowhere. (For more on Toulmin argument, see Chapter 7.)

Equivocation

Equivocations — half truths or arguments that give lies an honest appearance — are usually based on tricks of language. Consider the plagiarist who copies a paper word for word from a source and then declares that "I wrote the entire paper myself" — meaning that she physically copied the piece on her own. But the plagiarist is using *wrote* equivocally and knows that most people understand the word to mean composing and not merely copying words. In the first decade of the twenty-first century, critics of the Bush administration said its many denials that *torture* was being used on U.S. prisoners abroad amounted to a

Baseball star Alex Rodriguez admitted that he had taken performance-enhancing drugs during the 2003 season, but said that "I don't know exactly what" and hinted that they may have been legal substances. Some expert observers think that's an equivocation—a dishonest play on the word *know*—since he tested positive for drugs that can't be obtained legally in the United States.

long series of equivocations. What Bush described as the CIA's use of "an alternative set of procedures" was just another equivocal phrase used to cover up what was really going on, which was torture, at least as defined by the Geneva Convention.

Non Sequitur

A **non sequitur** is an argument whose claims, reasons, or warrants don't connect logically. Children are notably adept at framing non sequiturs like this one: *You don't love me or you'd buy me that bicycle!* Taking a look at the implied warrant shows no connection between love and bikes:

Claim	You must not love me . . .
Reason	. . . because you haven't bought me that bicycle.
Warrant	Buying bicycles for children is essential to loving them.

A five-year-old might buy that warrant, but no responsible adult would because love doesn't depend on buying bicycles.

Non sequiturs occur when writers omit a step in an otherwise logical chain of reasoning. For example, it's a non sequitur to argue that the poor performance of American students on international math exams means that the country should spend more money on math education. Such a conclusion might be justified if a correlation were known or found to exist between mathematical ability and money spent on education. But the students' performance might be poor for reasons other than education funding alone, so the logical connection fails.

Straw Man

Those who resort to the **straw man** fallacy attack an argument that isn't really there, often a much weaker or more extreme one than the opponent is actually making. The speaker or writer "sets up a straw man" in this way to create an argument that's easy to knock down, proceeds to do so, and then claims victory over the opponent whose real argument was quite different. In *Arguing with Idiots*, Glenn Beck argues against "the idiot" who says that if we spent as much on education as we do on defense, all would be well, saying that:

> We are all familiar with the bumper stickers pining for the day that the defense budget goes to the schools and the Pentagon has to hold a bake sale, but comparing educational spending with national defense isn't particularly fair, clever, or logical.
>
> First of all, we have to spend money on defense because if we don't defend our country — well, the schools won't matter much. Take the Republic of Georgia, for instance. Do you really think citizens there are worried about standardized test scores or drunk Russian soldiers driving tanks down their streets?

Writing for *Media Matters* about "Glenn Beck and the Great Straw Man Massacre," critic Simon Maloy takes Beck to task for using the strategy in this passage:

> I'm not familiar with those bumper stickers, nor am I familiar with any public education advocates who argue that we stop spending money on national defense. And what does Georgia have to do with any of this? Does anyone begrudge Georgia for spending on its national defense? None of this makes any sense.

By suggesting that those who want to cut defense spending don't want to "defend our country," Beck is setting up a straw man.

Red Herring

This fallacy gets its name from the old British hunting practice of dragging a dried herring across the path of the fox in order to throw the hounds off the trail. A **red herring** fallacy does just that: it changes the subject abruptly to throw readers or listeners off the trail.

In the highly political item above, from spring 2009, cartoonist William Warren depicts the red herring fallacy when he has President Obama interrupt his Supreme Court nominee Sonia Sotomayor as she replies to a question from a reporter about the Constitution. Obama's words represent what the cartoonist regards as red herring qualifications offered in defense of her appointment. When presented comically like this, red herrings may seem easy to spot. But be on the lookout for them whenever you read, and avoid them in your own writing. If you must resort to red herrings to support an argument, you probably should rethink your claim.

Faulty Analogy

Comparisons can help to clarify one concept by measuring it against another that is more familiar. Consider how quickly you make a judgment about Britney Spears after reading this comparison with Madonna in a blog posting:

> She's, regardless of how hard she tries, not Madonna. To be fair, Madonna wasn't Madonna at first either, but emulating someone else—even if they're as successful as Madonna—usually doesn't work in the end.
> —Erik J. Barzeski, NSLog ( ); (blog)

When comparisons are extended, they become *analogies*—ways of understanding unfamiliar ideas by comparing them with something that's already known. But useful as such comparisons are, they may prove false either taken on their own and pushed too far, or taken too seriously. At this point, they become **faulty analogies**—inaccurate or inconsequential comparisons between objects or concepts. An editorial in the *Taipei Times,* for example, found fault with analogies between Egypt and Taiwan in 2011:

> Following weeks of demonstrations in Egypt that ultimately forced former Egyptian president Hosni Mubarak to step down on Friday, some commentators have suggested that events in North Africa could serve as a catalyst for discontent with President Ma Ying-jeou. There are, however, a number of reasons why this analogy is wrongheaded and Taiwanese not only cannot—but should not—go down that road.
> For one, the situations in Egypt and Taiwan are very different. Taiwan does not have a radicalized and easily mobilized political opposition such as Egypt's Muslim Brotherhood, which has a long tradition of opposing despotic rule.

This editorial writer goes on to write a lengthy column analyzing the flaws in this analogy.

RESPOND●

1. Examine each of the following political slogans or phrases for logical fallacies.

    "Resistance is futile." (Borg message on *Star Trek*)

    "It's the economy, stupid." (sign on the wall at Bill Clinton's campaign headquarters)

    "Remember the Alamo." (battle cry)

    "Make love, not war." (antiwar slogan popularized during the Vietnam War)

    "A chicken in every pot." (campaign slogan)

"Guns don't kill, people do." (NRA slogan)

"If you can't stand the heat, get out of the kitchen." (attributed to Harry S. Truman)

"Yes we can." (Obama campaign slogan)

2. Choose a paper you've written for a college class and analyze it for signs of fallacious reasoning. Then find an editorial, a syndicated column, and a news report on the same topic and look for fallacies in them. Which has the most fallacies—and what kind? What may be the role of the audience in determining when a statement is fallacious?

3. Find a Web site that is sponsored by an organization (the Future of Music Coalition, perhaps), business (Coca-Cola, Pepsi), or other group (the Democratic or Republican National Committee), and analyze the site for fallacious reasoning. Among other considerations, look at the relationship between text and graphics and between individual pages and the pages that surround or are linked to them. How does the technique of separating information into discrete pages affect the argument?

4. Political blogs such as DailyKos.com and InstaPundit.com typically provide quick responses to daily events and detailed critiques of material in other media sites, including national newspapers. Study one such blog for a few days to see whether and how the blogger critiques the material he or she links to. Does the blogger point to fallacies in arguments? If so, does he or she explain them or just assume readers understand them? Summarize your findings in an oral report to your class.

6
Rhetorical Analysis

What do Bob Dylan, Lady Gaga, and Kanye West all have in common—beside the fact that all are successful and famous singers? *They all make commercial endorsements.* Lady Gaga's music videos are full of lucrative product placements, and she is now "creative director" for Polaroid, with her own line of "Grey Label" products. Kanye West launched a hangbag line with designer label Fendi. Even counterculture folk legend Bob Dylan—long considered a "virgin," that is, a celebrity who refused to give endorsements—eventually succumbed. In 2004, Dylan took the plunge, making his first-ever commercial—for women's underwear. (Check YouTube for related ads and videos.)

Such endorsements, and the contexts surrounding them, offer strong possibilities for analysis: Do such marketing strategies work? Are they truly effective? Media critic Seth Stevenson, writing in *Slate*, devoted a full column to analyzing Dylan's 2004 TV spot for Victoria's Secret, trying first to figure out why an artist of Dylan's stature would do a commercial endorsement for, of all things, women's lingerie, before turning to another intriguing question — how such ads work their persuasive magic:

> Why would a brand that's about sexiness, youth, and glamour want any connection at all with a decrepit, sixtysomething folksinger? The answer, my friend, is totally unclear. The answer is totally unclear.
>
> Even if Victoria's Secret hopes to bring in more boomer women, do those women want their underwear to exude the spirit and essence of Bob Dylan? Or, conversely, is Bob Dylan the sort of man they're hoping to attract? Even if you're of the belief that men frequently shop at VS for their ladies, I still don't see the appeal of this ad. I, for instance, am a man, and I can assure you that Bob Dylan is not what I'm looking for in a woman's undergarment. (And if I found him there — man, would that be disturbing.)
>
> Victoria's Secret wouldn't return my calls, but media reports say the idea of putting Dylan's face in the ad (they'd been using his song — "Love Sick" — in ads for the past year or so) came straight from corporate chief Les Wexner. To the company's surprise, Dylan accepted their offer. It's at this point that someone at Victoria's Secret should have stopped the madness. Just because you can hire Bob Dylan as the figurehead for your lingerie line, doesn't mean you should. Perhaps no one was willing to say no to the big boss, or perhaps they fully expected Dylan to say no. Joke's on them.
>
> — Seth Stevenson, "Tangled Up in Boobs"

To address the questions, Stevenson performs a brief **rhetorical analysis** — a close reading of a text to find how and whether it persuades. In these few paragraphs from a longer piece, Stevenson considers some of the basic strategies of argument we've explored in earlier chapters: First he identifies the ethos of Victoria's Secret ("sexiness, youth, and glamour") and finds it hard to reconcile with the ethos of the celebrity in the ad ("decrepit, sixtysomething"). He goes on to consider whether the ad might entice older men to buy expensive underwear for women but then rejects that approach: even men who shop for underwear at Victoria's Secret certainly don't want to think about Dylan when they do.

Along the way, Stevenson adds some humor with allusions to Dylan's songs, including his rendition of "Blowin' in the Wind" ("The answer, my friend, is totally unclear") and "Tangled Up in Blue" (the title of his article, "Tangled Up in Boobs"). Then Stevenson takes a step beyond the ad itself to ask whether having a superstar spokesperson like Bob Dylan might seem so cool that the advertisers don't even think about the other messages they might be sending. Stevenson's conclusion? "Joke's on them."

But was it? If Stevenson had dug a little deeper in his analysis, he might have discovered that during a 1960s press conference, when asked which he would choose if he ever decided to "sell out to a commercial interest," Dylan paused, smiled, and said "ladies' garments."[1] This bit of historical context suggests that Stevenson's conclusion ("Joke's on them") may be premature: Might Dylan have simply decided to honor his "promise" from decades earlier? Did someone at Victoria's Secret remember Dylan's comment and see if he would make good on what reporters at the time took as a facetious remark? Had he had this bit of information, Stevenson could have contextualized his analysis and possibly added another layer of irony to it.

As this example suggests, when you begin a rhetorical analysis, be prepared to follow every lead, to dig as deep as you can into the context in which the text you are analyzing exists. Especially when you encounter puzzling, troubling, or very successful appeals, a rhetorical analysis can help you to understand how they work. Begin by asking yourself what strategies the piece employs to move your heart, win your trust, and change your mind—and why it does or doesn't do so. Here's how.

Composing a Rhetorical Analysis

Exactly how does an iPad ad make you want to buy one immediately? How does an op-ed piece in the *Washington Post* suddenly change your thinking about immigration? A rhetorical analysis might help you understand.

You perform a rhetorical analysis by analyzing how well the components of an argument work together to persuade or move an audience. You can study arguments of any kind—advertisements (as we've seen), editorials, political cartoons, and even songs, movies, or photographs. In every case, you'll need to focus your rhetorical analysis on elements that stand out or make the piece intriguing or problematic. You could begin by exploring issues such as the following:

- What is the purpose of this argument? What does it hope to achieve?
- Who is the audience for this argument?

---

[1] Thanks to Ryan Ireland of Wright State University for sending us the footage of Dylan's press conference and for noting that "in studying Dylan, one can never mistake a seemingly oddball maneuver for a misfire until significant time has passed."

- What appeals or techniques does the argument use—emotional, logical, ethical?

- What genre of argument is it, and how does the genre affect the argument? (While you might well challenge an argument in an op-ed that lacked sufficient evidence, you wouldn't make the same complaint about a bumper sticker.)

- Who is making the argument? What ethos does it create, and how does it do so? What values does the ethos evoke? How does it make the writer or creator seem trustworthy?

- What authorities does the argument rely on or appeal to?

- What facts, reasoning, and evidence are used in the argument? How are they presented?

- What claims does the argument make? What issues are raised—or ignored or evaded?

- What are the contexts—social, political, historical, cultural—for this argument? Whose interests does it serve? Who gains or loses by it?

- How is the argument organized or arranged? What media does the argument use?

- How does the language or style of the argument work to persuade an audience?

In answering such questions, try to show *how* the key devices in an argument actually make it succeed or fail. Quote freely from a written piece, or describe the elements in a visual argument. (Annotating a visual text is one option.) Show readers where and why an argument makes sense and where it falls apart. If you believe that an argument startles, challenges, insults, or lulls audiences, explain just why that's so, and provide evidence. Don't be surprised when your rhetorical analysis itself becomes an argument. That's what it should be.

Understanding the Purpose of Arguments You Are Analyzing

To understand how well any argument works, begin with its purpose: Is it to sell running shoes? To advocate for limits to college tuition? To push a political agenda? In many cases, that purpose may be obvious. A conservative blog will likely advance right-wing causes; ads from a baby food company will likely show happy infants delighted with stewed prunes.

But some projects may be indirect about their persuasive intentions. Perhaps you've responded to a mail survey or telephone poll only to discover that the questions are leading you to switch your cell phone service. Does such a stealthy argument succeed? Answering this question provides material for a thoughtful rhetorical analysis in which you measure the strengths, risks, and ethics of such strategies.

Understanding Who Makes an Argument

Knowing *who* is claiming *what* is key to any rhetorical analysis. That's why persuasive appeals usually have a name attached to them. Remember the statements included in TV ads during the last federal election: "Hello, I'm X—and I approve this ad"? Federal law requires such statements so we can tell the difference between ads a candidate endorses and ones sponsored by groups not even affiliated with the campaigns. Their interests and motives might be very different.

But knowing a name is just a starting place for analysis. You need to dig deeper, and you could do worse than to Google such people or groups to discover more about them. What else have they produced? Who publishes them: the *Wall Street Journal*, the blog DailyKos, or even a LiveJournal celebrity gossip site such as *Oh No They Didn't*? Check out related Web sites for information about goals, policies, contributors, and funding.

Funny, offensive, or both?

WHO **IS THAT**? FLOATING ASIAN KID ■

See floating asian kid to the right? That would be me. I'm Sean Geng . I started working on the web many years ago. Since then, I have been creating clean , elegant , and *creative* designs for the web. I've worked on everything from Video Effects and Animation to Graphics and Web Design. I've learned and tried to master languages such as HTML , CSS , PHP , and much more. I've also worked with many of the popular CMS (content-management systems) such as Wordpress and Drupal. Through my experience on the internet, I've come to meet some of the most talented people, who have taught me much. When I design, I always try to be unique and *push the boundaries* . So now you know a bit about me. Check out my portfolio, or if you are really interested, head over to the contact area and shoot me an email.

The blogger bio: required reading for rhetorical analysis

RESPOND ●

Describe a persuasive moment that you can recall from a speech, an editorial, an advertisement, a YouTube clip, or a blog posting. Or research one of the following famous persuasive moments and describe the circumstances — the historical situation, the issues at stake, the purpose of the argument — that make it so memorable.

Abraham Lincoln's "Gettysburg Address" (1863)

Elizabeth Cady Stanton's "Declaration of Sentiments" at the Seneca Falls Convention (1848)

Chief Tecumseh's address to General William Henry Harrison (1810)

Winston Churchill's addresses to the British people during World War II (1940)

Martin Luther King Jr.'s "Letter from Birmingham Jail" (1963)

Ronald Reagan's tribute to the *Challenger* astronauts (1986)

Toni Morrison's speech accepting the Nobel Prize (1993)

Will.i.am and the Black Eyed Peas' "Yes We Can" song/collage on YouTube (2008)

Identifying and Appealing to Audiences

Most arguments are composed with specific audiences in mind, and their success depends, in part, on how well their strategies, content, tone, and language meet the expectations of that audience. So your rhetorical analysis of an argumentative piece should identify its target readers or viewers (see Audiences for Arguments on pp. 22–25) if possible, or make an educated guess about the audience, since most arguments suggest whom they intend to reach and in what ways.

Both a flyer stapled to a bulletin board in a college dorm ("Why you shouldn't drink and drive") and a forty-foot billboard for Bud Lite might be aimed at the same general population—college students. But each will adjust its appeals for the different moods of that group in different moments. For starters, the flyer will appeal to students in a serious vein, while the beer ad will probably be visually stunning and virtually text-free.

You might also examine how a writer or an argument establishes credibility with an audience. One effective means of building credibility is to show respect for your readers or viewers, especially if they may not agree with you. In introducing an article on problems facing African American women in the workplace, editor in chief of *Essence* Diane Weathers considers the problems that she faced with respecting all her potential readers:

> We spent more than a minute agonizing over the provocative cover line for our feature "White Women at Work." The countless stories we had heard from women across the country told us that this was a workplace issue we had to address. From my own experience at several major magazines, it was painfully obvious to me that Black and White women are not on the same track. Sure, we might all start out in the same place. But early in the game, most sisters I know become stuck—and the reasons have little to do with intelligence or drive. At some point we bump our heads against that ceiling. And while White women may complain of a glass ceiling, for us, the ceiling is concrete.
>
> So how do we tell this story without sounding whiny and paranoid, or turning off our White-female readers, staff members, advertisers and girlfriends? Our solution: Bring together real women (several of them highly successful senior corporate executives), put them in a room, promise them anonymity and let them speak their truth.
>
> —Diane Weathers, "Speaking Our Truth"

Retailers like Walmart build their credibility by simple "straight talk" to shoppers: our low prices make your life better.

Both paragraphs affirm Weathers's determination to treat audiences fairly *and* to deal honestly with a difficult subject. The strategy would merit attention in any rhetorical analysis.

Look, too, for signals that writers share values with readers or at least understand an audience. In the following passage, writer Jack Solomon is clear about one value that he hopes readers have in common—a preference for "straight talk":

> There are some signs in the advertising world that Americans are getting fed up with fantasy advertisements and want to hear some straight talk. Weary of extravagant product claims . . . consumers trained by years of advertising to distrust what they hear seem to be developing an immunity to commercials.
> —Jack Solomon, "Masters of Desire: The Culture of American Advertising"

It's increasingly important for writers of novels and film scripts to appeal to more than just a small niche audience. Here Amazon.com reviewer Andi Miller gives her take on Brian Selznick's *The Invention of Hugo*

Cabret, which was the inspiration for the recent Martin Scorsese film *Hugo*: "Selznick's creation navigates the grey area between picture book and graphic novel in what certainly constitutes a visual and narrative achievement and a truly original book." After a quick summary, Miller goes on to provide a brief rhetorical analysis that backs up her claim, that *The Invention of Hugo Cabret* is compelling for readers of all ages:

> While the novel largely defies categorization, it closely resembles a silent film in many respects, and fittingly so. In addition to the novel's rich illustrations, Selznick employs photos and movie stills to show the reader his story as opposed to simply telling it. In the tradition of graphic narrative (or sequential art, whatever your term of choice), the illustrations play as integral a role in the overall story as the text. The use of illustrations is hardly gratuitous, for the pictures quite literally take over and carry out the narrative when the text disappears. And, really, who would care if the illustrations were gratuitous? They're gorgeous.
>
> *The Invention of Hugo Cabret* is full of magic—for the child reader, for the adult reader, the film lover, the art lover, for anyone willing to give it a go. If you're scared of the size or the concept, don't be. Open your mind, pour Selznick's creation in, and be reminded of the dream of childhood.

Examining Arguments Based on Emotion: Pathos

Some emotional appeals are just ploys to win over readers with a pretty face, figurative or real. You've seen ads promising an exciting life and attractive friends if only you drink the right soda or wear a particular brand of clothes. Are you fooled by such claims? Probably not, if you pause to think about them. But that's the strategy—to distract you from thought just long enough to make a bad choice. It's a move worth commenting on in a rhetorical analysis.

Yet emotions can add real muscle to arguments, too, and that's worth noting. For example, persuading people not to drink and drive by making them fear death, injury, or arrest seems like a fair use of an emotional appeal. The public service announcement on page 99 uses an emotion-laden image to remind drivers to think of the consequences.

In a rhetorical analysis, you might note the juxtaposition of image with text, leading readers to connect casual notes left on windshields with the very serious consequences of drunk driving.

How well does the emotional appeal here work?

In analyzing emotional appeals, judge whether the emotions raised—anger, sympathy, fear, envy, joy, or love—advance the claims offered. Consider how columnist and novelist Lionel Shriver uses concrete and graphic language to evoke disgust with SUVs—and anyone who owns one—at a time of soaring gas prices:

> Filling the tank of an SUV in the U.S. has now crossed the psychologically traumatizing $100 mark. The resale value of these monsters is plummeting, and many owners are getting stuck with the things, like holding the Old Maid in cards. I greet this news with sadistic glee. People who bought SUVs were fools and I want them to suffer. Not just because I'm a sanctimonious greenie, but because I'm an aesthete. Sure, SUVs are petro-pigs, and they side-swipe cyclists into the curb. Yes, they emblemize everything about Americans the rest of the world detests: greedy, wasteful, and oblivious to the future. But on top of all that, they're ugly.
>
> —Lionel Shriver, "If the U.S. Election Were a Novel"

Does the use of pathos ("monsters," "petro-pigs") convince you, or does it distract from or undermine the claim that SUVs are ugly? Your task in a rhetorical analysis is to study an author's words, the emotions they evoke, and the claims they support and then to make this kind of judgment.

RESPOND●

Browse YouTube or another Web site to find an example of a powerful emotional argument that's made visually, either alone or using words as well. In a paragraph, defend a claim about how the argument works. For example, does an image itself make a claim, or does it draw you in to consider a verbal claim? What emotion does the argument generate? How does that emotion work to persuade you?

Examining Arguments Based on Character: Ethos

It should come as no surprise: readers believe writers who seem honest, wise, and trustworthy. So in analyzing the effectiveness of an argument, look for evidence of these traits. Does the writer have the experience or authority to write on this subject? Are all claims qualified reasonably? Is evidence presented in full, not tailored to the writer's agenda? Are important objections to the author's position acknowledged and addressed? Are sources documented? Above all, does the writer sound trustworthy?

When a Norwegian anti-immigration extremist killed seventy-six innocent people in July 2011, Prime Minister Jens Stoltenberg addressed the citizens of Norway (and the world), and in doing so evoked the character or ethos of the entire nation:

> **We will not let fear break us! The warmth of response from people in Norway and from the whole world makes me sure of this one thing: evil can kill a single person, but never defeat a whole people. The strongest weapon in the world—that is freedom of expression and democracy.**

In analyzing this speech, you would do well to look at the way this passage deploys the deepest values of Norway—freedom of expression and democracy—to serve as a response to fear of terrorism. In doing so, Stoltenberg evokes ethical ideals to hold onto in a time of tragedy.

Or take a look at the following paragraph from a blog posting by Timothy Burke, a teacher at Swarthmore College and parent of a preschool child who is trying to think through the issue of homework for elementary school kids:

> So I've been reading a bit about homework, and comparing notes with parents. There is a lot of variation across districts, not just in the amount of homework that kids are being asked to do, but in the kind of homework. Some districts give kids a lot of time-consuming busywork, other districts try to concentrate on having homework assignments be substantive work that is best accomplished independently. Some give a lot from a very early point in K–12 education, some give relatively little. As both a professional educator and an individual with personal convictions, I'd tend to argue against excessive amounts of homework and against assigning busywork. But what has ultimately interested me more about reading various discussions of homework is how intense the feelings are swirling around the topic, and how much that intensity strikes me as a problem in and of itself. Not just as a symptom of a kind of civic illness, an inability to collectively and democratically work through complex issues, but also in some cases as evidence of an educational failure in its own right.

Burke establishes his ethos by citing his reading and his talks with other parents.

Burke considers alternatives (though he then states his tentative preference).

He criticizes immoderate arguments as "a kind of civic illness" (and suggests that he will demonstrate the opposite of such an approach).

In considering the role of ethos in rhetorical analyses, you must pay attention to the details, right down to the choice of words or, in an image, the shapes and colors. The modest, tentative tone that Burke uses in his blog is an example of the kind of choice that can shape an audience's perception of ethos. But these details need your interpretation. Language that's hot and extreme can mark a writer as either passionate or loony. Work that's sober and carefully organized can paint an institution as competent or overly cautious. Technical terms and abstract phrases can make a writer seem either knowledgeable or pompous.

Examining Arguments Based on Facts and Reason: Logos

In analyzing most arguments, you'll have to decide whether an argument makes a plausible claim and offers good reasons for you to believe it. Not all arguments will package such claims in a single neat sentence, or **thesis**—nor should they. A writer may tell a story from which you have to infer the claim. Visual arguments may work the same way: viewers have to assemble the parts and draw inferences before they get the point.

Some conventional arguments (like those on an editorial page), may be perfectly obvious: writers stake out a claim and then present reasons that you consider, or they may first present reasons and lay out a case that leads you to accept a claim in the conclusion. Consider the following examples. The first comes from the conclusion of an August 22, 2008, editorial in the *New York Times*; the second from a petition letter for a "nuclear-free California" sponsored by change.org:

> To win the right to host [the Olympic] Games, China promised to honor the Olympic ideals of nonviolence, openness to the world and individual expression. Those promises were systematically broken, starting with this spring's brutal repression in Tibet and continuing on to the ugly farce of inviting its citizens to apply for legal protest permits and then arresting them if they actually tried to do so. . . .
>
> Surely one of the signature events of these Games was the sentencing of two women in their late 70s to "re-education through labor." Their crime? Applying for permission to protest the inadequate compensation they felt they had received when the government seized their homes years ago for urban redevelopment.
>
> A year ago, the I.O.C. predicted that these Games would be "a force for good" and a spur to human-rights progress. Instead, as Human Rights Watch has reported, they became a catalyst for intensified human-rights abuse.
>
> —"Beijing's Bad Faith Olympics," *New York Times*

Ban Nuclear Power Plants in California

Greetings:

The Fukushima, Three Mile Island, and Chernobyl nuclear power disasters have shown us that nuclear power is not safe. As an area prone to frequent earthquakes, California is an especially dangerous place to host a nuclear power plant.

We, the undersigned call for:

—No new nuclear plants.
—Closing existing plants as quickly as safely possible.
—Seeking and implementing greener energy solutions.

[Your Name]

When you analyze explicit claims like these, you look at how they are supported by good reasons and reliable evidence. A lengthy essay may, in fact, contain a series of claims, each developed to support an even larger point. Indeed, every paragraph in an argument may develop a specific and related idea. In a rhetorical analysis, you need to identify all these separate propositions and examine the relationships among them: Are they solidly linked? Are there inconsistencies that the writer should acknowledge? Does the end of the piece support what the writer said (and promised) at the beginning?

You'll also need to examine the quality of the information presented in an argument, assessing how accurately such information is reported, how conveniently it's displayed (in charts or graphs, for

This protester's T-shirt asks you to consider the dangers of nuclear power.

example), and how well the sources cited represent a range of *respected* opinion on a topic. (For more information on the use of evidence, see Chapter 4.)

Knowing how to judge the quality of sources is more important now than ever before because the digital universe is full of junk. In some ways, the computer terminal has become the equivalent of a library reference room, but the sources available online vary widely in quality and have not been evaluated by a library professional. As a consequence, you must know the difference between reliable, firsthand, or fully documented sources and those that don't meet such standards. (For using and documenting sources, see Chapters 18, 19, and 21.)

Examining the Arrangement and Media of Arguments

Aristotle carved the structure of logical argument to its bare bones when he observed that it had only two parts:

- statement
- proof

You could do worse, in examining an argument, than to make sure that every claim a writer makes is backed by sufficient evidence. Some arguments are written on the fly in the heat of the moment. Most arguments that you read and write, however, will be more than mere statements followed by proofs. Some writers will lay their cards on the table immediately; others may lead you carefully through a chain of claims toward a conclusion. Writers may even interrupt their arguments to offer background information or cultural contexts for readers. Sometimes they'll tell stories or provide anecdotes that make an argumentative point. They'll qualify the arguments they make, too, and often pause to admit that other points of view are plausible.

In other words, there are no formulas or acceptable patterns that fit all successful arguments. In writing a rhetorical analysis, you'll have to assess the organization of a persuasive text on its own merits.

It's fair, however, to complain about what may be *absent* from an argument. Most arguments of proposal (see Chapter 12), for example, include a section that defends the feasibility of a new idea, explaining how it might be funded or managed. In a rhetorical analysis, you might fault an editorial that supports a new stadium for a city without addressing feasibility issues. Similarly, analyzing a movie review that reads like an off-the-top-of-the-head opinion, you might legitimately ask what criteria of evaluation are in play (see Chapter 10).

Rhetorical analysis also calls for you to look carefully at an argument's transitions, headings and subheadings, documentation of sources, and overall tone or voice. Don't take such details for granted, since all of them contribute to the strength — or weakness — of an argument.

Nor should you ignore the way a writer or an institution uses media. Would an argument originally made in a print editorial, for instance, work better as a spoken presentation (or vice versa)? Would a lengthy paper have more power if it included more images? Or do these images distract from a written argument's substance?

Finally, be open to the possibility of new or nontraditional structures of arguments. The visual arguments that you analyze may defy conventional principles of logic or arrangement—for example, making juxtapositions rather than logical transitions between elements or using quick cuts, fades, or other devices to link ideas. Quite often, these non-traditional structures will also resist the neatness of a thesis, leaving readers to construct at least a part of the argument in their heads. Advertisers are growing fond of soft-sell multimedia productions that can seem more like entertainment than what they really are — product pitches. We're asked not just to buy a product but also to live its lifestyle. Is that a reasonable or workable strategy for an argument? Your analysis might entertain such possibilities.

Looking at Style

Even a coherent argument full of sound evidence may not connect with readers if it's dull, off-key, or offensive. Readers naturally judge the credibility of arguments in part by how stylishly the case is made — even when they don't know exactly what style is. Consider how these simple, blunt sentences from the opening of an argument shape your image of the author and probably determine whether you're willing to continue to read the whole piece:

> We are young, urban, and professional. We are literate, respectable, intelligent, and charming. But foremost and above all, we are unemployed.
> —Julia Carlisle, "Young, Privileged, and Unemployed"

The strong, straightforward tone and the stark juxtaposition of being "intelligent" with "unemployed" set the style for this letter to the editor.

Now consider the humorous and slightly sarcastic tone of the following series of questions that makes an argument about the intelligence of voters in South Florida during the electoral disaster of 2000:

> The question you're asking yourself is: Does South Florida contain the highest concentration of morons in the entire world? Or just in the United States? The reason you're asking this, of course, is South Florida's performance in Tuesday's election.
> —Dave Barry, "How to Vote in One Easy Step"

Both styles probably work, but they signal that the writers are about to make very different kinds of cases. Here, style alone tells readers what to expect.

Manipulating style also enables writers to shape readers' responses to their ideas. Devices as simple as sentence length, alliteration, or parallelism can give sentences remarkable power. Consider this passage from a review of *The Other Barack*, about President Obama's father:

> [I]f Obama Sr. were only a jerk, there wouldn't be any reason to read about him, regardless of who his son turned out to be. But there is. Like the president, Obama Sr. was also a brilliant, ambitious idealist who overcame the limited circumstances of his background to attend the best schools in the world, then set out to participate in a movement of vast political promise. That he failed so spectacularly, and that his son succeeded, says a lot about the qualities of character that can distinguish a leader from a lout.
> —Andrew Romano, "Who Was Barack Obama's Father?"

In this short passage, Romano uses a very short sentence ("But there is."), alliteration ("a leader from a lout"), and parallelism ("failed so spectacularly" and "succeeded") to paint a complex picture of Barack Obama Sr.

In a rhetorical analysis, you can explore such stylistic choices. Why does a formal style work for discussing one type of subject matter but not another? How does a writer use humor or irony to underscore an important point or to manage a difficult concession? Do stylistic choices, even something as simple as the use of contractions or personal pronouns, bring readers close to a writer, or do technical words and an impersonal voice signal that an argument is for experts only?

To describe the stylistic effects of visual arguments, you may use a different vocabulary and talk about colors, camera angles, editing, balance, proportion, fonts, perspective, and so on. But the basic principle is

This poster, promoting travel to the bicycle-friendly city of Münster, Germany, demonstrates visually the amount of space needed to transport the same number of people by car, bicycle, and bus.

this: the look of an item — whether a poster, an editorial cartoon, or a film documentary — can support the message that it carries, undermine it, or muddle it. In some cases, the look will *be* the message. In a rhetorical analysis, you can't ignore style.

RESPOND●

Find a recent example of a visual argument, either in print or on the Internet. Even though you may have a copy of the image, describe it carefully in your paper on the assumption that your description is all readers may have to go on. Then make a judgment about its effectiveness, supporting your claim with clear evidence from the "text."

Examining a Rhetorical Analysis

On the following pages, well-known political commentator and columnist for the *New York Times*, David Brooks, argues that today's college graduates have been poorly prepared for life after college because of what he sees as a radical excess of supervision. Responding to it with a detailed analysis is Rachel Kolb, a student at Stanford University.

It's Not about You

DAVID BROOKS

Over the past few weeks, America's colleges have sent another class of graduates off into the world. These graduates possess something of inestimable value. Nearly every sensible middle-aged person would give away all their money to be able to go back to age 22 and begin adulthood anew.

But, especially this year, one is conscious of the many ways in which this year's graduating class has been ill served by their elders. They enter a bad job market, the hangover from decades of excessive borrowing. They inherit a ruinous federal debt.

More important, their lives have been perversely structured. This year's graduates are members of the most supervised generation in American history. Through their childhoods and teenage years, they have been monitored, tutored, coached and honed to an unprecedented degree.

Yet upon graduation they will enter a world that is unprecedentedly wide open and unstructured. Most of them will not quickly get married, buy a home and have kids, as previous generations did. Instead, they will confront amazingly diverse job markets, social landscapes and lifestyle niches. Most will spend a decade wandering from job to job and clique to clique, searching for a role.

No one would design a system of extreme supervision to prepare people for a decade of extreme openness. But this is exactly what has emerged in modern America. College students are raised in an environment that demands one set of navigational skills, and they are then cast out into a different environment requiring a different set of skills, which they have to figure out on their own.

Worst of all, they are sent off into this world with the whole baby-boomer theology ringing in their ears. If you sample some of the commencement addresses being broadcast on C-Span these days, you see that many graduates are told to: Follow your passion, chart your own course, march to the beat of your own drummer, follow your dreams and find yourself. This is the litany of expressive individualism, which is still the dominant note in American culture.

But, of course, this mantra misleads on nearly every front.

College grads are often sent out into the world amid rapturous talk of limitless possibilities. But this talk is of no help to the central business of adulthood, finding serious things to tie yourself down to. The successful young adult is beginning to make sacred commitments—to a spouse, a community and calling—yet mostly hears about freedom and autonomy.

Today's graduates are also told to find their passion and then pursue their dreams. The implication is that they should find themselves first and then go off and live their quest. But, of course, very few people at age 22 or 24 can take an inward journey and come out having discovered a developed self.

Most successful young people don't look inside and then plan a life. They look outside and find a problem, which summons their life. A relative suffers from Alzheimer's and a young woman feels called to help cure that disease. A young man works under a miserable boss and must develop management skills so his department can function. Another young woman finds herself confronted by an opportunity she never thought of in a job category she never imagined. This wasn't in her plans, but this is where she can make her contribution.

Most people don't form a self and then lead a life. They are called by a problem, and the self is constructed gradually by their calling.

The graduates are also told to pursue happiness and joy. But, of course, when you read a biography of someone you admire, it's rarely the things that made them happy that compel your admiration. It's the things they did to court unhappiness—the things they did that were arduous and miserable, which sometimes cost them friends and aroused hatred. It's excellence, not happiness, that we admire most.

Finally, graduates are told to be independent-minded and to express their inner spirit. But, of course, doing your job well often means suppressing yourself. As Atul Gawande mentioned during his countercultural address last week at Harvard Medical School, being a good doctor often means being part of a team, following the rules of an institution, going down a regimented checklist.

Today's grads enter a cultural climate that preaches the self as the center of a life. But, of course, as they age, they'll discover that the tasks of a life are at the center. Fulfillment is a byproduct of how people engage their tasks, and can't be pursued directly. Most of us are egotistical and most are self-concerned most of the time, but it's nonetheless true that life comes to a point only in those moments when the self dissolves into some task. The purpose in life is not to find yourself. It's to lose yourself.

Understanding Brooks's Binaries

RACHEL KOLB

As a high school and college student, I was given an incredible range of educational and extracurricular options, from interdisciplinary studies to summer institutes to student-organized clubs. Although today's students have more opportunities to adapt their educations to their specific personal goals, as I did, David Brooks argues that the structure of the modern educational system nevertheless leaves young people ill-prepared to meet the challenges of the real world. In his *New York Times* editorial "It's Not about You," Brooks illustrates excessive supervision and uncontrolled individualistic rhetoric as opposing problems that complicate young people's entry into adult life, which then becomes less of a natural progression than an outright paradigm shift. Brooks's argument itself mimics the pattern of moving from "perversely structured" youth to "unprecedentedly wide open" adulthood: it operates on the basis of binary oppositions, raising familiar notions about how to live one's life and then dismantling them. Throughout the piece, it relies less on factual evidence than on Brooks's own authoritative tone and skill in using rhetorical devices.

In his editorial, Brooks objects to mainstream cultural messages that sell students on individuality, but bases his conclusions more on general observations than on specific facts. His argument is, in itself, a loose form of rhetorical analysis. It opens by telling us to "sample some of the commencement addresses being broadcast on C-Span these days," where we will find messages such as: "Follow your passion, chart your own course, march to the beat of your own drummer, follow your dreams and find yourself." As though moving down a checklist, it then scrutinizes the problems with this rhetoric of "expressive individualism." Finally, it turns to Atul Gawande's "countercultural address" about working collectively, en route to confronting the individualism of modern America. C-Span and Harvard Medical School aside, however, Brooks's argument is astonishingly short on external sources. He cites no basis for claims such as "this year's graduates are members of the most supervised generation in American history" or "most successful young people don't look inside and then plan a life," despite the fact that these claims are fundamental to his observations. Instead, his argument persuades through painting a picture—first of "limitless possibilities," then of young men and women called into action by problems that "summon their life"—and hoping that we will find the illustration familiar.

Instead of relying on the logos of his argument, Brooks assumes that his position as a baby boomer and *New York Times* columnist will provide a sufficient enough ethos to validate his claims. If this impression of age and social status did not enter our minds along with his bespectacled portrait, Brooks reminds us of it. Although he refers to the theology of the baby boomer generation as the "worst of all," from the beginning of his editorial he allots himself as another "sensible middle-aged person" and distances himself from college graduates by referring to them as "they" or as "today's grads," contrasting with his more inclusive reader-directed "you." Combined with his repeated use of passive sentence constructions that create a confusing sense of responsibility ("The graduates are sent off into the world"; "the graduates are told"), this sense of distance could be alienating to the younger audiences for which this editorial seems intended. Granted, Brooks compensates for it by embracing themes of "excellence" and "fulfillment" and by opening up his message to "most of us" in his final paragraph, but nevertheless his self-defined persona has its limitations. Besides dividing his audience, Brooks risks reminding us that, just as his observations belong only to this persona, his arguments apply only to a subset of American society. More specifically, they apply only to the well-educated middle to upper class who might be more likely to fret after the implications of "supervision" and "possibilities," or the

Comments critically on author's use of evidence.

Analyzes author's intended audience.

readers who would be most likely to flip through the *New York Times*.

Brooks overcomes his limitations in logos and ethos through his piece's greatest strength: its style. He effectively frames cultural messages in binaries in order to reinforce the disconnect that exists between what students are told and what they will face as full members of society. Throughout his piece, he states one assumption after another, then prompts us to consider its opposite. "Serious things" immediately take the place of "rapturous talk"; "look[ing] inside" replaces "look[ing] outside"; "suppressing yourself" becomes an alternative to being "independent-minded." Brooks's argument is consumed with dichotomies, culminating with his statement "It's excellence, not happiness, that we admire most." He frames his ideas within a tight framework of repetition and parallel structure, creating muscular prose intended to engage his readers. His repeated use of the phrase "but, of course" serves as a metronomic reminder, at once echoing his earlier assertions and referring back to his air of authority.

Closely analyzes Brooks's style.

Brooks illustrates the power of words in swaying an audience, and in his final paragraph his argument shifts beyond commentary. Having tested our way of thinking, he now challenges us to change. His editorial closes with one final binary, the claim that "The purpose in life is not to find yourself" but "to lose yourself." And, although some of Brooks's previous binaries have clanged with oversimplification, this one rings truer. In accordance with his adoption of the general "you," his concluding message need not apply only to college graduates. By unfettering its restrictions at its climax, Brooks liberates his argument. After all, only we readers bear the responsibility of reflecting, of justifying, and ultimately of determining how to live our lives.

Analyzes author's conclusion.

WORK CITED

Brooks, David. "It's Not about You." *Everything's an Argument*. Ed. Andrea A. Lunsford and John J. Ruszkiewicz. 6th ed. Boston: Bedford, 2013, 108–10. Print. Rpt. of "It's Not about You." *New York Times* 30 May 2011.

GUIDE to writing a rhetorical analysis

● Finding a Topic

A rhetorical analysis is usually assigned: you're asked to show how an argument works and to assess its effectiveness. When you can choose your own subject for analysis, look for one or more of the following qualities:

- a complex verbal or visual argument that challenges you—or disturbs or pleases you
- a text that raises current or enduring issues of substance
- a text that you believe should be taken more seriously

Look for arguments to analyze in the editorial and op-ed pages of any newspaper, political magazines such as the *Nation* or *National Review*, Web sites of organizations and interest groups, political blogs such as DailyKos.com or Powerline.com, corporate Web sites that post their TV ad spots, videos and statements posted to YouTube, and so on.

● Researching Your Topic

Once you've got a text to analyze, find out all you can about it. Use the library or resources of the Web to explore:

- who the author is and what his or her credentials are
- if the author is an institution, what it does, what its sources of funding are, who its members are, and so on
- who is publishing or sponsoring the piece, and what the organization typically publishes
- what the leanings or biases of the author and publisher might be
- what the context of the argument is—what preceded or provoked it and how others have responded to it

● Formulating a Claim

Begin with a hypothesis. A full thesis might not become evident until you're well into your analysis, but your final thesis should reflect the complexity of the piece that you're studying. In developing a thesis, consider questions such as the following:

- How can I describe what this argument achieves?
- What is the purpose, and is it accomplished?
- What audiences does the argument address and what audiences does it ignore, and why?
- Which of its rhetorical features will likely influence readers most: Ethos of the author? Emotional appeals? Style?
- What aspects of the argument work better than others?
- How do the rhetorical elements interact?

Here's the hardest part for most writers of rhetorical analyses: whether you agree or disagree with an argument doesn't matter in a rhetorical analysis. You've got to stay out of the fray and pay attention only to how—and to how well—the argument works.

● Examples of Possible Claims for a Rhetorical Analysis

- Many people admire the vision and eloquence of President Obama; others are put off by his often distant tone and his "professorial" stance. A close look at several of his speeches will illuminate both sides of this debate.
- Today's editorial in the *Daily Collegian* about campus crimes may scare first-year students, but its anecdotal reporting doesn't get down to hard numbers—and for a good reason. Those statistics don't back the position taken by the editors.
- The imageboard 4chan has been called an "Internet hate machine," yet others claim it as a great boon to creativity. A close analysis of its home-page can help to settle this debate.
- The original design of New York's Freedom Tower, with its torqued surfaces and evocative spire, made a stronger argument about American values than its replacement, a fortress-like skyscraper stripped of imagination and unable to make any statement except "I'm 1,776 feet tall."

● Preparing a Proposal

If your instructor asks you to prepare a proposal for your rhetorical analysis, here's a format you might use:

- Provide a copy of the work you're analyzing, whether it's a print text, a photograph, digital image, or URL, for instance.

- Offer a working hypothesis or tentative thesis.

- Indicate which rhetorical components seem especially compelling and worthy of detailed study and any connections between elements. For example, does the piece seem to emphasize facts and logic so much that it becomes disconnected from potential audiences? If so, hint at that possibility in your proposal.

- Indicate background information—about the author, institution, and contexts (political, economic, social, and religious) of the argument—you intend to research.

- Define the audience you'd like to reach. If you're responding to an assignment, you may be writing primarily for a teacher and classmates. But they make up a complex audience in themselves. If you can do so within the spirit of the assignment, imagine that your analysis will be published in a local newspaper, Web site, or blog.

- Suggest the media that you might use. Will a traditional essay work best? Could you use highlighting or other word-processing tools to focus attention on stylistic details? Would it be possible to use balloons, boxes, or other callouts to annotate a visual argument?

- Conclude by briefly discussing the key challenges you anticipate in preparing.

Thinking about Content and Organization

Your rhetorical analysis is likely to include the following:

- Facts about the text you're analyzing: Provide the author's name; the title or name of the work; its place of publication or its location; the date it was published or viewed.

- Contexts for the argument: Readers need to know where the text is coming from, to what it may be responding, in what controversies it might be embroiled, and so on. Don't assume that they can infer the important contextual elements.

- A synopsis of the text that you're analyzing: If you can't attach the original argument, you must summarize it in enough detail so that a reader can imagine it. Even if you attach a copy of the piece, the analysis should include a summary.

- Some claim about the work's rhetorical effectiveness: It might be a simple evaluative claim or something more complex. The claim can come early in the paper, or you might build up to it, providing the evidence that leads toward the conclusion you've reached.

- A detailed analysis of how the argument works: Although you'll probably analyze rhetorical components separately, don't let your analysis become a dull roster of emotional, ethical, and logical appeals. Your rhetorical analysis should be an argument itself that supports a claim; a simple list of rhetorical appeals won't make much of a point.

- Evidence for every part of the analysis.

- An assessment of alternative views and counterarguments to your own analysis.

● Getting and Giving Response: Questions for Peer Response

If you have access to a writing center, discuss the text that you intend to analyze with a writing consultant before you write the paper. Try to find people who agree with the argument and others who disagree, and take notes on their observations. Your instructor may assign you to a peer group for the purpose of reading and responding to one another's drafts; if not, share your draft with someone on your own. You can use the following questions to evaluate a draft. If you're evaluating someone else's draft, be sure to illustrate your points with examples. Specific comments are always more helpful than general observations.

The Claim

- Does the claim address the rhetorical effectiveness of the argument itself rather than the opinion or position that it takes?

- Is the claim significant enough to interest readers?

- Does the claim indicate important relationships between various rhetorical components?

- Would the claim be one that the creator of the piece would regard as serious criticism?

Evidence for the Claim

- Is enough evidence given to support all your claims? What evidence do you still need?

- Is the evidence in support of the claim simply announced, or are its significance and appropriateness analyzed? Is a more detailed discussion needed?

- Do you use appropriate evidence, drawn from the argument itself or from other materials?

- Do you address objections readers might have to the claim, criteria, or evidence?

- What kinds of sources might you use to explain the context of the argument? Do you need to use sources to check factual claims made in the argument?

- Are all quotations introduced with appropriate signal phrases (such as "As Peggy Noonan points out"), and do they merge smoothly into your sentences?

Organization and Style

- How are the parts of the argument organized? How effective is this organization? Would some other structure work better?

- Will readers understand the relationships among the original text, your claims, your supporting reasons, and the evidence you've gathered (from the original text and any other sources you've used)? If not, what could be done to make those connections clearer? Are more transitional words and phrases needed? Would headings or graphic devices help?

- Are the transitions or links from point to point, sentence to sentence, and paragraph to paragraph clear and effective? If not, how could they be improved?

- Is the style suited to the subject and appropriate to your audience? Is it too formal? Too casual? Too technical? Too bland or boring?

- Which sentences seem particularly effective? Which ones seem weakest, and how could they be improved? Should some short sentences be combined, or should any long ones be separated into two or more sentences?

- How effective are the paragraphs? Do any seem too skimpy or too long? Do they break the analysis at strategic points?

- Which words or phrases seem particularly effective, accurate, and powerful? Do any seem dull, vague, unclear, or inappropriate for the audience or your purpose? Are definitions provided for technical or other terms that readers might not know?

Spelling, Punctuation, Mechanics, Documentation, and Format

- Check the spelling of the author's name, and make sure that the name of any institution involved with the work is correct. Note that the names of many corporations and institutions use distinctive spelling and punctuation.

- Get the name of the text you're analyzing right.

- Are there any errors in spelling, punctuation, capitalization, and the like?

- Does the assignment require a specific format? Check the original assignment sheet to be sure.

RESPOND•

Find an argument on the editorial page or op-ed page in a recent newspaper. Then analyze it rhetorically, using principles discussed in this chapter. Show how it succeeds, fails, or does something else entirely. Perhaps you can show that the author is unusually successful in connecting with readers but then has nothing to say. Or perhaps you discover that the strong logical appeal is undercut by a contradictory emotional argument. Be sure that the analysis includes a summary of the original essay and basic publication information about it (its author, place of publication, and publisher).

PART 2

WRITING
arguments

7

Structuring Arguments

I get hives after eating ice cream.
My mouth swells up when I eat cheese.
Yogurt triggers my asthma.

↓

Dairy products make me sick.

Dairy products make me sick.
Ice cream is a dairy product.

↓

Ice cream makes me sick.

These two sets of statements illustrate the most basic ways in which Western culture structures logical arguments. The first piles up specific examples and draws a conclusion from them: that's **inductive reasoning** and structure. The second sets out a general principle (the major premise of a syllogism) and applies it to a specific case (the minor premise) in order to reach a conclusion: that's **deductive reasoning** and structure. In everyday reasoning, we often omit the middle statement, resulting in what Aristotle called an *enthymeme*: "Since dairy products make me sick, I better leave that ice cream alone." (See p. 68 for more on enthymemes.)

But the arguments you will write in college call for more than just the tight reasoning offered within inductive and deductive reasoning. You will also need to define claims, explain the contexts in which you are offering them, defend your assumptions, offer convincing evidence, deal with those who disagree with you, and more. And you will have to do so using a clear structure that moves your argument forward. This chapter introduces you to three helpful ways to structure arguments. Feel free to borrow from all of them!

The Classical Oration

The authors of this book once examined a series of engineering reports and found that—to their great surprise—they were generally structured in ways similar to those used by Greek and Roman rhetors two thousand years ago. Thus, this ancient structuring system is alive and well in twenty-first-century culture. The classical oration has six parts, most of which will be familiar to you, despite their Latin names:

Exordium: The speaker/writer tries to win the attention and goodwill of an audience while introducing a subject or problem.

Narratio: The speaker/writer presents the facts of the case, explaining what happened when, who is involved, and so on. The *narratio* puts an argument in context.

Partitio: The speaker/writer divides up the subject, explaining what the claim is, what the key issues are, and in what order the subject will be treated.

Confirmatio: The speaker/writer offers detailed support for the claim, using both logical reasoning and factual evidence.

Refutatio: The speaker/writer recognizes and refutes opposing claims or evidence.

Peroratio: The speaker/writer summarizes the case and moves the audience to action.

This structure is powerful because it covers all the bases: readers or listeners want to know what your subject is, how you intend to cover it, and what evidence you have to offer. And you probably need a reminder to present a pleasing *ethos* when beginning a presentation and to conclude with enough *pathos* to win an audience over completely. Here, in outline form, is a five-part updated version of the classical pattern, which you may find useful on many occasions:

Introduction

- gains readers' interest and willingness to listen
- establishes your qualifications to write about your topic
- establishes some common ground with your audience
- demonstrates that you're fair and evenhanded
- states your claim

Background

- presents information, including personal narrative, that's important to your argument

Lines of Argument

- presents good reasons, including logical and emotional appeals, in support of your claim

Alternative Arguments

- examines alternative points of view and opposing arguments
- notes the advantages and disadvantages of these views
- explains why your view is better than others

Conclusion

- summarizes the argument
- elaborates on the implications of your claim
- makes clear what you want the audience to think or do
- reinforces your credibility and perhaps offers an emotional appeal

Not every piece of rhetoric, past or present, follows the structure of the oration or includes all its components. But you can identify some of its elements in successful arguments if you pay attention to their design. Here are the words of the 1776 Declaration of Independence:

> When in the Course of human events, it becomes necessary for one people to dissolve the political bands which have connected them with another, and to assume among the powers of the earth, the separate and equal station to which the Laws of Nature and of Nature's God entitle them, a decent respect to the opinions of mankind requires that they should declare the causes which impel them to the separation.
>
> We hold these truths to be self-evident, that all men are created equal, that they are endowed by their Creator with certain unalienable Rights, that

Opens with a brief *exordium* explaining why the document is necessary, invoking a broad audience in acknowledging a need to show "a decent respect to the opinions of mankind." Important in this case, the lines that follow explain the assumptions on which the document rests.

among these are Life, Liberty, and the pursuit of Happiness—that to secure these rights, Governments are instituted among Men, deriving their just powers from the consent of the governed— That whenever any Form of Government becomes destructive to these ends, it is the Right of the People to alter or to abolish it and to institute new Government, laying its Foundation on such principles and organizing its powers in such form, as to them shall seem most likely to effect their Safety and Happiness. Prudence, indeed, will dictate that Governments long established should not be changed for light and transient causes; and accordingly all experience hath shewn that mankind are more disposed to suffer, while evils are sufferable, than to right themselves by abolishing the forms to which they are accustomed. But when a long train of abuses and usurpations, pursuing invariably the same Object evinces a design to reduce them under absolute Despotism, it is their right, it is their duty, to throw off such Government and to provide new Guards for their future security. —Such has been the patient sufferance of these Colonies; and such is now the necessity which constrains them to alter their former Systems of Government. The history of the present King of Great Britain is a history of repeated injuries and usurpations, all having in direct object the establishment of an absolute Tyranny over these States. To prove this, let Facts be submitted to a candid world.

A *narratio* follows, offering background on the situation: because the government of George III has become destructive, the framers of the Declaration are obligated to abolish their allegiance to him.

Arguably, the *partitio* begins here, followed by the longest part of the document (not reprinted here), a *confirmatio* that lists the "long train of abuses and usurpations" by George III.

—Declaration of Independence, July 4, 1776

The Declaration of Independence

The authors might have structured this argument by beginning with the last two sentences of the excerpt and then listing the facts intended to prove the king's abuse and tyranny. But by choosing first to explain the purpose and "self-evident" assumptions behind their argument and only then moving on to demonstrate how these "truths" have been denied by the British, the authors forge an immediate connection with readers and build up to the memorable conclusion. The structure is both familiar and inventive — as your own use of key elements of the oration should be in the arguments you compose.

Rogerian and Invitational Arguments

In trying to find an alternative to confrontational and angry arguments like those that so often erupt in legislative bodies around the world, scholars and teachers of rhetoric adapted the nonconfrontational principles psychologist Carl Rogers employed in personal therapy sessions. In simple terms, Rogers argued that people involved in disputes should not respond to each other until they could fully, fairly, and even sympathetically state the other person's position. Scholars of rhetoric Richard E. Young, Alton L. Becker, and Kenneth L.

Pike developed a four-part structure that is now known as Rogerian argument:

- **Introduction:** The writer describes an issue, a problem, or a conflict in terms rich enough to show that he/she fully understands and respects any alternative position or positions.
- **Contexts:** The writer describes the contexts in which alternative positions may be valid.
- **Writer's position:** The writer states his/her position on the issue and presents the circumstances in which that opinion would be valid.
- **Benefits to opponent:** The writer explains to opponents how they would benefit from adopting his/her position.

The key to Rogerian argumentation is a willingness to think about opposing positions and to describe them fairly. In a Rogerian structure, you have to acknowledge that alternatives to your claims exist and that they might be reasonable under certain circumstances. In tone, Rogerian arguments steer clear of heated and stereotypical language, emphasizing instead how all parties in a dispute might gain from working together.

In the same vein, feminist scholars Sonja Foss and Cindy Griffin have outlined a form of argument described as "invitational," one that begins with careful attention to and respect for the person or the audience you are in conversation with. Foss and Griffin show that such listening—in effect, walking in the other person's shoes—helps you see that person's points of view more clearly and thoroughly and thus offers a basis for moving together toward new understandings. The kind of argument they describe is what another rhetorician, Krista Ratcliffe, calls "rhetorical listening," which helps to establish productive connections between people and thus especially aids crosscultural communications.

Invitational rhetoric has as its goal not winning over opponents but getting people and groups to work together and identify with each other; it strives for connection, collaboration, and the mutually informed creation of knowledge. You may have opportunities to practice invitational rhetoric in peer-review sessions, when each member of a group listens carefully in order to work through problems and issues. You may also practice invitational rhetoric looking at any contested issue from other people's points of view, taking them into account, and engaging them fairly and respectfully in your own argument. Invitational arguments, then, call up structures that more resemble good two-way conversations or free-ranging dialogues than straight-line marches from thesis to conclusion. Even conventional arguments benefit from invitational strategies by giving space early on to a full range of perspectives, making sure to present them thoroughly and clearly. Remember that in such arguments, your goal is enhanced understanding so that you can open up a space for new perceptions and fresh ideas.

Consider how Frederick Douglass tried to broaden the outlook of his audiences when he delivered a Fourth of July oration in 1852. Most nineteenth-century Fourth of July speeches followed a pattern of praising the Revolutionary War heroes and emphasizing freedom, democracy, and justice. Douglass, a former slave, had that tradition in mind as he delivered his address, acknowledging the "great principles" that the "glorious anniversary" celebrates. But he also asked his (white) listeners to see the occasion from another point of view:

Fellow-citizens, pardon me, allow me to ask, why am I called upon to speak here today? What have I, or those I represent, to do with your national independence? Are the great principles of political freedom and natural justice, embodied in the Declaration of Independence, extended to us? And am I, therefore, called upon to bring our humble offering to the national altar, and to confess the benefits and express devout gratitude for the blessings resulting from your independence to us? . . . I say it with a sad sense of the disparity between us. I am not included within the pale of this glorious anniversary! Your high independence only reveals the immeasurable distance between us. The blessings in which you, this day, rejoice, are not enjoyed in common. The rich inheritance of justice, liberty, prosperity and independence, bequeathed by your fathers, is shared by you, not by me. The sunlight that brought life

Frederick Douglass

and healing to you, has brought stripes and death to me. This Fourth of July is yours, not mine. You may rejoice, I must mourn.

—Frederick Douglass, "What to the Slave Is the Fourth of July?"

Although his speech may seem confrontational, Douglass is inviting his audience to recognize a version of reality that they could have discovered on their own had they dared to imagine the lives of African Americans living in the shadows of American liberty. But the solution to the conflict between slavery and freedom, black and white, oppression and justice, was a long time in coming.

It was helped along by the arguments of another African American orator. Speaking at the foot of the Lincoln Memorial in Washington, D.C., on August 28, 1963, Martin Luther King Jr. clearly had Douglass's address (and Abraham Lincoln's Emancipation Proclamation) in mind in the opening of his "I Have a Dream" speech:

Martin Luther King Jr. on the steps of the Lincoln Memorial

Five score years ago, a great American, in whose symbolic shadow we stand today, signed the Emancipation Proclamation. This momentous decree came as a great beacon light of hope to millions of Negro slaves who had been seared in the flames of withering injustice. It came as a joyous daybreak to end the long night of their captivity.

But one hundred years later, the Negro still is not free. One hundred years later, the life of the Negro is still sadly crippled by the manacles of segregation and the chains of discrimination. One hundred years later, the Negro lives on a lonely island of poverty in the midst of a vast ocean of material prosperity. One hundred years later, the Negro is still languished in the corners of American society and finds himself an exile in his own land.

—Martin Luther King Jr., "I Have a Dream"

King goes on to delineate the many injustices still characteristic of U.S. society. Then, in one of the most brilliant perorations in the history of speechmaking, he invokes a dream of a future in which the United States would live up to the highest ideals of the Declaration of Independence. The outcome he imagines is a Rogerian-style win/win deliverance for all:

> . . . when we allow freedom to ring, when we let it ring from every village and every hamlet, from every state and every city, we will be able to speed up that day when all of God's children, black men and white men, Jews and Gentiles, Protestants and Catholics, will be able to join hands and sing in the words of the old Negro spiritual: "Free at last! Free at last! Thank God Almighty, we are free at last!"
>
> —Martin Luther King Jr., "I Have a Dream"

Such moments in political life are rare, but in spite of much evidence to the contrary (think of the repeatedly demonstrated effectiveness of political attack ads), the public claims to prefer nonpartisan and invitational rhetoric to one-on-one, winner-take-all battles, suggesting that such an approach strikes a chord in many people, especially in a world that is increasingly open to issues of diversity. The lesson to take from Rogerian or invitational argument is that it makes good sense in structuring your own arguments to learn opposing positions well enough to state them accurately and honestly, to strive to understand the points of view of your opponents, to acknowledge those views fairly in your own work, and to look for solutions that benefit as many people as possible.

RESPOND●

Choose a controversial topic that is frequently in the news, and decide how you might structure an argument on the subject, using the general principles of the classical oration. Then look at the same subject from a Rogerian or invitational perspective. How might your argument differ? Which approach would work better for your topic? For the audiences you might want to address?

Toulmin Argument

In *The Uses of Argument* (1958), British philosopher Stephen Toulmin presented structures to describe the way that ordinary people make reasonable arguments. Because Toulmin's system acknowledges the complications of life—situations when we qualify our thoughts with words such as *sometimes, often, presumably, unless,* and *almost*—his method isn't as airtight as formal logic that uses syllogisms (see p. 123 in this chapter and p. 67 in Chapter 4). But for that reason, Toulmin logic has become a powerful and, for the most part, practical tool for understanding and shaping arguments in the real world. We use his concepts and terminology in subsequent chapters in Part 2.

Toulmin argument will help you come up with ideas and test them and also figure out what goes where in many kinds of arguments. Let's take a look at the basic elements of Toulmin's structure:

Claim	the argument you wish to prove
Qualifiers	any limits you place on your claim
Reason(s)/ Evidence	support for your claim
Warrants	underlying assumptions that support your claim
Backing	evidence for warrant

If you wanted to state the relationship between them in a sentence, you might say:

> My claim is true, to a qualified degree, because of the following reasons, which make sense if you consider the warrant, backed by these additional reasons.

These terms—claim, evidence, warrants, backing, and qualifiers—are the building blocks of the Toulmin argument structure. Let's take them one at a time.

Making Claims

Toulmin arguments begin with **claims**, debatable and controversial statements or assertions you hope to prove.

Many writers stumble when it comes to making claims because facing issues squarely takes thought and guts. A claim answers the question *So what's your point?* or *Where do you stand on that?* Some writers might like to ignore these questions and avoid stating a position. But when you make a claim worth writing about, then it's worth standing up and owning it.

Is there a danger that you might oversimplify an issue by making too bold a claim? Of course. But making that sweeping claim is a logical first step toward eventually saying something more reasonable and subtle. Here are some fairly simple, undeveloped claims:

> The filibuster tactic in the legislatures of both the United States and Canada ought to be abolished.
>
> It's time to legalize the medical use of marijuana.
>
> NASA should launch a human expedition to Mars.
>
> Vegetarianism is the best choice of diet.
>
> Same-sex unions deserve the same protections as those granted to marriage between a man and a woman.

Good claims often spring from personal experiences. You may have relevant work or military or athletic experience — or you may know a lot about music, film, sustainable agriculture, social networking, inequities in government services — all fertile ground for authoritative, debatable, and personally relevant claims.

RESPOND●

Claims aren't always easy to find. Sometimes they're buried deep within an argument, and sometimes they're not present at all. An important skill in reading and writing arguments is the ability to identify claims, even when they aren't obvious.

Collect a sample of six to eight letters to the editor of a daily newspaper (or a similar number of argumentative postings from a political blog). Read each item, and then identify every claim that the writer makes. When you've compiled your list of claims, look carefully at the words that the writer or writers use when stating their positions. Is there a common vocabulary? Can you find words or phrases that signal an impending claim? Which of these seem most effective? Which ones seem least effective? Why?

Offering Evidence and Good Reasons

You can begin developing a claim by drawing up a list of reasons to support it or finding **evidence** that backs up the point.

Evidence and Reason(s) ⟶ So Claim

One student writer wanted to gather good reasons in support of an assertion that his college campus needed more official spaces for parking bicycles. He did some research, gathering statistics about parking-space allocation, numbers of people using particular designated slots, and numbers of bicycles registered on campus. Before he went any further, however, he listed his primary reasons for wanting to increase bicycle parking:

- **Personal experience:** At least twice a week for two terms, he was unable to find a designated parking space for his bike.
- **Anecdotes:** Several of his friends told similar stories. One even sold her bike as a result.
- **Facts:** He found out that the ratio of car to bike parking spaces was 100 to 1, whereas the ratio of cars to bikes registered on campus was 25 to 1.
- **Authorities:** The campus police chief told the college newspaper that she believed a problem existed for students who tried to park bicycles legally.

On the basis of his preliminary listing of possible reasons in support of the claim, this student decided that his subject was worth more research. He was on the way to amassing a set of good reasons and evidence that were sufficient to support his claim.

In shaping your own arguments, try putting claims and reasons together early in the writing process to create enthymemes. Think of these enthymemes as test cases or even as topic sentences:

> **Bicycle parking spaces should be expanded because the number of bikes on campus far exceeds the available spots.**

> **It's time to lower the drinking age because I've been drinking since I was fourteen and it hasn't hurt me.**

> **Legalization of the medical use of marijuana is long overdue since it has been proven an effective treatment for symptoms associated with cancer.**

> **Violent video games should be carefully evaluated and their use monitored by the industry, the government, and parents because these games cause addiction and psychological harm to players.**

As you can see, attaching a reason to a claim often spells out the major terms of an argument.

Anticipate challenges to your claims.

"I know your type, you're the type who'll make me prove every claim I make."

But your work is just beginning when you've put a claim together with its supporting reasons and evidence—because readers are certain to begin questioning your statement. They might ask whether the reasons and evidence that you're offering really do support the claim: Should the drinking age really be changed just because you've managed to drink since you were fourteen? They might ask pointed questions about your evidence: Exactly how do you know that the number of bikes on campus far exceeds the number of spaces available? Eventually, you've got to address potential questions about the quality of your assumptions and the quality of your evidence. The connection between claim and reason(s) is a concern at the next level in Toulmin argument.

Determining Warrants

Crucial to Toulmin argument is appreciating that there must be a logical and persuasive connection between a claim and the reasons and data supporting it. Toulmin calls this connection the **warrant**. It answers the question *How exactly do I get from the data to the claim?* Like the warrant in legal situations (a search warrant, for example), a sound warrant in an argument gives you authority to proceed with your case.

The warrant tells readers what your (often unstated) assumptions are—for example, that any practice that causes serious disease should be banned by the government. If readers accept your warrant, you can then present specific evidence to develop your claim. But if readers dispute your warrant, you'll have to defend it before you can move on to the claim itself.

Stating warrants can be tricky because they can be phrased in various ways. What you're looking for is the general principle that enables you to justify the move from a reason to a specific claim—the bridge connecting them. The warrant is the assumption that makes the claim seem believable. It's often a value or principle that you share with your readers. Let's demonstrate this logical movement with an easy example:

Don't eat that mushroom: it's poisonous.

The warrant supporting this enthymeme can be stated in several ways, always moving from the reason (*it's poisonous*) to the claim (*Don't eat that mushroom*):

Anything that is poisonous shouldn't be eaten.

If something is poisonous, it's dangerous to eat.

Here's the relationship, diagrammed:

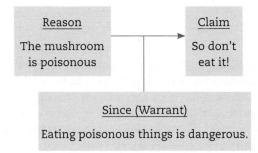

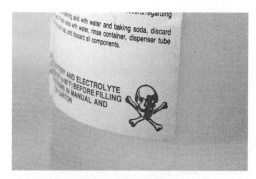

A simple icon—a skull and crossbones—can
make a visual argument that implies a claim, a
reason, and a warrant.

Perfectly obvious, you say? Exactly—and that's why the statement is so
convincing. If the mushroom in question is a death cap or destroying
angel (and you might still need expert testimony to prove that it is), the
warrant does the rest of the work, making the claim that it supports
seem logical and persuasive.

Let's look at a similar example, beginning with the argument in its
basic form:

> **We'd better stop for gas because the gauge has been reading empty
> for more than thirty miles.**

In this case, you have evidence that is so clear (a gas gauge reading
empty) that the reason for getting gas doesn't even have to be stated: the
tank is almost empty. The warrant connecting the evidence to the claim
is also pretty obvious:

> **If the fuel gauge of a car has been reading empty for more than thirty
> miles, then that car is about to run out of gas.**

Since most readers would accept this warrant as reasonable, they would
also likely accept the statement the warrant supports.

Naturally, factual information might undermine the whole argument:
the fuel gauge might be broken, or the driver might know that the car
will go another fifty miles even though the fuel gauge reads empty. But
in most cases, readers would accept the warrant.

Now let's consider how stating and then examining a warrant can help you determine the grounds on which you want to make a case. Here's a political enthymeme of a familiar sort:

> **Flat taxes are fairer than progressive taxes because they treat all taxpayers in the same way.**

Warrants that follow from this enthymeme have power because they appeal to a core American value—equal treatment under the law:

> **Treating people equitably is the American way.**
>
> **All people should be treated in the same way.**

You certainly could make an argument on these grounds. But stating the warrant should also raise a flag if you know anything about tax policy. If the principle is obvious and universal, then why do federal and many progressive state income taxes require people at higher levels of income to pay at higher tax rates than people at lower income levels? Could the warrant not be as universally popular as it seems at first glance? To explore the argument further, try stating the contrary claim and warrants:

> **Progressive taxes are fairer than flat taxes because people with more income can afford to pay more, benefit more from government, and shelter more of their income from taxes.**
>
> **People should be taxed according to their ability to pay.**
>
> **People who benefit more from government and can shelter more of their income from taxes should be taxed at higher rates.**

Now you see how different the assumptions behind opposing positions really are. If you decided to argue in favor of flat taxes, you'd be smart to recognize that some members of your audience might have fundamental reservations about your position. Or you might even decide to shift your entire argument to an alternative rationale for flat taxes:

> **Flat taxes are preferable to progressive taxes because they simplify the tax code and reduce the likelihood of fraud.**

Here, you have two stated reasons that are supported by two new warrants:

> **Taxes that simplify the tax code are desirable.**
>
> **Taxes that reduce the likelihood of fraud are preferable.**

Whenever possible, you'll choose your warrant knowing your audience, the context of your argument, and your own feelings.

Examples of Claims, Reasons, and Warrants

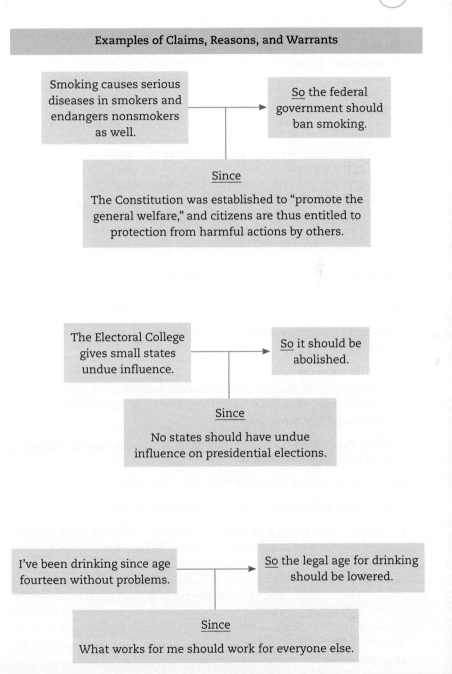

Be careful, though, not to suggest that you'll appeal to any old warrant that works to your advantage. If readers suspect that your argument for progressive taxes really amounts to *I want to stick it to people who work harder than me,* your credibility may suffer a fatal blow.

RESPOND●

At their simplest, warrants can be stated as "X is good" or "X is bad." Return to the letters to the editor or blog postings that you analyzed in the exercise on p. 133, this time looking for the warrant that is behind each claim. As a way to start, ask yourself these questions:

> If I find myself agreeing with the letter writer, what assumptions about the subject matter do I share with him/her?

> If I disagree, what assumptions are at the heart of that disagreement?

The list of warrants you generate will likely come from these assumptions.

Offering Evidence: Backing

The richest, most interesting part of a writer's work—backing—remains to be done after the argument has been outlined. Clearly stated claims and warrants show you how much evidence you will need. Take a look at this brief argument, which is both debatable and controversial, especially in tough economic times:

> **NASA should launch a human expedition to Mars because Americans need a unifying national goal.**

Here's one version of the warrant that supports the enthymeme:

> **What unifies the nation ought to be a national priority.**

To run with this claim and warrant, you'd first need to place both in context. The case of space exploration has been debated with varying intensity since the 1957 launch of the Soviet Union's *Sputnik* satellite, sparked after the losses of the U.S. space shuttles *Challenger* (1986) and *Columbia* (2003), and revisited again after the retirement of the Space Shuttle program in 2011. Acquiring such background knowledge through reading, conversation, and inquiry of all kinds will be necessary for making your case. (See Chapter 3 for more on gaining authority.)

There's no point in defending any claim until you've satisfied readers that questionable warrants on which the claim is based are defensible. In Toulmin argument, evidence you offer to support a warrant is called **backing**.

Sticker honoring the retirement of the Space Shuttle program

Warrant

What unifies the nation ought to be a national priority.

Backing

Americans want to be part of something bigger than themselves. (Emotional appeal as evidence)

In a country as diverse as the United States, common purposes and values help make the nation stronger. (Ethical appeal as evidence)

In the past, government investments such as the Hoover Dam and the *Apollo* moon program enabled many — though not all — Americans to work toward common goals. (Logical appeal as evidence)

In addition to evidence to support your warrant (backing), you'll need evidence to support your claim:

Argument in Brief (Enthymeme/Claim)

NASA should launch a human expedition to Mars because Americans now need a unifying national goal.

Evidence

The American people are politically divided along lines of race, ethnicity, religion, gender, and class. (Fact as evidence)

A common challenge or problem often unites people to accomplish great things. (Emotional appeal as evidence)

A successful Mars mission would require the cooperation of the entire nation — and generate tens of thousands of jobs. (Logical appeal as evidence)

A human expedition to Mars would be a valuable scientific project for the nation to pursue. (Appeal to values as evidence)

As these examples show, appeals to values and emotions can be just as appropriate as appeals to logic and facts, and all such claims will be stronger if a writer presents a convincing ethos. In most arguments, appeals work together rather than separately, reinforcing each other. (See Chapter 3 for more on ethos.)

Using Qualifiers

Experienced writers know that qualifying expressions make writing more precise and honest. Toulmin logic encourages you to acknowledge limitations to your argument through the effective use of **qualifiers**. You can save time if you qualify a claim early in the writing process. But you might not figure out how to limit a claim effectively until after you've explored your subject or discussed it with others.

Qualifiers

few	more or less	often
it is possible	in some cases	perhaps
rarely	many	under these conditions
it seems	typically	possibly
some	routinely	for the most part
it may be	most	if it were so
sometimes	one might argue	in general

Never assume that readers understand the limits you have in mind. Rather, spell them out as precisely as possible, as in the following examples:

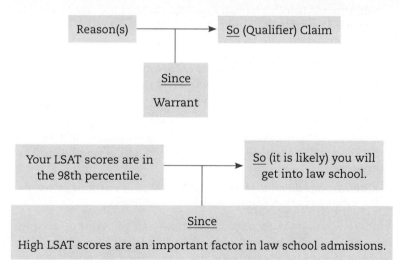

Unqualified Claim	People who don't go to college earn less than those who do.
Qualified Claim	*In most cases,* people who don't go to college earn less than those who do.

Understanding Conditions of Rebuttal

In the Toulmin system, potential objections to an argument are called **conditions of rebuttal.** Understanding and reacting to these conditions are essential to support your own claims where they're weak and also to understand the reasonable objections of people who see the world differently. For example, you may be a big fan of the Public Broadcasting Service (PBS) and the National Endowment for the Arts (NEA) and prefer that federal tax dollars be spent on these programs. So you offer the following claim:

Claim	**The federal government should support the arts.**

You need reasons to support this thesis, so you decide to present the issue as a matter of values:

Argument in Brief	**The federal government should support the arts because it also supports the military.**

Now you've got an enthymeme and can test the warrant, or the premises of your claim:

Warrant	**If the federal government can support the military, then it can also support other programs.**

But the warrant seems frail: you can hear a voice over your shoulder saying, "In essence, you're saying that *Because we pay for a military, we should pay for everything!*" So you decide to revise your claim:

Revised Argument	**If the federal government can spend huge amounts of money on the military, then it can afford to spend moderate amounts on arts programs.**

Now you've got a new warrant, too:

Revised Warrant	**A country that can fund expensive programs can also afford less expensive programs.**

This is a premise that you can defend, since you believe strongly that the arts are just as essential as a strong military is to the well-being of the

The new NEA logo

country. Although the warrant now seems solid, you still have to offer strong grounds to support your specific and controversial claim. So you cite statistics from reputable sources, this time comparing the federal budgets for the military and the arts. You break them down in ways that readers can visualize, demonstrating that much less than a penny of every tax dollar goes to support the arts.

But then you hear those voices again, saying that the "common defense" is a federal mandate; the government is constitutionally obligated to support a military and support for the arts is hardly in the same league! Looks like you need to add a paragraph explaining all the benefits the arts provide for very few dollars spent, and maybe you should suggest that such funding falls under the constitutional mandate to "promote the general welfare." Though not all readers will accept these grounds, they'll appreciate that you haven't ignored their point of view: you've gained credibility by anticipating a reasonable objection.

Dealing with conditions of rebuttal is an essential part of argument. But it's important to understand rebuttal as more than mere opposition. Anticipating objections broadens your horizons, makes you more open to alternative viewpoints, and helps you understand what you need to do to support your claim.

Within Toulmin argument, conditions of rebuttal remind us that we're part of global conversations: Internet newsgroups and blogs provide potent responses to positions offered by participants in discussions; instant messaging and social networking let you respond to and challenge others; links on Web sites form networks that are infinitely variable and open. In cyberspace, conditions of rebuttal are as close as your screen.

RESPOND •

Using a paper that you're writing, do a Toulmin analysis of the argument. When you're done, see which elements of the Toulmin scheme are represented. Are you short of evidence to support the warrant? Have you considered the conditions of rebuttal? Have you qualified your claim adequately? Next, write a brief revision plan: How will you buttress the argument in the places where it is weakest? What additional evidence will you offer for the warrant? How can you qualify your claim to meet the conditions of rebuttal? Then show your paper to a classmate and have him or her do a Toulmin analysis: a new reader will probably see your argument in different ways and suggest revisions that may not have occurred to you.

Outline of a Toulmin Argument

Consider the claim that was mentioned on p. 139:

Claim	The federal government should ban smoking.
Qualifier	The ban would be limited to public spaces.
Good Reasons	Smoking causes serious diseases in smokers. Nonsmokers are endangered by secondhand smoke.
Warrants	The Constitution promises to "promote the general welfare." Citizens are entitled to protection from harmful actions by others.
Backing	The United States is based on a political system that is supposed to serve the basic needs of its people, including their health.
Evidence	Numbers of deaths attributed to secondhand smoke Lawsuits recently won against large tobacco companies, citing the need for reparation for smoking-related health care costs Examples of bans already imposed in many public places
Authority	Cite the surgeon general.
Conditions of Rebuttal	Smokers have rights, too. Smoking laws should be left to the states. Such a ban could not be enforced.
Responses	The ban applies to public places; smokers can smoke in private.

The power of the federal government to impose other restrictions on smoking (such as warning labels on cigarettes and bans on cigarette advertisements on television) has survived legal challenges.

The experience of New York City, which has imposed such a ban, suggests that enforcement would not be a significant problem.

A Toulmin Analysis

You might wonder how Toulmin's method holds up when applied to an argument that is longer than a few sentences. Do such arguments really work the way that Toulmin predicts? In the following short argument, well-known linguist and author Deborah Tannen explores the consequences of a shift in the meaning of one crucial word: *compromise*. Tannen's essay, which originally appeared as a posting on Politico.com on June 15, 2011, offers a series of interrelated claims based on reasons, evidence, and warrants that culminate in the last sentence of the essay. She begins by showing that the word *compromise* is now rejected by both the political right and the political left and offers good reasons and evidence to support that claim. She then moves back to a time when "a compromise really was considered great," and offers three powerful pieces of evidence in support of that claim. The argument then comes back to the present, with a claim that the compromise and politeness of the nineteenth century have been replaced by "growing enmity." That claim is supported with reasoning and evidence that rest on an underlying warrant that "vituperation and seeing opponents as enemies is corrosive to the human spirit." The claims in the argument—that "compromise" has become a dirty word and that enmity and an adversarial spirit are on the rise—lead to Tannen's conclusion: rejecting compromise breaks the trust necessary for a democracy and thus undermines the very foundation of our society. While she does not use traditional qualifying words, she does say that the situation she describes is a "threat" to our nation, which qualifies the claim to some extent: the situation is not the "death" of our nation but rather a "threat." Tannen's annotated essay is on the following page.

Why Is Compromise Now a Dirty Word?

DEBORAH TANNEN

When did the word "compromise" get compromised?

When did the negative connotations of "He was caught in a compromising position" or "She compromised her ethics" replace the positive connotations of "They reached a compromise"?

Contextual information leading up to initial claim

House Speaker John Boehner said it outright on *60 Minutes* last year. When talking about "compromise," Boehner said, "I reject the word."

"When you say the word 'compromise,'" he explained, ". . . a lot of Americans look up and go, 'Uh-oh, they're gonna sell me out.'" His position is common right now.

In the same spirit, Tony Perkins wrote in a recent CNN.com op-ed piece, "When it comes to conservative principles, compromise is the companion of losers."

The political right is particularly vehement when it comes to compromise. Conservatives are now strongly swayed by the tea party movement, whose clarion call is a refusal to compromise, regardless of the practical consequences.

But the rejection of compromise is more widespread than that. The left regularly savages President Barack Obama for compromising too soon, too much or on the wrong issues. Many who fervently sought universal health coverage, for example, could not celebrate its near accomplishment because the president gave up the public option.

Initial claim

The death of compromise has become a threat to our nation as we confront crucial issues such as the debt ceiling and that most basic of legislative responsibilities: a federal budget. At stake is the very meaning of what had once seemed unshakable: "the full faith and credit" of the U.S. government.

Reason

Evidence

Back when the powerful nineteenth-century senator Henry Clay was called "the great compromiser," achieving a compromise really was considered great. On three occasions, the Kentucky statesman helped the Senate preserve the Union by crafting compromises between the deadlocked slave-holding South and the Northern free states. In 1820, his Missouri Compromise stemmed the spread of slavery. In 1833, when the South was poised to defy federal tariff laws favored by the North and the federal government was about to authorize military action, Clay found a last-minute compromise. And his Compromise of 1850 averted civil war for at least a decade.

It was during an 1850 Senate debate that Clay stated his conviction: "I go for honorable compromise whenever it can be made." Something else he said then holds a key to how the dwindling respect for compromise is related to larger and more dangerous developments in our nation today.

Warrant

"All legislation, all government, all society," Clay said, "is formed upon the principle of mutual concession, politeness, comity, courtesy; upon these, everything is based."

Claim

Concession, politeness, comity, courtesy—none of these words could be uttered now with the assurance of

Reason

listeners' approval. The word "comity" is rarely heard; "concession" sounds weak; "politeness" and "courtesy" sound quaint—much like the contemporary equivalent, "civility."

That Clay lauded both compromise and civil discourse in the same speech reveals the link between, on the one hand, the word "compromise" falling into disre-

Evidence

pute, and, on the other, the glorification of aggression that I wrote about in my book, *The Argument Culture: Stopping America's War of Words.*

Claim

Today we have an increasing tendency to approach every task—and each other—in an ever more adversarial spirit. Nowhere is this more evident, or more destructive, than in the Senate.

Rebuttal

Though the two-party system is oppositional by nature, there is plenty of evidence that a certain (yes) comity has been replaced by growing enmity. We don't have to look as

Evidence

far back as Clay for evidence. In 1996, for example, an unprecedented fourteen incumbent senators announced that they would not seek reelection. And many, in farewell essays, described an increase in vituperation and partisanship that made it impossible to do the work of the Senate.

Evidence

"The bipartisanship that is so crucial to the operation of Congress," Howell Heflin of Alabama wrote, "especially the Senate, has been abandoned." J. James Exon of Nebraska described an "ever-increasing vicious polarization of the electorate" that had "all but swept aside the former preponderance of reasonable discussion."

But this is not happening only in the Senate. There is a rising adversarial spirit among the people and the press. It isn't only the obvious invective on TV and radio. A newspaper story that criticizes its subject is praised as "tough"; one that refrains from criticism is scorned as a "puff piece." *Claim*

The notion of "balance" today often leads to a search for the most extreme opposing views — so they can be presented as "both sides," leaving no forum for subtlety, multiple perspectives or the middle ground, where most people stand. Framing issues in this polarizing way reinforces the impression that Boehner voiced: that compromising is selling out. *Reason* *Evidence*

Being surrounded by vituperation and seeing opponents as enemies is corrosive to the human spirit. It's also dangerous to our democracy. The great anthropologist Margaret Mead explained this in a 1962 speech. *Warrant* *Claim*

"We are essentially a society which must be more committed to a two-party system than to either party," Mead said. "The only way you can have a two-party system is to belong to a party formally and to fight to the death . . ." not for your party to win but "for the right of the other party to be there too." *Reason*

Today, this sounds almost as quaint as "comity" in political discourse.

Mead traced our two-party system to our unique revolution: "We didn't kill a king and we didn't execute a large number of our people, and we came into our own without the stained hands that have been associated with most revolutions." *Reason*

With this noble heritage, Mead said, comes "the obligation to keep the kind of government we set up" — where members of each party may "disagree mightily" but still "trust in each other and trust in our political opponents."

Losing that trust, Mead concluded, undermines the foundation of our democracy. That trust is exactly what is threatened when the very notion of compromise is rejected. *Conclusion*

What Toulmin Teaches

As Tannen's essay demonstrates, few arguments you read have perfectly sequenced claims or clear warrants, so you might not think of Toulmin's terms in building your own arguments. Once you're into your subject, it's easy to forget about qualifying a claim or finessing a warrant. But remembering what Toulmin teaches will always help you strengthen your arguments:

- Claims should be clear, reasonable, and carefully qualified.
- Claims should be supported with good reasons and evidence. Remember that a Toulmin structure provides the framework of an argument, which you fill out with all kinds of data, including facts, statistics, precedents, photographs, and even stories.
- Claims and reasons should be based on assumptions that readers will likely accept. Toulmin's focus on warrants can be confusing because it asks us to look at the assumptions that underlie our arguments—something many would rather not do. Toulmin pushes us to probe the values that support any argument and to think of how those values relate to particular audiences.
- Effective arguments respectfully anticipate objections readers might offer. Toulmin argument acknowledges that any claim can crumble under certain conditions, so it encourages a complex view that doesn't demand absolute or unqualified positions.

It takes considerable experience to write arguments that meet all these conditions. Using Toulmin's framework brings them into play automatically. If you learn it well enough, constructing good arguments can become a habit.

CULTURAL CONTEXTS FOR ARGUMENT

Organization

As you think about organizing your argument, remember that cultural factors are at work: patterns that you find persuasive are probably ones that are deeply embedded in your culture. In the United States, many people expect a writer to "get to the point" as directly as possible and to articulate that point efficiently and unambiguously. The organizational patterns favored by many in business hold many similarities to the classical oration—a highly explicit pattern that leaves little or nothing unexplained—introduction and thesis, background, overview of the parts that follow, evidence, other viewpoints, and conclusion. If a piece of writing follows this pattern, American readers ordinarily find it "well organized."

So it's no surprise that student writers in the United States are expected to make their structures direct and their claims explicit, leaving little unspoken. Their claims usually appear early in an argument, often in the first paragraph.

But not all cultures take such an approach. Some expect any claim or thesis to be introduced subtly, indirectly, and perhaps at the end of a work, assuming that audiences will "read between the lines" to understand what's being said. Consequently, the preferred structure of arguments (and face-to-face negotiations, as well) may be elaborate, repetitive, and full of digressions. Those accustomed to such writing may find more direct Western styles overly simple, childish, or even rude.

When arguing across cultures, look for cues to determine how to structure your presentations effectively. Here are several points to consider:

- Do members of your audience tend to be very direct, saying explicitly what they mean? Or are they restrained, less likely to call a spade a spade? Consider adjusting your work to the expectations of the audience.

- Do members of your audience tend to respect authority and the opinions of groups? They may find blunt approaches disrespectful or contrary to their expectations.

- Consider when to state your thesis: At the beginning? At the end? Somewhere else? Not at all?

- Consider whether digressions are a good idea, a requirement, or an element to avoid.

8
Arguments of Fact

Many people believe that taking vitamin E daily will prevent heart attacks, cataracts, colon cancer, impotence in men, and wrinkles. Evidence in scientific studies suggests that they are probably wrong.

In the past, female screen stars like Marilyn Monroe could be buxom and curvy, less concerned about their weight than actresses today. Or so the legend goes. But measuring the costumes worn by Monroe and other actresses reveals a different story.

When an instructor announces a tough new attendance policy for her course, a student objects that there is no evidence that students who regularly attend lectures classes perform any better than those who do not. The instructor begs to differ.

Understanding Arguments of Fact

Factual arguments come in many varieties, but they all try to establish whether something is or is not so, answering questions such as: *Is a historical legend true? Has a crime occurred?* or *Are the claims of a scientist accurate?* At first glance, you might object that these aren't arguments at all but just a matter of looking things up and then writing reports. And you'd be correct to an extent: people don't usually argue factual matters that are settled or undisputed (*The earth orbits the sun*), that might be decided with simple research (*Nelson Mandela was South Africa's first black president*), or that are the equivalent of a rule (*One foot equals 0.3048 meters*). Reporting facts, you might think, should be free of the friction of argument.

Yet facts become arguments whenever they're controversial on their own or challenge people's beliefs and lifestyles. Disagreements about childhood obesity, endangered species, or energy production ought to have a kind of clean, scientific logic to them. But that's rarely the case because the facts surrounding them must be interpreted. Those interpretations then determine what we feed children, where we can build a dam, or how we heat our homes. In other words, serious factual arguments almost always have consequences. *Can we rely on wind and solar power to solve our energy needs? Will the Social Security trust fund really go broke? Is it healthy to eat fatty foods?* People need well-reasoned factual arguments on subjects of this kind to make informed decisions. Such arguments educate the public.

For the same reason, we need arguments to challenge beliefs that are common in a society but held on the basis of inadequate or faulty information. Corrective arguments appear daily in the media, often based on studies written by scientists or researchers that the public would not encounter on their own. Many people, for example, believe that talking on a cell phone while driving is just like listening to the radio. But their intuition is not based on hard data: scientific studies show that using a cell phone in a car is comparable to driving under the influence of alcohol. That's a fact. As a result, some states have banned the use of handheld phones in cars.

Factual arguments also routinely address broad questions about how we understand the past. For example, are the accounts that we have of the American founding—or the Civil War, Reconstruction, or the heroics of the "Greatest Generation" in World War II—accurate? Or

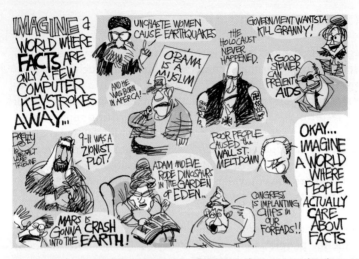

The Internet puts information at our fingertips, but we need to be sure to confirm that information as fact.

do the "facts" that we teach today sometimes reflect the perspectives and prejudices of earlier times or ideologies? The telling of history is almost always controversial and rarely settled: the British and Americans will always tell different versions of what happened in North America in 1776.

It's similarly important to have factual arguments to counterbalance what's narrowly or mistakenly reported—whether by news media, corporations, or branches of government. For good or ill, the words of public figures and the actions of institutions, from churches to news organizations, are now always on record and searchable. Corrective arguments can sometimes play like a game of "Gotcha!" but they broaden readers' perspectives and help them make judgments on the basis of better information. (They also suggest that our institutions are often just as inconsistent, fallible, and petty as the rest of us.)

As you can see, then, arguments of fact do much of the heavy lifting in our world. They report on what has been recently discovered or explore the implications of that new information. They also add interest and complexity to our lives, taking what might seem simple and adding new dimensions to it. In many situations, they're the precursors to other forms of analysis, especially causal and proposal arguments. Before we can explore why things happen as they do or solve problems, we need to know the facts on the ground.

RESPOND ●

For each topic in the following list, decide whether the claim is worth arguing to a college audience, and explain why or why not.

Hurricanes are increasing in number and ferocity.

Many people die annually of heart disease.

Fewer people would die of colon and prostate cancer each year if they drank more coffee.

Japan might have come to terms more readily in 1945 if the Allies in World War II hadn't demanded unconditional surrender.

Boys would do better in school if there were more men teaching in elementary and secondary classrooms.

The ongoing economic recession will lead drivers to buy more energy-efficient vehicles.

There aren't enough high-paying jobs for college graduates these days.

Hydrogen may never be a viable alternative to fossil fuels because it takes too much energy to change hydrogen into a usable form.

Its opponents have grossly exaggerated the costs of the Patient Protection and Affordable Care Act of 2010.

Characterizing Factual Arguments

Factual arguments are often motivated by simple human curiosity or suspicion: *Are people who earn college degrees happier than those who don't? If being fat is so unhealthy, why aren't mortality rates rising?* Researchers may notice a pattern that leads them to look more closely at some phenomenon or behavior, exploring questions such as *What if?* or *How come?* Or maybe a writer first notes something new or different or unexpected and wants to draw attention to that fact: *Contrary to expectations, suicide rates are much higher in rural areas than urban ones.*

Such observations can lead quickly to **hypotheses**—that is, toward tentative and plausible statements of fact whose merits need to be examined more closely. *Maybe being a little overweight isn't as bad for people as we've been told? Maybe people in rural areas have less access to mental health services?* To support such hypotheses, writers then have to uncover evidence that reaches well beyond the casual observations that triggered an initial interest—like a news reporter motivated to see whether there's a verifiable story behind a source's tip.

For instance, the authors of *Freakonomics*, Stephen J. Dubner and Steven Levitt, were intrigued by the National Highway Traffic Safety Administration's claim that car seats for children were 54 percent effective in preventing deaths in auto crashes for children below the age of four. In a *New York Times* op-ed column entitled "The Seat Belt Solution," they posed an important question about that factual claim:

> But 54 percent effective compared with what? The answer, it turns out, is this: Compared with a child's riding completely unrestrained.

Their initial question about that claim led them to a more focused inquiry, then to a database on auto crashes, and then to a surprising conclusion: for kids above age twenty-four months, those in car seats were statistically safer than those without any protection but weren't safer than those confined by seat belts (which are much simpler, cheaper, and more readily available devices). Looking at the statistics every which way, the authors wonder if children older than two years would be just as well off physically—and their parents less stressed and better off financially—if the government mandated seat belts rather than car seats for them.

What kinds of evidence typically appear in sound factual arguments? The simple answer might be "all sorts," but a case can be made that factual arguments try to rely on "hard evidence" more than on "constructed" arguments based on logic and reason (see Chapter 4). Even so, some pieces of evidence are harder and more convincing than others.

Developing a Factual Argument

Entire Web sites are dedicated to finding and posting errors from news and political sources. Some, like Media Matters for America and Accuracy in Media, take overtly partisan stands. Here's a one-day sampling of headlines from Media Matters:

Glenn Beck's Top 5 Most Inflammatory Moments

Fox Celebrated July 4 by Trying to Debunk Global Warming Again

Fox's Asman Unable to Acknowledge That Reagan Raised Taxes

And here's a listing from Accuracy in Media:

FACTS: Obama's Townhall Lacked Them

Media Deceptions Support Obama against Israel

More Proof That MSNBC Is Working for Obama

It would be hard to miss the political agendas at work on these sites.

Other fact-checking organizations have better reputations when it comes to assessing the truths behind political claims and media presentations. Though both are routinely charged with bias too, Pulitzer Prize–winning PolitiFact.com and FactCheck.org at least make an effort to be fair-minded across a broader political spectrum. FactCheck, for example, provides a detailed analysis of the claims it investigates in relatively neutral and denotative language, and lists the sources its researchers used—just as if its writers were doing a research paper. At its best, FactCheck.org demonstrates what one valuable kind of factual argument can accomplish.

Any factual argument that you might compose—from how you state your claim to how you present evidence and the language you use—should be similarly shaped by the occasion for the argument and a desire to serve the audiences that you hope to reach. We can offer some general advice to help you get started.

The Latest from PolitiFact

A scorecard separating fact from fiction

FLORIDA — Debbie Wasserman Schultz — Says Mitt Romney's campaign "has already spent more on negative ads than John McCain did during his entire presidential run." — FALSE — 2012 more than 2008 already? Nope.

VIRGINIA — Randy Forbes — "The national debt is equal to $48,700 for every American or $128,300 for every U.S. household. It is now equivalent to the size of our entire economy." — TRUE — The numbers add up

TENNESSEE — Stacey Campfield — AIDS was transmitted to humans because "one guy" had sex with "a monkey" and then started "having sex with men." — Completely ridiculous

Promise: Promote more pre-school education
Update: Money, guidelines dedicated to pre-school — Obame... PROMISE KEPT

PolitiFact uses a meter to rate political claims from "True" to "Pants on Fire."

RESPOND•

The Annenberg Public Policy Center at the University of Pennsylvania hosts FactCheck.org, a Web site dedicated to separating facts from opinion or falsehood in the area of politics. It claims to be politically neutral. Find a case that interests you, either a recent controversial item listed on its homepage or another from its archives. Carefully study the item. Pay attention to the devices that FactCheck uses to suggest or ensure objectivity and the way that it handles facts and statistics. Then offer your own brief *factual* argument about the site's objectivity. A full case from FactCheck.org appears at the end of this chapter as a sample reading.

Identifying an Issue

To offer a factual argument of your own, you need to identify an issue or problem that will interest you and potential readers. Look for situations or phenomena—local or national—that seem out of the ordinary in the expected order of things. For instance, you might notice that many people you know are deciding not to attend college. How widespread is this change, and who are the people making this choice?

Or follow up claims that strike you as at odds with the facts as you know them or believe them. Maybe you doubt explanations being offered for your favorite sport team's current slump or for the declining number of minority men in your college courses. Or you might give a local spin to factual questions that other people have already formulated on a national level. Did the recession have as deep an effect on jobs or schools in your community as elsewhere in the country? Do people in your town seem to be flocking to high-mpg vehicles or resisting bans on texting while driving or smoking in public places outdoors? You will likely write a better paper if you take on a factual question that genuinely interests you.

In fact, whole books are written when authors decide to pursue factual questions that intrigue them, even those that have been explored before. But you want to be careful not to argue matters that pose no challenge for you or your audiences. You're not offering anything new if you just try to persuade readers that smoking is harmful to their well-being. So how about something fresh in the area of health?

Quick preliminary research and reading might allow you to move from an intuition to a hypothesis, that is, a tentative statement of your claim: *Having a dog is good for your health.* As noted earlier, factual arguments often provoke other types of analysis. In developing this claim, you'd need to explain what "good for your health" means, potentially an argument of definition. You'd also likely find yourself researching causes of the phenomenon if you can demonstrate that it is factual. As it turns out, your canine hypothesis would have merit if you defined "good for health" as "encouraging exercise." Here's the lead to a *New York Times* story reporting recent research:

> If you're looking for the latest in home exercise equipment, you may want to consider something with four legs and a wagging tail.
>
> Several studies now show that dogs can be powerful motivators to get people moving. Not only are dog owners more likely to take regular walks, but new research shows that dog walkers are more active overall than people who don't have dogs.
>
> One study even found that older people are more likely to take regular walks if the walking companion is canine rather than human.
>
> —Tara Parker-Pope, "Forget the Treadmill. Get a Dog." March 14, 2011

As always, there's another side to the story: what if people likely to get dogs are the very sort already inclined to be more physically active? You could explore that possibility as well (and researchers have), and then either modify your initial hypothesis or offer a new one. That's what hypotheses are for. They are works in progress.

Moving is the best medicine.
Keeping active and losing weight are just two of the ways that you can fight osteoarthritis pain. In fact, for every pound you lose, that's four pounds less pressure on each knee. For information on managing pain, go to fightarthritispain.org.

Here's an actual ad based on the claim that exercise (and dog ownership) is good for health.

RESPOND•

Working with a group of colleagues, generate a list of twenty favorite "mysteries" explored on cable TV shows, in blogs, or in tabloid newspapers. Here are three to get you started—the alien crash landing at Roswell, the existence of Atlantis, and the uses of Area 51. Then decide which—if any—of these puzzlers might be resolved or explained in a reasonable factual argument and which ones remain eternally mysterious and improbable. Why are people attracted to such topics? Would any of these items provide material for a noteworthy factual argument?

Researching Your Hypothesis

How and where you research your subject will depend, naturally, on your subject. You'll certainly want to review Chapter 17, "Finding Evidence," Chapter 18, "Evaluating Sources," and Chapter 19, "Using Sources," before constructing an argument of fact. Libraries and the Web will provide you with deep resources on almost every subject. Your task will typically be to separate the best sources from all the rest. The word *best* here has many connotations: some reputable sources may be too technical for your audiences; some accessible sources may be pitched too low or be too far removed from the actual facts.

You'll be making judgment calls like this routinely. But do use primary sources whenever you can. For example, when gathering a comment from a source on the Web, trace it whenever possible to its original site, and read the comment in its full context. When statistics are quoted, follow them back to the source that offered them first to be sure that they're recent and reputable. Instructors and librarians can help you appreciate the differences. Understand that even sources with pronounced biases can furnish useful information, provided that you know how to use them, take their limitations into account, and then share what you know about the sources with your readers.

Sometimes, you'll be able to do primary research on your own, especially when your subject is local and you have the resources to do it. Consider conducting a competent survey of campus opinions and attitudes, for example, or study budget documents (often public) to determine trends in faculty salaries, tuition, student fees, and so on. Primary research of this sort can be challenging because even the simplest surveys or polls have to be intelligently designed and executed in a way that samples a representative population (see Chapter 4). But the work could pay off in an argument that brings new information to readers.

Refining Your Claim

As you learn more about your subject, you might revise your hypothesis to reflect what you've discovered. In most cases, these revised hypotheses will grow increasingly complex and specific. Following are three versions of essentially the same claim, with each version offering more information to help readers judge its merit:

- Americans really did land on the moon, despite what some people think!

- Since 1969, when the *Eagle* supposedly landed on the moon, some people have been unjustifiably skeptical about the success of the United States' *Apollo* program.

- Despite plentiful hard evidence to the contrary — from *Saturn V* launches witnessed by thousands to actual moon rocks tested by independent labs worldwide — some people persist in believing falsely that NASA's moon landings were actually filmed on deserts in the American Southwest as part of a massive propaganda fraud.

The additional details about the subject might also suggest new ways to develop and support it. For example, conspiracy theorists claim that the absence of visible stars in photographs of the moon landing is evidence that it was staged, but photographers know that the camera exposure needed to capture the foreground — astronauts in their bright space suits — would have made the stars in the background too dim to see. That's a key bit of evidence for this argument.

As you advance in your research, your thesis will likely pick up even more qualifying words and expressions, which help you to make reasonable claims. Qualifiers — words and phrases such as *some, most, few, for most people, for a few users, under specific conditions, usually, occasionally, seldom*, and so on — will be among your most valuable tools in a factual argument.

Sometimes it is important to set your factual claim into a context that helps explain it to others who may find it hard to accept. You might have to concede some ground initially in order to see the broader picture. For instance, professor of English Vincent Carretta anticipated strong objections after he uncovered evidence that Olaudah Equiano — the author of

The Interesting Narrative (1789), a much-cited autobiographical account of his Middle Passage voyage and subsequent life as a slave—may actually have been born in South Carolina and not in western Africa. Speaking to the *Chronicle of Higher Education*, Carretta explains why Equiano may have fabricated his African origins to serve a larger cause—a growing antipathy to slavery and slave markets:

> "Whether [Equiano] invented his African birth or not, he knew that what that movement needed was a first-person account. And because they were going after the slave trade, it had to be an account of someone who had been born in Africa and was brought across the Middle Passage. An African American voice wouldn't have done it."
>
> —Jennifer Howard, "Unraveling the Narrative"

Carretta asks readers to appreciate that the new facts that he has discovered about *The Interesting Narrative* do not undermine the work's historical significance. If anything, his research has added new dimensions to its meaning and interpretation.

Deciding Which Evidence to Use

In this chapter, we've blurred the distinction between factual arguments for scientific and technical audiences and those for the general public (in media such as magazines, blogs, and television documentaries). In the former kind of arguments, readers will expect specific types of evidence arranged in a formulaic way. Such reports may include a hypothesis, a review of existing research on the subject, a description of methods, a presentation of results, and finally a formal discussion of the findings. If you are thinking "lab report," you are already familiar with an academic form of a factual argument with precise standards for evidence.

Less scientific factual arguments—claims about our society, institutions, behaviors, habits, and so on—are seldom so systematic and they may draw on evidence from a great many different media. For instance, you might need to review old newspapers, scan videos, study statistics on government Web sites, read transcripts of Congressional hearings, record the words of eyewitnesses to an event, and so on. Very often, you will assemble your arguments from material found in credible though not always concurring authorities and resources—drawing upon the factual findings of scientists and scholars, but perhaps using their original insights in novel ways.

For example, when the National Endowment for the Arts (NEA) published a study entitled "Reading at Risk" in June 2004 to report "the declining importance of literature to our populace," it reached its pessimistic conclusions by studying a variety of phenomena in a large population:

> This survey investigated the percentage and number of adults, age eighteen and over, who attended artistic performances, visited museums, watched broadcasts of arts programs, or read literature. The survey sample numbered more than seventeen thousand individuals, which makes it one of the most comprehensive polls of art and literature consumption ever conducted.
>
> —National Endowment for the Arts, "Reading at Risk"

You might ponder the results of this study and wonder whether it defined literature too narrowly if it didn't consider that many people today favor nonprint, nontraditional, and electronic literary forms such as graphic novels or even video games. Your new study might challenge the conclusion of the earlier research by bringing fresh facts to the table.

Often, you may have only a limited number of words or pages in which to make a factual argument. What do you do then? You present your best evidence as powerfully as possible. But that's not difficult. You can make a persuasive factual case with just a few examples: three or four often suffice to make a point. Indeed, going on too long or presenting even good data in ways that make it seem uninteresting or pointless can undermine a claim.

Presenting Your Evidence

In *Hard Times* (1854), British author Charles Dickens poked fun at a pedagogue he named Thomas Gradgrind, who preferred hard facts before all things human or humane. When poor Sissy Jupe (called "girl number twenty" in his awful classroom) is unable at his command to define *horse*, Gradgrind turns to his star pupil:

> "Bitzer," said Thomas Gradgrind. "Your definition of a horse."
>
> "Quadruped. Graminivorous. Forty teeth, namely twenty-four grinders, four eyeteeth, and twelve incisive. Sheds coat in the spring; in marshy countries, sheds hoofs, too. Hoofs hard, but requiring to be shod with iron. Age known by marks in mouth." Thus (and much more) Bitzer.
>
> "Now girl number twenty," said Mr. Gradgrind. "You know what a horse is."
>
> —Charles Dickens, *Hard Times*

But does Bitzer? Rattling off facts about a subject isn't quite the same thing as knowing it, especially when your goal is, as it is in an argument of fact, to educate and persuade audiences. So you must take care how you present your evidence.

Factual arguments, like any others, take many forms. They can be as simple and pithy as a letter to the editor (or Bitzer's definition of a horse) or as comprehensive and formal as a senior thesis or even a dissertation. Such a thesis might have just two or three readers mainly interested in the facts you are presenting and the competence of your work. So your presentation can be lean and relatively simple.

But to earn the attention of readers in some more public forum, you may need to work harder to be persuasive. For instance, the National Commission on Adult Literacy's 2008 report, "Reach Higher, America: Overcoming Crisis in the U.S. Workforce," has the design of a formal scientific report, with sixty-five references, ten appendices, and a dozen figures and tables. Like many such studies, it also includes a foreword, an executive summary, and a detailed table of contents. All these elements help readers find the facts they need while also establishing the ethos of the work, making it seem serious, credible, well-conceived, and worth reading.

Considering Design and Visuals

When you prepare a factual argument, consider how you can present your evidence most effectively. Precisely because factual arguments often rely on evidence that can be measured, computed, or illustrated, they benefit from thoughtful, even artful presentation of data. If you have lots of examples, you might arrange them in a list (bulleted or otherwise) and keep the language in each item roughly parallel. If you have an argument that can be translated into a table, chart, or graph (see Chapter 14), try it. And if there's a more dramatic medium for your factual argument—a Prezi slideshow, a multimedia mash-up, a documentary video posted via a social network—experiment with it, checking to be sure it would satisfy the assignment.

Images and photos—from technical illustrations to imaginative recreations—have the power to document what readers might otherwise have to imagine, whether actual conditions of drought, poverty, or disaster like the earthquake and tsunami that devastated Japan in 2011, or the dimensions of the Roman forum as it existed in the time of

Infographics like this one turn facts and data into arguments.

Julius Caesar. Readers today expect the arguments they read to include visual elements, and there's little reason not to offer this assistance if you have the technical skills to create them.

Consider the rapid development of the genre known as infographics—basically data presented in bold visual form. These items can be humorous and creative, but many, such as "Learning Out of Poverty" on the preceding page, make powerful factual arguments even when they leave it to viewers to draw their own conclusions. Just search "infographics" on the Web to find many examples.

GUIDE to writing an argument of fact

● Finding a Topic

You're entering an argument of fact when you:

- make a claim about fact or existence that's controversial or surprising: *Climate change is threatening species in all regions by extending the range of non-native plants and animals.*

- correct an error of fact: *The overall abortion rate is not increasing in the United States, though rates are increasing in some states.*

- challenge societal myths: *Many Mexicans fought alongside Anglos in battles that won Texas its independence from Mexico.*

- wish to discover the state of knowledge about a subject or examine a range of perspectives and points of view: *The rationales of parents who homeschool their children reveal some surprising differences.*

● Researching Your Topic

Use both a library and the Web to locate the information you need. A research librarian can be a valuable resource, as are experts or eyewitnesses. Begin research by consulting the following types of sources:

- scholarly books on your subject
- newspapers, magazines, reviews, and journals (online and print)
- online databases
- government documents and reports
- Web sites, blogs, social networking sites, and listservs or newsgroups
- experts in the field, some of whom might be right on your campus

Do field research if appropriate—a survey, a poll, or systematic observation. Or invite people with a stake in the subject to present their interpretations of the facts. Evaluate all sources carefully, making sure that each is authoritative and credible.

● Formulating a Hypothesis

Don't rush into a thesis. Instead, begin with a hypothesis that expresses your beliefs at the beginning of the project but that may change as you learn more. It's OK to start with a question to which you don't have an answer or with a broad, general interest in a subject:

- **Question:** Have higher admissions standards at BSU reduced the numbers of entering first-year students from small, rural high schools?

- **Hypothesis:** Higher admissions standards at BSU are reducing the number of students admitted from rural high schools, which tend to be smaller and less well-funded than those in suburban and urban areas.

- **Question:** Have music sites like Pandora and Spotify reduced the amount of illegal downloading of music?

- **Hypothesis:** Services like Spotify and Pandora may have done more than lawsuits by record companies to discourage illegal downloads of music.

- **Question:** How dangerous is nuclear energy, really?

- **Hypothesis:** The danger posed by nuclear power plants is far less than that attributable to other viable energy sources.

- **Question:** Why can't politicians and citizens agree about the threat posed by the huge federal deficit?

- **Hypothesis:** People with different points of view read different threats into the budget numbers and so react differently.

● Examples of Arguable Factual Claims

- A campus survey that shows that far more students have read *Harry Potter and the Prisoner of Azkaban* than *Hamlet* indicates that our current core curriculum lacks depth.

- Evidence suggests that the European conquest of the Americas may have had more to do with infectious diseases than any superiority in technology or weaponry.

- In the long run, dieting may be more harmful than moderate overeating.

● Preparing a Proposal

If your instructor asks you to prepare a proposal for your project, here's a format that may help:

State your thesis or hypothesis completely. If you are having trouble doing so, try outlining it in Toulmin terms:

Claim:

Reason(s):

Warrant(s):

Alternatively, you might describe the complications of a factual issue you hope to explore in your project, with the thesis perhaps coming later.

- Explain why the issue you're examining is important, and provide the context for raising the issue. Are you introducing new information, making available information better known, correcting what has been reported incorrectly, or complicating what has been understood more simply?
- Identify and describe those readers you most hope to reach with your argument. Why is this group of readers most appropriate for your project? What are their interests in the subject? How might you involve them in the paper?
- Discuss the kinds of evidence you expect to use in the project and the research the paper will require.
- Briefly discuss the key challenges you anticipate in preparing your argument.
- Describe the format or genre you expect to use: Academic essay? Formal report? Wiki? Infographic? Will you need charts, tables, graphs, other illustrations?

● Thinking about Organization

The simplest structure for a factual argument is to make a claim and then prove it. But even a basic approach needs an introductory section that provides a context for the claim and a concluding section that assesses the implications of the argument. A factual argument that corrects an error or provides an alternative view of some familiar concept or historical event will also need a section early on explaining what the error or the common belief is. Be sure your opening section answers the *who, what, where, when, how,* and (maybe) *why* questions that readers will bring to the case.

Factual arguments offered in some academic fields follow formulas and templates. A typical paper in psychology will include an abstract, a review of literature, a discussion of method, an analysis, and a references list. When you have flexibility in the structure of your argument, it makes sense to lead with a striking example to interest readers in your subject and then to conclude with your strongest evidence. Pay particular attention to transitions between key points.

If you are defending a specific claim, anticipate the ways people with different points of view might respond to your argument. Consider how to address such differences respectfully in the body of your argument. But don't let a factual argument with a persuasive thesis end with concessions or refutations, especially in pieces for the general public. Such a strategy leaves readers thinking about problems with your claim at precisely the point when they should be impressed by its strengths. On the other hand, if your factual argument becomes exploratory, you may find yourself simply presenting a range of positions.

● Getting and Giving Response: Questions for Peer Response

Your instructor may assign you to a group for the purpose of reading and responding to each other's drafts. If not, ask for responses from serious readers or consultants at a writing center. Use the following questions to evaluate a colleague's draft. Since specific comments help more than general observations, be sure to illustrate your comments with examples. Some of the questions below assume a conventional, thesis-driven project, but more exploratory or invitational arguments of fact also need to be clearly phrased, organized, and supported with evidence.

The Claim

- Does the claim clearly raise a serious and arguable factual issue?
- Is the claim as clear and specific as possible?
- Is the claim qualified? If so, how?

Evidence for the Claim

- Is the evidence provided enough to persuade readers to believe your claim? If not, what additional evidence would help? Does any of the evidence seem inappropriate or ineffective? Why?

- Is the evidence in support of the claim simply announced, or do you explain its significance and appropriateness? Is more discussion needed?

- Are readers' potential objections to the claim or evidence addressed adequately? Are alternative positions understood thoroughly and presented fairly?

- What kinds of sources are cited? How credible and persuasive will they be to readers? What other kinds of sources might work better?

- Are all quotations introduced with appropriate signal phrases (such as "As Tyson argues, . . .") and blended smoothly into the writer's sentences?

- Are all visuals titled and labeled appropriately? Have you introduced them and commented on their significance?

Organization and Style

- How are the parts of the argument organized? Is this organization effective, or would some other structure work better?

- Will readers understand the relationships among the claims, supporting reasons, warrants, and evidence? If not, what could be done to make those connections clearer? Are more transitional words and phrases needed? Would headings or graphic devices help?

- How might you use visual elements to make facts you present more readable or persuasive?

- Are there helpful transitions or links from point to point, sentence to sentence, and paragraph to paragraph? If not, how could they be improved?

- Is the style suited to the subject? Is it too formal? Too casual? Too technical? Too bland? How can it be improved?

- Which sentences seem particularly effective? Which ones seem weakest, and how could they be improved? Should some short sentences be combined, or should any long ones be separated into two or more sentences?

- How well constructed are the paragraphs? Do any seem too skimpy or too long? How can they be improved?

- Which words or phrases seem particularly accurate, vivid, and memorable? Do any seem dull, vague, unclear, or inappropriate for the audience or the writer's purpose? Are definitions provided for technical or other terms that readers might not know?

Spelling, Punctuation, Mechanics, Documentation, and Format

- Are there any errors in spelling, punctuation, capitalization, and the like?
- Is an appropriate and consistent style of documentation used for parenthetical citations and the list of works cited or references? (See Chapter 21.)
- Does the paper or project follow an appropriate format? Is it appropriately designed and attractively presented? How could it be improved?

PROJECTS ●

1. Turn a database of information you find in the library or online into a traditional argument or, alternatively, into an infographic that offers a variety of potential claims. FedStats, a government Web site, provides endless data, but so can the sports or financial sections of a newspaper. Once you find a rich field of study, examine the data and draw your ideas from it, perhaps amplifying your ideas with material from other related sources of information. If you decide to create an infographic, you'll find good examples at VizWorld or Cool Infographics online. Software tools you can use to create infographics include Wordle and Google Public Data. Have fun.

2. Write an argument about one factual matter you are confident —based on personal experience or your state of knowledge—that most people get wrong, time and again. Use your expertise to correct this false impression.

3. Tough economic and political times sometimes reinforce and sometimes undermine cultural myths. With your classmates, generate a list of common beliefs about education, employment, family life, marriage, social progress, technology, and so on that seem to be under unusual scrutiny today. *Does it still pay to invest in higher education? Do two-parent households matter as much as they used to? Can children today expect to do better than their parents?* Pick one area to explore in depth, narrow the topic as much as you can, and then gather facts that inform it by doing research, perhaps working collaboratively to expand your findings. Turn your investigation into a factual argument.

4. Digital and electronic technologies have made still and video cameras cheap, small, and durable. As a result, they are now everywhere—in convenience stores, schools, public streets, subway stations, and so on. They are used by law enforcement and sports officials. And everyone with a cell phone has a camera and video recorder in hand. In all these circumstances, the cameras record what individuals on their own may not see or not remember well, presumably providing a more accurate account of an event.

   Does all this surveillance enhance our society, undermine it in some ways, or have perhaps unforeseen consequences? Study just one type of surveillance, including any others you think of not mentioned here. Read up on the subject in the library or on the Web and consult with a wide range of people interested in the subject, perhaps gathering them together for a discussion or panel discussion. Then offer a factual argument based on what you uncover, reflecting the range of perspectives and opinions you have encountered. For example, you might show whether and how people benefit from the technology, how it's being abused, or both.

Readers will certainly notice the title.

Why You Should Fear Your Toaster More Than Nuclear Power

TAYLOR PEARSON

A recent nuclear disaster in Japan provides a challenging context for Pearson's claim: we need nuclear energy.

For the past month or so, headlines everywhere have been warning us of the horrible crises caused by the damaged Japanese nuclear reactors. Titles like "Japan Nuclear Disaster Tops Scale" have fueled a new wave of protests against anything nuclear—namely, the construction of new nuclear plants or even the continued operation of existing plants. However, all this reignited fear of nuclear energy is nothing more than media sensationalism. We need nuclear energy. It's clean, it's efficient, it's economic, and it's probably the only thing that will enable us to quickly phase out fossil fuels.

The first person plural point of view (*we*) helps Pearson to connect with his audience.

DEATH TOLL

First, let's address what is probably everyone's main concern about nuclear energy: the threat it poses to us and the likelihood of a nuclear power plant killing large numbers of people. The actual number of deaths caused by nuclear power plant accidents, even in worst-case scenarios, have been few. Take the Chernobyl accident—the worst and most lethal nuclear incident

---

Taylor Pearson wrote "Why You Should Fear Your Toaster More Than Nuclear Power" while he was a sophomore at the University of Texas at Austin. The assignment asked for a public argument—one good enough to attract readers who could put it down if they lost interest. In other words, a purely academic argument wouldn't work. So Pearson allows himself to exercise his sense of humor. Nor did the paper have to be formally documented. However, Pearson was expected to identify crucial sources the way writers do in magazines and newspapers. The paper provides an example of a factual argument with a clear thesis: "We need nuclear energy."

to date. As tragic as it was, the incident has killed only eighty-two people. More specifically, according to a 2005 release by the World Health Organization, thirty-two were killed in the effort to put out the fires caused by the meltdown and thirty-eight died within months of the accident as a result of acute radiation poisoning. Since the accident occurred in 1986, an additional twelve people have died from the radiation they were exposed to during the accident. Almost all deaths were highly exposed rescue workers. Other nuclear power accidents have been few and never resulted in more than ten deaths per incident. Still think that's too dangerous? To provide some perspective, let's consider an innocuous household appliance, the toaster: over three thousand people died from toaster accidents the first year the appliances were produced and sold in the 1920s, and they still cause around fifty accident-related deaths every year in the United States. So your toaster is far more likely to kill you than any nuclear power plant and subsequently give you a painfully embarrassing epitaph.

> Pearson deflates fears by putting deaths caused by nuclear plants in perspective.

In fact, in comparison to the other major means of energy production in the United States, nuclear power is remarkably safe. According the U.S. Department of Labor, coal mining currently causes about sixty-five deaths and eleven thousand injuries per year, while oil drilling is responsible for approximately 125 deaths per year in the United States. Annual death tolls fluctuate depending upon the demand for these resources and the subsequent drilling or mining required, but the human cost is still exponentially more than that of nuclear energy. However, in the decades that nuclear power has been used in the United States, there have been zero deaths caused by nuclear power accidents—none at all. That's much better than the thousands of lives coal, oil, and toasters have cost us. If you care about saving human lives, then you should like nuclear energy.

RADIATION

Despite nuclear energy causing remarkably few deaths, people are also terrified of another aspect of nuclear power — radiation. Everyone's scared of developing a boulder-size tumor or our apples growing to similar size as a result of the awful radiation given off by nuclear power plants or their potential meltdowns. However, it should comfort you to know (or perhaps not) that you receive more radiation from a brick wall than from a nuclear power plant.

The paper uses technical terms, but makes sure they are accessible to readers.

We live in a radioactive world — nearly everything gives off at least a trace amount of radiation; that includes brick walls. Yes, while such a wall emits about 3.5 millirems of radiation per year, a nuclear power plant gives off about .3 millirems per year. (Millirem is just a unit of radiation dosage.) Of course, this low level of emission is a result of the numerous safeguards set up around the reactors to suppress radiation. So what happens if those safeguards fail? Will everyone surrounding the plant turn into a mutant?

To answer that question, let's examine the reactor failures in the recent Japanese nuclear crisis following several devastating earthquakes. The damage from the quakes took out the power to several nuclear plants, which caused their core cooling systems to go offline. To prevent reactor meltdowns, workers had to douse the failing reactors in thousands of gallons of seawater to cool the fuel rods, which contain all the radioactive materials. Worries about the resulting radioactive seawater contaminating the ocean and sea life flared as a result. But just how radioactive is the water? Officials from Tokyo Electric Power Company said the water "would have to be drunk for a whole year in order to accumulate one millisievert." People are generally exposed to about 1 to 10 millisieverts each year from background radiation caused by substances in the air and soil. "You would have to eat or drink an awful lot to get any level of radiation that would be harmful," said British nuclear expert Laurence Williams. You get

The paper is full of data and statistics from what seem to be reputable authorities and sources.

exposed to 5 millisieverts during a coast-to-coast flight across the United States. According to the U.S. Food and Drug Administration, you receive between 5 and 60 millisieverts in a CAT scan, depending on the type. So drinking water for a year that was in direct contact with containers of radioactive material used in those Japanese nuclear plants will expose you to a fifth of the radiation you would get from the weakest CAT scan. How dangerous!

As the paper explores various aspects of nuclear energy, headings keep the reader on track.

WASTE

But even if we have little to fear from nuclear power plants themselves, what about the supposedly deadly by-products of these plants? Opponents of nuclear energy cite the fact that while nuclear power plants don't emit greenhouse gases, they do leave behind waste that remains radioactive for thousands of years. However, this nuclear waste problem is exaggerated. According to Professor Emeritus of Computer Science at Stanford University, John McCarthy, a 1,000-megawatt reactor produces only 1.5 cubic meters of waste after a year of operation. The current solution is to put the waste in protective containers and store them in caverns cut in granite. At the very least, with such a small amount of waste per reactor, the caverns don't have to be dug very fast.

Pearson strategically concedes a downside of nuclear energy.

Nuclear power plants do produce waste that needs to be kept away from living things, but the actual amount of waste produced is small and therefore manageable. If the United States got all its power from nuclear plants, the amount of waste produced would be equivalent to one pill of aspirin per person, per year—tiny compared to the amount of waste produced by plants that use fossil fuels; the U.S. Energy Information Administration notes that coal alone produces about 1.8 billion metric tons of CO_2 emissions per year.

Quantity is not the only factor that has been exaggerated—the amount of time the waste remains dangerously radioactive has also been inflated. After about five hundred years, the fission products' radiation levels drop to below the level at which we typically find them in nature; the thousands of years opponents of nuclear energy refer to are the years the waste will be radioactive, not excessively so. You don't want to stand right next to this material even after those first five hundred years, but if it can exist in nature without doing any noticeable damage, then it doesn't pose any serious threat. Essentially, everything is radioactive; to criticize something for being radioactive without specifying the level of radioactivity means nothing.

Meeting Our Energy Demands

Although I've done a lot here in an attempt to defend nuclear energy, I still acknowledge it's not perfect. While the nuclear waste problem isn't something to be too worried about, it would still be better if we could satisfy our demand for energy without producing waste, radioactive or otherwise. However, I believe nuclear energy is the only realistic option we have to one day achieve an entirely clean energy reality.

We live in an age dominated by energy—to power our cars, our homes, and our computers. Let's face it: we're not going to give up the lifestyle that energy gives us. But under the current means of energy production—primarily coal in the United States—we're pumping out billions of tons of greenhouse gases that will eventually destroy our planet. So we have a dilemma. While we want to do something about global warming, we don't want to change our high-energy-consumption way of life. What are our options?

The concluding paragraphs compare nuclear power to potential alternatives.

Currently, completely clean sources of energy haven't been developed enough to make them a realistic option to supply all our energy needs. For solar energy to match the energy production of nuclear power plants presently in use, we would have to cover an area the size of New Jersey with solar panels. That's not a realistic option; we're not going to build that many panels just to get ourselves off of our addiction to fossil fuels. The same is true of the other renewable energy sources: wind, geothermal, hydroelectric, etc. The technologies simply aren't mature enough.

However, nuclear power is realistic. We have the means and the technology to make enough nuclear power plants to satisfy our electricity demands. Nuclear plants produce a lot of power with relatively little waste. Moving from coal to nuclear plants could provide us with adequate power until we develop more efficient renewable sources of electricity.

So what's stopping us? Of course, those heavily invested in coal and other fossil fuels lobby the government to keep their industries profitable, but a large source of opposition is also the American public. Because of the atom bombs of World War II, the Cold War, and Chernobyl, we're scared of all things nuclear. Anytime we hear the word "radiation," images of mushroom clouds and fallout enter our minds. But nuclear power plants aren't bombs. No matter what happens to them, they will never explode. Strong as it might be, our fear of nuclear power is overblown and keeping us from using a source of energy that could literally save our planet. We need to stop the fearmongering before we burn our planet to a crisp.

Pearson ends his argument by asking readers to acknowledge that their fears of nuclear power aren't based in fact.

Of course, that's if our toasters don't kill us first.

Democrats Deny Social Security's Red Ink

February 25, 2011

Some claim it doesn't contribute to the federal deficit, but it does.

SUMMARY

Some senior Democrats are claiming that Social Security does not contribute "one penny" to the federal deficit. That's not true. The fact is, the federal government had to borrow $37 billion last year to finance Social Security, and will need to borrow more this year. The red ink is projected to total well over half a trillion dollars in the coming decade.

President Barack Obama was closer to the mark than some of his Democratic allies when he said that Social Security is "not the huge contributor to the deficit that [Medicare and Medicaid] are." That's correct: Medicare and Medicaid consume more borrowed funds than Social Security, and their costs are growing more rapidly. But Obama's own budget director, Jacob Lew, was misleading when he wrote recently that "Social Security benefits are entirely self-financing." That's not true, except in a very narrow, legalistic sense, and doesn't change the fact that Social Security is now a small but growing drain on the government's finances.

Payroll taxes exceeded benefit payments regularly until 2010. But the fact is that Social Security has now passed a tipping point, beyond which the Congressional Budget Office projects that it will permanently pay out more in benefits than it gathers from Social Security taxes. The imbalance is made even larger this year by a one-year "payroll tax holiday" that was

---

"Democrats Deny Social Security's Red Ink" was written by Brooks Jackson, the director of FactCheck.org, which is a project of the Annenberg Public Policy Center. Its mission statement says, "We are a nonpartisan, nonprofit 'consumer advocate' for voters that aims to reduce the level of deception and confusion in U.S. politics. We monitor the factual accuracy of what is said by major U.S. political players in the form of TV ads, debates, speeches, interviews, and news releases. Our goal is to apply the best practices of both journalism and scholarship, and to increase public knowledge and understanding." The site is sponsored by the Annenberg Public Policy Center at the University of Pennsylvania and is not funded by corporations or political groups of any kind. Note that this article does include a list of sources, but they are not listed or cited within the text in any conventional way, such as MLA or APA style.

enacted as part of last year's compromise on extending the Bush tax cuts. The lost Social Security tax revenues are being made up with billions from general revenues that must all be borrowed. The combined effect is to add $130 billion to the deficit in the current fiscal year.

It's important to note that benefit payments are not in immediate danger. Under current law, scheduled benefits can be paid until about 2037, according to the most recent projections. But keeping those benefits flowing is already requiring the use of funds borrowed from the public. So we judge the claim that Social Security is not currently contributing to the deficit to be false.

ANALYSIS

As always, we take no position on whether Social Security should be changed, either to reduce the deficit or to shore up its troubled finances for future generations. Our job here is simply to establish facts and hold politicians accountable for any misinformation.

We'll start with the basic numbers. The nonpartisan Congressional Budget Office issued its most recent projections for Social Security's income and outgo Jan. 26, along with its twice-yearly "Budget and

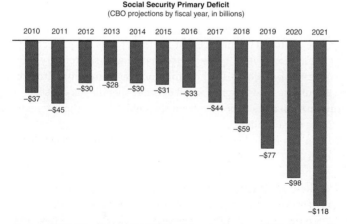

Social Security Primary Deficit
(CBO projections by fiscal year, in billions)

Source: CBO "Combined OASDI Trust Funds; January 2011 Baseline."
26 Jan 2011.
Note: See "Primary Surplus" line (which is negative, indicating a deficit).

Economic Outlook." What those numbers show is that Social Security ran a $37 billion deficit last year, is projected to run a $45 billion deficit this year, and more red ink every year thereafter.

Matters are even worse than this chart shows. In December, Congress passed a Social Security tax reduction. Workers are temporarily paying 2 percentage points less, from 6.2 percent to 4.2 percent, in Social Security payroll taxes this calendar year. Since the government is making up the shortfall out of general revenues, CBO's deficit projections for the trust funds do not include that. But CBO's figures predict that the "payroll tax holiday" will cost the government's general fund $85 billion in this fiscal year and $29 billion in fiscal year 2012 (which starts Oct. 1, 2011). Since every dollar of that will have to be borrowed, the combined effect of the "tax holiday" and the annual deficits will amount to a $130 billion addition to the federal deficit in the current fiscal year, and $59 billion in fiscal 2012.

Social Security has passed a tipping point. For years it generated more revenue than it consumed, holding down the overall federal deficit and allowing Congress to spend more freely for other things. But those days are gone. Rather than lessening the federal deficit, Social Security has at last—as long predicted—become a drag on the government's overall finances.

As recently as October, CBO was projecting that it would be 2016 before outlays regularly exceed revenues. But Social Security's fiscal troubles are more severe than was thought, and the latest projections show the permanent deficits started several years ahead of earlier predictions.

Don't be confused by the fact that the trust funds are projected to continue growing for several more years. That's because Treasury must still credit interest payments to the funds on the borrowings from earlier years. But unless taxes are increased or other spending is cut severely, the government will have to borrow from the public to pay the interest that it owes to the trust funds.

And don't be misled by those who say the system can pay full benefits until about 2037 without making any changes to the law. That's true, but does not change the fact that Social Security taxes no longer cover those benefits. The government is now borrowing money to pay them, and will do so every year for the foreseeable future. And keep in mind, if nothing is done, when those trust funds are exhausted, benefits would have to be cut by 22 percent in 2037, and more each year after that, according to the most recent report of the system's trustees. By 2084, the system will generate only enough revenue to pay for 75 percent of promised benefit levels.

Facts vs. Spin

Those are the facts. But they haven't stopped some Democrats from claiming over and over that Social Security doesn't contribute "one penny" to the deficit. Examples:

Feb. 20, 2011: Sen. Richard Durbin of Illinois, on NBC's *Meet the Press*:

> *Durbin:* Social Security does not add one penny to the deficit. Social Security untouched will make every promised payment for more than 25 years.

Feb. 20, 2011: Sen. Chuck Schumer of New York, on CNN's *State of the Union* with Candy Crowley:

> *Schumer:* Social Security, however, does not contribute one penny to the deficit and won't until 2037.

Feb. 16, Senate Majority Leader Harry Reid of Nevada:

> *Reid:* Social Security has contributed not a single penny to the deficit. So we can talk about entitlements as long as you eliminate Social Security. . . . Social Security is not part of the problem we have in America with the deficit.

President Barack Obama's budget director, Jacob Lew, doesn't go quite that far. But he did write a Feb. 22 opinion piece in *USA Today* claiming that Social Security "does not cause our deficits" and is "entirely self-financing."

> *Lew:* [L]ooking to the next two decades, Social Security does not cause our deficits. Social Security benefits are entirely self-financing. They are paid for with payroll taxes collected from workers and their employers throughout their careers.

USA Today's editorial writers rebutted Lew and took him to task for making a similar claim earlier, saying, "That would be nice if it were true. It's not." The newspaper stated:

> *USA Today:* Social Security is a cash-in/cash-out program. It went into the red last year, when payroll tax revenue came up about $37 billion short of the benefits paid to retirees.

And as we've shown, *USA Today* is correct.

Interestingly, the president has stopped short of this sort of misleading talk. On Feb. 15, Obama held a White House news conference to defend his budget proposal for fiscal year 2012. And here's what he said about cutting entitlement spending:

> *Obama:* Now, you talked about Social Security, Medicare and Medicaid. The truth is Social Security is not the huge contributor to the deficit that the other two entitlements are.

That's true enough. As Obama concedes, Social Security is a "contributor" to the deficit—$37 billion last year. So how can his fellow Democrats claim that it isn't? When we asked Sen. Schumer's spokesman Brian Fallon, we got this on-the-record response:

> *Brian Fallon:* This is nitpicking to the nth degree. Social Security is a standalone program and is fully solvent. Our deficit problem lies not with Social Security, but with the rest of the budget.

And from Sen. Durbin's spokesman Max Gleischman, we got this:

> *Max Gleischman:* We can argue line items and budget allocations all day—our position is that SS doesn't add to the deficit. Jack Lew and the President agree.

But as we've seen, the president's statement doesn't back up what Durbin said, and Lew chose his words carefully in his *USA Today* article. We agree with Lew that Social Security does not "cause our deficits," at least not by itself. But it already contributes some of the deficit, and that will grow over time unless changes are made somewhere.

When Lew says Social Security is "entirely self-financing," he refers to the trust funds that have built up assets of more than $2.5 trillion over the years. That's what the rest of the government has borrowed and spent on other things. Those trust funds and the future interest payments will keep benefits funded at promised levels for years to come, it's true. But unless the government raises taxes or cuts other spending substantially, the government will need to borrow more from the public to finance its obligations to the trust funds.

In an opinion piece published Dec. 2 on Politico.com, David M. Walker—a former U.S. comptroller general who heads a nonprofit dedicated to reducing the deficit—flatly disagreed with "liberals" who deny Social Security's contribution to the deficit:

> *Walker, Dec. 2:* [C]ontrary to assertions by some liberals, Social Security is now adding to the federal deficit, since it currently pays out more than it

takes in. This negative cash flow position will accelerate and become permanent by 2015.

That was before the CBO's latest projections, which show the negative cash flow has become permanent ahead of schedule.

One of Washington's leading experts on Social Security financing, Eugene Steuerle of the Urban Institute, says that Social Security unambiguously adds to the nation's "fiscal woes" and that quibbling over how trust fund income and expenditures are accounted for is "somewhat silly." In an exchange of e-mails with FactCheck.org, he said:

> *Eugene Steuerle:* I think the right way to phrase the issue is whether an increasing portion of the population receiving benefits and decreasing portions paying taxes adds currently and in the coming years to our fiscal woes. There the answer is an unambiguous, "Yes."

For more on the future effect of Social Security on the budget, see "Social Security and the Budget," a report co-authored by Steuerle for the Urban Institute last May. A figure on page 4 graphically illustrates that Social Security's expenses are projected to outrun its income. The gap is projected to grow to close to 2 percent of the national gross domestic product and remain there for decades, as far in the future as 2080 and beyond.

SOURCES

"The 2010 OASDI Trustees Report." Social Security Board of Trustees, 5 Aug 2010.

CNN. "State of the Union with Candy Crowley." Transcript, 20 Feb 2011.

Congressional Budget Office. "CBO's 2010 Long-Term Projections for Social Security: Additional Information." Oct 2010.

Congressional Budget Office. "Combined OASDI Trust Funds, January 2011 Baseline." 26 Jan 2011.

Duggan, James E., and Christopher J. Soares. "Social Security and Medicare Trust Funds and the Federal Budget." U.S. Department of Treasury, Office of Economic Policy, May 2009.

Espo, David. "Reid Wants No Cuts to Social Security." The Associated Press, 16 Feb 2011.

Exchange of emails with Brian Fallon, 23 Feb 2011.

Exchange of emails with Max Gleischman, 22–23 Feb 2011.

Lew, Jacob. "Opposing View: Social Security Isn't the Problem." *USA Today*, 22 Feb 2011.

NBC News. "*Meet the Press* Transcript for Feb. 20, 2011." 20 Feb 2011.

Ohlemacher, Stephen. "CBO: Social Security to Run Permanent Deficits." The Associated Press, 26 Jan 2011.

The Raw Story. "Exclusive: 'Social Security Has Nothing to Do with the Deficit,' Sanders Tells Raw." 19 Jan 2011.

Steuerle, Eugene, and Stephanie Rennane. "Social Security and the Budget." Urban Institute, May 2010.

Telephone interview and exchange of emails with Eugene Steuerle, 23–24 Feb 2011.

USA Today. "Our View: Fix Social Security Sooner, Not Later." Editorial, 22 Feb 2011.

The White House. "Press Conference by the President." Transcript, 15 Feb 2011.

9
Arguments of Definition

A student submits a "senior thesis" in history made up almost entirely of music and still images projected onto a wall in a gallery. She wants to redefine current definitions of *thesis*.

A conservative student group accuses the student government on campus of sponsoring a lecture series featuring a disproportionate number of "left-wing" writers and celebrities. A spokesperson for the student government defends its program by questioning the definition of *left-wing* used to classify some of the speakers.

A panel of judges must decide whether computer-enhanced images will be eligible in a contest for landscape photography. At what point is an electronically manipulated image no longer a *photograph*?

Understanding Arguments of Definition

Definitions matter. Just ask a scientist, a mathematician, an engineer, or a judge. In 2007, the United States Supreme Court decided that the United States Environmental Protection Agency (EPA) had the authority to regulate carbon dioxide (CO_2) if it could show that the naturally occurring chemical compound—which humans exhale—met the Clean Air Act's definition of *air pollutant*. Many businesses objected. But Justice John Paul Stevens, writing for the majority in a five to four decision, put it this way:

> Because greenhouse gases fit well within the Act's capacious definition of "air pollutant," the EPA has statutory authority to regulate emissions of such gases from new motor vehicles.

As a result, we'll all be driving much different cars and trucks soon in order to reduce CO_2 concentrations in the atmosphere.

What the EPA example demonstrates is that arguments of definition aren't abstract academic exercises: they are almost always contentious and often consequential. That's because they wield the power to say what someone or something is or can be. Such arguments can both include or exclude: A wolf in Montana either is an endangered species or it isn't. An unsolicited kiss is or is not sexual harassment. A person merits official political refugee status in the United States or doesn't. Another way of approaching definitional arguments, however, is to think of what falls between *is* and *is not* in a definitional claim. In fact, many definitional disputes occur in that murky realm.

Consider the controversy over how to define *human intelligence*. Some argue that human intelligence is a capacity that is measured by tests of verbal and mathematical reasoning. In other words, it's defined by IQ and SAT scores. Others define *intelligence* as the ability to perform specific practical tasks. Still others interpret *intelligence* in emotional terms as a competence in relating to other people. Any of these positions could be defended reasonably, but perhaps the wisest approach would be to construct a definition of *intelligence* that is rich enough to incorporate all these perspectives—and maybe more.

The fact is that crucial political, social, and scientific terms—such as *intelligence, social justice,* or *war*—are constantly reargued, reshaped, and updated for the times. For instance, in 2011, in order to avoid calling a martial incursion into Libya a "war," the White House defined the strategy as a "kinetic military action." It took heat for the euphemism, but the term makes a useful distinction, as Byron York explains:

> "Kinetic" is a word that's been used around the Pentagon for many years to distinguish between actions like dropping bombs, launching cruise missiles, or shooting people and newer forms of non-violent fighting like cyber-warfare. At times, it also appears to mean just taking action.

If you don't like the new expression, you are free to make an argument of definition against it—as many did.

Important arguments of definition can't be decided simply by running to a dictionary. Dictionaries reflect the way that particular groups of people use words at a specified time and place. And like any form of writing, these reference books mirror the prejudices of their makers—as shown, perhaps most famously, in the entries of lexicographer Samuel Johnson (1709–1784), who gave the English language its first great dictionary. Johnson, no friend of the Scots, defined *oats* as "a grain which in England is generally given to horses, but in Scotland supports the people." (To be fair, he also defined *lexicographer* as "a writer of dictionaries, a harmless drudge.") Thus, it's possible to disagree with dictionary definitions or to regard them merely as starting points for arguments.

A cartoonist finds political implications in a euphemism.

RESPOND•

Briefly discuss how you might define the italicized terms in the following controversial claims of definition. Compare your definitions of the terms with those of your classmates.

Graphic novels are *serious literature*.

Burning a nation's flag is a *hate crime*.

Matt Drudge and Arianna Huffington aren't *journalists*.

College sports programs have become *big businesses*.

Plagiarism can be an act of *civil disobedience*.

Satanism is a *religion* properly protected by the First Amendment.

Campaign contributions are acts of *free speech* that should never be regulated.

The District of Columbia should not have all the privileges of an American *state*.

Polygamous couples should have the legal privileges of *marriage*.

Kinds of Definition

Because there are different kinds of definitions, there are also different ways to make a definition argument. Fortunately, identifying a particular type of definition is less important than appreciating when an issue of definition is at stake. Let's explore some common definitional issues.

Formal Definitions

Formal definitions are what you find in dictionaries. Such definitions place a term in its proper **genus** and **species**—first determining its class and then identifying the features or criteria that distinguish it from other members of that class. That sounds complicated, but a definition will help you see the principle. To define *hybrid car*, you might first place it in a general class—*passenger vehicles*. Then the formal definition would distinguish hybrid cars from other passenger vehicles: *they can move using two or more sources of power, either separately or in combination.* So the full definition might look like this: *a hybrid car is a passenger vehicle (genus) that can operate using two or more sources of power, separately or in combination (species).*

Buick LaCrosse: full hybrid or poseur? The big sedan now uses a variety of technologies, including a small electric motor, to get more than thirty-five miles per gallon on the highway. But it cannot run on electricity alone.

Many arguments involve deciding whether an object meets the criteria set by a formal definition. For instance, suppose that you are considering whether a Toyota Prius and a Buick LaCrosse are actually hybrid cars. Both are clearly passenger cars, so the genus raises no questions. But not all vehicles that claim to be hybrids are powered by two sources: some of them are just electrically *assisted* versions of a regular gasoline car. That's the species question. Looking closely, you discover that a Prius can run on either gas or electric power alone. But does the LaCrosse have that flexibility? If not, should it be labeled something other than *hybrid*—perhaps, *mild hybrid*? This definitional question obviously has consequences for consumers concerned about the CO_2 emissions discussed earlier.

Operational Definitions

Operational definitions identify an object or idea by what it does or by what conditions create it. For example, someone's offensive sexual imposition on another person may not meet the technical definition of *harassment* unless it is considered *unwanted*, *unsolicited*, and *repeated*. These three conditions then define what makes an act that might be acceptable in some situations turn into harassment. But they might also then become part of a highly contentious debate: were the conditions actually present in a given case? For example, could an offensive act really be harassment if the accused believed sexual interest was mutual and therefore solicited?

As you might imagine, arguments arise from operational definitions whenever people disagree about what the conditions define or whether these conditions have been fulfilled. Here are some examples of those types of questions:

Questions Related to Conditions

- Can institutional racism occur in the absence of specific and individual acts of racism?
- Can someone who is paid for their community service still be called a volunteer?
- Does someone who uses steroids to enhance home-run-hitting performance deserve the title Hall of Famer?

Questions Related to Fulfillment of Conditions

- Has an institution supported traditions or policies that have led to widespread racial inequities?
- Was the compensation given to a volunteer really "pay" or simply "reimbursement" for expenses?
- Should Player X, who used steroids prescribed for a medical reason, be ineligible for the Hall of Fame?

RESPOND •

This chapter opens with several rhetorical situations that center on definitional issues. Select one of these situations, and then, using the strategy of formal definition, set down some criteria of definition. For example, identify the features of a photograph that make it part of a larger class (*art, communication method, journalistic technique*). Next, identify the features that make it distinct from other members of that larger class. Then use the strategy of operational definition to establish criteria for the same object: what does it do? Remember to ask questions related to conditions (*Is a computer-scanned photograph still a photograph?*) and questions related to fulfillment of conditions (*Does a good photocopy of a photograph achieve the same effect as the photograph itself?*).

Prince Charming considers whether an action would fulfill the conditions for an operational definition.

© www.cartoonstock.com

Definitions by Example

Resembling operational definitions are **definitions by example**, which define a class by listing its individual members. Such definitions can be helpful when it is easier to illustrate or show what related people or things have in common than to explain each one in precise detail. For example, one might define the broad category of *smart phones* by listing the major examples of these products or define *heirloom tomatoes* by recalling all those available at the local farmers' market.

An app like Discovr Music defines musical styles by example when it connects specific artists or groups to others who make similar sounds.

Arguments of this sort may focus on who or what may be included in a list that defines a category—*classic movies, worst natural disasters, groundbreaking painters*. Such arguments often involve comparisons and contrasts with the items that most readers would agree belong in this list. One could ask why Washington, D.C., is denied the status of a state: how does it differ from the fifty recognized American states? Or one might wonder why the status of planet is denied to asteroids, when both planets and asteroids are bodies that orbit the sun. A comparison between planets and asteroids might suggest that size is one essential feature of the eight recognized planets that asteroids don't meet. (In a recent famous exercise in definition argument, astronomers decided to deny poor Pluto its planetary classification.)

Developing a Definitional Argument

Definitional arguments don't just appear out of the blue; they often evolve out of daily life. You might get into an argument over the definition of *ordinary wear and tear* when you return a rental car with some soiled upholstery. Or you might be asked to write a job description for a

new position to be created in your office: you have to define the job position in a way that doesn't step on anyone else's turf. Or maybe employees on your campus object to being defined as *temporary workers* when
they've held their same jobs for years. Or someone derides one of your
best friends as *just a nerd.* In a dozen ways every day, you encounter situations that are questions of definition. They're so frequent and indispensable that you barely notice them for what they are.

Formulating Claims

In addressing a question of definition, you'll likely formulate a *tentative
claim*—a declarative statement that represents your first response to
such situations. Note that such initial claims usually don't follow a single definitional formula.

Claims of Definition

A person paid to do public service is not a *volunteer.*

Institutional racism can exist—maybe even thrive—in the absence of
overt civil rights violations.

Political bias has been consistently practiced by the mainstream media.

Theatergoers shouldn't confuse *musicals* with *operas.*

White lies are hard to define but easy to recognize.

None of the statements listed here could stand on its own because it
likely reflects a first impression and gut reaction. But that's fine because
making a claim of definition is typically a starting point, a cocky moment that doesn't last much beyond the first serious rebuttal or challenge. Statements of this sort aren't arguments until they're attached to
reasons, data, warrants, and evidence. (See Chapter 7.)

Finding good reasons to support a claim of definition usually requires
formulating a general definition by which to explore the subject. To be
persuasive, the definition must be broad and not tailored to the specific
controversy:

A volunteer is . . .

Institutional racism is . . .

Political bias is . . .

A musical is . . . but an opera is . . .

A white lie is . . .

Now consider how the following claims might be expanded with a general definition to become full-fledged definitional arguments:

Arguments of Definition

Someone paid to do public service is not a volunteer because volunteers are people who . . .

Institutional racism can exist even in the absence of overt violations of civil rights because, by definition, institutional racism is . . .

Political bias in the media is evident when . . .

Musicals focus on words while operas . . .

The most important element of a white lie is its destructive nature; the act of telling one hurts both the receiver and the sender.

Notice, too, that some of the issues can involve comparisons between things—such as operas and musicals.

Crafting Definitions

Imagine that you decide to tackle the concept of *paid volunteer* in the following way:

> Participants in the federal AmeriCorps program are not really volunteers because they receive "education awards" for their public service. Volunteers are people who work for a cause without receiving compensation.

In Toulmin terms, as explained in Chapter 7, the argument looks like this:

Claim	Participants in AmeriCorps aren't volunteers . . .
Reason	. . . because they are paid for their service.
Warrant	People who are compensated for their services are, ordinarily, employees.

As you can see, the definition of *volunteers* will be crucial to the shape of the argument. In fact, you might think you've settled the matter with this tight little formulation. But now it's time to listen to the readers over your shoulder (again, see Chapter 7), who are pushing you further. Do the terms of your definition account for all pertinent cases of volunteerism—in particular, any related to the types of public service AmeriCorps members might be involved in? What do you do with unpaid interns: how do they affect your definition of *volunteers*? Consider, too, the word *cause* in your original claim of the definition:

> **Volunteers are people who work for a cause without receiving compensation.**

Cause has political connotations that you may or may not intend. You'd better clarify what you mean by *cause* when you discuss its definition in your paper. Might a phrase such as *the public good* be a more comprehensive or appropriate substitute for *a cause*? And then there's the matter of *compensation* in the second half of your definition:

> **Volunteers are people who work for a cause without receiving compensation.**

Aren't people who volunteer to serve on boards, committees, and commissions sometimes paid, especially for their expenses? What about members of the so-called all-volunteer military? They're financially compensated during their years of service, and they enjoy benefits after they complete their tours of duty.

As you can see, you can't just offer up a definition as part of an argument and expect that readers will accept it. Every part of a definition has to be interrogated, critiqued, and defended. So investigate your subject in the library, on the Internet, and in conversation with others, including experts if you can. You might then be able to present your definition in a single paragraph, or you may have to spend several pages coming to terms with the complexity of the core issue.

After conducting research of this kind, you'll be in a better position to write an extended definition that explains to your readers what you believe makes a volunteer a volunteer, how to identify institutional racism, or how to distinguish between a musical and an opera.

Matching Claims to Definitions

Once you've formulated a definition that readers will accept — a demanding task in itself — you might need to look at your particular subject to see if it fits your general definition. It should provide evidence of one of the following:

- It is a clear example of the class defined.
- It clearly falls outside the defined class.

- It falls between two closely related classes or fulfills some conditions of the defined class but not others.

- It defies existing classes and categories and requires an entirely new definition.

How do you make this key move in an argument? Here's an example from an article by Anthony Tommasini entitled "Opera? Musical? Please Respect the Difference." Early in the piece, Tommasini argues that a key element separates the two musical forms:

> Both genres seek to combine words and music in dynamic, felicitous and, to invoke that all-purpose term, artistic ways. But in opera, music is the driving force; in musical theater, words come first.

His claim of definition (or of difference) makes sense because it clarifies aspects of the two genres.

> This explains why for centuries opera-goers have revered works written in languages they do not speak. . . . As long as you basically know what is going on and what is more or less said, you can be swept away by a great opera, not just by music, but by visceral drama.
>
> In contrast, imagine if the exhilarating production of Cole Porter's *Anything Goes* now on Broadway . . . were to play in Japan without any kind of titling technology. The wit of the musical is embedded in its lyrics. . . .

But even after having found a distinction so perceptive, Tommasini (like most writers making arguments of definition) still has to acknowledge exceptions.

> Theatergoing audiences may not care much whether a show is a musical or an opera. But the best achievements in each genre . . . have been from composers and writers who grounded themselves in a tradition, *even while reaching across the divide.* [emphasis added]

If evidence you've gathered while developing an argument of definition suggests that similar limitations may be necessary, don't hesitate to modify your claim. It's amazing how often seemingly cut-and-dry matters of definition become blurry—and open to compromise and accommodation—as you learn more about them. That has proved to be the case as various campuses across the country have tried to define *hate speech* or *sexual harassment*—tricky matters. And even the Supreme Court has never said exactly what *pornography* is. Just when matters seem to be settled, new legal twists develop. Should virtual child pornography created with software be illegal, as is the real thing? Or is a virtual image—even a lewd one—an artistic expression that is protected (as other works of art are) by the First Amendment?

Considering Design and Visuals

In thinking about how to present your argument of definition, you may find a simple visual helpful, such as the Venn diagram below from Wikimedia Commons that defines *sustainability* as the place where our society and its economy intersect with the environment. Such a visual might even suggest a structure for an oral presentation.

Remember, too, that visuals like photographs, charts, and graphs can also help you make your case. Such items might demonstrate that the conditions for a definition have been met—as the widely circulated and horrific photographs from Abu Ghraib prison in Iraq in 2004 helped to define *torture*. Or you might create a graphic yourself to illustrate a concept you are defining, perhaps through comparison and contrast.

Finally, don't forget that basic design elements—such as boldface and italics, headings, or links in online text—can contribute to (or detract from) the credibility and persuasiveness of your argument of definition.

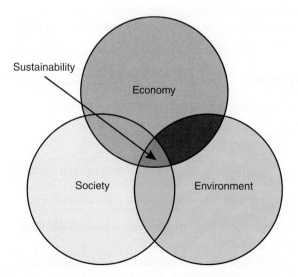

GUIDE to writing an argument of definition

● Finding a Topic

You're entering an argument of definition when you:

- formulate a controversial or provocative definition: *The American Dream, which once meant a McMansion in a gated community, now has taken on a new definition.*

- challenge a definition: *For most Americans today, the American Dream involves not luxury but the secure pensions, cheap energy costs, and health insurance that workers in the 1950s and 1960s supposedly enjoyed.*

- try to determine whether something fits an existing definition: *Expanding opportunity is (or is not) central to the American Dream.*

- seek to broaden an existing definition or create a new definition to accommodate wider or differing perspectives: *In a world where information is easily and freely shared, it may be time to explore alternative definitions of plagiarism.*

Look for issues of definition in your everyday affairs — for instance, in the way that jobs are classified at work, that key terms are used in your academic major, that politicians characterize social issues that concern you, and so on. Be especially alert to definitional arguments that may arise when you or others deploy adjectives such as *true, real, actual,* or *genuine: a true patriot, real reform, authentic Mexican food.*

● Researching Your Topic

You can research issues of definition by using the following sources:

- college dictionaries and encyclopedias
- unabridged dictionaries
- specialized reference works and handbooks, such as legal and medical dictionaries
- your textbooks (check their glossaries)
- newsgroups and blogs that focus on particular topics, particularly political ones
- community or advocacy groups that are engaged in legal or social issues

Browse in your library reference room and use the electronic indexes and databases to determine how often disputed or contentious terms or phrases occur in influential online newspapers, journals, and Web sites.

When dealing with definitions, ask librarians about the most appropriate and reliable sources. For instance, to find the definition of a legal term, *Black's Law Dictionary* or a database such as FindLaw may help. Check USA.gov for how the government defines terms.

● Formulating a Claim

After exploring your subject, try to formulate a thesis that lets readers know where you stand or what issues are at stake. Begin with the following types of questions:

- questions related to genus: *Is assisting in suicide a crime?*

- questions related to species: *Is marijuana a harmful addictive drug or a useful medical treatment?*

- questions related to conditions: *Must the imposition of sexual attention be both unwanted and unsolicited to be considered sexual harassment?*

- questions related to fulfillment of conditions: *Has our college kept in place traditions or policies that might constitute racial discrimination?*

- questions related to membership in a named class: *Is any pop artist today in a class with Bob Dylan, the Beatles, Aretha Franklin, or the Rolling Stones?*

If you start with a thesis, it should be a complete statement that makes a claim of definition and states the reasons supporting it. You may later decide to separate the claim from its supporting reasons. But a working thesis should be a fully articulated thought that spells out all the details and qualifications: *Who? What? Where? When? How many? How regularly? How completely?*

However, since arguments of definition are often exploratory and tentative, an initial thesis (if you have one) may simply describe problems in formulating a particular definition: *What we mean by X is likely to remain unsettled until we can agree more fully about Y and Z; The key to understanding what constitutes X may be in appreciating how different groups approach Y and Z.*

● Examples of Definitional Claims

- Assisting a gravely ill person in committing suicide should not be considered *murder* when the motive for the act is to ease a person's suffering and not to benefit from the death.

- Although somewhat addictive, marijuana should not be classified as a *dangerous drug* because it damages individuals and society less than heroin or cocaine and because it helps people with life-threatening diseases live more comfortably.

- Giving college admission preference to all racial minorities can be an example of *class discrimination* because such policies may favor middle- and upper-class students who are already advantaged.

- Attempts to define the concept of *freedom* need to take into account the way the term is historically understood in cultures worldwide, not just in the countries of Western Europe and North America.

Preparing a Proposal

If your instructor asks you to prepare a proposal for your project, here's a format that may help:

State your thesis or hypothesis completely. If you're having trouble doing so, try outlining it in Toulmin terms:

Claim:

Reason(s):

Warrant(s):

Alternatively, you might describe the complications of a definitional issue you hope to explore in your project, with a thesis perhaps coming later.

- Explain why this argument of definition deserves attention. What's at stake? Why is it important for your readers to consider?

- Identify whom you hope to reach through your argument and why these readers would be interested in it. How might you involve them in the paper?

- Briefly discuss the key challenges that you anticipate in preparing your argument.

- Determine what sources you expect to consult: Web? Databases? Dictionaries? Encyclopedias? Periodicals?

- Determine what visuals to include in your definitional argument.

- Describe the format you expect to use: Research essay? Letter to the editor? Web page?

● Thinking about Organization

Your argument of definition is likely to include some of the following parts:

- a claim involving a question of definition
- a general definition of some key concept
- a careful look at your subject in terms of that general definition
- evidence for every part of the argument, including visual evidence if appropriate
- a careful consideration of alternative views and counterarguments
- a conclusion drawing out the implications of the argument

It's impossible, however, to predict what emphasis each of those parts might receive or what the ultimate shape of an argument of definition will be. Try to account for the ways people with different points of view will likely respond to your argument. Then, consider how to address such differences civilly in the body of your argument.

● Getting and Giving Response: Questions for Peer Response

Your instructor may assign you to a group for the purpose of reading and responding to each other's drafts. If not, ask for responses from serious readers or consultants at a writing center. Use the following questions to evaluate a colleague's draft. Be sure to illustrate your comments with examples; specific comments help more than general observations.

The Claim

- Is the claim clearly an issue of definition?
- Is the claim significant enough to interest readers?
- Are clear and specific criteria established for the concept being defined? Do the criteria define the term adequately? Using this definition, could most readers identify what's being defined and distinguish it from other related concepts?

Evidence for the Claim

- Is enough evidence furnished to explain or support the definition? If not, what kind of additional evidence is needed?

- Is the evidence in support of the claim simply announced, or are its significance and appropriateness analyzed? Is a more detailed discussion needed?

- Are all the conditions of the definition met in the concept being examined?

- Are any objections readers might have to the claim, criteria, evidence, or way the definition is formulated adequately addressed? Have you represented other points of view completely and fairly?

- What kinds of sources are cited? How credible and persuasive will they be to readers? What other kinds of sources might work better?

- Are all quotations introduced with appropriate signal phrases (such as "As Tyson argues, . . .") and blended smoothly into the writer's sentences?

Organization and Style

- How are the parts of the argument organized? Is this organization effective?

- Will readers understand the relationships among the claims, supporting reasons, warrants, and evidence? If not, how might those connections be clearer? Is the function of every visual clear? Are more transitions needed? Would headings or graphic devices help?

- Are the transitions or links from point to point, sentence to sentence, and paragraph to paragraph clear and effective? If not, how could they be improved?

- Is the style suited to the subject? Is it too formal, casual, or technical? Can it be improved?

- Which sentences seem effective? Which ones seem weaker, and how could they be improved? Should short sentences be combined, and any longer ones be broken up?

- How effective are the paragraphs? Too short or too long? How can they be improved?

- Which words or phrases seem effective? Do any seem vague or inappropriate for the audience or the writer's purpose? Are technical or unfamiliar terms defined?

Spelling, Punctuation, Mechanics, Documentation, and Format

- Are there any errors in spelling, punctuation, capitalization, and the like?

- Is the documentation appropriate and consistent? (See Chapter 21.)

- Does the paper or project follow an appropriate format? Is it appropriately designed and attractively presented?

PROJECTS •

1. Write an argument of definition about a term such as *kinetic military action* (see p. 189) that has suddenly become culturally significant or recently changed in some important way. Either defend the way the term has come to be defined or raise questions about its appropriateness, offensiveness, inaccuracy, and so on. Consider words or expressions such as *terrorism, marriage equality, racist, death panel, enhanced interrogation, tea partier, academic bulimia, occupy anything,* etc.

2. Write an essay in which you compare or contrast the meaning of two related terms, explaining the differences between them by using one or more methods of definition: formal definition, operational definition, definition by example. Be clever in your choice of the intial terms: look for a pairing in which the differences might not be immediately apparent to people unfamiliar with how the terms are used in specific communities. Consider terms such as liberal/progressive, classy/cool, intellectual/egghead, student athlete/jock, and so on.

3. In an essay at the end of this chapter, Jennifer Pier explores the definition of *white lie,* trying to understand not only how it differs from other lies, but also how serious it is. Her conclusion is perhaps startling: "the white lie is the most dangerous form of lying." After reading this selection carefully, respond to Pier's argument in an argument of definition of your own. Or, alternatively, explore a concept similar to *white lie* with the same intensity that Pier brings to her project. Look for a term to define and analyze either from your major or from an area of interest to you.

4. Because arguments of definition can have such important consequences, it helps to develop one by first getting input from lots of "stakeholders," that is, from people or groups likely to be affected by any change in the way a term is defined. Working with a small group, identify a term in your school or wider community that might need a fresh formulation or a close review. It could be a familiar campus word or phrase such as *nontraditional student, diversity, scholastic dishonesty,* or *social justice*; or it may be a term that has newly entered the local environment, perhaps reflecting an issue of law enforcement, safety, transportation, health, or even entertainment. Once you have settled on a significant term, identify a full range of stakeholders. Then, through some systematic field research (interviews, questionnaires) or by examining existing documents and materials (such as library sources, Web sites, pamphlets, publications), try to understand how the term currently functions in your community. Your definitional argument will, in effect, be what you can learn about the meanings that word or phrase has today for a wide variety of people.

The Reprehensibility of the White Lie

JENNIFER PIER

Opening
paragraph
defines *white
lies* through
familiar
examples.

The white lie wears many hats, and he is tricky in his disguise. He is hard to define but easy to recognize. Do you like this dress on me? *Of course.* Did you enjoy the party? *It was a blast.* Did you break this vase? *It wasn't me!* This tactic pervades our society, and many times, we don't even notice that we're employing it. The white lie is so enticing and available. It has become almost second nature for people to slip in an untruth that ameliorates a situation. But why do we do this? It's not as if our words actually mean something, as if our lies and truths matter in the grand scheme of things. Perhaps this evasion of responsibility is a sign that they do.

Pier offers a first
criterion for
white lie.

Therein lies the first criterion that defines a white lie. It means something. A listener can deduce a meaning, whether it's the intended one or not, from our words. Take the question that begets the prototypical white lie, a woman asking a man: "Do I look fat in this dress?" Assuming that the dress does indeed make the questioner look fat, what is one to say? If you say that it doesn't, then the woman could technically deduce that she does look fat, but she just happens not to in this dress. Or perhaps she is fat, and she will always look fat?

Jennifer Pier wrote this essay for an "Advanced Writing" class during her junior year at the University of Texas at Austin. In her topic proposal, she begins with her sense that "[a] lie is a lie, no matter what color or degree of politeness accompanies it." Then she offered the following as her working thesis: "Although society considers the white lie to be the most benign form of lying, it actually is the most malignant: it meets the criteria for the vilest of lies while also carrying the guise of benevolence (which we bestow upon it through societal convention)." These notions are explored in considerable detail in the final version reprinted here.

So it doesn't matter what type of clothing she dons because in whatever she wears, she will still look fat. Noticing myself going through these conclusions after I've posed the question, I've learned just not to ask it, for my own sanity and for the sanity of the people around me.

Yet white lies, as innocent as they seem, have a meaning behind them. If my sister were to tell me, "Yes, that dress makes you look as hideous and large as the Eiffel Tower," I wouldn't believe her for a second. The absurdity of her statement allows me to see that she is making a gross overstatement. White lies, however, are not so transparent. Within their politeness, they carry a judgment that satisfies a social convention. The liar provides the desired answer to a question or situation because this is his proper role at that moment. When a guest tells his hostess that an obviously lame party was (to him, the hostess, and everyone else there) "Terrific!" he, as well as everyone within hearing range, knows that he is lying. But because it is socially acceptable to tell this type of falsehood, no one passes judgment. The question here shouldn't be whether the guest lied. He did. The ethical issue should be whether in telling this fib his actions are reprehensible. Why is it okay to lie blatantly when one is fulfilling a social convention? It's because his white lie establishes that he is playing by the rules of society: he's being polite.

Pier then explores what makes white lies tolerable.

What is it about the politeness of a white lie that makes it acceptable? I don't think that I can supply a complete answer. But perhaps it is in comparison to the alternative that we tolerate it. Honesty and simplicity don't thrive in our society today. We cling to euphemisms and walk on tiptoes so that we remain politically correct, not allowing ourselves to offend others or hurt ourselves. A painting is art until it offends my culture, free speech exists until it encroaches on my freedoms, and honesty is a virtue only until it gets me into trouble. Nothing can exist by itself as good or bad, right or wrong, without a point of contrast. A white lie is acceptable in comparison

Pier makes a second key distinction here to separate white lies from other types of duplicity: their politeness.

to every other form of lying because, in the short run, it does the least amount of damage.

Over the years, linguists have developed the definition of a paradigmatic lie. Not coincidentally, the formula for a lie mirrors the formula for a mortal sin in the Catholic tradition. Perhaps that makes perfect sense, since one of the Ten Commandments is "you shall not bear false witness against your neighbor." To reach the status of "mortal" sin, an act must go against divine law, the person performing the act must know that the sin is grave, and despite this, he must do it voluntarily. In like manner, to qualify as a lie, a statement must first be false. Then the speaker must know that the statement is false, and finally, in telling someone the statement, the speaker must intend to deceive his audience (Coleman).

The essay now provides an operational definition of *common lying*: three conditions must be in place.

A common "perfect" lie, then, fits all three of these qualifications. What makes a white lie more despicable than the common lie is that a white lie fits all three while carrying with it the duplicity of politeness. Sometimes a person tells a white lie to benefit his audience or to save face. But more often, white lies hide under the ruse of social convention. A white lie is still morally reprehensible—it's still a lie. The innocence associated with a white lie tricks us into looking past its addictive nature. Much like a gateway drug, the white lies we tell initiate a spiral downward into heavier, more serious lies that have lethal effects on our reputations and interpersonal relationships.

The third criterion of a white lie—its destructiveness— is also the most important.

The most important element of a white lie is its destructiveness; the act of telling one hurts both the receiver and the sender. On the surface, it's a handy fix-all for an uncomfortable situation or a loaded question that begs evasion. But a deeper look reveals the disconnect in communication between a speaker and his audience. On one hand, the receiver of the lie is never allowed to hear the truth. Yet, on the other hand, the speaker cannot trust the situation he is in enough to allow himself to speak honestly. Rather than face this vulnerability, he protects himself under the shield of a white lie because, after all, this is a socially acceptable option. But then the speaker grows dependent on this shield. His words lose their truthfulness, and he is conquered by the ease of evasion that the white lie offers.

Going back to the *Do I look fat in this dress?* example, say that this question was asked in the context of a marriage. A wife asks this of her husband as they rush out the door, late for a dinner appointment. The husband, not wanting to waste more time by his wife changing her clothes, says immediately, "No, you look fine." This lie creates a first crack in the foundation of their relationship. As soon as he understands that he's gotten away with this lie, he sees no problem with one or two more. Before long, the foundation will crumble. His wife, perceiving his lies, no matter the severity, begins to doubt any statement or excuse that he makes. Is he really working late, or is he with someone else? What perhaps seemed like a ready and easy answer at the time, in the long run, is only the first step toward the destruction of their marriage.

Pier dramatizes the danger of white lies by describing a slippery slope (see p. 76).

The ease and politeness that we associate with white lies prevents the liar from looking beyond the here-and-now to the problems and consequences that will inevitably arise from its use. This is why the white lie is the most dangerous form of lying. This is why the white lie is morally and ethically reprehensible. I don't mean to condemn those who tell white lies. We all do. Heck, I do—daily. And I don't propose that no one should ever tell a white lie again. Rather, I mean to reveal the white lie for what it truly is and to make us aware of its insidiousness. Perhaps the next time you're grappling between the decision to tell the truth or to slide your way out of confrontation with a white lie, you'll think twice before choosing the latter.

Essay concludes by considering how to deal with white lies.

Work Cited

Coleman, Linda, and Paul Kay. "Prototypes Semantics: The English Word *Lie*." *Language* 57 (Mar. 1981): 26–44. 14 Apr. 2009. Web.

The Meaning of Friendship in a Social-Networked World

ALEX PATTAKOS

"What is a friend? A single soul dwelling in two bodies." This quote is attributed to the ancient Greek philosopher Aristotle who wrote extensively about the notion and importance of true friendship as a determinant of *meaningful* living.

Aristotle's view on this matter stands in sharp contrast to what is depicted in the newly-released movie *The Social Network,* destined to become a cult classic, about the founding of the Internet social networking site "Facebook." With the advertising tag line, "You don't get to 500 million friends without making a few enemies," you have to wonder what the definition of "friends" is in this kind of social networking context. And as you watch the relationships depicted in the film, especially that between founder Mark Zuckerberg and his network of "friends," it is obvious that they don't meet the quality standards espoused by Aristotle!

In this connection (no pun intended), computer whiz Zuckerberg and his best friend Eduardo Saverin, also a principal co-founder of Facebook, become embroiled in enough fights, including a nasty legal battle, to establish that there is not a single soul dwelling in their two bodies. The notion of "friend," of course, is used rather loosely in the online world of Facebook. What do you think Aristotle would have to say about the meaning of—and path to—friendship that has come to popularize the new millennium? Have we gone too far in our quest for connection with others in a world that has become increasingly disconnected even if, according to American journalist Thomas Friedman, it is supposedly "flat"?

And in a world of hyper-connectivity driven by technology that knows no bounds, what is happening to true friendship? Is it dying away? Or are

---

Alex Pattakos is a frequent contributor to publications such as *Fast Company* and the *Huffington Post* and the author of the book *Prisoners of Our Thoughts* (2008). He is the founder of the Center for Meaning in Santa Fe, New Mexico.

the various social media "platforms" such as Facebook, Twitter, and LinkedIn simply redefining or transforming our modern-day notion of friendship? If so, what are the implications for life as we know it on this planet? Will we be more happy? Will it promote the kind of meaningful existence that Aristotle was seeking and advocating?

The search for meaning is not only the primary intrinsic motivation of human beings, it is also a megatrend of the twenty-first century. From such a meaning-focused perspective, where does friendship fit in? And how might the social media "advances" referred to here influence, directly and indirectly, the nature of friendships between people and the human quest for meaning?

To be sure, I have more questions than answers, although there are some trends that are worthy of mention on the subject. A recent article in *USA Today* by Mark Vernon, a research fellow at Birkbeck College in London, England, addressed the issue of the social media's influence and concluded, "Just as our daily lives are becoming more technologically connected, we're losing other more meaningful relationships. Yes, we're losing our friends." In other words, the joys of real human contact are being replaced by electronic stimuli and *shallow* friendships, that is, "social connections" rather than the kind of true friendships described and espoused by Aristotle. In our post-modern society, there is evidence that while we have plenty of acquaintances, more and more of us have few individuals to whom we can turn and share our authentic selves, our deep intimacies.

Moreover, according to research published in the *American Sociological Review*, a highly-reputable professional journal, the average American has only two close friends and some twenty-five percent don't have any friends! We're not just "bowling alone," to borrow the title from a book by sociologist Robert Putman, we're effectively *living alone* in the midst of a socially-networked world! Now how ironic is that? Parenthetically, this is an illustration of what I call in my book, *Prisoners of Our Thoughts,* paradoxical intention or working against ourselves. We have become our worst enemy as we seek to navigate the sea of so-called "friends" that we've been promised through Facebook and other social networking sites.

Aristotle once asked his fellow Athenians, "Who would live without friends even if they had every other thing?" Importantly, he believed that good friends were superior to any material possessions one might have. Stop and think, then, for a moment about the quality of friends that we may make online, such as via Facebook, and compare this quality of relationships with other kinds of friends with whom we have actual face-to-face contact—be it infrequent, work-related, social, and intimate, perhaps even loving. Which of these contacts represent meaningful relationships and, by implication, true friendships? Which of these contacts, when all is said and done, really matters the most to you? In addition to feeding your soul, you can feel a single soul dwelling in two bodies?

In his classic work *Ethics*, Aristotle also offered the following ageless wisdom: "The desire for friendship comes quickly. Friendship does not." This is a very profound and perhaps provocative statement, especially in light of the powerful forces behind social networking. ("What do you mean you don't have a Facebook page?") It takes time and effort to build true friendships; relationships through which you are able and willing to disclose your *authentic* self—close thoughts, intimate feelings, and sensitive vulnerabilities including fears. While a social connection on Facebook may be only a click away, cultivating a true friendship is not that easy or straightforward if you believe in and take Aristotle's advice.

Now, in the spirit of full disclosure, I must admit that I'm a "techie" (formerly called a "nerd") and have been for as long as I can remember. Among other things, I was credited by the World Future Society with inventing the concept of the "Electronic Visiting Professor," an innovation in online distance learning when the Information Highway was still a dirt road. I've also been a "Crackberry" (an obsessive-compulsive user of the Blackberry device), and was an early adopter of the iPhone which now keeps me "connected" to family, friends, acquaintances, and others whenever I choose to let it. (Note the "I choose" reference; I am very conscious of the need to manage the technology, not the other way around!) I also regularly use most of the social networking platforms mentioned, explicitly or implicitly, in this blog article. Moreover, I'm very familiar with the propensity among people today to share themselves online with complete strangers-as-friends, presumably feeling safe in the deceptive shadows of cyberspace.

I also recognize that in today's busy, fast-paced world, many people are more likely to tell their hopes and troubles to bartenders, taxi drivers, hair stylists, and therapists than they are to the people who are regularly in their lives. In my opinion, this is a sad commentary on post-modern society for many people seem to have drifted away from true friendships and a sense of "community" and are now living very private, even lonely, lives. It's time to resurrect the meaning and value of authentic relationships with others. It's time to refocus on and allow friendships to flourish in *meaningful* ways, both in our personal and work lives. "A friend is another self," Aristotle also told us. True friendships, which admittedly are a blast from the past, are not simply a manifestation of what is being called "social connectivity" in social networking parlance. No, true friendships are the key to a flourishing, meaningful life, well-being, and a truly-connected society and world. Now would you like to Facebook me?

10
Evaluations

"We don't want to go there for coffee. Their beans aren't fair trade, the drinks are high in calories, and the stuff is *way* overpriced."

Three students who have cochaired the campus Arts Festival for six semesters are all graduating. Their leadership has led to significant improvements in the diversity and quality of cultural activities. So the group calls a special meeting to talk about what qualities it needs in its next leaders to sustain the progress.

Orson Welles's masterpiece *Citizen Kane* is playing at the Student Union for only one more night, but the new *Spider-Man* is featured across the street in THX sound. Guess which movie your roomie wants to see? You intend to set him straight.

Understanding Evaluations

Evaluations are everyday arguments. By the time you leave home in the morning, you've likely made a dozen informal evaluations: You've selected dressy clothes because you have a job interview with a law firm. You've chosen low-fat yogurt and fruit over the pancakes you really love. You've queued up the perfect playlist on your iPod for your hike to campus. In each case, you've applied criteria to a particular problem and then made a decision. That's evaluating on the fly.

Some professional evaluations require more elaborate standards, evidence, and paperwork (imagine an aircraft manufacturer certifying a new jet for passenger service), but they don't differ structurally from the simpler choices that people make all the time. People love to voice their opinions, and they always have. In fact, a mode of ancient rhetoric—called the **ceremonial**, or **epideictic**—was devoted entirely to speeches of praise and blame. (See Chapter 1.)

Today, rituals of praise and blame are a significant part of American life. Adults who would choke at the notion of debating causal or definitional claims will happily spend hours appraising the Oakland Raiders, Boston Red Sox, or Detroit Pistons. Other evaluative spectacles in our culture include awards shows, beauty pageants, most-valuable-player presentations, lists of best-dressed or worst-dressed celebrities, "sexiest people"

Arguments about sports are usually evaluations of some kind.

magazine covers, literary prizes, political opinion polls, consumer product magazines, and — the ultimate formal public gesture of evaluation — elections. Indeed, making evaluations is a form of entertainment in America and generates big audiences (think of *American Idol*) and revenues.

RESPOND •

In the last ten years, there has been a proliferation of awards programs for movies, musicians, sports figures, and other categories. For example, before the Academy of Motion Picture Arts and Sciences hands out the Oscars, a half-dozen other organizations have given prizes to the annual crop of films. Write a short opinion piece assessing the merits of a particular awards show or a feature such as *People*'s annual "Sexiest Man Alive" issue. What should a proper event of this kind accomplish? Does the event you're reviewing do so?

Criteria of Evaluation

Arguments of evaluation can produce simple rankings and winners or can lead to profound decisions about our lives, but they always involve standards. The particular standards we establish for judging anything — whether an idea, a work of art, a person, or a product — are called **criteria of evaluation**. Sometimes criteria are self-evident: a car that gets fifteen miles per gallon is a gas hog, and a piece of fish that smells even a little off shouldn't be eaten. But criteria get complicated when a subject is abstract: *What features make a song a classic? What constitutes a fair wage? How do we measure a successful foreign policy or college career?* Struggling to identify such difficult criteria of evaluation can lead to important insights into your values, motives, and preferences.

Why make such a big deal about criteria when many acts of evaluation seem effortless? We should be suspicious of our judgments especially when we make them casually. It's irresponsible simply to think that spontaneous and uninformed quips should carry the same weight as well-informed and well-reasoned opinions. Serious evaluations always require reflection, and when we look deeply into our judgments, we sometimes discover important questions that typically go unasked, many prefaced by *why*:

- You challenge the grade you received in a course, but you don't question the practice of grading.

- You argue passionately that a Republican Congress is better for America than a Democratic alternative, but you fail to ask why voters get only two choices.

- You argue that buying a hybrid car makes more sense than keeping an SUV, but you don't ask whether taking alternative forms of transportation (like the bus or a bike) makes the most sense of all.

Push an argument of evaluation hard enough, and even simple judgments become challenging and intriguing.

In fact, for many writers, grappling with criteria is the toughest step in producing an evaluation. When you offer an opinion about a topic you know reasonably well, you want readers to learn something from your judgment. So you need time to think about and then justify the criteria for your opinion, whatever the subject.

Do you think, for instance, that you could explain what (if anything) makes a veggie burger good? Though many people have eaten veggie burgers, they probably haven't spent much time thinking about them. But it wouldn't be enough to claim merely that a proper one should be juicy or tasty—such trite claims are not even interesting. The following criteria offered on the *Cook's Illustrated* Web site show what happens when experts give the issue a closer look:

> We wanted to create veggie burgers that even meat eaters would love. We didn't want them to taste like hamburgers, but we did want them to act like hamburgers, *having a modicum of chew, a harmonious blend of savory ingredients, and the ability to go from grill to bun without falling apart.* [emphasis added]
>
> —*Cook's Illustrated*

After a lot of experimenting, *Cook's Illustrated* came up with a recipe that met these criteria.

Criteria of evaluation aren't static, either. They differ according to time and audience. Much market research, for example, is designed to find out what particular consumers want now

What criteria of evaluation are embedded in this visual argument?

and may want in the future—what their criteria are for buying a product. In good times, people may demand homes with soaring entryways, lots of space, and premium appliances. In tougher times, they may care more about efficient use of space, quality insulation, and energy-efficient stoves and dishwashers. Shifts in values, attitudes, and criteria happen all the time.

RESPOND •

Choose one item from the following list that you understand well enough to evaluate. Develop several criteria of evaluation that you could defend to distinguish excellence from mediocrity in the area. Then choose an item that you don't know much about and explain the research you might do to discover reasonable criteria of evaluation for it.

digital cameras	U.S. vice presidents
NFL quarterbacks	organic vegetables
social networking sites	hot water heaters
TV journalists	spoken word poetry
video games	athletic shoes
fashion designers	country music bands
Navajo rugs	hip-hop bands

Characterizing Evaluation

One way of understanding evaluative arguments is to consider the types of evidence they use. A distinction explored in Chapter 4 between hard evidence and constructed arguments based on reason is helpful here: we defined **hard evidence** as facts, statistics, testimony, and other kinds of arguments that can be measured, recorded, or even found—the so-called smoking gun in a criminal investigation. We defined constructed arguments based on reason as those that are shaped by language, using various kinds of logic.

We can talk about arguments of evaluation the same way, looking at some as quantitative and others as qualitative. **Quantitative arguments** of evaluation rely on criteria that can be measured, counted, or demonstrated in some mechanical fashion (something is taller, faster, smoother, quieter, or more powerful than something else). In contrast, **qualitative arguments** rely on criteria that must be explained through language and media, relying on such matters as values, traditions, and emotions (something is more ethical, more beneficial, more handsome, or more noble than something else). A claim of evaluation might be supported by arguments of both sorts.

Quantitative Evaluations

At first glance, quantitative evaluations seem to hold all the cards, especially in a society as enamored of science and technology as our own is. Making judgments should be easy if all it involves is measuring and counting—and in some cases, that's the way things work out. *Who's the tallest or heaviest or loudest person in your class?* If your classmates allow themselves to be measured, you could find out easily enough, using the right equipment and internationally sanctioned standards of measurement—the meter, the kilo, or the decibel.

But what if you were to ask, *Who's the smartest person in class?* You could answer this more complex question quantitatively, using IQ tests or college entrance examinations that report results numerically. In fact, almost all college-bound students in the United States submit to this kind of evaluation, taking either the SAT or ACT to demonstrate their verbal and mathematical prowess. Such measures are widely accepted by educators and institutions, but they are also vigorously challenged. What do they actually measure? They predict likely academic success only in college, which is one kind of intelligence.

Quantitative measures of evaluation can be enormously useful, but even the most objective measures have limits. They've been devised by fallible people who look at the world from their own inevitably limited perspectives.

Qualitative Evaluations

Many issues of evaluation that are closest to people's hearts aren't subject to quantification. *What makes a movie great?* If you suggested a quantitative measure like length, your friends would probably hoot, "Get serious!" But what about box-office receipts, adjusted for inflation? Would films that made the most money—an easily quantifiable measure—be the "best pictures"? That select group would include movies such as *Star Wars, The Sound of Music, Gone with the Wind, Titanic,* and *Avatar.* An interesting group of films—but the best?

To define the criteria for "great movie," you'd more likely look for the standards and evidence that serious critics explore in their arguments, abstract or complicated issues such as their societal impact, cinematic technique, dramatic structures, intelligent casting, and so on. Most of these markers of quality could be defined and identified with some precision but not measured or counted. You'd also have to make your case rhetorically, convincing the audience to accept the markers of quality you are offering and yet appreciating that they might not. A movie reviewer making qualitative judgments might spend as much time defending criteria of evaluation as providing evidence that these standards are present in a particular film. But putting those standards into action can be what makes a review something worth reading. Consider how Roger Ebert, in writing about the classic film *The Godfather*, actually teaches his readers how to find evidence of quality in a great director's choices:

> [Francis Ford] Coppola populates his dark interior spaces with remarkable faces. The front-line actors—Brando, Pacino, Caan, Duvall—are attractive in one way or another, but those who play their associates are chosen for their fleshy, thickly lined faces—for huge jaws and deeply set eyes. Look at Abe Vigoda as Tessio, the fearsome enforcer. The first time we see him, he's dancing with a child at the wedding, her satin pumps balanced on his shoes. The sun shines that day, but

Web sites such as Netflix do offer recommendations for films based on users' past selections and the ratings of other users and critics. Sometimes those judgments are at odds. Then whom do you trust?

never again: He is developed as a hulking presence who implies the possibility of violent revenge. Only at the end is he brightly lit again, to make him look vulnerable as he begs for his life.

RESPOND●

For examples of powerful evaluation arguments, search the Web or your library for eulogies or obituaries of famous, recently deceased individuals. Try to locate at least one such item, and then analyze the types of claims it makes about the accomplishments of the deceased. What types of criteria of evaluation hold the obituary or eulogy together? Why should we respect or admire the person?

Developing an Evaluative Argument

Developing an argument of evaluation can seem like a simple process, especially if you already know what your claim is likely to be. To continue the movie theme for one more example:

Citizen Kane is the finest film ever made by an American director.

Having established a claim, you would then explore the implications of your belief, drawing out the reasons, warrants, and evidence that might support it:

Claim	*Citizen Kane* is the finest film ever made by an American director . . .
Reason	. . . because it revolutionizes the way we see the world.
Warrant	Great films change viewers in fundamental ways.
Evidence	Shot after shot, *Citizen Kane* presents the life of its protagonist through cinematic images that viewers can never forget.

The warrant here is, in effect, an implied statement of criteria—in this case, the quality that defines "great film" for the writer. It may be important for the writer to share that assumption with readers and perhaps to identify other great films that similarly make viewers appreciate new perspectives.

As you can see, in developing an evaluative argument, you'll want to pay special attention to criteria, claims, and evidence.

Formulating Criteria

Although even casual evaluations (*The band sucks!*) might be traced to reasonable criteria, most people don't defend their positions until they are challenged (*Oh yeah?*). Similarly, writers who address readers with whom they share core values rarely discuss their criteria in great detail. A film critic like Roger Ebert (see p. 220) isn't expected to restate all his principles every time he writes a movie review. Ebert assumes that his readers will—over time—come to appreciate his standards. Still, criteria can make or break a piece.

So spend time developing your criteria of evaluation. What exactly makes a shortstop an all-star? Why is a standardized test an unreliable measure of intelligence? Fundamentally, what distinguishes an inspired fashion designer from a run-of-the-mill one? List the possibilities and then pare the possibilities down to the essentials. If you offer vague, dull, or unsupportable principles, expect to be challenged.

You're most likely to be vague about your beliefs when you haven't thought (or read) enough about your subject. Push yourself at least as far as you imagine readers will. Anticipate readers looking over your shoulder, asking difficult questions. Say, for example, that you intend to argue that anyone who wants to stay on the cutting edge of personal technology will obviously want Apple's latest iPad because it does so many amazing things. But what does that mean exactly? What makes the device "amazing"? Is it that it gives access to email and the Web, has a high-resolution screen, offers an astonishing number of apps, and makes a good e-reader? These are particular features of the device. But can you identify a more fundamental quality to explain the product's appeal, such as an iPad user's experience, enjoyment, or feeling of productivity? (For one answer, see Virginia Postrel's "Why We Prize That Magical Mystery Pad" on p. 240.) You'll often want to raise your evaluation to a higher level of generality like this so that your appraisal of a product, book, performance, or political figure works as a coherent argument, and not just as a list of random observations.

Be certain, too, that your criteria of evaluation apply to more than just your topic of the moment. Your standards should make sense on their own merits and apply across the board. If you tailor your criteria to get the outcome you want, you are doing what is called "special pleading." You might be pleased when you prove that the home team is awesome, but it won't take skeptics long to figure out how you've cooked the books.

RESPOND •

Local news and entertainment magazines often publish "best of" issues or articles that catalog their readers' and editors' favorites in such categories as "best place to go on a first date," "best ice cream sundae," and "best dentist." Sometimes the categories are specific: "best places to say 'I was retro before retro was cool'" or "best movie theater seats." Imagine that you're the editor of your own local magazine and that you want to put out a "best of" issue tailored to your hometown. Develop ten categories for evaluation. For each category, list the evaluative criteria that you would use to make your judgment. Next, consider that because your criteria are warrants, they're especially tied to audience. (The criteria for "best dentist," for example, might be tailored to people whose major concern is avoiding pain, to those whose children will be regular patients, or to those who want the cheapest possible dental care.) For several of the evaluative categories, imagine that you have to justify your judgments to a completely different audience. Write a new set of criteria for that audience.

Making Claims

In evaluations, claims can be stated directly or, more rarely, strongly implied. For most writers, strong statements followed by reasonable qualifications work best. Consider the differences between the following three claims and how much greater the burden of proof is for the first claim:

The most outrageous of them all? Margaret Cho in 2008 lamé mode.

Margaret Cho is the most shocking comedian ever.

Margaret Cho is one of the three or four most outrageous comedians around today.

Margaret Cho may come to be regarded as one of the most outspoken comedians of her time.

Here's a second set of examples demonstrating the same principle, that qualifications generally make a claim of evaluation easier to deal with and smarter:

No Child Left Behind sure was a dumb idea.

The No Child Left Behind educational reform likely did more harm than good.

While laudable in its intentions to improve American schools, the No Child Left Behind Act of 2001 put so high a premium on testing that it undermined more fundamental aspects of elementary and secondary education.

The point of qualifying a statement isn't to make evaluative claims bland but to make them responsible and reasonable. Consider how Reagan Tankersley uses the criticisms of a musical genre he enjoys to frame a claim he makes in its defense:

> Structurally, dub step is a simple musical form, with formulaic progressions and beats, something that gives a musically tuned ear little to grasp or analyze. For this reason, a majority of traditionally trained musicians find the genre to be a waste of time. These people have a legitimate position. . . . However, I hold that it is the simplicity of dub step that makes it special: the primal nature of the song is what digs so deeply into fans. It accesses the most primitive area in our brains that connects to the uniquely human love of music.
> —Reagan Tankersley, "Dub Step: Why People Dance"

Tankersley doesn't pretend that dub step is something it's not, nor does he expect his argument to win over traditionally minded critics. Yet he still makes a claim worth considering.

One tip: Nothing adds more depth to an opinion than letting others challenge it. When you can, use the resources of the Internet or local

Dub step DJs Benga, Artwork, and Skream of Magnetic Man perform.

discussion boards to get responses to your opinions or topic proposals. It can be eye-opening to realize how strongly people react to ideas or points of view that you regard as perfectly normal. Share your claim and, then when you're ready, your first draft with friends and classmates, asking them to identify places where your ideas need additional support, either in the discussion of criteria or in the presentation of evidence.

Presenting Evidence

Generally, the more evidence in an evaluation the better, provided that the evidence is relevant. For example, in evaluating the performance of two laptops, the speed of their processors would be essential, but the quality of their keyboards or the availability of service might be less crucial yet still worth mentioning. But you have to decide how much detail your readers want in your argument. For technical subjects, you might make your basic case briefly and then attach additional supporting documents at the end—tables, graphs, charts—for those who want more data.

Just as important as relevance in selecting evidence is presentation. Not all pieces of evidence are equally convincing, nor should they be treated as such. Select evidence that is most likely to influence your readers, and then arrange the argument to build toward your best material. In most cases, that best material will be evidence that's specific, detailed, memorable, and derived from credible sources. The details in these paragraphs from Sean Wilsey's review of *Fun Home: A Family Tragicomic*, a graphic novel by Alison Bechdel, tell you precisely what makes the work "lush," "absorbing," and well worth reading:

> It is a pioneering work, pushing two genres (comics and memoir) in multiple new directions, with panels that combine the detail and technical proficiency of R. Crumb with a seriousness, emotional complexity, and innovation completely its own. Then there are the actual words. Generally this is where graphic narratives stumble. Very few cartoonists can also write—or, if they can, they manage only to hit a few familiar notes. But *Fun Home* quietly succeeds in telling a story, not only through well-crafted images but through words that are equally revealing and well chosen. Big words, too! In 232 pages this memoir sent me to the dictionary five separate times (to look up "bargeboard," "buss," "scutwork," "humectant," and "perseverated").
>
> A comic book for lovers of words! Bechdel's rich language and precise images combine to create a lush piece of work—a memoir where

concision and detail are melded for maximum, obsessive density. She has obviously spent years getting this memoir right, and it shows. You can read *Fun Home* in a sitting, or get lost in the pictures within the pictures on its pages. The artist's work is so absorbing you feel you are living in her world.

—Sean Wilsey, "The Things They Buried"

The details in this passage make the case that Alison Bechdel's novel is one that pushes both comics and memoirs in new directions.

In evaluation arguments, don't be afraid to concede a point when evidence goes contrary to the overall claim you wish to make. If you're really skillful, you can even turn a problem into an argumentative asset, as Bob Costas does in acknowledging the flaws of baseball great Mickey Mantle in the process of praising him:

None of us, Mickey included, would want to be held to account for every moment of our lives. But how many of us could say that our best moments were as magnificent as his?

—Bob Costas, "Eulogy for Mickey Mantle"

RESPOND

Take a close look at the cover of Alison Bechdel's graphic novel *Fun Home: A Family Tragicomic*. In what various ways does it make an argument of evaluation designed to make you want to buy the work? Examine other books, magazines, or media packages (such as video game or software boxes) and describe any strategies they use to argue for their merit.

Considering Design and Visuals

Visual components play a significant role in many arguments of evaluation, especially those based on quantitative information. As soon as numbers are involved in supporting a claim, think about ways to arrange them in tables, charts, graphs, or infographics to make the information more accessible to readers. Visual elements are especially helpful when comparing items. Indeed, a visual spread like those in the federal government's "Buy a Safer Car" pamphlet (see p. 228) becomes an argument in itself about the vehicles the government has crash-tested for safety. The facts seem to speak for themselves because they are arrayed with care and deliberation. Similarly, you need to consider how you might present your facts visually to inform and persuade readers.

But don't ignore other basic design features of a text—such as headings for the different criteria you're using or, in online evaluations, links to material related to your subject. Such details can enhance your authority, credibility, and persuasiveness.

PURCHASING WITH SAFETY IN MIND

Code key on page 8

More Stars, Safer Cars. ★ 2

MAKE	MODEL	Body Style	RATINGS — Frontal Crash (Driver)	Frontal Crash (Passenger)	Overall Frontal	Side Barrier (Driver)	Side Barrier (Passenger–Rear Seat)	Side Pole (Driver)	Overall Side	Rollover	Overall Vehicle Score	SAFETY FEATURES — Lane Departure Warning	Forward Collision Warning	Electronic Stability Control
Cadillac	Escalade RWD	SUV	★★★★	★★★★	★★★★	★★★★	★★★★	★★★★★	★★★★	★★★	★★★★	0	0	S
Cadillac	STS FWD/AWD	4 DR	NR	NR	NR	NR	NR	NR	NR	★★★★	NR			S
Chevrolet	Cruze FWD	4 DR	★★★★★	★★★★★	★★★★★	★★★★★	★★★★★	★★★★★	★★★★★	★★★★	★★★★★			S
Chevrolet	Equinox AWD	SUV	★★★★	★★★★	★★★★	★★★★★	★★★★	★★★★★	★★★★	★★★★	★★★★			S
Chevrolet	Equinox FWD	SUV	★★★★	★★★★	★★★★	★★★★★	★★★★	★★★★★	★★★★	★★★★	★★★★			S
Chevrolet	Malibu FWD	4 DR	★★★★★	★★★	★★★★	★★★★★	★★★★★	★★★★	★★★★★	★★★★	★★★★			S
Chevrolet	Silverado 1500 Crew Cab 4WD	PU	★★★★	★★★★	★★★★	★★★★★	★★★★★	★★★★★	★★★★★	★★★	★★★★			S
Chevrolet	Silverado 1500 Crew Cab Hybrid 4WD	PU	★★★★	★★★★	★★★★	★★★★★	★★★★★	★★★★★	★★★★★	★★★	★★★★			S
Chevrolet	Silverado 1500 Crew Cab Hybrid RWD	PU	★★★★	★★★★	★★★★	★★★★★	★★★★★	★★★★★	★★★★★	★★★	★★★★			S
Chevrolet	Silverado 1500 Crew Cab RWD	PU	★★★★	★★★★	★★★★	★★★★★	★★★★★	★★★★★	★★★★★	★★★	★★★★			S
Chevrolet	Silverado 1500 Extended Cab 4WD	PU	★★★★★	★★★★	★★★★	★★★★★	★★★★★	★★★★★	★★★★★	★★★	★★★★			S
Chevrolet	Silverado 1500 Extended Cab RWD	PU	★★★★	★★★★	★★★★	★★★★★	★★★★★	★★★★★	★★★★★	★★★	★★★★			S
Chevrolet	Silverado 1500 Regular Cab RWD	PU	★★★★★	★★★★	★★★★	★★★★★	N/A	★★★★★	★★★★★	★★★	★★★★			S
Chevrolet	Tahoe 4WD	SUV	★★★★★	★★★★★	★★★★★	★★★★★	★★★★★	★★★★★	★★★★★	★★★	★★★★★			S
Chevrolet	Tahoe Hybrid 4WD	SUV	★★★★★	★★★★★	★★★★★	NR	NR	NR	NR	★★★	NR			S
Chevrolet	Tahoe Hybrid RWD	SUV	★★★★	★★★★★	★★★★	NR	NR	NR	NR	★★★★	NR			S
Chevrolet	Tahoe RWD	SUV	★★★★★	★★★★★	★★★★★	★★★★★	★★★★★	★★★★★	★★★★★	★★★★	★★★★★			S
Chevrolet	Traverse AWD	SUV	★★★★★	★★★★★	★★★★★	★★★★★	★★★★★	★★★★★	★★★★★	★★★★	★★★★★			S
Chevrolet	Traverse FWD	SUV	★★★★★	★★★★★	★★★★★	★★★★★	★★★★★	★★★★★	★★★★★	★★★★	★★★★★			S
Chevrolet	Volt FWD	5 HB	★★★★★	★★★★★	★★★★★	★★★★★	★★★★★	★★★★★	★★★★★	★★★★	★★★★★			S
Dodge	Caliber FWD	5 HB	★★★★★	★★★★★	★★★★★	★★★★	★★★★	★	★★★★	★★★★	★★★★			S
Ford	Edge AWD	SUV	★★★	★★★★	★★★★	★★★★★	★★★★★	★★★★★	★★★★★	★★★★	★★★★	0	0	S
Ford	Edge FWD	SUV	★★★★	★★★	★★★★	★★★★★	★★★★★	★★★★★	★★★★★	★★★★	★★★★		0	S
Ford	Escape 4WD	SUV	★★	★★★★	★★★	★★★★	★★★★	★★★★★	★★★★	★★★★	★★★			S
Ford	Escape FWD	SUV	★★★	★★★★	★★★	★★★★	★★★★	★★★★★	★★★★	★★★★	★★★			S
Ford	Escape Hybrid FWD	SUV	★★	★★★★	★★★	★★★★	★★★★	★★★★★	★★★	★★★★	★★★			S
Ford	Escape Hybrid FWD	SUV	★★	★★★★	★★★	★★★★	★★★★	★★★★★	★★★	★★★★	★★★			S
Ford	Escape FWD	SUV	★★	★★★★	★★★	★★★	★★★	★★★★★	★★★	★★★	★★★			S

This panel uses numerous devices to convey information and make comparisons. How many devices or features can you identify?

| GUIDE | to writing an evaluation |

● Finding a Topic

You're entering an argument of evaluation when you:

- make a judgment about quality: Citizen Kane is *probably the finest film ever made by an American director.*

- challenge such a judgment: Citizen Kane is *vastly overrated by most film critics.*

- construct a ranking or comparison: Citizen Kane is *a more intellectually challenging movie than* Casablanca.

- explore criteria that might be used in making evaluative judgments: *Criteria for judging films are evolving as the production and audiences of films become ever more international.*

Issues of evaluation arise daily—in the judgments you make about public figures or policies; in the choices you make about instructors and courses; in the recommendations you offer about books, films, or television programs; in the preferences you exercise in choosing products, activities, or charities. Evaluations typically use terms that indicate value or rank—*good/bad, effective/ineffective, best/worst, competent/incompetent, successful/unsuccessful.* When you can choose a topic for an evaluation, write about something on which others regularly ask your opinion or advice.

● Researching Your Topic

You can research issues of evaluation by using the following sources:

- journals, reviews, and magazines (for current political and social issues)
- books (for assessing judgments about history, policy, etc.)
- biographies (for assessing people)
- research reports and scientific studies
- books, magazines, and Web sites for consumers
- periodicals and Web sites that cover entertainment and sports
- blogs for exploring current affairs

Surveys and polls can be useful in uncovering public attitudes: *What books are people reading? Who are the most admired people in the country? What activities or businesses are thriving or waning?* You'll discover that Web sites, newsgroups, and blogs thrive on evaluation. (Ever keep track of who "Likes" what you post on Facebook as evidence of how funny or interesting your Wall is?) Browse these public forums for ideas, and, when possible, explore your own topic ideas there. But remember that all sources need to be evaluated themselves; examine each source carefully, making sure that it is legitimate and credible.

● Formulating a Claim

After exploring your subject, try to draw up a full and specific claim that lets readers know where you stand and on what criteria you'll base your judgments. Come up with a thesis that's challenging enough to attract readers' attention. In developing a thesis, you might begin with questions like these:

- What exactly is my opinion? Where do I stand?
- Can I make my judgment more clear-cut?
- Do I need to narrow or qualify my claim?
- By what standards will I make my judgment?
- Will readers accept my criteria, or will I have to defend them, too? What criteria might others offer?
- What evidence or major reasons can I offer in support of my evaluation?

For a conventional evaluation, your thesis should be a complete statement. In one sentence, make a claim of evaluation and state the reasons that support it. Be sure your claim is specific. Anticipate the questions readers might have: *Who? What? Where? Under what conditions? With what exceptions? In all cases?* Don't expect readers to guess where you stand.

For a more exploratory argument, you might begin (and even end) with questions about the process of evaluation itself. *What are the qualities we seek—or ought to—in our political leaders? What does it say about our cultural values when we find so many viewers entertained by so-called reality shows on television? What might be the criteria for collegiate athletic programs consistent with the values of higher education?* Projects that explore topics like these might not begin with straightforward theses or have the intention to persuade readers.

● Examples of Evaluative Claims

- Though they may never receive Oscars for their work, Tom Cruise and Keanu Reeves deserve credit as actors who have succeeded in a wider range of film roles than most of their contemporaries.

- People are returning to cities because they find life there more civilized than in the suburbs.

- Barack Obama's speech on race, delivered in Philadelphia on March 18, 2008, is the most honest presentation of this issue we have heard since Martin Luther King Jr.'s time.

- Jimmy Carter has been highly praised for his work as a former president of the United States, but history may show that even his much-derided term in office laid the groundwork for the foreign policy and economic successes now attributed to later administrations.

- Because knowledge changes so quickly and people switch careers so often, an effective education today may be one that focuses more on training people how to learn than on teaching them what to know.

● Preparing a Proposal

If your instructor asks you to prepare a proposal for your project, here's a format that may help:

State your thesis completely. If you're having trouble doing so, try outlining it in Toulmin terms:

Claim:

Reason(s):

Warrant(s):

Alternatively, you might describe your intention to explore a particular question of evaluation in your project, with the thesis perhaps coming later.

- Explain why this issue deserves attention. What's at stake?

- Identify whom you hope to reach through your argument and why these readers would be interested in it.

- Briefly discuss the key challenges you anticipate in preparing your argument.

- Determine what research strategies you'll use. What sources do you expect to consult?

- Describe the format you expect to use: Conventional research essay? Letter to the editor? Web page?

● Thinking about Organization

Your evaluation will likely include elements such as the following:

- an evaluative claim that makes a judgment about a person, idea, or object
- the criterion or criteria by which you'll measure your subject
- an explanation or justification of the criteria (if necessary)
- evidence that the particular subject meets or falls short of the stated criteria
- consideration of alternative views and counterarguments

All these elements may be present in arguments of evaluation, but they won't follow a specific order. In addition, you'll often need an opening paragraph to explain what you're evaluating and why. Tell readers why they should care about your subject and take your opinion seriously.

● Getting and Giving Response: Questions for Peer Response

Your instructor may assign you to a group for the purpose of reading and responding to each other's drafts. If not, ask for responses from serious readers or consultants at a writing center. Use the following questions to evaluate a colleague's draft. Be sure to illustrate your comments with examples; specific comments help more than general observations.

The Claim

- Is the claim an argument of evaluation? Does it make a judgment about something?
- Does the claim establish clearly what's being evaluated?
- Is the claim too sweeping? Does it need to be qualified?
- Will the criteria used in the evaluation be clear to readers? Do the criteria need to be defined more precisely?
- Are the criteria appropriate ones to use for this evaluation? Are they controversial? Should they be defended?

Evidence for the Claim

- Is enough evidence provided to show that what's being evaluated meets the established criteria? If not, what additional evidence is needed?
- Is the evidence in support of the claim simply announced, or are its significance and appropriateness analyzed? Is more detailed discussion needed?

- Are any objections readers might have to the claim, criteria, or evidence adequately addressed?

- What kinds of sources are cited? How credible and persuasive will they be to readers? What other kinds of sources might work better?

- Are all quotations introduced with appropriate signal phrases (such as "As Tyson argues, . . .") and blended smoothly into the writer's sentences?

Organization and Style

- How are the parts of the argument organized? Is this organization effective?

- Will readers understand the relationships among the claims, supporting reasons, warrants, and evidence? If not, how might those connections be clearer? Is the function of every visual clear? Are more transitions needed? Would headings or graphic devices help?

- Are the transitions or links from point to point, sentence to sentence, and paragraph to paragraph clear and effective? If not, how could they be improved?

- Are all visuals carefully integrated into the text? Is each visual introduced and commented on to point out its significance? Is each visual labeled as a figure or a table and given a caption as well as a citation?

- Is the style suited to the subject? Is it too formal, casual, or technical? Can it be improved?

- Which sentences seem effective? Which ones seem weaker, and how could they be improved? Should short sentences be combined, and any longer ones be broken up?

- How effective are the paragraphs? Too short or too long? How can they be improved?

- Which words or phrases seem effective? Do any seem vague or inappropriate for the audience or the writer's purpose? Are technical or unfamiliar terms defined?

Spelling, Punctuation, Mechanics, Documentation, and Format

- Are there any errors in spelling, punctuation, capitalization, and the like?

- Is the documentation appropriate and consistent? (See Chapter 21.)

- Does the paper or project follow an appropriate format? Is it attractively designed and presented?

PROJECTS •

1. What kinds of reviews or evaluations do you consult most often or read religiously—those of TV shows, sports stars, video games, fashions, fishing gear, political figures? Try composing an argument of evaluation in your favorite genre: make and defend a claim about the quality of some object, item, work, or person within your area of interest or special knowledge. Let the paper demonstrate an expertise you have gained by your reading. If it helps, model your evaluation upon the work of a reviewer or expert you particularly respect.

2. Prepare a project in which you challenge what you regard as a wrongheaded evaluation, providing sound reasons and solid evidence for challenging this existing and perhaps commonly held view. Maybe you believe that a classic novel you had to read in high school is overrated or that people who criticize video games really don't understand them. Explain why the topic of your evaluation needs to be reconsidered and provide reasons, evidence, and, if necessary, different criteria of evaluation for doing so. For an example of this type of evaluation, see Sean Kamperman's "The Wikipedia Game" on pp. 235–39.

3. Write an evaluation in which you compare or assess the contributions or achievements of two or three notable people working within the same field or occupation. They may be educators, entrepreneurs, artists, legislators, editorial cartoonists, fashion designers, programmers, athletes—you name it. While your first instinct might be to rank these individuals and pick a "winner," this evaluation will work just as well if you can help readers appreciate the different paths by which your subjects have achieved distinction.

4. Within this chapter, the claim is made that criteria of evaluation can change depending on times and circumstances: "In good times, people may demand homes with soaring entryways, lots of space, and premium appliances. In tougher times, they'll likely care more about efficient use of space, quality insulation, and energy-efficient stoves and dishwashers." Working in a group, discuss several scenarios of change and then explore how those circumstances could alter the way we evaluate particular objects, activities, or productions. For example, what impact might global warming have upon the way we determine desirable places to live or vacation? How might a continued economic downturn change the criteria by which we judge successful careers or good educational paths for our children? If people across the globe continue to put on weight, how might standards of personal beauty or fashion alter? If government institutions continue to fall in public esteem, how might we modify our expectations for elected officials? Following the discussion, write a paper or prepare a project in which you explore how one scenario for change might revise customary values and standards of evaluation.

The Wikipedia Game: Boring, Pointless, or Neither?

SEAN KAMPERMAN

When most people think about Wikipedia—the self-styled "free, Web-based, collaborative, multilingual encyclopedia project"—they are likely reminded of the preliminary research they did for that term paper on post-structuralism, or of the idle minutes they may've spent exploring an interesting topic just for the heck of it—the neuroanatomy of purple-striped jellyfish, for example, or *Jersey Shore*. First and foremost a layman's tool, Wikipedia has struggled to find legitimacy alongside more reputable reference sources such as *Encyclopaedia Britannica*, even in spite of the outstanding quality of many of its entries. But fortunately for the makers of the Free Encyclopedia—and for the rest of us—Wikipedia's usefulness goes far beyond its intended "encyclopedic" purpose. Under the right circumstances, it can be as much a source of entertainment as one of knowledge and self-improvement.

A prime example of this fact is a phenomenon identified as the Wikipedia game—or, as it's now known to users of Apple and Android smart phones, "WikiHunt." WikiHunt is a simple game whose rules draw upon the unique

Sean Kamperman wrote "The Wikipedia Game: Boring, Pointless, or Neither?" in spring 2010 for a lower-division course on rhetoric and media at the University of Texas at Austin. In his topic proposal he briefly described Wikipedia games familiar to many students and then indicated what he intended to explore: "A lot of scholars have been very critical of Wikipedia—some going so far as to discourage its use altogether, even for the purpose of gathering background info. Does the fact that games like these use Wikipedia detract from their educational value? Or do the games in some way rebut these criticisms, demonstrating that the practical uses of user-generated online encyclopedias go beyond traditional research and, by extension, considerations of factual correctness?" His paper is the answer to those questions.

Opening paragraph provides a context and a subtle evaluative thesis: "Wikipedia's usefulness goes far beyond its intended 'encyclopedic' purpose."

WikiHunt is introduced as a cultural phenomenon.

architectural features of wikis, in that players perform "moves" by following the links that connect one Wikipedia entry to another. Driven by cultural conditions of dilettantism and the spurts of creativity that tend to come on in times of extreme boredom, dozens if not hundreds of Wikipedia users in high school computer labs, college dormitories, and professional workspaces around the globe have "discovered" the game on their own. Some have even gone so far as to claim sole proprietorship—as in the case of two of my friends, who swear they invented the game while sitting through a lecture on academic dishonesty. Questions of original authorship aside, the Wikipedia game would appear to be a bona fide grassroots phenomenon—and one well worth examining if we consider its possible implications for learning and education.

Understanding that not every reader will know WikiHunt, Kamperman offers a detailed explanation.

If you've never played the Wikipedia game, it's fun—educational—and, for the most part, free; indeed, all you'll need is one or more friends, two computers, and an Internet connection. To begin, navigate to the Wikipedia homepage and click the "Random article" link on the left-hand side of the screen. As advertised, this link will lead you and your friend to two randomly generated Wikipedia articles. The objective from here is to get from your article to your opponent's using nothing but links to other articles. These links, which appear within the text of the articles themselves, are bits of hypertext denoted in blue; click on any of them, and you'll be instantly transported to another article and another set of links. Depending on which version of the rules you're going by, either the player who finishes first or the one who gets to his or her opponent's page using the fewest number of links is the winner. Easy, right?

The paper returns to its thesis when it notes how unexpectedly hard WikiHunt is.

Not exactly. What makes the Wikipedia game hard—and coincidentally, what makes it so much fun—is the vastness of the Web site's encyclopedic content. Click the "Random article" button enough times, and you'll see a pattern emerge: the majority of articles that pop up are short ones covering extremely obscure topics, usually having to do with something related to European club soccer. Entries such as these, labeled "orphans" for their relative paucity of length and links, in fact comprise the majority of Wikipedia articles. So the chances of you or your opponent hitting the randomly-generated-article jackpot and getting a "Jesus" or an "Adolf Hitler"—two pages with tons of links—are pretty slim. Rather, the task at hand usually requires that players navigate from orphan to orphan, as was the case in a game I played just last night with my friends David and Paige. They were unlucky enough to pull up an article on the summer village of Whispering Hills, Alberta, and I was no less unfortunate to get one on "blocking," an old 3D computer animation technique that makes characters and objects look like they're moving. Between these two pages, we were supplied with a total of nineteen links—they had nine doors to choose from, whereas I had ten. That's not a lot to work with. As you can probably surmise, games like this one take more than a few idle minutes—not to mention a heck of a lot of brainpower and spontaneous strategizing.

Indeed, what makes the Wikipedia game interesting is that it welcomes comparison between the players' respective strategies and methods for getting from point A to point B, highlighting differences between their thought processes and respective knowledge sets. To elaborate using the aforementioned example, I initially knew nothing about either Whispering Hills, Alberta, or "Blocking (animation)." What I did know, however, was that in order to get to Canada, I'd have to go through the good old U.S. of A. So I clicked a link at the bottom of the page entitled "Categories: animation techniques," and from there looked for a well-known technique that I knew to be associated with an American software company. Selecting "PowerPoint animation," I was led from there to the article on Microsoft—which, thanks to the company's late '90s monopolistic indiscretions, furnished me with a link to the U.S. Department of Justice. Five clicks later and I was in Alberta, looking for a passageway to Whispering Hills, one

Kamperman uses his own experience to show precisely how WikiHunt tracks users' processes of thought and "knowledge sets."

of the province's smallest, obscurest villages. I finally found it in a series of lists on communities in Alberta—but not before my opponents beat me to the punch and got to my page on "blocking" first. David, a computer science major, had taken a different approach to clinch the win; rather than drawing upon his knowledge of a macroscopic, big-picture subject like geography, he skipped from the article on Canada to a page entitled "Canadian industrial research and development organizations," from which he quickly bored through twelve articles on various topics in the computer sciences before falling on "Blocking (animation)." In his case, specialized knowledge was the key to winning.

But did David and Paige really win? Perhaps—but in the wide world of the Wikipedia game, there are few hard-and-fast rules to go by. Whereas my opponents got to their destination quicker than I, my carefully planned journey down the funnel from big ("United States") to small ("List of summer villages in Alberta") got me to Whispering Hills using two fewer links than they. So in this example, one sees not a clear-cut lesson on how to win the game, but rather a study in contrasting styles. A player can rely on specialized knowledge, linking quickly to familiar domains and narrowing the possibilities from there; or, she/he may choose to take a slower, more methodical approach, employing abstract, top-down reasoning skills to system-atically sift through broader categories of information. Ultimately, victory is possible in either case.

Its more casual, entertaining uses aside, Wikipedia gets a bad rap, especially in the classroom. Too many college professors and high school English teachers have simply written it off, some even going so far as to expressly forbid their students from using it while at school. These stances and attitudes are understandable. Teaching students how to find good sources and properly credit them is hard enough without the competing influence of the Wikipedia community, whose definition of an acceptably accurate source seems to extend not only to professionally or aca-demically vetted articles, but to blogs as well, some obvi-ously plagiarized. But to deny Wikipedia a place in the classroom is to deny both students and teachers alike the valuable experience of playing a game that shows us not only what we know, but how we know—how our brains work when posed with the everyday challenge of having to connect ostensibly unrelated pieces of information, and furthermore, how they work differently in that respect.

Knowledge building is a connective or associative process, as the minds behind Wikipedia well know. A casual perusal of any Wikipedia article reveals reams and reams of blue hypertext—bits of text that, when set in isolation, roughly correspond to discrete categories of information about the world. In a sense, the visual rhetoric of Wikipedia invokes the verbal rhetoric of exploration, prompting intrepid Web-using truth seekers to go sailing through a bright blue sea of information that is exciting by virtue of its seeming limitlessness. It should comfort teachers to know that, in quickly navigating through linked knowledge categories to reach their respective destinations, Wikipedia gamers aren't relying too much on their understanding of the articles themselves; rather, what they're relying on is their ability to understand relationships.

The fact that so many people have independently found the fun at the heart of Wikipedia should be a heads-up. The Wikipedia game is a grassroots technological innovation that sheds new light on what it means to know— and, perhaps more importantly, one that reminds us that, yes, learning can be fun. It isn't too hard to imagine versions of the game that could be played by kids in school, and how teachers could then use the game to learn more about the stuff of their trade—namely, learning and how it works. So the next time you hear a friend, teacher, or coworker dismiss the Free Encyclopedia as "unreliable" or "unacademic," do knowledge a favor and challenge them to the following:

"Villa of Livia" to "List of Montreal Expos broadcasters" . . .

. . . no click-backs . . .

. . . twenty links or less.

Go.

Acknowledging reservations about Wikipedia, the paper asserts that WikiHunt shows players "how we know."

Argues that WikiHunt is about learning relationships between ideas.

Defends Wikipedia as supporting a game that proves to be about "learning and how it works."

Why We Prize That Magical Mystery Pad

VIRGINIA POSTREL

When Apple introduced the iPad last year, it added a new buzzword to technology marketing. The device, it declared, was not just "revolutionary," a tech-hype cliché, but "magical." Skeptics rolled their eyes, and one Apple fan even started an online petition against such superstitious language.

But the company stuck with the term. When Steve Jobs appeared on stage last week to unveil the iPad 2, which hit stores Friday, he said, "People laughed at us for using the word 'magical,' but, you know what, it's turned out to be magical."

Apple has long had an aura of trend-setting cool, but magic is a bolder—and more provocative—claim. In a promotional video, Jonathan Ive, the company's design chief, explains it this way: "When something exceeds your ability to understand how it works, it sort of becomes magical, and that's exactly what the iPad is." Mr. Ive is paraphrasing the famous pronouncement by Arthur C. Clarke, the science-fiction author and futurist, that "any sufficiently advanced technology is indistinguishable from magic."

So in celebrating the iPad as magical, Apple is bragging that its customers haven't the foggiest idea how the machine works. The iPad is completely opaque. It is a sealed box. You can't see the circuitry or read the software code. You can't even change the battery.

The iPad represents the final repudiation of the original iMacs that in 1998 heralded Mr. Jobs's return to the company. With their translucent, jellybean-colored shells, those machines seemed friendly in part because consumers could see their insides. The iMacs' "translucence celebrates those inscrutable internal components that most of us think of as black magic," wrote the influential design theorists Katherine and Michael McCoy in a 1999 *Fast Company* article. Back then, the challenge was to make technological magic seem benign—white (or Bondi blue) rather than black.

Virginia Postrel, author of *The Future and Its Enemies* (1998) and *The Substance of Style* (2003), writes frequently about issues of design and culture. "Why We Prize That Magical Mystery Pad" was published in the *Wall Street Journal* on March 12, 2011.

A closed box offends geeks' tinkering impulse, which demands swappable components and visible source code. But most of us aren't looking to hack our own computers. In fact, the very characteristics that empower enthusiasts tend to frustrate and infantilize ordinary users, making them dependent on the occult knowledge of experts. The techies who so often dismiss Apple products as toys take understandable pride in their own knowledge. They go wrong in expecting everyone to share the same expertise.

Hence Mr. Ive's second boast about the iPad's magic: "I don't have to change myself to fit the product. It fits me." A capable machine makes you feel powerful even if you don't understand it and can't fix it. The perfect tool is invisible, an extension of the user's own will.

With its utterly opaque yet seemingly transparent design, the iPad affirms a little-recognized fact of the supposedly "disenchanted" modern world. We are surrounded by magic. Clarke's Law applies not just to technology from advanced alien civilizations but to the everyday components of our own. We live in a culture made rich by specialization, with enormous amounts of knowledge embedded in the most everyday of artifacts.

Even the "maker ethic" of do-it-yourself hobbyists depends on having the right ingredients and tools, from computers, lasers, and video cameras to plywood, snaps, and glue. Extraordinarily rare even among the most accomplished seamstresses, chefs, and carpenters are those who spin their own fibers, thresh their own wheat, or trim their own lumber—all once common skills. Rarer still is the Linux hacker who makes his own chips. Who among us can reproduce from scratch every component of a pencil or a pencil skirt? We don't notice their magic—or the wonder of electricity or eyeglasses, anesthesia or aspirin—only because we're used to them.

"Between a wish and its fulfillment there is, in magic, no gap," wrote the anthropologist Marcel Mauss in *A General Theory of Magic*. Effortlessly, instantly, the magical alters reality with a tap of the finger or wave of the hand. Sound familiar?

Unfortunately, that magic operates only in the world of bits, where metaphors rule. In the world of atoms, a new iPad won't materialize free.

11
Causal Arguments

Millions of bats in the United States are dying as a result of white-nose syndrome, a bacterial infection that has destroyed entire bat populations. Are spelunkers carrying contaminated equipment spreading it from cave to cave? Some scientists think that's a possibility.

Small business owners and big companies alike seem reluctant to hire new employees. Is it because of complex government regulations, uncertainties about health care costs, worries about debt, improvements in productivity—or all of the above? People needing jobs want to know.

Most state governments use high taxes to discourage the use of tobacco products. But when antismoking campaigns and graphic warning labels convince people to quit smoking, tax revenues decline, reducing support for health and education programs. Will raising taxes even higher restore that lost revenue?

Understanding Causal Arguments

The eye-catching title image of a *National Geographic* story poses a simple question: "Why Are We So Fat?" You can probably guess that simple questions like this rarely have simple answers. But in this case, the author, Cathy Newman, argues that there are no real surprises:

> [I]n one sense, the obesity crisis is the result of simple math. It's a calories in, calories out calculation. The First Law of Fat says that anything you eat beyond your immediate need for energy, from avocados to ziti, converts to fat. . . . The Second Law of Fat: The line between being in and out of energy balance is slight. Suppose you consume a mere 5 percent over a 2,000-calorie-a-day average. "That's just one hundred calories; it's a glass of apple juice," says Rudolph Leibel, head of molecular genetics at Columbia University College of Physicians and Surgeons. "But those few extra calories can mean a huge weight gain." Since one pound of body weight is roughly equivalent to 3,500 calories, that glass of juice adds up to an extra ten pounds over a year.
> —Cathy Newman, "Why Are We So Fat?"

And yet you know that there's more to it than that—as Newman's full story reveals. "Calories in, calories out" may explain the physics of weight gain. But why in recent years have we so drastically shifted the equation

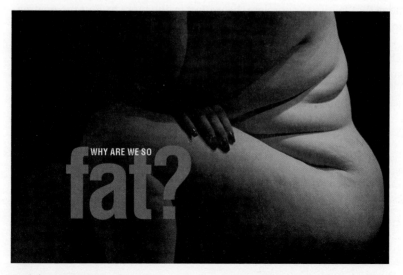

And the answer is . . . ?

from out to in? Because people instinctually crave fatty foods? Because we've grown addicted to giant portions? Because fast-food restaurants and junk-food corner stores are the only ones available in some neighborhoods? Because we walk less? Because we've become Internet or video game addicts? Whatever the reasons for our increased weight, the consequences can be measured by everything from the width of airliner seats to the rise of diabetes in the general population. Many explanations are offered by scientists, social critics, and health gurus, and some are refuted. Figuring out what's going on is a national concern—and an important exercise in cause-and-effect argument.

Causal arguments—from the causes of poverty in rural communities to the consequences of ocean pollution around the globe—are at the heart of many major policy decisions, both national and international. But arguments about causes and effects also inform many choices that people make every day. Suppose that you need to petition for a grade change because you were unable to turn in a final project on time. You'd probably enumerate the reasons for your failure—the death of your cat, followed by an attack of the hives, followed by a crash of your computer—hoping that an associate dean reading the petition might see these explanations as tragic enough to change your grade. In identifying the causes of the situation, you're implicitly arguing that the effect (your failure to submit the project on time) should be considered in a new light. Unfortunately, the administrator might accuse you of faulty causality (see p. 83) and judge that failure to complete the project is due more to your procrastination than to the reasons you offer.

Causal arguments exist in many forms and frequently appear as part of other arguments (such as evaluations or proposals). It may help focus your work on causal arguments to separate them into three major categories:

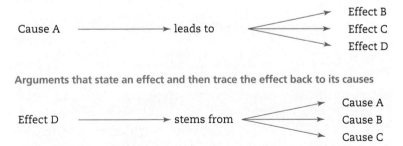

Arguments that state a cause and then examine its effects

Cause A   ⟶   leads to   ⟶ Effect B
  ⟶ Effect C
  ⟶ Effect D

Arguments that state an effect and then trace the effect back to its causes

Effect D   ⟶   stems from   ⟶ Cause A
  ⟶ Cause B
  ⟶ Cause C

Arguments that move through a series of links: A causes B, which leads to C and perhaps to D

Cause A →► leads to Cause B →► leads to Cause C →► leads to Effect D

ARGUMENTS THAT STATE A CAUSE AND THEN EXAMINE ITS EFFECTS

What would happen if immigration reform suddenly gave millions of people currently already in the United States a legal pathway to citizenship? The possible effects of this "cause" could be examined in detail and argued intensely. Groups on various sides of this hot-button issue would likely present very different scenarios. In this debate, you'd be successful if you could convincingly describe the consequences of this change. Alternatively, you could challenge the causal explanations made by people you don't agree with. But speculation about causes and effects is always risky because life is complicated.

Consider the opening of a May 2007 article from the *Christian Science Monitor* describing possible consequences of then-new U.S. government subsidies to increase the production of ethanol from corn:

> Policymakers and legislators often fail to consider the law of unintended consequences. The latest example is their attempt to reduce the United States' dependence on imported oil by shifting a big share of the nation's largest crop—corn—to the production of ethanol for fueling automobiles.
>
> Good goal, bad policy. In fact, ethanol will do little to reduce the large percentage of our fuel that is imported (more than 60 percent), and the ethanol policy will have ripple effects on other markets. Corn farmers and ethanol refiners are ecstatic about the ethanol boom and are enjoying the windfall of artificially enhanced demand. But it will be an expensive and dangerous experiment for the rest of us.
>
> —Colin A. Carter and Henry I. Miller, "Hidden Costs
> of Corn-Based Ethanol"

Note that the researchers here begin with a cause—raising the percentage of the corn crop used for ethanol—and then point to the potential effects of that policy change. As it turns out, using corn for fuel did have many unintended consequences, for example, inflating the price not only of corn but of wheat and soybeans as well, leading to food shortages around the globe and even food riots.

Paresh Nath, cartoonist for India's *National Herald*, personifies the causes for a world food crisis in this item from March 2011.

ARGUMENTS THAT STATE AN EFFECT AND THEN TRACE THE EFFECT BACK TO ITS CAUSES

This type of argument might begin with a specific effect (a catastrophic drop in sales of music CDs) and then trace it to its most likely causes (the introduction of MP3 technology, new modes of music distribution, a preference for single song purchases). Or you might examine the reasons that music executives offer for their industry's dip and decide whether their causal analyses pass muster.

Like other kinds of causal arguments, those tracing effects to a cause can have far-reaching significance. In 1962, for example, the scientist Rachel Carson seized the attention of millions with a famous causal argument about the effects that the overuse of chemical pesticides might have on the environment. Here's an excerpt from the beginning of her book-length study of this subject. Note how she begins with the effects before saying she'll go on to explore the causes:

[A] strange blight crept over the area and everything began to change. Some evil spell had settled on the community: mysterious maladies swept the flocks of chickens; the cattle and sheep sickened and died. Everywhere was a shadow of death. The farmers spoke of much illness among their families. . . . There had been several sudden and unexplained deaths, not only among adults but even among children, who would be stricken suddenly while at play and die within a few hours. The roadsides, once so attractive, were now lined with browned and withered vegetation as though swept by fire. These, too, were silent, deserted by all living things. Even the streams were now lifeless. Anglers no longer visited them, for all the fish had died.

In the gutters under the eaves and between the shingles of the roofs, a white granular powder still showed a few patches; some weeks before it had fallen like snow upon the roofs and lawns, the fields and streams. No witchcraft, no enemy action had silenced the rebirth of new life in this stricken world. The people had done it themselves. . . . What has silenced the voices of spring in countless towns in America? This book is an attempt to explain.

—Rachel Carson, *Silent Spring*

Today, one could easily write a causal argument of the first type about *Silent Spring* and the environmental movement that it spawned.

ARGUMENTS THAT MOVE THROUGH A SERIES OF LINKS: A CAUSES B, WHICH LEADS TO C AND PERHAPS TO D

In an environmental science class, for example, you might decide to argue that, despite reductions in acid rain, tightened national regulations regarding smokestack emissions from utility plants are still needed for the following reasons:

1. Emissions from utility plants in the Midwest still cause significant levels of acid rain in the eastern United States.
2. Acid rain threatens trees and other vegetation in eastern forests.
3. Powerful lobbyists have prevented midwestern states from passing strict laws to control emissions from these plants.
4. As a result, acid rain will destroy most eastern forests by 2020.

In this case, the first link is that emissions cause acid rain; the second, that acid rain causes destruction in eastern forests; and the third, that states have not acted to break the cause-and-effect relationship that is established by the first two points. These links set the scene for the fourth link, which ties the previous points together to argue from effect: unless X, then Y.

RESPOND•

The causes of some of the following events and phenomena are well-known and frequently discussed. But do you understand these causes well enough to spell them out to someone else? Working in a group, see how well (and in how much detail) you can explain each of the following events or phenomena. Which explanations are relatively clear, and which seem more open to debate?

earthquakes/tsunamis

popularity of Lady Gaga or *Jersey Shore*

Cold War

subprime mortgage crisis or GM bankruptcy

AIDS pandemic in Africa

popularity of the *Transformers* films

swelling caused by a bee sting

sharp rise in cases of autism or asthma

climate change

Characterizing Causal Arguments

Causal arguments tend to share several characteristics.

THEY ARE OFTEN PART OF OTHER ARGUMENTS.

Many stand-alone causal arguments address questions that are fundamental to our well-being: *Why are juvenile asthma and diabetes increasing so dramatically in the United States? What are the causes of the rise in cases of malaria in Africa, and what can we do to counter this rise? What will happen to Europe if its birthrate continues to decline?*

But causal analyses often work to support other arguments—especially proposals. For example, a proposal to limit the time that children spend playing video games might first draw on a causal analysis to establish that playing video games can have bad results—such as violent behavior, short attention spans, and decreased social skills. The causal analysis provides a rationale that motivates the proposal. In this way, causal analyses can be useful in establishing good reasons for arguments in general.

THEY ARE ALMOST ALWAYS COMPLEX.

The complexity of most causal relationships makes it difficult to establish causes and effects. For example, in 2011 researchers at Northwestern University reported a startling correlation: youths who participated in church activities were far more likely to grow into obese adults than their counterparts who were not engaged in religious activities. How does one even begin to explain such a peculiar and unexpected finding? Too many church socials? Unhealthy food at potluck meals? More regular social engagement? Perhaps.

Or consider the complexity of analyzing the causes of food poisoning when they strike large populations: in 2008, investigators spent months trying to discover whether tomatoes, cilantro, or jalapeño peppers were the cause of a nationwide outbreak of salmonella. More than seventeen states were affected. But despite such challenges, whenever it is possible to demonstrate convincing causal connections between X and Y, we gain important knowledge and powerful arguments. That's why, for example, great effort went into establishing an indisputable link between smoking and lung cancer. Once proven, decisive legal action could finally be taken to warn smokers.

THEY ARE OFTEN DEFINITION BASED.

One reason that causal arguments are complex is that they often depend on careful definitions. Recent figures from the U.S. Department of Education, for example, show that the number of high school dropouts is

"The rise in unemployment, however, which was somewhat offset by an expanding job market, was countered by an upturn in part-time dropouts, which, in turn, was diminished by seasonal factors, the anticipated summer slump, and, over-all, a small but perceptible rise in actual employment."

Causal arguments can also be confusing.

rising and that this rise has caused an increase in youth unemployment. But exactly how does the study define *dropout*? A closer look may suggest that some students (perhaps a lot) who drop out later "drop back in" and complete high school or that some who drop out become successful entrepreneurs or business owners. Further, how does the study define *employment*? Until you can provide definitions for all key terms in a causal claim, you should proceed cautiously with your argument.

THEY USUALLY YIELD PROBABLE RATHER THAN ABSOLUTE CONCLUSIONS.

Because causal relationships are almost always complex or subtle, they seldom can yield more than a high degree of probability. Consequently, they are almost always subject to criticism or open to charges of false causality. (We all know smokers who defy the odds to live long, cancer-free lives.) Scientists in particular are wary when making causal claims.

Even after an event, proving precisely what caused it can be hard. During the student riots of the late 1960s, for example, a commission was charged with determining the causes of riots on a particular campus. After two years of work and almost a thousand pages of evidence and reports, the commission was unable to pinpoint anything but a broad network of contributing causes and related conditions. And how many years is it likely to take to unravel all the factors responsible for the extended recession and economic decline in the United States that began in 2008? After all, serious scholars are still arguing about the forces responsible for the Great Depression of 1929.

To demonstrate that X caused Y, you must find the strongest possible evidence and subject it to the toughest scrutiny. But a causal argument doesn't fail just because you can't find a single compelling cause. In fact, causal arguments are often most effective when they help readers appreciate how tangled our lives and landscapes really are.

Developing Causal Arguments

Exploring Possible Claims

To begin creating a strong causal claim, try listing some of the effects—events or phenomena—that you'd like to know the causes of:

- Why do college tuition costs routinely outstrip the rate of inflation?

- Who's really responsible for rises and falls in gasoline prices?
- What has led to recent warnings of contamination along your favorite creek?
- Why has the divorce rate leveled off in recent decades?
- Why do so few younger Americans vote, even in major elections?

Or try moving in the opposite direction, listing some phenomena or causes you're interested in and then hypothesizing what kinds of effects they may produce:

- How will the growing popularity of e-readers change our relationships to books?
- What will happen to health care in the United States as a result of recent legislation?
- What will be the consequences if more liberal (or conservative) judges are appointed to the U.S. Supreme Court?
- What will happen as China and India become dominant industrialized nations?

Read a little about the causal issues that interest you most, and then try them out on friends and colleagues. They might suggest ways to refocus or clarify what you want to do or offer leads to finding information about your subject. After some initial research, map out the causal relationship you want to explore in simple form:

> **X might cause (or might be caused by) Y for the following reasons:**
>
> 1.
> 2.
> 3.

Such a statement should be tentative because writing a causal argument should be an exercise in which you uncover facts, not assume them to be true. Often, your early assumptions (*Tuition was raised to renovate the stadium*) might be undermined by the facts you later discover (*Tuition doesn't fund the construction or maintenance of campus buildings*).

You might even decide to write a wildly exaggerated or parodic causal argument for humorous purposes. Humorist Dave Barry does this when he explains the causes of El Niño and other weather phenomena: "So we see that the true cause of bad weather, contrary to what they have been claiming all these years, is TV weather forecasters, who have also single-handedly destroyed the ozone layer via overuse of hair spray." Most of the causal reasoning you do, however, will take a serious approach to subjects that you, your family, and your friends care about.

RESPOND ●

Working with a group, write a big *Why?* on a sheet of paper or computer screen, and then generate a list of *why* questions. Don't be too critical of the initial list:

Why?

—*do people laugh?*

—*do birds build nests?*

—*do college students binge drink?*

—*do teenagers drive fast?*

—*do babies cry?*

—*do politicians take risks on social media?*

Generate as lengthy a list as you can in fifteen minutes. Then decide which of the questions might make plausible starting points for intriguing causal arguments.

Defining the Causal Relationships

In developing a causal claim, you can examine the various types of causes and effects in play in a given argument and define their relationship. Begin by listing all the plausible causes or effects you need to consider. Then decide which are the most important for you to analyze or the easiest to defend or critique. The following chart on "Causes" may help you to appreciate some important terms and relationships.

Type of Causes	What It Is or Does	What It Looks Like
Sufficient cause	Enough for something to occur on its own	Lack of oxygen is sufficient to cause death Cheating on exam is sufficient to fail a course
Necessary cause	Required for something to occur (but in combination with other factors)	Fuel is necessary for fire Capital is necessary for economic growth

Type of Causes	What It Is or Does	What It Looks Like
Precipitating cause	Brings on a change	Protest march ignites a strike by workers Plane flies into strong thunderstorms
Proximate cause	Immediately present or visible cause of action	Strike causes company to declare bankruptcy Powerful wind shear causes plane to crash
Remote cause	Indirect or underlying explanation for action	Company was losing money on bad designs and inept manufacturing Wind shear warning failed to sound in cockpit
Reciprocal causes	One factor leads to a second, which reinforces the first, creating a cycle	Lack of good schools leads to poverty, which further weakens education, which leads to even fewer opportunities . . .

Even the most everyday causal analysis can draw on such distinctions among reasons and causes. What persuaded you, for instance, to choose the college you decided to attend? *Proximate* reasons might be the location of the school or the college's curriculum in your areas of interest. But what are the *necessary* reasons — the ones without which your choice of that college could not occur? Adequate financial support? Good test scores and academic record? The expectations of a parent?

Once you've identified a causal claim, you can draw out the reasons, warrants, and evidence that can support it most effectively:

Claim	Certain career patterns cause women to be paid less than men.
Reason	Women's career patterns differ from men's.
Warrant	Successful careers are made during the period between ages twenty-five and thirty-five.
Evidence	Women often drop out of or reduce work during the decade between ages twenty-five and thirty-five to raise families.

Claim	Lack of community and alumni support caused the football coach to lose his job.
Reason	Ticket sales and alumni support have declined for three seasons in a row despite a respectable team record.
Warrant	Winning over fans is as important as winning games for college coaches in smaller athletic programs.
Evidence	Over the last ten years, coaches at several programs have been sacked because of declining support and revenues.

RESPOND•

Here's a schematic causal analysis of one event, exploring the difference among precipitating, necessary, and sufficient causes. Critique and revise the analysis as you see fit. Then create another of your own, beginning with a different event, phenomenon, incident, fad, or effect.

> **Event:** Traffic fatality at an intersection
>
> **Precipitating cause:** A pickup truck that runs a red light, totals a Miata, and injures its driver
>
> **Necessary cause:** Two drivers who are navigating Friday rush-hour traffic (if no driving, then no accident)
>
> **Sufficient cause:** A truck driver who is distracted by a cell-phone conversation

Supporting Your Point

In drafting your causal argument, you'll want to do the following:

- Show that the causes and effects you've suggested are highly probable and backed by evidence, or show what's wrong with the faulty causal reasoning you may be critiquing.

- Assess any links between causal relationships (what leads to or follows from what).

- Show that your explanations of any causal chains are accurate, or identify where links in a causal chain break down.

- Show that plausible cause-and-effect explanations haven't been ignored or that the possibility of multiple causes or effects has been considered.

In other words, you will need to examine your subject carefully and find appropriate ways to support your claims. There are different ways to do that.

For example, in studying effects that are physical (as they would be with diseases or climate conditions), you can offer and test *hypotheses*, or theories about possible causes. That means researching such topics thoroughly because you'll need to draw upon authorities and research articles for your explanations and evidence. (See Chapter 16, "Academic Arguments," and Chapter 17, "Finding Evidence.") Don't be surprised if you find yourself debating which among conflicting authorities make the most plausible causal or explanatory arguments. Your achievement as a writer may be simply that you present these differences in an essay, leaving it to readers to make judgments of their own—as John Tierney does in "Can a Playground Be Too Safe?" at the end of this chapter (see p. 269).

But not all the evidence in compelling causal arguments needs to be strictly scientific or scholarly. Many causal arguments rely on **ethnographic observations**—the systematic study of ordinary people in their daily routines. How would you explain, for example, why some people step aside when they encounter someone head-on and others do not? In an argument that attempts to account for such behavior, investigators Frank Willis, Joseph Gier, and David Smith observed "1,038 displacements involving 3,141 persons" at a Kansas City shopping mall. In results that surprised the investigators, "gallantry" seemed to play a significant role in causing people to step aside for one another—more so than other causes that the investigators had anticipated (such as deferring to someone who's physically stronger or higher in status). Doubtless you've read of other such studies, perhaps in psychology courses. You may even decide to do a little fieldwork on your own—which raises the possibility of using personal experiences in support of a causal argument.

Indeed, people's experiences generally lead them to draw causal conclusions about things they know well. Personal experience can also help build your credibility as a writer, gain the empathy of listeners, and thus support a causal claim. Although one person's experiences cannot ordinarily be universalized, they can still argue eloquently for causal relationships. Listen to Sara Barbour, a recent graduate of Columbia University, as she draws upon her own carefully described experiences to bemoan what may happen when e-readers finally displace printed books:

> In eliminating a book's physical existence, something crucial is lost forever. Trapped in a Kindle, the story remains but the book can no longer be scribbled in, hoarded, burned, given, or received. We may be able to read it, but we can't share it with others in the same way, and its ability to connect us to people, places, and ideas is that much less powerful.
>
> I know the Kindle will eventually carry the day—an electronic reader means no more embarrassing coffee stains, no more library holds and renewals, no more frantic flipping through pages for a lost quote, or going to three bookstores in one afternoon to track down an evasive title. Who am I to advocate the doom of millions of trees when

the swipe of a finger can deliver all 838 pages of *Middlemarch* into my waiting hands?

But once we all power up our Kindles something will be gone, a kind of language. Books communicate with us as readers—but as important, we communicate with each other through books themselves. When that connection is lost, the experience of reading—and our lives—will be forever altered.

—Sara Barbour, "Kindle vs. Books: The Dead Trees Society,"
Los Angeles Times, June 17, 2011

All these strategies—testing hypotheses, presenting experimental evidence, and offering personal experience—can help you support a causal argument or undermine a causal claim you regard as faulty.

RESPOND●

One of the fallacies of argument discussed in Chapter 5 is the *post hoc, ergo propter hoc* ("after this, therefore because of this") fallacy. Causal arguments are particularly prone to this kind of fallacious reasoning, in which a writer asserts a causal relationship between two entirely unconnected events. When Angelina Jolie gave birth to twins in 2008, for instance, the stock market rallied by nearly six hundred points, but it would be difficult to argue that either event is related to the other.

Because causal arguments can easily fall prey to this fallacy, you might find it instructive to create and defend an absurd connection of this kind. Begin by asserting a causal link between two events or phenomena that likely have no relationship: *The enormous popularity of* Jersey Shore *is partially due to global warming.* Then spend a page or so spinning out an imaginative argument to defend the claim. It's OK to have fun with this exercise, but see how convincing you can be at generating plausibly implausible arguments.

Considering Design and Visuals

You may find that the best way to illustrate a causal relationship is to present it visually. Even a simple bar graph or chart can demonstrate a relationship between two variables that might be related to a specific cause, like the one on the facing page showing the dramatic effects of lowered birthrates. The report that uses this figure explores the effects that such a change would have on the economies of the world.

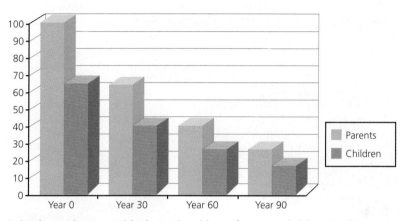

The comparative size of successive generations across time when fertility is constant at 1.3 births per woman

A simple graph can provide dramatic evidence for a causal claim—in this case, the effect of reduced fertility rates on a population.

Or you may decide that the most dramatic way to present important causal information about a single issue or problem is via an infographic, cartoon, or public service announcement. Our arresting example on page 258 is part of a campaign by People for the Ethical Treatment of Animals (PETA). An organization that advocates for animal rights, PETA promotes campaigns that typically try to sway people to adopt vegetarian diets by depicting the practices of the agriculture industry as cruel (many of us have also seen their celebrity antifur campaigns). Their "Meat's Not Green!" campaign, however, attempts to reach an audience that might not buy into the animal rights argument. Instead, it appeals to people who have environmentalist beliefs by presenting data that claims a causal link between animal farming and environmental destruction. How much of this data surprises you?

PETA's ad campaign expands its focus to environmentalists by explaining through causal links why they should consider vegetarian diets.

GUIDE | to writing a causal argument

● Finding a Topic

You're entering a causal argument when you:

- state a cause and then examine its effects: *The ongoing economic downturn has led more people to return to college to enhance their job market credentials.*

- describe an effect and trace it back to its causes: *There has been a recent surge in the hiring of contract workers, likely due to the reluctance of businesses to hire permanent employees who would be subject to new health care regulations.*

- trace a string of causes to figure out why something happened: *The housing and financial markets collapsed in 2008 after government mandates to encourage homeownership led banks to invent questionable financial schemes in order to offer subprime mortgages to borrowers who bought homes they could not afford with loans they could not pay back.*

- explore plausible consequences (intended or not) of a particular action, policy, or change: *The recent ban on incandescent lightbulbs may draw more attention to climate change than any previous government action.*

Spend time brainstorming possibilities for causal arguments. Many public issues lend themselves to causal analysis and argument: browse the homepage of a newspaper or news source on any given day to discover plausible topics. Consider topics that grow from your own experiences.

It's fair game, too, to question the accuracy or adequacy of existing arguments about causality. You can write a strong paper by raising doubts about the facts or assumptions that others have made and perhaps offering a better causal explanation on your own.

● Researching Your Topic

Causal arguments will lead you to many different resources:

- current news media—especially magazines and newspapers (online or in print)

- online databases

- scholarly journals

- books written on your subject (here you can do a keyword search, either in your library or online)

- blogs, Web sites, or social networking sites

In addition, why not carry out some field research? Conduct interviews with appropriate authorities on your subject, create a questionnaire aimed at establishing a range of opinion on your subject, or arrange a discussion forum among people with a stake in the issue. The information you get from interviews, questionnaires, or open-ended dialogue might provide ideas to enrich your argument or evidence to back up your claims.

● Formulating a Claim

For a conventional causal analysis, try to formulate a claim that lets readers know where you stand on some issue involving causes and effects. First, identify the kind of causal argument that you expect to make (see pp. 243–47 for a review of these kinds of arguments) or decide whether you intend, instead, to debunk an existing cause-and-effect claim. Then explore your relationship to the claim. What do you know about the subject and its causes and effects? Why do you favor (or disagree with) the claim? What significant reasons can you offer in support of your position?

End this process by formulating a thesis—a complete sentence that says, in effect, A *causes (or does not cause or is caused by)* B, followed by a summary of the reasons supporting this causal relationship. Make your thesis as specific as possible and be sure that it's sufficiently controversial or interesting to hold a reader's interest. Of course, feel free to revise any such claim as you learn more about a subject.

For causal topics that are more open-ended and exploratory, you may not want to take a strong position, particularly at the outset. Instead, your argument might simply present a variety of reasonable (and possibly competing) explanations and scenarios.

● Examples of Causal Claims

- Right-to-carry gun laws are, in part, responsible for decreased rates of crime in states that have approved such legislation.

- Sophisticated use of social media is now a must for any political candidate who hopes to win.

- The proliferation of images in film, television, and computer-generated texts is changing the way we read and use information.

- Grade inflation is lowering the value of a college education.

- Experts don't yet agree on the long-term impact that sophisticated use of social media will have on American political campaigns, though some effects are already evident.

● Preparing a Proposal

If your instructor asks you to prepare a proposal for your project, here's a format that may help:

State your thesis or hypothesis completely. If you are having trouble doing so, try outlining it in Toulmin terms:

Claim:

Reason(s):

Warrant(s):

Alternatively, you might indicate an intention to explore a particular causal question in your project, with the thesis perhaps coming later.

- Explain why this issue deserves attention. What's at stake?
- Identify whom you hope to reach through your argument and why this group of readers would be interested in it.
- Briefly discuss the key challenges you anticipate in preparing your argument.
- Determine what research strategies you'll use. What sources do you expect to consult?
- Briefly identify and explore the major stakeholders in your argument and what alternative perspectives you may need to consider as you formulate your argument.
- Describe the format you expect to use: Conventional research essay? Letter to the editor? Web page? Press release? Op-ed for the local paper?

● Thinking about Organization

Your causal argument will likely include elements such as the following:

- a specific causal claim somewhere in the paper—or the identification of a significant causal issue
- an explanation of the claim's significance or importance
- evidence sufficient to support each cause or effect—or, in an argument based on a series of causal links, evidence to support the relationships among the links
- a consideration of other plausible causes and effects, and evidence that you have thought carefully about these alternatives before offering your own ideas

● Getting and Giving Response: Questions for Peer Response

Your instructor may assign you to a group for the purpose of reading and responding to each other's drafts. If not, ask for responses from serious readers or consultants at a writing center. Use the following questions to evaluate a colleague's draft. Be sure to illustrate your comments with examples; specific comments help more than general observations.

The Claim

- Does the claim state a causal argument?
- Does the claim identify clearly what causes and effects are being examined?
- What about the claim will make it appeal to readers?
- Is the claim too sweeping? Does it need to be qualified? How might it be narrowed and focused?
- How strong is the relationship between the claim and the reasons given to support it? How could that relationship be made more explicit?

Evidence for the Claim

- What's the strongest evidence offered for the claim? What, if any, evidence needs to be strengthened?
- Is enough evidence offered to show that these causes are responsible for the identified effect, that these effects result from the identified cause, or that a series of causes and effects are linked? If not, what additional evidence is needed? What kinds of sources might provide this evidence?
- How credible will the sources be to potential readers? What other sources might be more persuasive?
- Is evidence in support of the claim analyzed logically? Is more discussion needed?
- Have alternative causes and effects been considered? Have objections to the claim been carefully considered and presented fairly? Have these objections been discussed?

Organization and Style

- How are the parts of the argument organized? Is this organization effective?
- Will readers understand the relationships among the claims, supporting reasons, warrants, and evidence? If not, how might those connections be clearer? Is the function of every visual clear? Are more transitions needed? Would headings or graphic devices help?

- Are the transitions or links from point to point, sentence to sentence, and paragraph to paragraph clear and effective? If not, how could they be improved?

- Are all visuals carefully integrated into the text? Is each visual introduced and commented on to point out its significance? Is each visual labeled as a figure or a table and given a caption as well as a citation?

- Is the style suited to the subject? Is it too formal, casual, or technical? Can it be improved?

- Which sentences seem effective? Which ones seem weaker, and how could they be improved? Should short sentences be combined, and any longer ones be broken up?

- How effective are the paragraphs? Too short or too long? How can they be improved?

- Which words or phrases seem effective? Do any seem vague or inappropriate for the audience or the writer's purpose? Are technical or unfamiliar terms defined?

Spelling, Punctuation, Mechanics, Documentation, and Format

- Are there any errors in spelling, punctuation, capitalization, and the like?

- Is the documentation appropriate and consistent? (See Chapter 21.)

- Does the paper or project follow an appropriate format? Is it appropriately designed and attractively presented?

PROJECTS •

1. Develop an argument exploring one of the cause-and-effect topics mentioned in this chapter. Just a few of those topics are listed below:

    Declining population of bats in the United States

    Causes of long-term unemployment or declining job markets

    Using the tax code to discourage/encourage specific behaviors (i.e., smoking, eating unhealthy foods, hiring more workers)

    Increasing numbers of obese children and/or adults

    Ramifications of ocean pollution

    Aftermaths of immigration reform

    Repercussions of U.S. ethanol policy

    Effects of declining solar activity

2. Write a causal argument about a subject you know well, even if the topic does not strike you as particularly "academic": *What accounts for the popularity of* The Hunger Games *trilogy? What are the likely consequences of students living more of their lives via social media? How are video games changing the way students you know learn? Why do women love shoes?* In this argument, be sure to separate precipitating or proximate causes from sufficient or necessary ones. In other words, do a deep and revealing causal analysis about your subject, giving readers new insights.

3. John Tierney's essay "Can a Playground Be Too Safe?" (see p. 269) explores some unintended consequences of noble-minded efforts in recent decades to make children's playgrounds safer. After reading the Tierney piece, list any comparable situations you know of where unintended consequences may have undermined the good (or maybe even bad?) intentions of those who took action or implemented some change. Choose the most intriguing situation, do the necessary research, and write a causal argument about it.

4. Lia Hardin's "Cultural Stress Linked to Suicide" on the facing page describes a variety of causal relationships focused on Asian American women in academic environments. Although the newspaper report doesn't make an explicit argument, its implicit message is that specific actions could be taken to lessen the stress the women feel and improve their mental health. In a project of your own, describe a causal situation at your own school, in your community, or at a place of work that is raising issues, problems, or maybe even opportunities that might be addressed. Like Hardin's, your paper need not be overtly persuasive: instead, use it to invite readers to consider a range of plausible causal explanations and relationships.

Cultural Stress Linked to Suicide

LIA HARDIN

May 31, 2007

Asian American women demonstrate a high rate of suicide when compared with women of other ethnicities, California State–Fullerton researcher Eliza Noh found in a recent empirical study.

> The causal claim is introduced: several factors lead to mental health problems. Credentials of researchers are established.

Noh and Stanford mental health professionals Alejandro Martinez, the director of Counseling and Psychological Services (CAPS), and Rona Hu, director of the Acute Inpatient Unit at Stanford Hospital, told *The Daily* that parental pressure, cultural differences between the United States and Asian countries, and avoidance of mental health issues in Asian American families can contribute to the prevalence of mental health problems.

> Examples of deaths attributed to the identified factors are given.

Following the death of graduate student Mengyao "May" Zhou earlier this year and the recent revelation that Azia Kim had been squatting in Stanford dorms for eight months despite the fact that she was not a student, suicide and mental health issues in the Asian American community have become widely discussed on the Stanford campus.

Citing the ongoing study, Noh said that the tendency of Asian American women to ignore or deny stress, depression, and other mental health problems can cause the larger anxieties that lead to suicide.

Lia Hardin wrote this article as a staff writer for her campus newspaper, the *Stanford Daily*. In it, she explores the factors that contribute to the relatively high rate of suicide among Asian American women. Because she is writing for a newspaper, Hardin does not provide any formal documentation of her sources but simply identifies the three authorities who supplied most of her information.

Expert testimony in support of claim is introduced.

"There are multiple factors that contribute to suicidality," Noh said. "[For Asian American women] there is this pressure to do well in school and that pressure comes from their family members. There is a miscommunication or a lack of communication with their parents. There is a cultural division between them and their parents."

"They are expected to listen to their parents," she said, "to do well in school, not to ask questions and not to talk back."

All those cultural pressures can lead Asian American women to treat mental health issues like an elephant in the room, exacerbating existing problems and generating others.

A second expert researcher is cited.

Hu argued that, for many Asian American women, culturally related issues can contribute directly to mental health problems. She cited young women she knew who had been disowned by their families because of circumstances that parents interpreted as failures.

"The whole concept in the Asian family is that the family is not a democracy," Hu said. "Parents feel entitled to make decisions for their children, including what major or career to choose, or whom to marry. There's a line from a movie where they say, 'There's no word for *privacy* in Chinese.'"

"The sense of shame can be a big part of Asian American culture and that's something that Americans don't understand so much," she added. "If Hugh Grant is caught doing something [shameful,] he apologizes and goes on with his movie career. In Asia, shame can endure for generations. The default Asian coping mechanism is denial."

A third researcher is cited.

Martinez added that differences between education systems in America and Asian countries can lead to misunderstandings within families.

"Specifically in some Asian countries, people have to make career decisions almost when they get to high school," Martinez said. Coming from such a background, parents often misinterpret their children's decision to explore different fields in college.

"If someone did that in their country of origin, it would be a dramatic setback," he said. "They may not be familiar with how much flexibility is possible in the United States."

Martinez cited Korea's suicide rate, which is far higher than the United States.

"The consequences of someone getting a 'B' in a class at Stanford really aren't that great in the context of career decisions and career opportunities," he said. "In other cultures they can be significant."

Noh said that open discussion of mental health issues in the community, along with the availability of resources that can cater specifically to Asian Americans, can be used to counter the problem.

"There has to be some serious commitment on the part of the community," Noh said. "[Resources] need to be appropriate for Asian American students. Counselors should be trained in the languages that they speak and have some level of cultural awareness of [students'] backgrounds."

Without those specially tailored resources, she said, Asian American women in her study often chose to reject counseling and therapy altogether.

"The big fear was that they didn't want to go to strangers who didn't know about their situation," she said. "Asian Americans have the lowest rates of utilization of mental health services. There is something about traditional mental health services that doesn't appeal to Asian Americans."

Hu and Martinez said that Stanford has resources for Asian Americans available at campus mental health facilities.

"We address this in two ways," Martinez said. "An important one is to have diversity on our staff. In

Ways to address the problem are introduced.

Campus resources for addressing the problem are reviewed.

addition to that, we do commit some of our resources to making sure that all of our staff have sensitivity to the communities that make up Stanford students."

Hu said that at the Stanford Hospital, some of the attending physicians and residents in psychiatry are Asian and that staff members fluent in Mandarin are available.

Hu and Noh both said that in addition to providing ethnicity-specific resources, fostering discussion of suicide and mental health is important because avoidance of the issue is pervasive in the Asian American community.

"Helping to de-stigmatize things is very helpful," Hu said. "I don't see people disowned so frequently in other cultures."

"The number one factor that [study participants] felt in terms of contributing to suicide is that they felt alone and helpless and that they didn't have any place to turn," Noh said. "I've received lots of emails of thanks . . . from people happy that there is dialogue taking place."

A final contributing factor to suicide: feeling alone and helpless.

Can a Playground Be Too Safe?

JOHN TIERNEY

A childhood relic: jungle gyms, like this one in Riverside Park in Manhattan, have disappeared from most American playgrounds in recent decades.

When seesaws and tall slides and other perils were disappearing from New York's playgrounds, Henry Stern drew a line in the sandbox. As the city's parks commissioner in the 1990s, he issued an edict concerning the ten-foot-high jungle gym near his childhood home in northern Manhattan.

"I grew up on the monkey bars in Fort Tryon Park, and I never forgot how good it felt to get to the top of them," Mr. Stern said. "I didn't want to see that playground bowdlerized. I said that as long as I was parks commissioner, those monkey bars were going to stay."

His philosophy seemed reactionary at the time, but today it's shared by some researchers who question the value of safety-first playgrounds. Even if children do suffer fewer physical injuries — and the evidence for

John Tierney is a journalist and coauthor of the book *Willpower: Rediscovering the Greatest Human Strength* (2011). He writes the science column "Findings" for the *New York Times*, where this piece was originally published on July 18, 2011.

that is debatable—the critics say that these playgrounds may stunt emotional development, leaving children with anxieties and fears that are ultimately worse than a broken bone.

"Children need to encounter risks and overcome fears on the playground," said Ellen Sandseter, a professor of psychology at Queen Maud University in Norway. "I think monkey bars and tall slides are great. As playgrounds become more and more boring, these are some of the few features that still can give children thrilling experiences with heights and high speed."

After observing children on playgrounds in Norway, England, and Australia, Dr. Sandseter identified six categories of risky play: exploring heights, experiencing high speed, handling dangerous tools, being near dangerous elements (like water or fire), rough-and-tumble play (like wrestling), and wandering alone away from adult supervision. The most common is climbing heights.

"Climbing equipment needs to be high enough, or else it will be too boring in the long run," Dr. Sandseter said. "Children approach thrills and risks in a progressive manner, and very few children would try to climb to the highest point for the first time they climb. The best thing is to let children encounter these challenges from an early age, and they will then progressively learn to master them through their play over the years."

Sometimes, of course, their mastery fails, and falls are the common form of playground injury. But these rarely cause permanent damage, either physically or emotionally. While some psychologists—and many parents—have worried that a child who suffered a bad fall would develop a fear of heights, studies have shown the opposite pattern: A child who's hurt in a fall before the age of nine is less likely as a teenager to have a fear of heights.

By gradually exposing themselves to more and more dangers on the playground, children are using the same habituation techniques developed by therapists to help adults conquer phobias, according to Dr. Sandseter and a fellow psychologist, Leif Kennair, of the Norwegian University for Science and Technology.

"Risky play mirrors effective cognitive behavioral therapy of anxiety," they write in the journal *Evolutionary Psychology*, concluding that this "anti-phobic effect" helps explain the evolution of children's fondness for thrill-seeking. While a youthful zest for exploring heights might not seem adaptive—why would natural selection favor children who risk death before they have a chance to reproduce?—the dangers seemed to be out-weighed by the benefits of conquering fear and developing a sense of mastery.

"Paradoxically," the psychologists write, "we posit that our fear of children being harmed by mostly harmless injuries may result in more fearful children and increased levels of psychopathology."

The old tall jungle gyms and slides disappeared from most American playgrounds across the country in recent decades because of parental concerns, federal guidelines, new safety standards set by manufacturers and—the most frequently cited factor—fear of lawsuits.

Shorter equipment with enclosed platforms was introduced, and the old pavement was replaced with rubber, wood chips, or other materials designed for softer landings. These innovations undoubtedly prevented some injuries, but some experts question their overall value.

"There is no clear evidence that playground safety measures have lowered the average risk on playgrounds," said David Ball, a professor of risk management at Middlesex University in London. He noted that the risk of some injuries, like long fractures of the arm, actually increased after the introduction of softer surfaces on playgrounds in Britain and Australia.

"This sounds counterintuitive, but it shouldn't, because it is a common phenomenon," Dr. Ball said. "If children and parents believe they are in an environment which is safer than it actually is, they will take more risks. An argument against softer surfacing is that children think it is safe, but because they don't understand its properties, they overrate its performance."

Reducing the height of playground equipment may help toddlers, but it can produce unintended consequences among bigger children. "Older children are discouraged from taking healthy exercise on playgrounds because they have been designed with the safety of the very young in mind," Dr. Ball said. "Therefore, they may play in more dangerous places, or not at all."

Fear of litigation led New York City officials to remove seesaws, merry-go-rounds, and the ropes that young Tarzans used to swing from one platform to another. Letting children swing on tires became taboo because of fears that the heavy swings could bang into a child.

"What happens in America is defined by tort lawyers, and unfortunately that limits some of the adventure playgrounds," said Adrian Benepe, the current parks commissioner. But while he misses the Tarzan ropes, he's glad that the litigation rate has declined, and he's not nostalgic for asphalt pavement.

"I think safety surfaces are a godsend," he said. "I suspect that parents who have to deal with concussions and broken arms wouldn't agree that playgrounds have become too safe." The ultra-safe enclosed platforms of the 1980s and 1990s may have been an overreaction, Mr. Benepe said, but lately there have been more creative alternatives.

"The good news is that manufacturers have brought out new versions of the old toys," he said. "Because of height limitations, no one's building the old monkey bars anymore, but kids can go up smaller climbing walls and rope nets and artificial rocks."

Still, sometimes there's nothing quite like being ten feet off the ground, as a new generation was discovering the other afternoon at Fort Tryon Park. A soft rubber surface carpeted the pavement, but the jungle gym of Mr. Stern's youth was still there. It was the prime destination for many children, including those who'd never seen one before, like Nayelis Serrano, a ten-year-old from the South Bronx who was visiting her cousin.

When she got halfway up, at the third level of bars, she paused, as if that was high enough. Then, after a consultation with her mother, she continued to the top, the fifth level, and descended to recount her triumph.

"I was scared at first," she explained. "But my mother said if you don't try, you'll never know if you could do it. So I took a chance and kept going. At the top I felt very proud." As she headed back for another climb, her mother, Orkidia Rojas, looked on from a bench and considered the pros and cons of this unfamiliar equipment.

"It's fun," she said. "I'd like to see it in our playground. Why not? It's kind of dangerous, I know, but if you just think about danger you're never going to get ahead in life."

12
Proposals

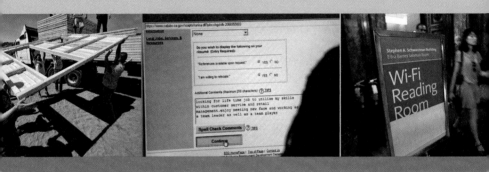

A student looking forward to spring break proposes to two friends that they join a group that will spend the vacation helping to build a school in a Guatemalan village.

The members of a club for undergrad business majors talk about their common need to create informative, appealing résumés. After much talk, three members suggest that the club develop a résumé app especially for business majors looking for a first job.

A project team at a large architectural firm works for three months developing a response to an RFP (request for proposal) to convert a university library into a digital learning center.

Understanding and Categorizing Proposals

We live in an era of big proposals—complex programs for health care reform, bold dreams to privatize space exploration, multibillion-dollar designs for high-speed rail systems, ceaseless calls to reform education, and so many other such ideas brought down to earth by sobering proposals for budget reform and deficit reduction. As a result, there's often more talk than action because persuading people (or legislatures) to do something—or *anything!*—is always hard. But that's what *proposal arguments* do: they provide thoughtful reasons for supporting or sometimes resisting change.

Such arguments, whether national or local, formal or casual, are important in all of our lives. How many proposals do you make or respond to in one day? A neighbor might suggest that the two of you volunteer to clean up an urban creek bed; a campus group might demand that students get better seats at football games; a supervisor might ask for ideas to improve customer satisfaction at a restaurant; you might offer an ad agency reasons to hire you as a summer intern. In each case, the proposal implies that some action should take place and suggests that there are sound reasons why it should.

Cartoonist Dave Granlund illustrates objections to President Obama's high-speed rail proposal.

In their simplest form, proposal arguments look something like this:

A should do B because of C.

```
  ┌───── A ─────┐┌───────── B ─────────┐
```
Our student government should endorse the Academic Bill of Rights

```
  ┌────────────── C ──────────────┐
```
because students should not be punished in their courses for their personal political views.

Proposals come at us so routinely that it's not surprising that they cover a dizzyingly wide range of possibilities. So it may help to think of proposal arguments as divided roughly into two kinds—those that focus on specific practices and those that focus on broad matters of policy. Here are several examples:

Proposals about Practices

- The college should allow students to pay tuition on a month-by-month basis.
- Hotels should once again wash sheets in hot water to curb bedbug infestations.
- The NCAA should not implement a playoff system to determine its Division I football champion.

Proposals about Policies

- The college should adopt a policy guaranteeing that students in all majors can graduate in four years.
- The United Nations should make saving the oceans from pollution a global priority.
- The U.S. Congress needs to apply the same fiscal restraints on its spending that state legislatures do.

RESPOND•

People write proposal arguments to solve problems and to change the way things are. But problems aren't always obvious: what troubles some people might be no big deal to others. To get an idea of the range of problems people face on your campus (some of which you may not even have thought of as problems), divide into groups, and brainstorm about things that annoy you on and around campus, including wastefulness in the cafeterias, 8:00 a.m. classes, and long lines for football or concert tickets. Ask each group to aim for at least a dozen gripes. Then choose three problems, and as a group, discuss how you'd prepare a proposal to deal with them.

Characterizing Proposals

Proposals have three main characteristics:

- They call for change, often in response to a problem.
- They focus on the future.
- They center on the audience.

Proposals always call for some kind of action. They aim at getting something done—or sometimes at *preventing* something from being done. Proposals marshal evidence and arguments to persuade people to choose a course of action: *Let's build a completely green house. Let's oppose the latest Supreme Court ruling on Internet privacy. Let's create a campus organization for first-generation college students. Let's resist the proposal for yet another campus outreach program.* But you know the old saying, "You can lead a horse to water, but you can't make it drink." It's usually easier to *convince* audiences what a good course of action is than to *persuade* them to take it (or pay for it). Even if you present a cogent proposal, you may still have work to do.

Proposal arguments must appeal to more than good sense. Ethos matters, too. It helps if a writer suggesting a change carries a certain gravitas earned by experience or supported by knowledge and research. If your word and credentials carry weight, then an audience is more likely to listen to your proposal. So when the commanders of three Apollo moon missions, Neil Armstrong, James Lovell, and Eugene Cernan, wrote an open letter to President Obama expressing their dismay at his administration's decision to cancel NASA's plans for advanced spacecraft and new lunar missions, they won a wide audience:

> For The United States, the leading space faring nation for nearly half a century, to be without carriage to low Earth orbit and with no human exploration capability to go beyond Earth orbit for an indeterminate time into the future, destines our nation to become one of second or even third rate stature. While the President's plan envisages humans traveling away from Earth and perhaps toward Mars at some time in

the future, the lack of developed rockets and spacecraft will assure that ability will not be available for many years.

Without the skill and experience that actual spacecraft operation provides, the USA is far too likely to be on a long downhill slide to mediocrity. America must decide if it wishes to remain a leader in space. If it does, we should institute a program which will give us the very best chance of achieving that goal.

But even their considerable ethos was not enough to carry the day with the space agency and the man who made the decision.

Yet, as the space program example obviously demonstrates, proposal arguments focus on the future—what people, institutions, or governments should do over the upcoming weeks, months, or, in the NASA moon-mission example, decades. This orientation toward the future presents special challenges, since few of us have crystal balls. Proposal arguments must therefore offer the best evidence available to suggest that actions we recommend will achieve what they promise.

In April 2011, for example, Republican Congressman Paul Ryan, serving as Chair of the House Budget Committee, offered a federal budget plan designed to significantly reduce government spending over the next decade. The title of the seventy-three-page document, "The Path to Prosperity: Restoring America's Plan," emphasized its overtly political mission—to outline a detailed alternative to the spending priorities of

All that remains of the American space program?

Wisconsin Representative Paul Ryan presents "The Path to Prosperity."

the Obama administration. Available online, along with a summary, comparison chart, and response to critics, what quickly became known as the Ryan Plan turned into a political football, embraced by the Republican-dominated House of Representatives and members of the Tea Party, but rejected by the president, many interest groups, and a wide swath of the media. Still, the Ryan Plan did accomplish one implicit goal of many proposal arguments: to put an issue squarely on the table by making specific recommendations. It got people talking and, occasionally, even thinking.

Which raises the matter of audiences. Some proposals are tailored to general audiences; consequently, they avoid technical language, make straightforward and relatively simple points, and sometimes use charts, graphs, and tables to make data comprehensible. You can find such arguments, for example, in newspaper editorials, letters to the editor, and political documents like the Ryan Plan. And such appeals to a broad group make sense when a proposal—say, to finance new toll roads or build an art museum—must surf on waves of community support and financing.

But often proposals need to win the approval of specific groups or individuals (such as financiers, developers, public officials, and legislators) who have the power to make change actually happen. Such arguments will usually be more technical, detailed, and comprehensive than those aimed at the general public because people directly involved with an issue have a stake in it. They may be affected by it themselves and

Proposals have to take audience values into account. Shooting deer, even when they're munching on garden flowers, is unacceptable to most suburbanites.

thus have in-depth knowledge of the subject. Or they may be responsible for implementing the proposal. You can expect them to have specific questions about it and, possibly, formidable objections. So identifying your potential audiences is critical to the success of any proposal. On your own campus, for example, a plan to alter admissions policies might be directed both to students in general and (perhaps in a different form) to the university president, members of the faculty council, and admissions officers.

An effective proposal also has to be compatible with the values of the audience. Some ideas may make good sense but cannot be enacted. For example, many American towns and cities have a problem with expanding deer populations. Without natural predators, the deer are moving closer to homes, dining on gardens and shrubbery, and endangering traffic. Yet one obvious and feasible solution—culling the herds through hunting—is usually not saleable to communities (perhaps too many people remember *Bambi*).

RESPOND•

Work in a group to identify about half a dozen problems on your campus or in the local community, looking for a wide range of issues. (Don't focus on problems in individual classes.) Once you have settled on these issues, then use various resources—the Web, the phone book (if you can find one), a campus directory—to locate specific people, groups, or offices whom you might address or influence to deal with the issues you have identified.

Developing Proposals

In developing a proposal, you will have to do some or all of the following:

- Define a problem that needs a solution or describe a need that is not currently addressed.
- Make a strong claim that addresses the problem or need. Your solution should be an action directed at the future.
- Show why your proposal will fix the problem or address the need.
- Demonstrate that your proposal is feasible.

This might sound easy, but writing a proposal argument can be a process of discovery. At the outset, you think you know exactly what ought to be done, but by the end, you may see (and even recommend) other options.

Defining a Need or Problem

To make a proposal, first establish that a need or problem exists. You'll typically dramatize the problem that you intend to fix at the beginning of your project and then lead up to a specific claim. But in some cases, you could put the need or problem right after your claim as the major reason for adopting the proposal:

> Let's ban cell phones on campus now. Why? Because we've become a school of walking zombies. No one speaks to or even acknowledges the people they meet or pass on campus. Half of our students are so busy chattering to people that they don't participate in the community around them.

How can you make readers care about the problem you hope to address? Following are some strategies:

- Paint a vivid picture of the need or problem.
- Show how the need or problem affects people, both those in the immediate audience and the general public as well.
- Underscore why the need or problem is significant and pressing.
- Explain why previous attempts to address the issue may have failed.

For example, in proposing that the military draft be restored in the United States or that all young men and women give two years to national service (a tough sell!), you might begin by drawing a picture of a younger generation that is self-absorbed, demands instant gratification, and doesn't understand what it means to participate as a full member of society. Or you might note how many young people today fail to develop the life skills they need to strike out on their own. Or like Congressional Representative Charles Rangel (D–New York), who regularly proposes a Universal National Service Act, you could define the issue as a matter of fairness, arguing that the current all-volunteer army shifts the burden of national service to a small and unrepresentative sample of the American population:

> The test for Congress . . . is to require all who enjoy the benefits of our democracy to contribute to the defense of the country. . . . The largest segment of our fighting force comes from large urban centers with high unemployment, and from economically depressed small towns. This small portion of the population forces many soldiers to take multiple tours of duty, sometimes as many as six deployments. . . . We make decisions about war without worry over who fights them. Those who do the fighting have no choice; when the flag goes up, they salute and follow orders.
>
> —Office of Charles B. Rangel, "Press Release: Rangel Introduces Universal National Service Act," March 17, 2011

Of course, you would want to cite authorities and statistics to prove that any problem you're diagnosing is real and that it touches your likely audience. Then readers *may* be ready to hear your proposal.

File this cartoon under "anticipate objections to your proposal."

In describing a problem that your proposal argument intends to solve, be sure to review earlier attempts to fix it. Many issues have a long history that you can't afford to ignore (or be ignorant of). For example, if you were arguing for a college football playoff, you might point out that the current bowl championship series represents an attempt—largely unsuccessful—to crown a widely recognized national champion. Understand too that some problems seem to grow worse every time someone tinkers with them. You might pause before proposing any new attempt to reform the current system of financing federal election campaigns when you discover that previous reforms have resulted in more bureaucracy, more restrictions on political expression, and more unregulated money flowing into the system. *"Enough is enough"* can be a potent argument when faced with such a mess.

RESPOND •

If you review "Ugly? You May Have a Case" at the end of this chapter, an essay by Daniel S. Hamermesh, a professor at the University of Texas at Austin, you'll discover that he spends most of his essay addressing potential objections to his proposal that we compensate unattractive people for society's prejudicial attitudes toward them. Do you think it makes sense for him to argue this way? Or does Hamermesh need to do more to convince his audience (or you, specifically) that attractive people really do enjoy privileges to such an extent that the government needs to compensate unattractive people in the same ways it protects other disadvantaged groups? What kinds of audience issues does Hamermesh face in making his argument in a newspaper as widely read as the *New York Times?*

Making a Strong and Clear Claim

After you've described and analyzed a problem, you're prepared to offer a fix. Begin with your claim (a proposal of what X or Y should do) followed by the reason(s) that X or Y should act and the effects of adopting the proposal:

Claim	Communities should encourage the development of charter schools.
Reason	Charter schools are not burdened by the bureaucracy that is associated with most public schooling.

Effects   Instituting such schools will bring more effective education to communities and offer an incentive to the public
schools to improve their programs.

Having established a claim, you can explore its implications by drawing out
the reasons, warrants, and evidence that can support it most effectively:

Claim   In light of a recent U.S. Supreme Court decision that
ruled that federal drug laws cannot be used to prosecute
doctors who prescribe drugs for use in suicide, our state
should immediately pass a bill legalizing physician-
assisted suicide for patients who are terminally ill.

Reason   Physician-assisted suicide can relieve the suffering of
those who are terminally ill and will die soon.

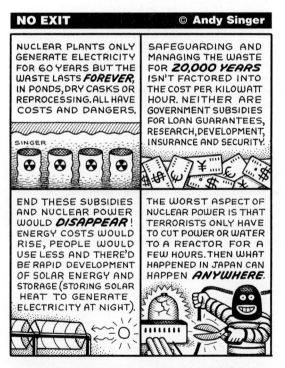

A proposal argument in four panels. You might
compare this argument with Taylor Pearson's "Why
You Should Fear Your Toaster More Than Nuclear
Power" in Chapter 8.

Warrant	The relief of suffering is desirable.
Evidence	Oregon voters have twice approved the state's Death with Dignity Act, which has been in effect since 1997, and to date the suicide rate has not risen sharply nor have doctors given out a large number of prescriptions for death-inducing drugs. Several other states are considering ballot initiatives in favor of doctor-assisted suicide.

In this proposal argument, the *reason* sets up the need for the proposal, whereas the *warrant* and *evidence* demonstrate that the proposal is just and could meet its objective. Your actual argument would develop each point in detail.

RESPOND ●

For each problem and solution below, make a list of readers' likely objections to the solution offered. Then propose a solution of your own, and explain why you think it's more workable than the original.

Problem	Future deficits in the Social Security system
Solution	Raise the age of retirement to seventy-two.

Problem	Severe grade inflation in college courses
Solution	Require a prescribed distribution of grades in every class: 10% A; 20% B; 40% C; 20% D; 10% F

Problem	Increasing rates of obesity in the general population
Solution	Ban the sale of high-fat sandwiches and entrees in fast-food restaurants.

Problem	Inattentive driving because drivers are texting
Solution	Institute a one-year mandatory prison sentence for the first offense.

Problem	Increase in sexual assaults on and around campus
Solution	Establish a 10:00 p.m. curfew on weekends.

Showing That the Proposal Addresses the Need or Problem

An important but tricky part of making a successful proposal lies in relating the claim to the need or problem that it addresses. Facts and probability are your best allies. Take the time to show precisely how your solution will fix a problem or at least improve upon the current situation. Sometimes an emotional appeal is fair play, too. Here's former NBA player John Amaechi using that approach when he asks superstar Kobe Bryant of the L.A. Lakers not to appeal a $100,000 penalty he received for hurling an antigay slur at a referee:

> Kobe, stop fighting the fine. You spoke ill-advised words that shot out like bullets, and if the emails I received from straight and gay young people and sports fans in Los Angeles alone are anything to go by, you did serious damage with your outburst.
>
> A young man from a Los Angeles public school emailed me. You are his idol. He is playing up, on the varsity team, he has your posters all over his room, and he hopes one day to play in college and then in the NBA with you. He used to fall asleep with images of passing you the ball to sink a game-winning shot. He watched every game you played this season on television, but this week he feels less safe and less positive about himself because he stared adoringly into your face as you said the word that haunts him in school every single day.
>
> Kobe, stop fighting the fine. Use that money and your influence to set a new tone that tells sports fans, boys, men, and the society that looks up to you that the word you said in anger is not OK, not ever. Too many athletes take the trappings of their hard-earned success and leave no tangible legacy apart from "that shot" or "that special game."
>
> —John Amaechi, "A Gay Former NBA Player Responds to Kobe Bryant"

John Amaechi (left) and Kobe Bryant (right)

The paragraph describing the reaction of the schoolboy provides just the tie that Amaechi needs between his proposal and the problem it would address. The story also gives his argument more power.

Alternatively, if you oppose an idea, these strategies work just as well in reverse: if a proposal doesn't fix a problem, you have to show exactly why. Here are a few paragraphs from a column by *Washington Post* writer Robert Samuelson in which he refutes, point by point, a proposal by the federal government to spend $53 billion to develop what might seem like a sensible piece of infrastructure: a national high-speed rail system:

> **The reasons why passenger rail service doesn't work in America are well-known:** Interstate highways shorten many trip times; suburbanization has fragmented destination points; air travel is quicker and more flexible for long distances (if fewer people fly from Denver to Los Angeles and more go to Houston, flight schedules simply adjust). Against history and logic is the imagery of high-speed rail as "green" and a cutting-edge technology.
>
> It's a triumph of fancy over fact. Even if ridership increased fifteen-fold over Amtrak levels, the effects on congestion, national fuel consumption and emissions would still be trivial. Land use patterns would change modestly, if at all; cutting twenty minutes off travel times between New York and Philadelphia wouldn't much alter real estate development in either. Nor is high-speed rail a technology where the United States would likely lead; European and Asian firms already dominate the market.
>
> Governing ought to be about making wise choices. What's disheartening about the Obama administration's embrace of high-speed rail is that it ignores history, evidence, and logic. The case against it is overwhelming. The case in favor rests on fashionable platitudes. High-speed rail is not an "investment in the future"; it's mostly a waste of money. Good government can't solve all our problems, but it can at least not make them worse.
>
> —Robert Samuelson, "The Enemies of Good
> Government," *Washington Post*, February 14, 2011

Finally, if your own experience backs up your claim or demonstrates the need or problem that your proposal aims to address, then consider using it to develop your proposal (as John Amaechi does in addressing his proposal to Kobe Bryant). Consider the following questions in deciding when to include your own experiences in showing that a proposal is needed or will in fact do what it claims:

- Is your experience directly related to the need or problem that you seek to address or to your proposal about it?
- Will your experience be appropriate and speak convincingly to the audience? Will the audience immediately understand its significance, or will it require explanation?
- Does your personal experience fit logically with the other reasons that you're using to support your claim?

Be careful. If a proposal seems crafted to serve mainly your own interests, you won't get far.

Showing That the Proposal Is Feasible

To be effective, proposals must be *feasible*—that is, the action proposed can be carried out in a reasonable way. Demonstrating feasibility calls on you to present evidence—from similar cases, from personal experience, from observational data, from interview or survey data, from Internet research, or from any other sources—showing that what you propose can indeed be done with the resources available. "Resources available" is key: if the proposal calls for funds, personnel, or skills beyond reach or reason, your audience is unlikely to accept it. When that's the case, it's time to reassess your proposal, modify it, and test any new ideas against these revised criteria. This is also when you can reconsider proposals that others might suggest are better, more effective, or more workable than yours. There's no shame in admitting that you may have been wrong. When drafting a proposal, ask friends to think of counterproposals. If your own proposal can stand up to such challenges, it's likely a strong one.

Considering Design and Visuals

Because proposals often address specific audiences, they can take a number of forms—a letter, memo, Web page, feasibility report, brochure, prospectus, or even an editorial cartoon (see Andy Singer's "No Exit" item on p. 283). Each form has different design requirements. Indeed, the design may add powerfully to—or detract significantly from—the effectiveness of the proposal. Typically, though, proposals are heavy in photographs, tables, graphs, comparison charts, and maps, all designed to help readers understand the nature of a problem and how to solve it. Needless to say, any visual items should be handsomely presented: they contribute to your ethos.

Lengthy reports also usually need headings—or, in an oral report, slides—that clearly identify the various stages of the presentation. Those headings, which will vary, would include items such as Introduction, Nature of the Problem, Current Approaches or Previous Solutions, Proposal/Recommendations, Advantages, Counterarguments, Feasibility, Implementation, and so on. So before you produce a final copy of any proposal, be sure its design enhances its persuasiveness.

A related issue to consider is whether a graphic image might help readers understand key elements of the proposal—what the challenge is, why it demands action, and what exactly you're suggesting—and help make the idea more attractive. That strategy is routinely used in professional proposals by architects, engineers, and government agencies.

For example, the artist rendering on page 289 shows the Bionic Arch, a proposed skyscraper in Taiwan designed by architect Vincent Callebaut. As a proposal, this one stands out because it not only proposes an addition to the city skyline, but it proposes an architectural addition that is self-sufficient and carbon nuetral by incorporating solar and wind power as well as bioreactors that purify water and aid in recycling and waste elimination efforts. If you look closely, you'll notice that each floor of the building includes suspended "sky gardens" that, according to the proposal, will help solve the problem of city smog by siphoning away toxic fumes. According to Callebaut, "The skyscraper reduces our ecological footprint in the urban area. It respects the environment and gives a new symbiotic ecosystem for the biodiversity of Taiwan. The Bionic Arch is the new icon of sustainable development." Who wouldn't support a building that looked great *and* helped clean the air?

The Bionic Arch proposes to do more than add retail and office space.

GUIDE to writing a proposal

● Finding a Topic or Identifying a Problem

You're entering a proposal argument when you:

- make a claim that supports a change in practice: *Water sold in plastic bottles should carry a warning label describing its environmental impact.*

- make a claim that supports a change in policy: *Government workers, especially legislators and administrative officials, should never be exempt from laws or programs imposed on other citizens.*

- make a claim that resists suggested changes in practice or policy: *The surest way to guarantee that HOV lanes on freeways improve traffic flow is not to build any.*

- explore options for addressing existing issues or investigate opportunities for change: *Urban planners need to examine the long-term impact digital technologies may have on transportation, work habits, housing patterns, power usage, and entertainment opportunities in cities of the future.*

Since your everyday experience often calls on you to consider problems and to make proposals, begin your brainstorming for topics with practical topics related to your life, education, major, or job. Or make an informal list of proposals that you would like to explore in broader academic or cultural areas—problems you see in your field or in the society around you. Or do some freewriting on a subject of political concern, and see if it leads to a call for action.

● Researching Your Topic

For many proposals, you can begin your research by consulting the following types of sources:

- newspapers, magazines, reviews, and journals (online and print)
- online databases
- government documents and reports
- Web sites, blogs, social networking sites, listservs, or newsgroups
- books
- experts in the field, some of whom might be right on your campus

Consider doing some field research, if appropriate—a survey of student opinions on Internet accessibility, for example, or interviews with people who have experienced the problem you are trying to fix.

Finally, remember that your proposal's success can depend on the credibility of the sources you use to support it, so evaluate each source carefully (see Chapter 18).

● Formulating a Claim

As you think about and explore your topic, begin formulating a claim about it. To do so, come up with a clear thesis that makes a proposal and states the reasons that this proposal should be adopted. To start formulating a claim, explore and respond to the following questions:

- What do I know about the proposal that I'm making?
- What reasons can I offer to support my proposal?
- What evidence do I have that implementing my proposal will lead to the results I want?

Rather than make a specific proposal, you may sometimes want to explore the range of possibilities for addressing a particular situation or circumstance. In that case, a set of open-ended questions might be a more productive starting point than a focused thesis, suggesting, for instance, what goals any plausible proposal might have to meet.

● Examples of Proposal Claims

- Because Congress has proved itself unable to rein in spending and because debt is threatening the economic stability of the country, increases in federal spending should be capped annually at 2 percent below the rate of inflation in all departments, programs, and entitlements for a decade.
- Every home should be equipped with a well-stocked emergency kit that can sustain inhabitants for at least three days in a natural disaster.
- Congress should repeal the Copyright Extension Act, since it disrupts the balance between incentives for creators and the right of the public to information as set forth in the U.S. Constitution.
- To simplify the lives of consumers and eliminate redundant products, industries that manufacture rechargeable batteries should agree on a design for a universal power adapter.

- People from different economic classes, age groups, political philosophies, and power groups (government, Main Street, Wall Street) all have a stake in reforming current budget and tax policies. But how do we get them to speak and to listen to each other? That is the challenge we face if we hope to solve our national economic problems.

● Preparing a Proposal

If your instructor asks you to prepare a proposal for your project, here's a format that may help:

State the thesis of your proposal completely. If you're having trouble doing so, try outlining it in Toulmin terms:

Claim:

Reason(s):

Warrant(s):

Alternatively, you might describe your intention to explore a particular problem in your project, with the actual proposal (and thesis) coming later.

- Explain why this issue deserves attention. What's at stake?
- Identify and describe those readers whom you hope to reach with your proposal. Why is this group of readers appropriate? Can you identify individuals who can actually fix a problem?
- Briefly discuss the major difficulties that you foresee for your proposal. How will you: Demonstrate that the action you propose is necessary and workable? Persuade the audience to act? Pay for the proposal?
- Determine what research strategies you'll use. What sources do you expect to consult?
- Describe the format you expect to use: Conventional research essay? Letter to the editor? PowerPoint presentation? Press release? Discussion forum? Op-ed for the local paper?

● Thinking about Organization

Proposals can take many different forms but generally include the following elements:

- a description of the problem you intend to address or the state of affairs that leads you to propose the action

- a strong and specific proposal, identifying the key reasons for taking the proposed action and the effects that taking this action will have

- a clear connection between the proposal and a significant need or problem

- a demonstration of ways in which the proposal addresses the need

- evidence that the proposal will achieve the desired outcome

- a consideration of alternative ways to achieve the desired outcome and a discussion of why these may not be feasible

- a demonstration that the proposal is feasible and an explanation of how it may be implemented

● Getting and Giving Response: Questions for Peer Response

Your instructor may assign you to a group for the purpose of reading and responding to each other's drafts. If not, ask for responses from serious readers or consultants at a writing center. Use the following questions to evaluate a colleague's draft. Since specific comments help more than general observations, be sure to illustrate your comments with examples. Some of the questions below assume a conventional, thesis-driven project, but more exploratory, open-ended proposal arguments also need to be clearly phrased, organized, and supported with evidence.

The Claim

- Does the claim clearly call for action? Is the proposal as clear and specific as possible?

- Is the proposal too sweeping? Does it need to be qualified? If so, how?

- Does the proposal clearly address the problem that it intends to solve? If not, how could the connection be strengthened?

- Is the claim likely to get the audience to act rather than just to agree? If not, how could it be revised to do so?

Evidence for the Claim

- Is enough evidence furnished to get the audience to support the proposal? If not, what kind of additional evidence is needed? Does any of the evidence provided seem inappropriate or otherwise ineffective? Why?

- Is the evidence in support of the claim simply announced, or are its significance and appropriateness analyzed? Is a more detailed discussion needed?

- Are objections that readers might have to the claim or evidence adequately and fairly addressed?
- What kinds of sources are cited? How credible and persuasive will they be to readers? What other kinds of sources might work better?
- Are all quotations introduced with appropriate signal phrases (such as "As Tyson argues, . . .") and blended smoothly into the writer's sentences?

Organization and Style

- How are the parts of the argument organized? Is this organization effective?
- Will readers understand the relationships among the claims, supporting reasons, warrants, and evidence? If not, how might those connections be clearer? Is the function of every visual clear? Are more transitions needed? Would headings or graphic devices help?
- Are the transitions or links from point to point, sentence to sentence, and paragraph to paragraph clear and effective? If not, how could they be improved?
- Are all visuals carefully integrated into the text? Is each visual introduced and commented on to point out its significance? Is each visual labeled as a figure or a table and given a caption as well as a citation?
- Is the style suited to the subject? Is it too formal, casual, or technical? Can it be improved?
- Which sentences seem effective? Which ones seem weaker, and how could they be improved? Should short sentences be combined, and any longer ones be broken up?
- How effective are the paragraphs? Too short or too long? How can they be improved?
- Which words or phrases seem effective? Do any seem vague or inappropriate for the audience or the writer's purpose? Are technical or unfamiliar terms defined?

Spelling, Punctuation, Mechanics, Documentation, and Format

- Are there any errors in spelling, punctuation, capitalization, and the like?
- Is the documentation appropriate and consistent? (See Chapter 21.)
- Does the paper or project follow an appropriate format? Is it appropriately designed and attractively presented?

PROJECTS

1. Identify a proposal currently in the news or one advocated unrelentingly by the media that you *really* don't like. It may be a political initiative, a cultural innovation, a transportation alternative, or a lifestyle change. Spend time studying the idea more carefully than you have before. And then compose a proposal argument based on your deeper understanding of the proposal. You may still explain why you think it's a bad idea. Or you may endorse it, using your new information and your interesting perspective as a former dissenter.

2. The uses and abuses of technology and media—from smart phones to social networks—seem to be on everyone's mind. Write a proposal argument about some pressing dilemma caused by the digital screens that are changing (ruining?) our lives. You might want to explain how to bring traditional instructors into the digital age or establish etiquette for people who walk in traffic using handheld electronic devices. Or maybe you want to keep parents off of social networks. Or maybe you have a great idea for separating professional and private lives online. Make your proposal in some pertinent medium: paper, op-ed, cartoon, photo essay.

3. Write a proposal to yourself diagnosing some minor issue you would like to address, odd behavior you'd like to change, or obsession you'd like to curb. Explore the reasons behind your mania and the problems it causes you and others. Then come up with a plausible proposal to resolve the issue and prove that you can do it. Make the paper hilarious.

4. Working in a group initially, come up with a list of problems—local, national, or international—that seem just about insoluble, from persuading nations to cut down on their CO_2 emissions to figuring out how to keep tuition costs in check. After some discussion, focus on just one or two of these matters and then discuss not the issues themselves but the general reasons that the problems have proven intractable. What exactly keeps people from agreeing on solutions? Are some people content with the status quo? Do some groups profit from the current arrangements? Are alternatives to the status quo just too costly or not feasible for other reasons? Do people find change uncomfortable? Following the discussion, work alone or collaboratively on an argument that examines the general issue of *change*: What makes it possible in any given case? What makes it difficult? Use the problems you have discussed as examples to illustrate your argument. Your challenge as a writer may be to make such an open-ended discussion interesting to general readers.

A Call to Improve Campus Accessibility for the Mobility Impaired

MANASI DESHPANDE

INTRODUCTION

Wes Holloway, a sophomore at the University of Texas at Austin (UT), never considered the issue of campus accessibility during his first year on campus. But when an injury his freshman year left him wheelchair-bound, he was astonished to realize that he faced an unexpected challenge: maneuvering around the UT campus. Hills that he had effortlessly traversed became mountains; doors that he had easily opened became anvils; and streets that he had mindlessly crossed became treacherous terrain. Says Wes: "I didn't think about accessibility until I had to deal with it, and I think most people are the same way."

For the ambulatory individual, access for the mobility impaired on the UT campus is easy to overlook. Automatic door entrances and bathrooms with the universal handicapped symbol make the campus seem sufficiently accessible. But for many students and faculty at UT, including me, maneuvering the UT campus in a wheelchair is a daily experience of stress and frustration. Although the University has made a concerted and continuing effort to improve access, students and faculty with physical disabilities still suffer from discriminatory hardship, unequal opportunity to succeed, and lack of independence.

Manasi Deshpande wrote a longer version of this essay for a course preparing her to work as a consultant in the writing center at the University of Texas at Austin. We have edited it to emphasize the structure of her complex proposal. Note, too, how she reaches out to a general audience to make an argument that might seem to have a narrow constituency. This essay is documented using MLA style.

The University must make campus accessibility a higher priority and take more seriously the hardship that the campus at present imposes on people with mobility impairments. Better accessibility would also benefit the numerous students and faculty with temporary disabilities and help the University recruit a more diverse body of students and faculty.

The introduction's final paragraph summarizes the argument.

Assessment of Current Efforts

The current state of campus accessibility leaves substantial room for improvement. There are approximately 150 academic and administrative buildings on campus (Grant). Eduardo Gardea, intern architect at the Physical Plant, estimates that only about nineteen buildings comply fully with the Americans with Disabilities Act (ADA). According to Penny Seay, PhD, director of the Center for Disability Studies at UT Austin, the ADA in theory "requires every building on campus to be accessible." However, as Bill Throop, associate director of the Physical Plant, explains, there is "no legal deadline to make the entire campus accessible"; neither the ADA nor any other law mandates that certain buildings be made compliant by a certain time. Though not bound by specific legal obligation, the University should strive to fulfill the spirit of the law and recognize campus accessibility as a pressing moral obligation.

The author's fieldwork (mainly interviews) enhances her authority and credibility.

The Benefits of Change

Benefits for People with Permanent Mobility Impairments

Improving campus accessibility would significantly enhance the quality of life of students and faculty with mobility impairments. The campus at present poses discriminatory hardship on these individuals by making daily activities such as getting to class and using the bathroom unreasonably difficult. Before Wes Holloway leaves home, he must plan his route carefully to avoid hills, use ramps that are easy to maneuver, and enter the side of the building with the accessible entrance. As he

The paper uses several layers of headings to organize its diverse materials.

The author outlines the challenges faced by a student with mobility impairment.

goes to class, Wes must go out of his way to avoid poorly paved sidewalks and roads. Sometimes he cannot avoid them and must take an uncomfortable and bumpy ride across potholes and uneven pavement. If his destination does not have an automatic door, he must wait for someone to open the door for him because it is too heavy for him to open himself. To get into Burdine Hall, he has to ask a stranger to push him through the heavy narrow doors because his fingers would get crushed if he pushed himself. Once in the classroom, Wes must find a suitable place to sit, often far away from his classmates because stairs block him from the center of the room.

Accessibility problems are given a human face with examples of the problems that mobility-impaired people face on campus.

Other members of the UT community with mobility impairments suffer the same daily hardships as Wes. According to Mike Gerhardt, student affairs administrator of Services for Students with Disabilities (SSD), approximately eighty students with physical disabilities, including twenty to twenty-five students using wheelchairs, are registered with SSD. However, the actual number of students with mobility impairments is probably higher because some students choose not to seek services from SSD. The current state of campus accessibility discriminates against all individuals with physical disabilities in the unnecessary hardship it imposes and in the ways it denies them independence.

Benefits for People with Temporary Mobility Impairments

The author broadens the appeal of her proposal by showing how improved accessibility will benefit everyone on campus.

In addition to helping the few members of the UT campus with permanent mobility impairments, a faster rate of accessibility improvement would also benefit the much larger population of people with temporary physical disabilities. Many students and faculty will become temporarily disabled from injury at some point during their time at the University. They will encounter difficulties similar to those facing people with permanent disabilities, including finding accessible entrances, opening doors without automatic entrances, and finding convenient classroom seating. And, according to Dr. Jennifer

Maedgen, assistant dean of students and director of SSD, about 5 to 10 percent of the approximately one thousand students registered with SSD at any given time have temporary disabilities. By improving campus accessibility, the University would in fact reach out to all of its members, even those who have never considered the possibility of mobility impairment or the state of campus accessibility.

Numbers provide hard evidence for an important claim.

Benefits for the University

Better accessibility would also benefit the University as a whole by increasing recruitment of handicapped individuals and thus promoting a more diverse campus. When prospective students and faculty with disabilities visit the University, they might decide not to join the UT community because of poor access. On average, about one thousand students, or 2 percent of the student population, are registered with SSD. Mike Gerhardt reports that SSD would have about 1,500 to 3,000 registered students if the University reflected the community at large with respect to disability. These numbers suggest that the University can recruit more students with disabilities by taking steps to ensure that they have an equal opportunity to succeed.

The author offers a new but related argument: enhanced accessibility could bolster recruitment efforts.

COUNTERARGUMENTS

Arguments against devoting more effort and resources to campus accessibility have some validity but ultimately prove inadequate. Some argue that accelerating the rate of accessibility improvements and creating more efficient services require too much spending on too few people. However, this spending actually enhances the expected quality of life of all UT community members rather than just the few with permanent physical disabilities. Unforeseen injury can leave anyone with a permanent or temporary disability at any time. In making decisions about campus accessibility, administrators must realize that having a disability is not a choice and that bad luck

The paper briefly notes possible objections to the proposal.

does not discriminate. They should consider how their decisions would affect their campus experience if they became disabled. Despite the additional cost, the University should make accessibility a priority and accommodate more accessibility projects in its budget.

RECOMMENDATIONS

Foster Empathy and Understanding for Long-Term Planning

After establishing a case for enhanced campus accessibility, the author offers specific suggestions for action.

The University should make campus accessibility a higher priority and work toward a campus that not only fulfills legal requirements but also provides a user friendly environment for the mobility impaired. It is difficult for the ambulatory person to empathize with the difficulties faced by these individuals. Recognizing this problem, the University should require the administrators who allocate money to ADA projects to use wheelchairs around the campus once a year. Administrators must realize that people with physical disabilities are not a small, distant, irrelevant group; anyone can join their ranks at any time. Administrators should ask themselves if they would find the current state of campus accessibility acceptable if an injury forced them to use a wheelchair on a permanent basis.

In addition, the University should actively seek student input for long-term improvements to accessibility. The University is in the process of creating the ADA Accessibility Committee, which, according to the office of the Dean of Students' Web site, will "address institutionwide, systemic issues that fall under the scope of the Americans with Disabilities Act." Students should play a prominent and powerful role in this new ADA Accessibility Committee. The Committee should select its student representatives carefully to make sure that they are driven individuals committed to working for progress and representing the interests of students with disabilities. The University should consider making Committee positions paid so that student representatives can devote sufficient time to their responsibilities.

Improve Services for the Mobility Impaired

The University should also work toward creating more useful, transparent, and approachable services for its members with physical disabilities by making better use of online technology and helping students take control of their own experiences.

First, SSD can make its Web site more useful by updating it frequently with detailed information on construction sites that will affect accessible routes. The site should delineate alternative accessible routes and approximate the extra time required to use the detour. This information would help people with mobility impairments to plan ahead and avoid delays, mitigating the stress of maneuvering around construction sites.

The University should also develop software for an interactive campus map. The software would work like MapQuest or Google Maps but would provide detailed descriptions of accessible routes on campus from one building to another. It would be updated frequently with new ADA improvements and information on construction sites that impede accessible routes.

Since usefulness of services are most important for students during their first encounters with the campus, SSD should hold one-on-one orientations for new students with mobility impairments. SSD should inform students in both oral and written format of their rights and responsibilities and make them aware of problems that they will encounter on the campus. Beyond making services more useful, these orientations would give students the impression of University services as open and responsive, encouraging students to report problems that they encounter and assume the responsibility of self-advocacy.

As a continuing resource for people with physical disabilities, the SSD Web site should include an anonymous forum for both general questions and specific complaints and needs. Many times, students notice problems but do not report them because they find visiting or calling SSD time-consuming or because they do not wish to be a burden. The anonymity and immediate feedback provided by the forum would allow for more freedom of expression and provide students an easier way to solve the problems they face.

Services for the mobility impaired should also increase their transparency by advertising current accessibility projects on their Web sites. The University should give its members with mobility impairments a clearer idea of its efforts to improve campus accessibility. Detailed online descriptions of ADA projects, including the cost of each project, would affirm its resolve to create a better environment for its members with physical disabilities.

Conclusion

Although the University has made progress in accessibility improvements on an old campus, it must take bolder steps to improve the experience of its members with mobility impairments. At present, people with permanent mobility impairments face unreasonable hardship, unequal opportunity to succeed, and lack of independence. To enhance the quality of life of all of its members and increase recruitment of disabled individuals, the University should focus its resources on increasing the rate of accessibility improvements and improving the quality of its services for the mobility impaired.

As a public institution, the University has an obligation to make the campus more inclusive and serve as an example for disability rights. With careful planning and a genuine desire to respond to special needs, practical and cost-effective changes to the University campus can significantly improve the quality of life of many of its members and prove beneficial to the future of the University as a whole.

WORKS CITED

Gardea, Eduardo. Personal interview. 24 Mar. 2005.

Gerhardt, Michael. Personal interview. 8 Apr. 2005.

Grant, Angela. "Making Campus More Accessible." *Daily Texan Online*. 14 Oct. 2003. Web. 1 Mar. 2005.

Holloway, Wesley Reed. Personal interview. 5 Mar. 2005.

Maedgen, Jennifer. Personal interview. 25 Mar. 2005.

Office of the Dean of Students, University of Texas at Austin. "ADA Student Forum." 6 Apr. 2005. Web. 23 Apr. 2005.

Seay, Penny. Personal interview. 11 Mar. 2005.

Throop, William. Personal interview. 6 Apr. 2005.

Ugly? You May Have a Case

DANIEL S. HAMERMESH

Being good-looking is useful in so many ways.

In addition to whatever personal pleasure it gives you, being attractive also helps you earn more money, find a higher-earning spouse (and one who looks better, too!) and get better deals on mortgages. Each of these facts has been demonstrated over the past twenty years by many economists and other researchers. The effects are not small: one study showed that an American worker who was among the bottom one-seventh in looks, as assessed by randomly chosen observers, earned 10 to 15 percent less per year than a similar worker whose looks were assessed in the top one-third—a lifetime difference, in a typical case, of about $230,000.

Beauty is as much an issue for men as for women. While extensive research shows that women's looks have bigger impacts in the market for mates, another large group of studies demonstrates that men's looks have bigger impacts on the job.

Why this disparate treatment of looks in so many areas of life? It's a matter of simple prejudice. Most of us, regardless of our professed attitudes, prefer as customers to buy from better-looking salespeople, as jurors to listen to better-looking attorneys, as voters to be led by better-looking politicians, as students to learn from better-looking professors. This is not a matter of evil employers' refusing to hire the ugly: in our roles as workers, customers and potential lovers we are all responsible for these effects.

How could we remedy this injustice? With all the gains to being good-looking, you would think that more people would get plastic surgery or makeovers to improve their looks. Many of us do all those things, but as studies have shown, such refinements make only small differences in our beauty. All that spending may make us feel better, but it doesn't help us much in getting a better job or a more desirable mate.

Daniel S. Hamermesh is a professor of psychology at the University of Texas at Austin and the author of *Beauty Pays* (2011). This essay originally appeared on August 27, 2011, in the *New York Times*.

A more radical solution may be needed: why not offer legal protections to the ugly, as we do with racial, ethnic and religious minorities, women and handicapped individuals?

We actually already do offer such protections in a few places, including in some jurisdictions in California, and in the District of Columbia, where discriminatory treatment based on looks in hiring, promotions, housing and other areas is prohibited. Ugliness could be protected generally in the United States by small extensions of the Americans With Disabilities Act. Ugly people could be allowed to seek help from the Equal Employment Opportunity Commission and other agencies in overcoming the effects of discrimination. We could even have affirmative-action programs for the ugly.

The mechanics of legislating this kind of protection are not as difficult as you might think. You might argue that people can't be classified by their looks—that beauty is in the eye of the beholder. That aphorism is correct in one sense: if asked who is the most beautiful person in a group of beautiful people, you and I might well have different answers. But when it comes to differentiating classes of attractiveness, we all view beauty similarly: someone whom you consider good-looking will be viewed similarly by most others; someone you consider ugly will be viewed as ugly by most others. In one study, more than half of a group of people were assessed identically by each of two observers using a five-point scale; and very few assessments differed by more than one point.

For purposes of administering a law, we surely could agree on who is truly ugly, perhaps the worst-looking 1 or 2 percent of the population. The difficulties in classification are little greater than those faced in deciding who qualifies for protection on grounds of disabilities that limit the activities of daily life, as shown by conflicting decisions in numerous legal cases involving obesity.

There are other possible objections. "Ugliness" is not a personal trait that many people choose to embrace; those whom we classify as protected might not be willing to admit that they are ugly. But with the chance of obtaining extra pay and promotions amounting to $230,000 in lost lifetime earnings, there's a large enough incentive to do so. Bringing anti-discrimination lawsuits is also costly, and few potential plaintiffs could afford to do so. But many attorneys would be willing to organize classes of plaintiffs to overcome these costs, just as they now do in racial-discrimination and other lawsuits.

Economic arguments for protecting the ugly are as strong as those for protecting some groups currently covered by legislation. So why not go ahead and expand protection to the looks-challenged? There's one legitimate concern. With increasingly tight limits on government resources, expanding rights to yet another protected group would reduce protection for groups that have commanded our legislative and other attention for over fifty years.

We face a trade-off: ignore a deserving group of citizens, or help them but limit help available for other groups. Even though I myself have demonstrated the disadvantages of ugliness in twenty years of research, I nonetheless would hate to see anything that might reduce assistance to groups now aided by protective legislation.

You might reasonably disagree and argue for protecting all deserving groups. Either way, you shouldn't be surprised to see the United States heading toward this new legal frontier.

PART 3

STYLE AND PRESENTATION IN arguments

13
Style in Arguments

The three images above all reflect strong individual styles: the graceful form of a very distinctive basketball player, the unique drawing style of a well-known graphic narrative artist, and the classic flair of the original iPod ads.

Even scientists, whose work might seem cut-and-dried at first glance, have style—and often lots of it! Five hundred years ago, Johann Bernoulli challenged the greatest mathematicians in the world to solve a problem that had eluded everyone to date. When an anonymous person solved the problem the very day he received it, it didn't matter that he was anonymous: the mathematics world knew that the savant was Isaac Newton. "You can tell the lion," they said, "by his claw." That "claw" was Newton's style.

So we know style when we see it—as in an elegant move in sports or in mathematics, a comic book, an Apple ad—but creating a style of your own is something else. This chapter will help you begin that process. Let's start with looking at how word choice contributes to style.

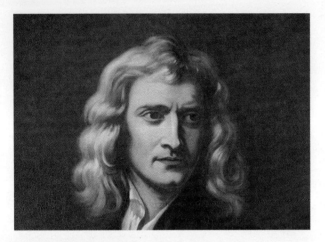

Sir Isaac Newton

Style and Word Choice

The words you choose for an argument help define its style—and yours. For most academic arguments, fairly formal language is appropriate. In an article that urges every member of society to care about energy issues, Chevron CEO Dave O'Reilly adopts a formal and serious tone: "We call upon scientists and educators, politicians and policy-makers, environmentalists, leaders of industry, and each one of you to be part of reshaping the next era of energy." Had he written "How 'bout we rally 'round and mix us up a new energy plan?" the effect would have been quite different.

Slang and *colloquial terms* may enliven an argument, but they also can bewilder readers. An article about arms-control negotiations that uses terms like *nukes* and *boomers* to refer to nuclear weaponry might confuse readers who assume that the shorthand portrays a flippant attitude toward a serious subject. Be alert, too, to the use of *jargon*, the special vocabulary of members of a profession, trade, or field. Although jargon serves as shorthand for experts, it can alienate readers who don't recognize technical words or acronyms.

Another key to an argument's style is its control of **connotation**, the associations that surround many words. Note the differences among the following three statements:

Students from the Labor Action Committee (LAC) carried out a hunger strike to call attention to the below-minimum wages that are being paid to campus temporary workers, saying, "The university must pay a living wage to all its workers."

Left-wing agitators and radicals tried to use self-induced starvation to stampede the university into caving in to their demands.

Champions of human rights put their bodies on the line to protest the university's tightfisted policy of paying temporary workers scandalously low wages.

The style of the first sentence is the most neutral, presenting facts and offering a quotation from one of the students. The second sentence uses loaded terms like *agitators, radicals,* and *stampede* to create a negative image of this event, while the final sentence uses other loaded words to create a positive view. As these examples demonstrate, words matter.

Finally, vivid *concrete* and *specific words* work better in arguments than abstract and general ones. Responding to a claim that American students are falling behind their counterparts in Asia and Europe, Jay Mathews uses memorable language to depict the stereotype:

Most commentary on the subject leaves the impression that China and India are going to bury the United States in an avalanche of new technology. Consider, for example, a much-cited *Fortune* article that included the claim that China turned out 600,000 engineers in the previous year, India graduated 350,000, and poor, declining America could manage only 70,000. The cover of *Fortune* showed a buff Chinese beach bully looming over a skinny Uncle Sam. The headline said, "Is the U.S. a 97-Pound Weakling?"

—Jay Mathews, "Bad Rap on the Schools"

Mathews' concrete language (*bury, avalanche,* and *buff Chinese beach bully looming over a skinny Uncle Sam*) creates a style that gets and keeps readers' attention.

Sentence Structure and Argument

Writers of effective arguments know that "variety is the spice of life" when it comes to stylish sentences. *Varying sentence length* can be especially effective. Here's Mary H. K. Choi introducing the twenty-third season of *The Simpsons:*

Let's make a pact. The next person who whines about how *The Simpsons* sucks gets flung in a well. The rest of us can tailgate. Spare us your blustery, pedantic indignation. There's nothing to add. No petition long enough, no outcry loud enough. Winter is coming, and so is the Fox series' twenty-third season and 500th episode. If this really upsets you . . . Just. Quit. Watching.

—Mary H. K. Choi

Choi opens with a dramatic first sentence, followed by one a little longer and then a series of short, staccato statements that lead up to the compound *Winter is coming, and so is.* . . . And note the special effects she creates by dividing up the last sentence for emphasis: *Just. Quit. Watching.*

Variety in the way sentences open can also help create a subtly pleasing style. Here is Lisa Miller writing about the spread of "Tiger Mom" tactics in child raising:

Happy Rogers, age eight, stands among her classmates in the schoolyard at dismissal time, immune, it seems, to the cacophonous din. A poised and precocious blonde, Hilton Augusta Parker Rogers, nicknamed Happy, would be at home in the schoolyard of any affluent American suburb or big-city private school. But here, at the elite, bilingual Nanyang Primary School in Singapore, Happy is in the minority, her Dakota Fanning hair shimmering in a sea of darker heads. This is what her parents have traveled halfway around the world for. While her American peers are feasting on the idiocies fed to them by junk TV and summer movies, Happy is navigating her friendships and doing her homework entirely in Mandarin.

—Lisa Miller, "How to Raise a Global Kid"

RESPOND•

Work with a classmate to revise Miller's paragraph, making sure that every sentence begins the same way, with the subject first. Then read the passage aloud and see if it sounds much less effective and memorable. It's the variety in sentence openings that does the trick!

Parallel structures in sentences also help create style. In a review of a biography of writer Henry Roth, Jonathan Rosen includes the following description:

His hands were warped by rheumatoid arthritis; the very touch of his computer keyboard was excruciating. But he still put in five hours a day, helped by Percocet, beer, a ferocious will, and the ministrations of several young assistants.

—Jonathan Rosen, "Writer, Interrupted"

In the first sentence, Rosen chooses parallel clauses, with the first one about Roth's arthritic hands balanced by the next one describing the results of putting those hands on a keyboard. In the second sentence, Rosen also uses a series of parallel specific nouns and noun phrases (*Percocet, beer, the ministrations*) to build up a picture of Roth as extremely persistent.

RESPOND•

Turn to something you read frequently—a blog, a sports or news magazine, or a friend's page on Twitter—and look closely at the sentences. What seems distinctive about them? Do they vary in terms of their length and the way that they begin? If so, how? Do they use parallel structures or other structural devices to good effect? How easy to read are they, and what accounts for that ease?

Punctuation and Argument

In a memorable comment, actor and director Clint Eastwood said, "You can show a lot with a look. . . . It's punctuation." Eastwood is right about punctuation's effect, and it is important that as you read and write

"You can show a lot with a look. . . . It's punctuation."

arguments, you consider punctuation closely. Here are some ways in which punctuation helps to enhance style.

The *semicolon* signals a pause that is stronger than a comma but not as strong as a period. Semicolons often connect two independent clauses that are linked by one idea. See how Romesh Ratnesar describes the results of the infamous "Stanford Prison Experiment" in which students were either "guards" or "prisoners":

> Some of [the "prisoners"] rebelled violently; others became hysterical or withdrew into despair.
>
> —Romesh Ratnesar, "The Menace Within"

Using a semicolon gives Ratnesar's sentence an abrupt rhythmic shift, in this case from rebellion to despair.

Writers also use end punctuation to create stylistic effects. Although the *exclamation point* can be irritating if overused (think of those Facebook status updates that bristle with them), it can be helpful for creating tone if used sparingly. In an argument about the treatment of prisoners at Guantanamo, consider how Jane Mayer evokes the sense of desperation in some of the suspected terrorists:

> As we reached the end of the cell-block, hysterical shouts, in broken English, erupted from a caged exercise area nearby. "Come here!" a man screamed. "See here! They are liars! . . . No sleep!" he yelled. "No food! No medicine! No doctor! Everybody sick here!"
>
> —Jane Mayer, "The Experiment"

While sometimes used interchangeably, the *dash* and the *colon* create different stylistic effects. Dashes offer a great way to call attention to a relevant detail that isn't itself necessary information in the sentence you're writing. Here are dashes used to insert such information in the opening of Philip Womack's London *Telegraph* review of *Harry Potter and the Deathly Hallows, Part 2*:

> *Harry Potter and the Deathly Hallows, Part 2*—the eighth and final film in the blockbusting series—begins with our teenage heroes fighting for their lives, and for their entire world.

The review continues with a sentence that makes good use of a colon, which often introduces explanations or examples:

> The first scene of David Yates's film picks up where his previous installment left off: with a shot of the dark lord Voldemort's noseless face in triumph as he steals the most powerful magic wand in the world from the tomb of Harry's protector, Professor Dumbledore.

And Womack concludes his review with a powerful *question mark* that signals not only the evaluation of the entire film but a prediction for the future:

> This is not an end. How could it be?
>
> —Philip Womack

As these examples suggest, punctuation is often key to creating the rhythm of an argument. Take a look at how Maya Angelou uses a dash along with another punctuation mark—ellipsis points—to indicate a pause or hesitation, in this case one that builds anticipation:

> Then the voice, husky and familiar, came to wash over us—"The winnah, and still heavyweight champeen of the world . . . Joe Louis."
>
> —Maya Angelou, "Champion of the World"

Creating rhythms can be especially important in online communication when writers are trying to invest their arguments with emotion or emphasis. Some writers still use asterisks in online communication to convey emphasis the way that italic or boldface type creates in print texts: "You *must* respond to this message today!" Others use emoticons or other new characters to establish a particular rhythm, tone, and style. In an argument where the stakes are high, though, most writers use conventional style. The use of asterisks and emoticons is so common in online communication that many chat and comments programs automatically convert type enclosed in asterisks to bold, or emoticons to graphics.

RESPOND•

Try writing a brief movie review for your campus newspaper, experimenting with punctuation as one way to create an effective style. See if using a series of questions might have a strong effect, whether exclamation points would add or detract from the message you want to send, and so on. When you've finished the review, compare it to one written by a classmate, and look for similarities and differences in your choices of punctuation.

Special Effects: Figurative Language and Argument

Any magazine or Web site will show how figurative language works in arguments. When a reviewer of new software that promises complete filtering of ads on the Web refers to the product as "a weedwhacker for the Web," he's using figurative language (in this case, metaphor) to advance an argument about the nature and function of that product. When a writer calls Disney World a "smile factory," she begins a stinging critique of the way pleasure is "manufactured" there.

Figurative language, which is indispensable to writers, brings two major strengths to arguments. First, it helps us understand things by drawing parallels between an unknown and a known. For example, to describe DNA, scientists Watson and Crick used the figures of a helix (spiral) and a zipper to help people understand this new concept.

Figures of speech are usually classified into two main types: **tropes** involve a change in the ordinary meaning of a word or phrase, and **schemes** involve a special arrangement of words. Here is a brief listing—with examples—of some of the most familiar kinds.

Tropes

METAPHOR

A bedrock of our language, **metaphor** implies a comparison between two things and thereby clarifies and enlivens many arguments. Columnist David Brooks depends on metaphors in an essay arguing that such figures are "at the very heart of how we think":

> Even the hardest of sciences depend on a foundation of metaphors. To be aware of metaphors is to be humbled by the complexity of the world, to realize that deep in the undercurrents of thought there are thousands of lenses popping up between us and the world, and that we're surrounded at all times by what Steven Pinker of Harvard once called "pedestrian poetry."
>
> —David Brooks, "Poetry for Everyday Life"

In the following passage, novelist and poet Benjamin Sáenz uses several metaphors to describe his relationship to the southern border of the United States:

> It seems obvious to me now that I remained always a son of the border, a boy never quite comfortable in an American skin, and certainly not comfortable in a Mexican one. My entire life, I have lived in a liminal space, and that space has both defined and confined me. That liminal space wrote and invented me. It has been my prison, and it has also been my only piece of sky.
>
> —Benjamin Sáenz, "Notes from Another Country"

In another example from Andrew Sullivan's blog, he quotes an 1896 issue of *Munsey's Magazine* that uses a metaphor to explain what, at that time, the bicycle meant to women and to clarify the new freedom it gave women who weren't accustomed to being able to ride around on their own:

> To men, the bicycle in the beginning was merely a new toy, another machine added to the long list of devices they knew in their work and play. To women, it was a steed upon which they rode into a new world.

SIMILE

A **simile** uses *like* or *as* to compare two things. Here's a simile from an essay on cosmology from the *New York Times*:

> Through his general theory of relativity, Einstein found that space, and time too, can bend, twist, and warp, responding much as a trampoline does to a jumping child.
>
> —Brian Greene, "Darkness on the Edge of the Universe"

And here is a series of similes, from an excerpt of a *Wired* magazine review of a new magazine for women:

> Women's magazines occupy a special niche in the cluttered infoscape of modern media. Ask any *Vogue* junkie: no girl-themed Web site or CNN segment on women's health can replace the guilty pleasure of slipping a glossy fashion rag into your shopping cart. Smooth as a pint of chocolate Häagen-Dazs, feckless as a thousand-dollar slip dress, women's magazines wrap culture, trends, health, and trash in a single, decadent package. But like the diet dessert recipes they print, these slick publications can leave a bad taste in your mouth.
>
> —Tiffany Lee Brown, "En Vogue"

Here, three similes—*smooth as a pint of chocolate Häagen-Dazs* and *feckless as a thousand-dollar slip dress* in the third sentence and *like the diet dessert recipes* in the fourth—add to the image of women's magazines as a mishmash of "trash" and "trends."

ANALOGY

Analogies compare two things, often point by point, either to show similarity or to argue that if two things are alike in one way, they are probably alike in other ways as well. Often extended in length, analogies can

This cartoon mocks the Republican presidential nominating process by using a familiar analogy.

clarify and emphasize points of comparison. In an argument about the failures of the aircraft industry, a writer uses an analogy for potent contrast:

> If the aircraft industry had evolved as spectacularly as the computer industry over the past twenty-five years, a Boeing 767 would cost five hundred dollars today, and it would circle the globe in twenty minutes on five gallons of fuel.
>
> —*Scientific American*

To be effective, analogies have to hold up to scrutiny. In reflecting on the congressional debacle of July 2011 that took the United States close to default, columnist Joe Nocera draws an analogy:

> You know what they say: Never negotiate with terrorists. It only encourages them. These last few months, much of the country has watched in horror as the Tea Party Republicans have waged jihad on the American people. Their intransigent demands for deep spending cuts, coupled with their almost gleeful willingness to destroy one of America's most invaluable assets, its full faith and credit, were incredibly irresponsible. But they didn't care. Their goal, they believed, was worth blowing up the country for, if that's what it took.
>
> —Joe Nocera

CULTURAL CONTEXTS FOR ARGUMENT

Levels of Formality and Other Issues of Style

At least one important style question needs to be asked when arguing across cultures: what level of formality is most appropriate? In the United States, a fairly informal style is often acceptable and even appreciated. Many cultures, however, tend to value formality. If in doubt, err on the side of formality:

- Take care to use proper titles as appropriate (*Ms.*, *Mr.*, *Dr.*, and so on).
- Don't use first names unless you've been invited to do so.
- Steer clear of slang and jargon. When you're communicating with members of other cultures, slang may not be understood, or it may be seen as disrespectful.
- Avoid potentially puzzling pop cultural allusions, such as sports analogies or musical references.

When arguing across cultures or languages, another stylistic issue might be clarity. When communicating with people whose native languages are different from your own, analogies and similes almost always aid in understanding. Likening something unknown to something familiar can help make your argument forceful—and understandable.

Nocera's comparison between Tea Partiers and terrorists offended many, who wrote to condemn the tone of the piece and to note that the analogy doesn't hold. Here's Michael from New York City, who says:

> I am not a tea partier, or a Republican, but I just have to comment on the tone of this article. Comparing tea partiers to terrorists now . . . interesting. They are not terrorists, they are citizens who banded together to push for what they believe in.

OTHER TROPES

Signifying, in which a speaker or writer cleverly and often humorously needles another person, is a distinctive trope found extensively in African American English. In the following passage, two African American men (Grave Digger and Coffin Ed) signify on their white supervisor (Anderson), who has ordered them to discover the originators of a riot:

> "I take it you've discovered who started the riot," Anderson said.
> "We knew who he was all along," Grave Digger said.
> "It's just nothing we can do to him," Coffin Ed echoed.
> "Why not, for God's sake?"
> "He's dead," Coffin Ed said.
> "Who?"
> "Lincoln," Grave Digger said.
> "He hadn't ought to have freed us if he didn't want to make provisions to feed us," Coffin Ed said. "Anyone could have told him that."
>
> —Chester Himes, *Hot Day, Hot Night*

Coffin Ed and Grave Digger demonstrate the major characteristics of effective signifying—indirection, ironic humor, fluid rhythm, and a surprising twist at the end. Rather than insulting Anderson directly by pointing out that he's asked a dumb question, they criticize the question indirectly by ultimately blaming a white man (and not just any white

In these *Boondocks* strips, Huey signifies on Jazmine, using indirection, ironic humor, and two surprising twists.

© 1999 Aaron McGruder. Reprinted by permission of Universal Press Syndicate. All rights reserved.

man, but one they're supposed to revere). This twist leaves the supervisor speechless, teaching him something and giving Grave Digger and Coffin Ed the last word—and the last laugh.

Take a look at the example of signifying from a *Boondocks* cartoon (see opposite page). Note how Huey seems to be sympathizing with Jazmine and then, in two surprising twists, reveals that he has been needling her all along.

Hyperbole is the use of overstatement for special effect, a kind of fireworks in prose. The tabloid gossip magazines that scream at you in the checkout line are champions of hyperbole. Everyone has seen these overstated arguments and perhaps marveled at the way they sell.

Hyperbole is also the trademark of serious writers. In a column arguing that men's magazines fuel the same kind of neurotic anxieties about appearance that have long plagued women, Michelle Cottle uses hyperbole and humor to make her point:

> My affection for *Men's Health* is driven by pure gender politics. . . . With page after page of bulging biceps and Gillette jaws, robust hairlines and silken skin, *Men's Health* is peddling a standard of male beauty as unforgiving and unrealistic as the female version sold by those dewy-eyed pre-teen waifs draped across covers of *Glamour* and *Elle.*
>
> —Michelle Cottle, "Turning Boys into Girls"

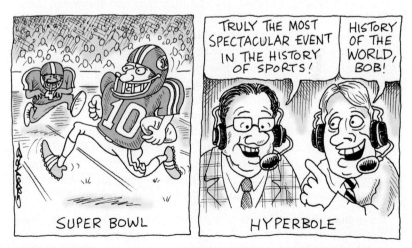

SUPER BOWL

HYPERBOLE

How does this cartoon make light of the frequent use of hyperbole in sports broadcasting?

As you might imagine, hyperbole can easily backfire. Blogging on the *Robinson Post*, Matthew Robinson deplores the use of hyperbole on both the right and the left:

> Glenn Beck, in a discussion on his show about some Americans' distaste for the recent healthcare overhaul, compared the U.S. government to pedophilic rapist Roman Polanski, and the American people to a thirteen-year-old girl. . . . Maureen Dowd compared her own experience as a Catholic woman to that of the subjugated women of Saudi Arabia, calling the Catholic Church, "an inbred and wealthy men's club cloistered behind walls and disdaining modernity . . . an autocratic society that repress[es] women and ignore[s] their progress in the secular world."
>
> —Matthew Robinson, "Sticks and Stones:
> How Hyperbole Is Hurting America"

Understatement uses a quiet message to make its point. In her memoir, Rosa Parks—the civil rights activist who made history in 1955 by refusing to give up her bus seat to a white passenger—uses understatement so often that it becomes a hallmark of her style. She refers to Martin Luther King Jr. simply as "a true leader," to Malcolm X as a person of "strong conviction," and to her own lifelong efforts as just a small way of "carrying on."

Understatement can be particularly effective in arguments that might seem to call for its opposite. When Watson and Crick published their first article on the structure of DNA, they felt that they had discovered the secret of life. (Imagine what a Fox News or MSNBC headline might have been for this story!) Yet in an atmosphere of extreme scientific competitiveness, they closed their article with a vast understatement: "It has not escaped our notice that the specific pairing we have postulated immediately suggests a possible copying mechanism for the genetic material." A half century later, considering the profound developments in genetics, the power of this understatement still resonates strongly.

Rhetorical questions, which we use frequently, don't really require answers. When you say "Who cares?" or "How should I know?" you're using such questions. Rhetorical questions also show up in arguments. In reviewing a book on power in the Disney dynasty, Linda Watts uses a series of rhetorical questions to introduce part of her argument:

> If you have ever visited one of the Disney theme parks, though, you have likely wondered at the labor—both seen and unseen—necessary to maintain these fanciful environments. How and when are the

grounds tended so painstakingly? How are the signs of high traffic erased from public facilities? What keeps employees so poised, meticulously groomed, and endlessly cheerful?

—Linda S. Watts, review of *Inside the Mouse*

And Erin Biba asks a potent rhetorical question in her analysis of Facebook "friending":

So if we're spending most of our time online talking to people we don't even know, how deep can the conversation ever get?

—Erin Biba, "Friendship Has Its Limits"

Antonomasia is probably most familiar to you from sports coverage: "His Airness" still means Michael Jordan, "The Great One," Wayne Gretzky. But it's also used in fields like politics, sometimes neutrally (Arnold Schwarzenegger as "The Governator"), sometimes as a compliment (Ronald Reagan as "The Great Communicator"), and sometimes as a crude and sexist put-down (Sarah Palin as "Caribou Barbie") or in the entertainment industry (as in calling Owen Wilson "The Butterscotch Stallion"). Such nicknames can pack arguments into just one phrase. What does calling Jordan "His Airness" argue about him?

Irony uses words to convey a meaning in tension with or opposite to their literal meanings to create special effects in argument. One of the most famous sustained uses of irony in literature occurs in Shakespeare's *Julius Caesar* as Antony punctuates his condemnation of Brutus with the repeated ironic phrase, "But Brutus is an *honourable* man." Publications such as the *Onion* and the online *Ironic Times* are noted for their satiric treatment of politics and popular culture, scoring points while provoking a chuckle.

RESPOND●

Use online sources (such as American Rhetoric's Top 100 Speeches at http://www.americanrhetoric.com/top100speechesall.html) to find the text of an essay or a speech by someone who uses figures of speech liberally. Pick a paragraph that is rich in figures and rewrite it, eliminating every bit of figurative language. Then read the original and your revised version aloud to your class. Can you imagine a rhetorical situation in which your pared-down version would be appropriate?

Schemes

Schemes, figures that depend on word order, can add stylistic "zing" to arguments. Here are ones that you're likely to see most often.

Parallelism involves the use of grammatically similar phrases or clauses for special effect:

> For African Americans, the progress toward racial equality over the last half century was summed up in a widely quoted sequence: "Rosa sat so that Martin could walk. Martin walked so that Obama could run. Obama ran so that our children could fly."

Antithesis is the use of parallel structures to mark contrast or opposition:

> Marriage has many pains, but celibacy has no pleasures.
> —Samuel Johnson

> Those who kill people are called murderers; those who kill animals, sportsmen.

Inverted word order, in which the parts of a sentence or clause are not in the usual subject-verb-object order, can help make arguments particularly memorable:

> Into this grey lake plopped the thought, I know this man, don't I?
> —Doris Lessing

> Hard to see, the dark side is.
> —Yoda

Anaphora, or effective repetition, can act like a drumbeat in an argument, bringing the point home. In an argument about the future of Chicago, Lerone Bennett Jr. uses repetition to link Chicago to innovation and creativity:

> [Chicago]'s the place where organized Black history was born, where gospel music was born, where jazz and the blues were reborn, where the Beatles and the Rolling Stones went up to the mountaintop to get the new musical commandments from Chuck Berry and the rock'n'roll apostles.
> —Lerone Bennett Jr., "Blacks in Chicago"

And speaking of the Rolling Stones, here's Dave Barry using repetition comically in his comments on their 2002 tour:

> Recently I attended a Rolling Stones concert. This is something I do every two decades. I saw the Stones in the 1960s, and then again in the 1980s. I plan to see them next in the 2020s, then the 2040s, then the 2060s, at their 100th anniversary concert.
> —Dave Barry, "OK, What Will Stones Do for 100th Anniversary?"

Reversed structures for special effect have been used widely in political argumentation.

> Ask not what your country can do for you; ask what you can do for your country.
> —President John F. Kennedy, 1961 Inaugural Address

> The Democrats won't get elected unless things get worse, and things won't get worse until the Democrats get elected.
> —Jeane Kirkpatrick

> Your manuscript is both good and original. But the part that is good is not original, and the part that is original is not good.
> —Samuel Johnson

RESPOND●

Identify the figurative language used in the following slogans:

"Energy drink with attitude." (Red Eye)

"Open happiness." (Coca-Cola)

"Melts in your mouth, not in your hands." (M&M's)

"Be all that you can be." (U.S. Army)

"Breakfast of champions." (Wheaties)

"America runs on Dunkin'." (Dunkin' Donuts)

"Got milk?" (America's Milk Processors)

14
Visual and Multimedia Arguments

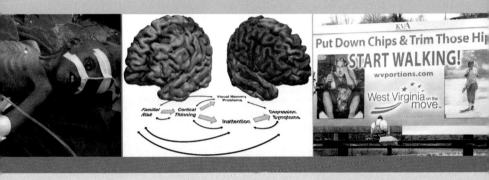

We don't need to be reminded that visual and multimedia images have clout. The images above, for example, all make powerful arguments — about the face of malnutrition in Somalia today, about how psychiatric drugs combat depression, about the need to confront and hopefully conquer obesity. Of course, some images are so iconic that they become part of our cultural memory. Just think of the first images you saw of planes slamming into the World Trade Center towers. Or the photographs of Japanese cities after the 2011 earthquake and tsunami. Or maybe you recall YouTube video of President Obama standing at the end of a long hall announcing the death of Osama bin Laden, or the dramatic opening ceremonies of the 2012 Summer Olympics in London. Images like these stick in our memories.

The Power of Visual Arguments

Yet even in mundane moments, images—from T-shirts to billboards to animated films and computer screens—influence us. Media analyst Kevin Kelly remarks on the "ubiquity" of screens and their images in our lives:

> Everywhere we look, we see screens. The other day I watched clips from a movie as I pumped gas into my car. The other night I saw a movie on the backseat of a plane. We will watch anywhere. Screens playing video pop up in the most unexpected places—like ATM machines and supermarket checkout lines and tiny phones; some movie fans watch entire films in between calls. These ever-present screens have created an audience for very short moving pictures, as brief as three minutes, while cheap digital creation tools have empowered a new generation of filmmakers, who are rapidly filling up those screens. We are headed toward screen ubiquity.
>
> —Kevin Kelly, "Becoming Screen Literate"

As technology makes it easier for us to create and transmit images, those images become more compelling than ever, brought to us via Blu-ray and high-definition television on our smartphones and computers, on our walls, in our pockets, in our cars. But visual arguments weren't invented by YouTube, and they've always had power. The pharaohs of Egypt lined the banks of the Nile River with statues of themselves to assert their authority, and over thirty thousand years ago, people in the south of France created magnificent cave paintings to celebrate and to communicate.

Still, the ease and speed with which all of us can create and share images seems unprecedented. Beginning with the introduction of personal computers with image-controlled interfaces in the 1980s, slowly and then with the force of a tsunami, these graphic computers (the only kind that people use now) moved society further away from an age of print into an era of electronic, image-saturated communications.

Most of us have adjusted to a world of seamless, multichannel, multimedia connections. The prophet of this time was Marshall McLuhan, who nearly fifty years ago proclaimed that "the medium is the massage," with the play on *message* and *massage* intentional. As McLuhan says, "We shape our tools and afterwards our tools shape us. . . . All media works us over completely."

Marshall McLuhan

RESPOND ●

Find an advertisement, either print or digital, that uses both verbal and visual elements. Analyze its argument by answering some of the questions on pages 329–33. Then switch ads with a classmate, and analyze his or her argument. Compare your responses to the two ads. If they're different—and they probably will be—how do you account for the differences? What effect does the audience have on the argument's reception? What differences appear between your own active reading and your classmate's?

Shaping the Message

Images make arguments of their own. A photograph, for example, isn't a faithful representation of reality; it's reality shaped by the photographer's point of view. That's probably one reason why so many Facebook users change their photos so often—to present themselves at their very best.

Those who produce images fashion the messages that those images convey, but those who "read" those images are by no means passive. To some extent, we actively shape what we see and have learned to see things according to their meanings within our culture. People don't always see things the same way, which explains why eyewitnesses to a particular event often report it differently. Even instant replays don't always solve disputed calls on football fields. The visual images that surround us today and compete for our attention, time, and money are designed to invite, perhaps even coerce, us into seeing them in a specific way. But we all have our own frames of reference and can resist such pressures—if we are sharp!

Analyzing Visual Elements of Arguments

To figure out how a visual or multimedia argument works, start by examining its key components:

- the creators and distributors
- the medium it uses
- the viewers and readers it hopes to reach
- its content and purpose
- its design

Following are brief analyses of several visual arguments, along with questions to explore when you encounter similar texts.

The Creators and Distributors

This image from Amnesty International calls on viewers to help "Abolish the use of child soldiers worldwide," noting that "Children have the right to be children." This group, a nongovernmental organization with three million members in 150 countries around the globe, has as its mission to end "grave abuses of human rights." Amnesty International has carried out many campaigns, including Stamp Out Torture, Stop Violence against Women, and Demand Dignity. How does this information help you "read" the image above? Why might the organization have chosen this image to support their campaign? How well does it achieve its purpose?

Questions about Creators and Distributors

- Who created this visual or multimedia text? Who distributed it?
- What can you find out about these people and other work that they have done?
- What does the creator's attitude seem to be toward the image(s)?
- What do the creator and the distributor intend its effects to be? Do they have the same intentions?

The Medium

During February 2011, protesters occupied Cairo's Tahrir Square and used their mobile devices as tools to let the world know what was happening. They tweeted and texted and sent cell phone pictures documenting police atrocities, and newspapers around the world printed tweets rather than formal reports from their journalists, like this one sent to London's *Globe and Mail*: "What's worse than being detained three hours by Egyptian army? Watching a four-year-old girl being detained with you even longer." Protesters kept their phones alive by hacking streetlamps to keep them charged. During this period, the medium was indeed a big part of the message. The photo above shows graffiti painted by protesters to promote the use of social media, including Facebook, to share information about the protests. What message is the graffiti sending? More importantly, how does media play a role in sending such a message?

Questions about the Medium

- Which media are used for this visual text? Images only? Words and images? Sound, video, animation, graphs, charts—and in what ways are they interactive?

- How are the media used to communicate words and images? How do various media work together?

- What effect does the medium have on the message of the text? How would the message be altered if different media were used?

- What role do words—if there are words—play in the visual text? How do they clarify, reinforce, blur, or contradict the image's message?

The Viewers and Readers

Questions about Viewers and Readers

- What does the visual text assume about its viewers and what they know and agree with?

- What overall impression does the visual text create in you?

- What positive or negative feelings about individuals, scenes, or ideas does the visual intend to evoke in viewers?

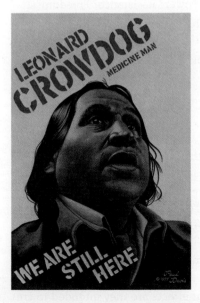

In 1977, Paul Davis created this poster celebrating Native American political activist Leonard Crowdog. The poster uses simple language and a strong image to express solidarity among Native Americans (and their political allies) and to affirm Crowdog's call for renewal of Native American traditions. In what ways can visual arguments invoke their audiences or even become a part of their cultural histories? With what similar visual items (such as posters or CD art) do you identify?

Take a close look at this photograph taken during the 2008 presidential campaign: is your eye drawn first to the earnest face in the middle, the one with a pink John McCain T-shirt on? If so, pull back and take in the whole photo: what's with that pair of legs? An Associated Press photographer took this photo of Sarah Palin, causing a flap: was the photo sexist and prurient, or was it upbeat and emblematic of a new kind of feminism? What was the photographer's purpose in taking the shot? How do you read its message?

The Content and Purpose

Questions about Content and Purpose

- What purpose does the visual text convey? What is it designed to convey?
- What cultural values does the visual evoke? The good life? Love and harmony? Sex appeal? Adventure? Power? Resistance? Freedom?
- Does the visual reinforce these values or question them? How does the visual strengthen the argument?
- What emotions does the visual evoke? Are these the emotions that it intends to evoke?

The Design

Questions about Design

- How is the visual text composed? What's your eye drawn to first? Why?
- What's in the foreground? In the background? What's in or out of focus? What's moving? What's placed high, and what's placed low? What's to the left, in the center, and to the right? What effect do these placements have on the message? If the visual text is interactive, how well does that element work and what does it add?
- Is any information (such as a name, face, or scene) highlighted or stressed to attract your attention?
- How are light and color used? What effects are they intended to create? What about video? Sound? Animation?

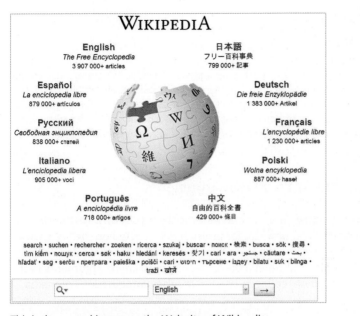

This is the central image on the Web site of Wikipedia, a collaborative nonprofit encyclopedia project. Since its launch (as Nupedia) in 2000, Wikipedia has grown to include 21 million articles in 282 languages, all of them authored by volunteers around the world. This central image acts as a logo, a portal to access the site's content, and, in a way, a mission statement for the organization. How does your eye construct this logo? What do you notice first, and how do your eyes move around the page? Do the parts make sense when you put them together?

- What details are emphasized? What details are omitted or deemphasized? To what effect? Is anything downplayed, ambiguous, confusing, distracting, or obviously omitted? Why?

- What, if anything, is surprising about the design of the visual text? What do you think is the purpose of that surprise?

- Is anything in the visual repeated, intensified, or exaggerated? Is anything presented as "supernormal" or idealistic? What effects do these strategies intend to create? What effects do they have on you? How do they clarify or reinforce (or blur or contradict) the message?

- How are you directed to move within the argument? Are you encouraged to read further? Click on a link? Scroll down? Fill out a form? Provide your email address? Place an order?

RESPOND •

Find three or four Web pages that exemplify good visual design, and then find three or four that don't. When you've picked the good and bad designs, draw a rough sketch of each page's physical layout. Where are the graphics? Where is the text? What are the size and position of text blocks relative to graphics? How is color used? Can you discern common design principles among the pages, or does each good page work well in its own way? Write up your findings, focusing on how the visual arguments influence audiences.

Using Visuals in Your Own Arguments

It's easy today to use images and multimedia in your own writing. In fact, many college classes now call for projects to be posted on the Web, which almost always involves the use of images. Other courses invite or require students to make multimedia presentations or to create arguments in the form of videos, photo collages, comics, or other combinations of media.

Using Images and Multimedia to Appeal to Emotion

Many advertisements, YouTube videos, political documentaries, rallies, marches, and even church services use images and multimedia to trigger emotions. You can't flip through a magazine, watch a video, or browse the Web without being cajoled or seduced by images of all kinds—most of them designed in some way to attract your eye and attention and many of them linked to other media or using animation or some sort of interactive element.

CHOOSE IMAGES CAREFULLY

You want to take advantage of technology to appeal effectively to your readers' emotions. To do so, think first of the purpose of your writing: you want every image or use of multimedia to carry out that purpose. Look at the famous *Apollo 8* photograph of our planet as a big blue marble hanging above the horizon of the moon. You could use this image to introduce an argument about the need for additional investment in the space program. Or it might become part of an argument about the need to preserve our frail natural environment, or an argument against nationalism: *From space, we are one world.* You could make any of these claims without the image, but the photograph—like most images—will probably touch members of your audience more powerfully than words alone could.

A striking image, like this *Apollo 8* photograph of the earth shining over the moon, can support many different kinds of arguments.

REMEMBER THE POWER OF COLOR

As the photo of the earth demonstrates, color can have great power: the blue earth floating in deep black space carries a message of its own. Our response to color is part of our biological and cultural makeup. So it makes sense to consider what colors are compatible with the kinds of arguments you're making.

In most situations, you can be guided in your selection of colors by your own good taste, by designs you admire, or by the advice of friends or helpful professionals. Some design and presentation software will even help you choose colors by offering dependable "default" shades or an array of pre-existing designs and compatible colors (for example, of presentation slides). To be emotionally effective, the colors you choose for a design should follow certain commonsense principles. If you're using background colors on a political poster, Web site, or slide, the contrast between words and background should be vivid enough to make reading easy. For example, white letters on a yellow background are not usually legible. Similarly, any bright background color should be avoided for a long document because reading is easiest with dark letters against a light or white background. Avoid complex patterns; even though they might look interesting and be easy to create, they often interfere with other more important elements of a presentation.

When you use visuals in your college projects, test them on prospective readers. That's what professionals do because they appreciate how delicate the choices of visual and multimedia texts can be. These responses will help you analyze your own arguments and improve your success with them.

Using Images and Multimedia to Appeal to Character

Careful use of images and multimedia can help to establish the character and credibility of your text as well as your own ethos as a writer. If you are on Facebook, LinkedIn, or other social networking sites, you will know how images especially create a sense of who you are and what you value. It's no accident that employers have been known not to hire people because of the images they find on their Facebook pages—or just the opposite: we know one person whose Facebook page use of images and multimedia so impressed a prospective employer that she got the job on the spot. So whether you are using images and multimedia on your personal pages or in your college work, it pays to attend to how they shape your ethos.

USE IMAGES AND MULTIMEDIA TO REINFORCE
YOUR CREDIBILITY AND AUTHORITY

Just like the Red Cross, the Department of Homeland Security, and the Canadian Olympic Committee, you want to use images and multimedia that will build your trustworthiness and authority. For a Web site about a

Take a look at these three images, each of which intends to convey credibility and authority. Do they accomplish their goals? Why or why not?

group or organization you belong to or represent, you might display its logo or emblem because such images can provide credibility. An emblem or a logo can also convey a wealth of cultural and historical implications. That's why university Web sites often include the seal of the institution somewhere on the homepage or why the president of the United States travels with a presidential seal to hang on the speaker's podium. Other kinds of media can also enhance ethos. For an essay on safety issues in competitive biking, you might include a photo of yourself in a key race, embed a video showing how serious accidents often occur, or include an audio file of an interview with an injured biker. The photo shows that you have personal experience with biking, while the video and audio files show that you have done research and know your subject well, thus helping to affirm your credibility.

CONSIDER HOW DESIGN REFLECTS YOUR CHARACTER

Almost every design element sends signals about character and ethos. For example, the type fonts that you select for a document can mark you as warm and inviting or as efficient and contemporary. The warm and inviting fonts often belong to a family called *serif*. The serifs are those little flourishes at the ends of the strokes that make the fonts seem handcrafted and artful:

warm and inviting (Bookman Old Style)

warm and inviting (Times New Roman)

warm and inviting (Georgia)

Cleaner, modern fonts go without those little flourishes and are called *sans serif*. These fonts are cooler, simpler, and, some argue, more readable on a computer screen (depending on screen resolution):

efficient and contemporary (Helvetica)

efficient and contemporary (Verdana)

efficient and contemporary (Comic Sans MS)

Other typographic elements shape your ethos as well. The size of type can make a difference. If your text or headings are in boldface and too large, you'll seem to be shouting:

LOSE WEIGHT! PAY NOTHING!*

Tiny type, on the other hand, might make you seem evasive:

*Excludes the costs of enrollment and required meal purchases. Minimum contract: 12 months.

Your choice of *color*—especially for backgrounds—can make a statement about your taste, personality, and common sense. For instance, you'll create a bad impression with a Web page whose dark background colors or busy patterns make reading difficult. If you want to be noticed, you might use bright colors—the same sort that would make an impression in clothing or cars. But subtle background shades are a better choice in most situations.

Don't ignore the power of *illustrations* and *photographs*. Because they reveal what you visualize, images can communicate your preferences,

Olympic champion Michael Phelps learned a quick lesson about ethos when a drug-related incident tarnished his reputation, costing him an endorsement deal with Kellogg's. His photograph had already appeared on boxes of Kellogg's Corn Flakes and Wheaties.

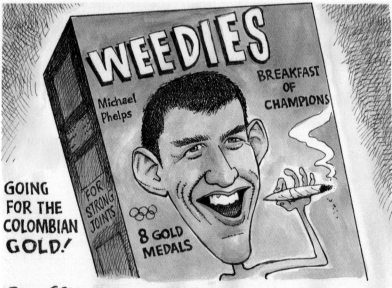

© Dave Granlund/Cagle Cartoons, Inc.

sensitivities, and inclusiveness. Conference planners, for example, are careful to create brochures that represent all participants, and they make sure that the brochure photos don't show only women, only men, or only members of one racial or ethnic group.

Even your choice of *medium* says something important about you. Making an appeal on a Web site sends signals about your technical skills, contemporary orientation, and personality. If you direct people to a Facebook or Flickr page, be sure that the images and items there present you in a favorable light.

RESPOND●

Choose a project or essay you have written recently and examine it for how well it establishes your credibility and how well it is designed. Ask a classmate or friend to look at it and tell you how effectively it is designed and how well it represents you. Then go back to the drawing board with a memo to yourself about how you might use images and multimedia to improve it.

You should also be careful that any *handouts* you use during a presentation or any slides you may show work to build your ethos and authority as well. And remember that you don't always have to be high-tech to be effective: when reporting on a children's story that you're writing, the most effective medium of presentation might be cardboard and paper made into an oversized book and illustrated by hand.

FOLLOW DESIGN CONVENTIONS

Many kinds of writing have required design conventions. When that's the case, follow them to the letter. It's no accident that lab reports for science courses are sober and unembellished. Visually, they reinforce the professional ethos of scientific work. The same is true of a college research paper. You might resent the tediousness of placing page numbers in the appropriate corner, aligning long quotations just so, and putting footnotes in the right place, but these visual details help convey your competence. So whether you're composing a term paper, résumé, film, animated comic, or Web site, look for competent models and follow them.

Visual Arguments Based on Facts and Reason

Not that long ago, media critics ridiculed the colorful charts and graphs in newspapers like *USA Today*. Now, comparable features appear in even the most traditional publications because they work: they convey information efficiently. We now expect information to be presented graphically, to see multiple streams of data on our screens, and to be able to interact with many of these presentations.

ORGANIZE INFORMATION VISUALLY

Graphic presentation calls for careful design, which can help readers and viewers look at an item and understand what it does. A brilliant, much-copied example of such an intuitive design is a seat adjuster invented many years ago by Mercedes-Benz (see below). It's shaped like a tiny seat. Push any element of the control, and the real seat moves in that direction—back and forth, up and down. No instructions are necessary.

Good visual design can work the same way in an argument by conveying information without elaborate instructions. Titles, headings, subheadings, enlarged quotations, running heads, and boxes are some common visual signals.

- Use headings to guide your readers through your print or electronic document. For long and complex pieces, use subheadings as well, and make sure they are parallel.

- Use type font, size, and color to show related information within headings.

- Plan how text should be arranged on a page by searching for relationships among items that should look alike.

- Use a list or a box to set off information that should be treated differently from the rest of the presentation or for emphasis. You can also use shading, color, and typography for emphasis.

  - Place your images and illustrations carefully: what you position front and center will appear more important than items in less conspicuous places. On a Web site, key headings should usually lead to subsequent pages on the site.

Mercedes-Benz's seat adjuster

Remember, too, that design principles evolve and change from medium to medium. A printed text or an overhead slide, for example, ordinarily works best when its elements are easy to read, simply organized, and surrounded by restful white space. But some types of Web pages thrive on visual clutter that attracts attention by packing a wide variety of information onto a relatively limited screen. Look closely, and you'll probably find the logic in these designs.

USE VISUALS TO CONVEY DATA EFFICIENTLY

Words are powerful and capable of precision and subtlety. But some information is conveyed more efficiently by charts, graphs, drawings, maps, or photos. When making an argument, especially to a large group, consider what information should be delivered in nonverbal form.

A *pie chart* is an effective way of comparing parts to the whole. You might use a pie chart to illustrate the ethnic composition of your school, the percentage of taxes paid by people at different income levels, or the consumption of energy by different nations. Pie charts depict such information memorably, as the one on p. 342 shows.

A *graph* is an efficient device for comparing items over time or according to other variables. You could use a graph to trace the rise and fall of test scores over several decades or to show college enrollment by sex, race, and Hispanic origin, as in the bar graph on p. 342.

Diagrams or *drawings* are useful for drawing attention to details. Use drawings to illustrate complex physical processes or designs of all sorts. After the 2001 attack on the World Trade Center, for example, engineers prepared drawings and diagrams to help citizens understand precisely what led to the total collapse of the buildings.

You can use *maps* to illustrate location and spatial relationships—something as simple as the distribution of office space in your student union or as complex as the topography of Utah. Such information would be far more difficult to explain in words alone. And you can now use tools like UMapper to customize maps.

Timelines allow you to represent the passage of time graphically, and online tools like Dipity can help you create them for insertion into your documents.

Web pages can also make for valuable illustrations. Programs like ShrinkTheWeb let you create snapshots of Web sites that can then be inserted easily into your writing.

Portrait of America

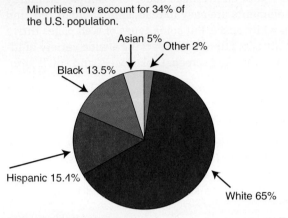

Minorities now account for 34% of
the U.S. population.

Asian 5% Other 2%

Black 13.5%

Hispanic 15.4%

White 65%

Source: Census Bureau

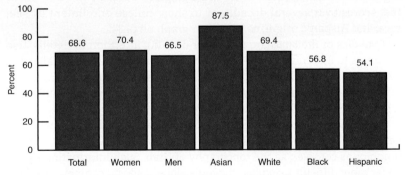

College enrollment of year 2005 high school graduates, by sex, race, and Hispanic origin

FOLLOW PROFESSIONAL GUIDELINES FOR PRESENTING VISUALS

Charts, graphs, tables, illustrations, timelines, snapshots of Web sites, and video clips play such an important role in many fields that professional groups have come up with guidelines for labeling and formatting these items. You need to become familiar with those conventions as you advance in a field. A guide such as the *Publication Manual of the American Psychological Association* (6th edition) or the *MLA Handbook for Writers of Research Papers* (7th edition) describes these rules in detail. See also Chapter 15, "Presenting Arguments."

REMEMBER TO CHECK FOR COPYRIGHTED MATERIAL

You also must be careful to respect copyright rules when using visual items that were created by someone else. It's relatively easy these days to download visual texts of all kinds from the Web. Some of these items—such as clip art or government documents—may be in the *public domain*, meaning that you're free to use them without requesting permission or paying a royalty. But other visual texts may require permission, especially if you intend to publish your work or use the item commercially. And remember: anything you place on a Web site is considered "published." (See Chapter 20 for more on intellectual property.)

15
Presenting Arguments

Sometimes you won't have a choice about how to present an argument: your instructor will say, "Write a report," or "Design a Web page." But often you'll be the one to decide what kind of presentation best fits your topic, purpose, and audience, just as the writers above chose a face-to-face oral presentation (Josette Sheeran's talk at a conference on World Food Security), the student site that contains additional materials linked to this text (accessible via the QR code provided), or a Web-based presentation (Lawrence Lessig's use of slides and Web tools to talk about Internet and wireless gambling).

Print Presentations

For many arguments that you make in college, print is still a major mode of delivery. Print texts are more permanent than most Web-based materials, they're inexpensive and easy to produce, and they offer a precise way to express abstract ideas or to set down complicated chains of reasoning. In making arguments in print today, though, you have an embarrassment of riches. What used to be confined to black print on 8½ x 11" white paper read left to right, top to bottom, today can be designed in a dizzying array of shapes, sizes, and colors.

As you think about presenting print-based arguments, try answering these questions:

- What overall tone do you want to create in this written argument? What's the purpose of your argument, and to whom is it addressed?

- What format will get your message across most effectively? A formal report? A newsletter? A triple-fold brochure? A poster? Whatever you choose, follow the conventions of that format by looking at good examples.

- What fonts will make your argument most readable? Will varying the font or type size help guide readers through your text? Will it draw attention to what's most important?

- Will you use subheads as another guide? If so, what size type will you select? Will you use all caps, boldface, or italics? In any case, be consistent in the style and the structure of subheads (all nouns, for example, or all questions).

- Should you use colors other than black ink and white paper in presenting your argument? What colors best evoke your tone and purpose? What colors will be most appealing?

- How will you use white or blank space in your argument? To give readers time to pause? To establish a sense of openness or orderliness?

- Will you use visuals in your print argument? If so, how will you integrate them smoothly into the text? (For more on the role of visuals in arguments, see Chapter 14.)

RESPOND ●

Choose a print presentation that you find particularly effective. Study it carefully, noting how its various elements—format, type sizes, typefaces, color, white space, visuals, and overall layout—work to deliver its message. If you find a particularly ineffective print presentation, carry out the same analysis to figure out why it's bad. Finally, prepare a five-minute presentation of your findings to deliver in class.

F2F Oral and Multimedia Presentations

You are probably being asked to make oral presentations in your classes, but you may be given few if any instructions in how to do so effectively. And students returning from summer internships say their employers expect them to be good at delivering arguments orally—and at accompanying their presentations with well-designed slides or illustrations.

It's hard to generalize here, but capable presenters attribute their success to several crucial elements:

- They have thorough knowledge of their subjects.
- They pay attention to the values, ideas, and needs of their listeners.
- They use structures and styles that make their spoken arguments easy to follow.
- They realize that oral arguments are interactive. (Live audiences can argue back!)
- They appreciate that most oral presentations involve visuals, and they plan accordingly.
- They practice, practice—and then practice some more.

Oral Arguments in Discussions

You are arguing all the time, whether exploring the meaning of a poem in English class, arguing against a writer's interpretation of an economics phenomenon, or speaking against a student government policy on funding political organizations. You can improve your performance in such situations by observing effective speakers and by joining conversations whenever you can. The more that you participate in lively discussions, the more comfortable you'll be with speaking your mind. Here are some tips to help you do so:

- Do the required reading so that you know what you're talking about.
- Listen carefully and purposefully, and jot down important points.
- Speak briefly to the point under discussion so that your comments are relevant. Don't do all the talking.
- Ask questions about issues that matter to you: others probably have the same thoughts.
- Occasionally offer brief summaries of points that have already been made to make sure that everyone is "on the same page."

CULTURAL CONTEXTS FOR ARGUMENT

Speaking Up in Class

Speaking up in class is viewed as inappropriate or even rude in some cultures. In the United States, however, doing so is expected and encouraged. Some instructors even assign credit for such class participation.

- Respond to questions or comments by others in specific rather than vague terms.
- Try to learn the names of people in the discussion, and then use them.
- When you are already part of a discussion, invite others to join in.

Formal Oral and Multimedia Presentations

When asked to make a formal presentation in class or on the job, consider the context carefully. Note how much time you have to prepare and how long the presentation should be: never infringe on the time of other speakers. Consider also what visual aids, slides, or handouts might make the presentation successful. Will you need an overhead projector, a flip chart, a whiteboard? What presentation software, if any, will you use?

Check out where your presentation will take place. In a classroom with fixed chairs? A lecture or assembly hall? An informal sitting area? Will you have a lectern? Other equipment? Will you sit or stand? Remain in one place or move around? What will the lighting be, and can you adjust it?

Sometimes oral presentations are group efforts. When that's the case, plan and practice accordingly. The work will need to be divvied up, and you will need to work out who speaks when. Finally, note any criteria for evaluation: how will your live oral argument be assessed?

In addition to these logistical matters, consider these rhetorical elements whenever you make a formal presentation:

Purpose. Determine your major argumentative purpose. Is it to inform? To convince or persuade? To explore? To make a decision? To entertain? Something else?

Audience. Who is your audience? An interested observer? A familiar face? A stranger? What will be the mix of age groups, of gender, etc.? Are you a peer of the audience members? Think carefully about what they know about your topic and what opinions they're likely to hold.

Structure. Structure your presentation so that it's easy to follow. Plan an introduction that gets the audience's attention and a conclusion that makes your argument memorable. You'll find more help with structure on p. 349.

Arguments to Be Heard

Even if you deliver a live presentation from a printed text, be sure to compose a script that is to be *heard* rather than *read*. Such a text—whether in the form of note cards, an overhead list, or a fully written-out script—should feature a strong introduction and conclusion, an unambiguous structure with helpful transitions and signposts, concrete diction, and straightforward syntax.

STRONG INTRODUCTIONS AND CONCLUSIONS

Like readers, listeners remember beginnings and endings best. Work hard, therefore, to make these elements of your spoken argument especially memorable. Consider including a provocative or puzzling statement, opinion, or question; a memorable anecdote; a powerful quotation; or a vivid visual image. If you can refer to the interests or experiences of your listeners in the introduction or conclusion, then do so.

Look at the introduction to Toni Morrison's acceptance speech to the Nobel Academy when she won the Nobel Prize for Literature:

> "Once upon a time there was an old woman. Blind but wise." Or was it an old man? A guru, perhaps. Or a griot soothing restless children. I have heard this story, or one exactly like it, in the lore of several cultures. "Once upon a time there was an old woman. Blind. Wise."
>
> —Toni Morrison

Here, Morrison uses a storytelling strategy, calling on the traditional "Once upon a time" to signal to her audience that she's doing so. Note also the use of repetition and questioning. These strategies raise interest and anticipation in her audience: how will she use this story in accepting the Nobel Prize?

Toni Morrison accepting the Nobel Prize for Literature in 1993

CLEAR STRUCTURES AND SIGNPOSTS

For a spoken argument, you want your organizational structure to be crystal clear. So offer an overview of your main points toward the beginning of the presentation, and make sure that you have a sharply delineated beginning, middle, and end. Throughout the report or lecture, remember to pause between major points and to offer *signposts* to mark your movement from one topic to the next. They can be transitions as obvious as *next, on the contrary,* or *finally.* Such words act as memory points in your spoken argument and thus should be explicit and concrete: *The second crisis point in the breakup of the Soviet Union occurred hard on the heels of the first,* rather than *The breakup of the Soviet Union came to another crisis.* You can also keep listeners on track by repeating key words and concepts and by using unambiguous topic sentences to introduce each new idea.

STRAIGHTFORWARD SYNTAX AND CONCRETE DICTION

Avoid long, complicated sentences and use straightforward syntax (subject-verb-object, for instance, rather than an inversion of that order). Remember, too, that listeners can hold onto concrete verbs and nouns more easily than they can grasp a steady stream of abstractions.

When you need to deal with abstract ideas, illustrate them with concrete examples.

Take a look at the following text that student Ben McCorkle wrote about *The Simpsons*, first as he prepared it for an essay and then as he adapted it for a live oral and multimedia presentation:

Print Version

The Simpson family has occasionally been described as a *nuclear* family, which obviously has a double meaning: first, the family consists of two parents and three children, and, second, Homer works at a nuclear power plant with very relaxed safety codes. The overused label "dysfunctional," when applied to the Simpsons, suddenly takes on new meaning. Every episode seems to include a scene in which son Bart is being choked by his father, the baby is being neglected, or Homer is sitting in a drunken stupor transfixed by the television screen. The comedy in these scenes comes from the exaggeration of commonplace household events (although some talk shows and news programs would have us believe that these exaggerations are not confined to the madcap world of cartoons).

—Ben McCorkle, "*The Simpsons:* A Mirror of Society"

Oral Version (with a visual illustration)

What does it mean to describe the Simpsons as a *nuclear* family? Clearly, a double meaning is at work. First, the Simpsons fit the dictionary meaning—a family unit consisting of two parents and some children. The second meaning, however, packs more of a punch. You see, Homer works at a nuclear power plant [pause here] with *very* relaxed safety codes!

Still another overused family label describes the Simpsons. Did everyone guess I was going to say *dysfunctional*? And like *nuclear*, when it comes to the Simpsons, *dysfunctional* takes on a whole new meaning.

Remember the scene when Bart is being choked by his father?

How about the many times the baby is being neglected?

Or the classic view—Homer sitting in a stupor transfixed by the TV screen!

My point here is that the comedy in these scenes often comes from double meanings—and from a lot of exaggeration of everyday household events.

Note that the second version presents the same information as the first, but this time it's written to be *heard*. The revision uses simpler syntax, so the argument is easy to listen to, and employs signposts, repetition, a list, and italicized words to prompt the speaker to give special emphasis where needed.

Homer Simpson in a typical pose

Arguments to Be Remembered

Some oral and multimedia arguments have power just because they stick in the memory—the way catchy song lyrics do. For instance, people who don't even know what the slogan means still recognize James Polk's 1844 rallying cry: "Fifty-Four Forty or Fight!" Or consider the impact of a song lyric like Lorrie Morgan's "What part of *no* don't you understand?"—which is a riff on an even simpler women's rights argument: "No means *no*."

More recently, Republican presidential hopeful Herman Cain used deliberate repetition and parallel structure to fashion a tax reform plan people might notice. Called simply 9-9-9, Cain proposed a 9 percent

Some arguments are memorable in part because they offer repetition.

personal income tax rate, 9 percent corporate tax rate, and 9 percent national sales tax. Even though economists criticized his idea roundly, Cain enjoyed a momentary boost in the polls in 2011 before his campaign foundered over other issues. (See Chapter 13 for more on using figurative language to make arguments vivid.)

RESPOND●

Take three or four paragraphs from an essay that you've recently written. Then, following the guidelines in this chapter, rewrite the passage to be heard by a live audience. Finally, make a list of every change that you made.

REPETITION, PARALLELISM, AND CLIMACTIC ORDER

Whether they're used alone or in combination, repetition, parallelism, and climactic order are especially appropriate for spoken arguments that sound a call to arms or that seek passionate engagement from the audience. Perhaps no person in the twentieth century used them more effectively than Martin Luther King Jr., whose sermons and speeches helped to spearhead the civil rights movement. Standing on the steps of the Lincoln Memorial in Washington, D.C., on August 23, 1963, with hundreds of thousands of marchers before him, King called on the nation to make good on the "promissory note" represented by the Emancipation Proclamation.

Look at the way that King uses repetition, parallelism, and climactic order in the following paragraph to invoke a nation to action:

> It is obvious today that America has defaulted on this promissory note insofar as her citizens of color are concerned. Instead of honoring this sacred obligation, America has given the Negro people a bad *check* which has come back marked "*insufficient funds*." But *we* refuse to believe that the bank of justice is bankrupt. *We* refuse to believe that there are *insufficient funds* in the great vaults of opportunity of this nation. So *we have come* to cash this *check*—a *check* that will give us upon demand the riches of freedom and the security of justice. *We have also come* to this hallowed spot to remind America of the fierce urgency of now. There is no time to engage in the luxury of cooling off or to take the tranquillizing drug of gradualism. *Now* is the time *to rise* from the dark and desolate valley of segregation to the sunlit path of racial justice. *Now* is the time *to open* the doors of opportunity to all of God's children. *Now* is the time *to lift* our nation from the quicksands of racial injustice to the solid rock of brotherhood.
>
> —Martin Luther King Jr., "I Have a Dream" (emphasis added)

The italicized words highlight the way that King uses repetition to drum home his theme and a series of powerful verb phrases (*to rise, to open, to lift*) to build to a strong climax. These stylistic choices, together with the vivid image of the "bad check," help to make King's speech powerful, persuasive—and memorable.

You don't have to be as highly skilled as King to take advantage of the power of repetition and parallelism. Simply repeating a key word in your argument can impress it on your audience, as can arranging parts of sentences or items in a list in parallel order.

The Role of Visuals in Oral and Multimedia Arguments

Visual materials—chart, graphs, posters, and presentation slides—are major tools for conveying your message and supporting your claims. In many cases, a picture can truly be worth a thousand words. (For more about visual argument, see Chapter 14.)

Be certain that any visuals that you use are large enough to be seen by all members of your audience. If you use slides or overhead projections, the information on each frame should be simple, clear, and easy to process. For slides, use 24-point type for major headings, 18 point for subheadings, and at least 14 point for other text. The same rule of clarity and simplicity holds true for posters, flip charts, and whiteboards.

And remember not to turn your back on your audience while you refer to these visuals. If you prepare supplementary materials (such as bibliographies or other handouts) for the audience, don't distribute them until the audience actually needs them. Or wait until the end of the presentation so that they don't distract listeners from your spoken argument.

If you've watched many PowerPoint presentations, you're sure to have seen some bad ones. But nothing is more deadly than a speaker who stands up and reads from each screen. It is fine to use presentation slides to furnish an overview for a presentation and to give visual signposts to listeners. But never read the slides word for word — or even put much prose on a screen. You'll just put your audience to sleep.

For an oral and multimedia presentation, Sach Wickramasekara used the PowerPoint slides shown on p. 356 to compare Frank Miller's graphic novel *Sin City* and its movie adaptation. Notice that the student uses text minimally, letting the pictures do the talking.

His choices in layout and font size also aim for clarity but without sacrificing visual appeal. The choice of white on a black background is appropriate for the topic — a stark black-and-white graphic novel and its shades-of-gray movie version. But be aware that light writing on a dark background can be hard to read and that dark writing on a white or cream-colored background is almost always a safer choice. Sach is not reading from his slides; rather the slides illustrate the point he is making orally. In this case, the words and the images work together beautifully.

(Note that if your presentation shows or is based on source materials — either text or images — your instructor may want you to include a slide that lists the sources at the end of the presentation.)

The best way to test the effectiveness of any images, slides, or other visuals is to try them out on friends, family members, classmates, or roommates. If they don't get the meaning of the visuals right away, revise and try again.

Remember, finally, that visuals and accompanying media tools can help make your presentation accessible but that some members of your audience may not be able to see your presentation or may have trouble seeing or hearing them. Here are a few key rules to remember:

- Use words to describe projected images. Something as simple as *That's Franklin Roosevelt in 1944* can help even sight-impaired audience members appreciate what's on a screen.

- Consider providing a written handout that summarizes your presentation or putting the text on an overhead projector—for those who learn better by reading *and* listening.

- If you use video, take the time to label sounds that might not be audible to audience members who are hearing impaired. (Be sure your equipment is caption capable and use the captions; they can be helpful to everyone when audio quality is poor.)

Oral and Multimedia Presentation Strategies

In spite of your best preparation, you may feel some anxiety before a live presentation. This is natural. (According to one Gallup poll, Americans often identify public speaking as a major fear—scarier than possible attacks from outer space.) Experienced speakers say that they have strategies for dealing with anxiety, and even that a little nervousness—and accompanying adrenaline—can act to a speaker's advantage.

The most effective strategy seems to be thoroughly knowing your topic and material. Confidence in your own knowledge goes a long way toward making you a confident speaker. In addition to being well prepared, you may want to try some of the following strategies:

- Practice a number of times, running through every part of the presentation. Leave nothing out, even audio or video clips. Work with the equipment you intend to use so that you are familiar with it. It also may help to visualize your presentation, imagining the scene in your mind as you run through your materials.

- Time your presentation to make sure you stay within your allotted slot.

- Tape yourself (video, if possible) at least once so that you can listen to your voice. Tone of voice and body language can dispose audiences for—or against—speakers. For most oral arguments, you want to develop a tone that conveys commitment to your position as well as respect for your audience.

Introduction

A frame from the *Sin City* graphic novel.

"Instead of trying to make it [*Sin City*] into a movie which would be terrible, I wanted to take cinema and try and make it into this book."

- Robert Rodriguez, DVD Interview

The same scene from the *Sin City* movie.

Technology

Right: The original scene from the graphic novel.

Left: The scene is filmed with live actors on a green screen set.

Right: The final version of the scene, after the colors have been changed to shades of black and white. Notice the sapphire shade of the convertible, and how it stands out from the background.

[Opening Slide: Title]

Hi, my name is Sach.

[Change Slide: Introduction]

Take a look at this pair of scenes. Can you tell which one's from a movie and which one's from a graphic novel? How can two completely different media produce such similar results? Stay tuned; you're about to hear how.

[Pause]

[Change Slide: Technology]

Part of what makes *Sin City* so innovative is the technology powering it. The movie captures the look of the graphic novel so well by filming actors on a green screen and using digital imagery to put detailed backdrops behind them. Computer technology also turns the movie's visuals into shades of black and white with rare dashes of color splashed in, reproducing the noir feel of the original novels. Thus, scenes in *Sin City* have a photorealistic yet stylized quality that differentiates them from both the plain black-and-white images of the comics and the real sets used in other movies.

- Think about how you'll dress for your presentation, remembering that audience members usually notice how a speaker looks. Dressing for an effective presentation depends on what's appropriate for your topic, audience, and setting, but most experienced speakers choose clothes that are comfortable, allow easy movement, and aren't overly casual. Dressing up a little indicates that you take pride in your appearance, have confidence in your argument, and respect your audience.

- Get some rest before the presentation, and avoid consuming too much caffeine.

- Relax! Consider doing some deep-breathing exercises. Then pause just before you begin, concentrating on your opening lines.

- Maintain eye contact with members of your audience. Speak to them, not to your text or to the floor.

- Interact with the audience whenever possible; doing so will often help you relax and even have some fun.

- Most speakers make a stronger impression standing than sitting, so stand if you have that option. Moving around a bit may help you maintain good eye contact.

- When using presentation slides, stand to the side so that you don't block the view. Look at the audience rather than the slide.

- Remember to allow time for audience responses and questions. Keep your answers brief so that others may join the conversation.

- Finally, at the very end of your presentation, thank the audience for its attention to your arguments.

A Note about Webcasts: Live Presentations over the Web

This discussion of live oral and multimedia presentations has assumed that you'll be speaking before an audience that's in the same room with you. Increasingly, though—especially in business, industry, and science—the presentations you make will be live, but you won't be in the same physical space as the audience. Instead, you might be in front of a camera that will capture your voice and image and relay them via the Web to attendees who might be anywhere in the world. In another type of Webcast, participants can see only your slides or the software that you're demonstrating, using a screen-capture relay without cameras, and you're not visible but still speaking live.

In either case, as you learn to adapt to Webcast environments, most of the strategies that work in oral and multimedia presentations for an audience that's physically present will continue to serve you well. But there are some significant differences:

- Practice is even more important in Webcasts, since you need to be able to access online any slides, documents, video clips, names, dates, and sources that you provide during the Webcast.

- Because you can't make eye contact with audience members, it's important to remember to look into the camera (if you are using one), at least from time to time. If you're using a stationary Webcam, perhaps one mounted on your computer, practice standing or sitting without moving out of the frame and yet without looking stiff.

- Even though your audience may not be visible to you, assume that if you're on camera, the Web-based audience can see you. If you slouch, they'll notice. Assume too that your microphone is always live. Don't mutter under your breath, for example, when someone else is speaking or asking a question.

RESPOND ●

Attend a presentation on your campus, and observe the speaker's delivery. Note the strategies that the speaker uses to capture and hold your attention (or not). What signpost language and other guides to listening can you detect? How well are visuals integrated into the presentation? What aspects of the speaker's tone, dress, eye contact, and movement affect your understanding and appreciation (or lack of it)? What's most memorable about the presentation, and why? Finally, write up an analysis of this presentation's effectiveness.

Web-Based Presentations

Even without the interactivity of Webcasts, most students have enough access to the Web to use its powers for effective presentations, especially in Web sites and blogs.

The Web site for the band Moonlight Social.

Web Sites

You may already have created a Web site for a class or an extracurricular group or project. Take a look at a site designed by Jeremy Burchard and specifically at the "About" page, shown above, for the band he is part of, Moonlight Social. Note that this page design is simple and clear, with a menu bar across the top and three images on the left balanced by a block of text on the right. Also note that it allows a free download and that the entire page makes an argument that we should listen to their music.

In planning any Web site, you'll need to pay careful attention to your rhetorical situation—the purpose of your site, its intended audience, and the overall impression that you want to make. To get started, you may want to visit several sites that you admire, looking for effective design ideas and ways of organizing navigation and information. Creating a map or storyboard for your site will help you to think through the links from page to page.

Experienced Web designers cite several important principles for Web-based presentations. The first of these is *contrast*, which is achieved through the use of color, icons, boldface, and so on; contrast helps guide readers through the site. The second principle, *proximity*, calls on you to keep together the parts of a page that are closely related, again for ease of reading. *Repetition* means using a consistent design throughout the site for the elements (such as headings and links) that help readers move smoothly through the environment. Finally, designers concentrate on an *overall impression* or mood for the site, which means that the colors and visuals on the pages should help to create that impression rather than challenge or undermine it.

Here are some additional tips that may help you design your site:

- The homepage should be eye-catching, inviting, and informative. Use titles and illustrations to make clear what the site is about.

- Think carefully about two parts of every page — the navigation area (menus or links) and the content areas. You want to make these two areas clearly distinct from one another. And make sure you *have* a navigation area for every page, including links to the key sections of the site and a link back to the homepage. Ease of navigation is one key to a successful Web site.

- Either choose a design template that is provided by Web-writing tools or create a template of your own that ensures that the elements of each page are consistent.

- Remember that some readers may not have the capacity to download heavy visuals or to access elements like Flash. If you want to reach a wide audience, stick with visuals that can be downloaded easily.

- Remember to include Web contact information on every page, but not your personal address or phone number.

Videos

When is a video the best medium for delivering a message? When it fits well with the purpose of the message and enables the writer to reach a wider audience than a live presentation can. And students today have opportunities to make arguments using this influential medium.

When Max Oswald became concerned that online communication was separating people rather than bringing them together in the way that face-to-face communication can, he decided that the best way to get his message across was through a short film. Called "Progress," the video features Max talking directly with his viewers about the distancing effects of online communication. We also see Max moving around a room as he

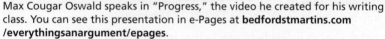
Max Cougar Oswald speaks in "Progress," the video he created for his writing class. You can see this presentation in e-Pages at **bedfordstmartins.com /everythingsanargument/epages**.

speaks, gesturing to slides that underscore the points he is making. At the end of the clip, however, Max steps into camera range and we realize he has been standing aside throughout. He looks at the audience and says he will end not with the video, which he argues has distanced us from him, but by talking to us face-to-face. The effect of the shift was a dramatic instantiation of the point his video was making.

Wikis

To make working on group projects easier, many classes have begun to use wikis, which are Web-based sites that enable writers to collaborate in the creation of a single project or database. The most famous group effort of this kind is, of course, Wikipedia, but software such as Doku-Wiki, MediaWiki, or Tiki Wiki helps people to manage similar, if less ambitious, efforts of their own, whether it be exploring questions raised in academic courses or examining and supporting needs within a community. Wiki projects can be argumentative in themselves, or they might furnish raw data and evidence for subsequent projects.

If asked to participate in a wiki, you should, naturally, learn how to use the assigned software and follow course or project guidelines for entering and documenting the material you contribute. Just as you will expect your colleagues to use reliable sources or make accurate observations, they will depend on you to do your part in shaping the project. Of course, within the wiki, participants will be able to draw upon each other's strengths and, ideally, to compensate for any weaknesses. So take your responsibilities seriously.

Blogs

No Web texts have captured the public imagination more swiftly than blogs, which are now too numerous to count as well as thoroughly interactive.

In many ways, these blogs offer an alternative to traditional newspapers, TV networks, and periodicals: blogs often break important news stories as well as give more breadth to the political spectrum. As such, blogs create an ideal space for building communities, engaging in arguments, and giving voice to views and opinions of ordinary, everyday folks. We seldom see these people writing or being written about in major print media—many of which now sponsor blogs themselves as part of their electronic versions.

The Web site for Moonlight Social contains a blog. Take a look at this posting from February 8, 2011:

Hi there
It looks like you've stumbled upon a blog! But why is Moonlight Social blogging? Well, people like to talk about themselves . . . and bands like to talk about themselves even more. But more importantly, we want to keep you, the fans, in the loop. So here's what you can expect: quick updates, some responses to questions from the comments posted in the contact section, and maybe a musical thought or three. We'll keep it brief, and you let us know if you like it enough to keep it around!

Music update: You can officially expect to hear two new songs at our next show.
HOW EXCITING!

Response to Jessica: Glad you like the music player! The song you're talking about is called "Even If"—the third song in the rotation. Click the little arrows under the play/pause button until it pops up.

Response to Mango: The song you're referring to is called "The Idea of Me," and it is certainly on the docket to be recorded. A video of a live version may pop up some time soon too, so keep an eye out. And we can't wait for the next show either!

Speaking of the next show, it's Feb. 17th at New World Deli at 8:30—see you there!

Wonkette

HOT AIR TPM

Political blogs Wonkette, Hot Air, and Talking Points Memo are well-known for their lively comments sections.

Note that the Moonlight Social blog is direct and personable and that it allows for readers to comment. The bloggers then respond to comments, thus setting up a dialogue with their fans.

Of course, like everything else, blogs can have downsides: they are idiosyncratic, can be self-indulgent and egoistic, and can distort issues by spreading misinformation very quickly. If you're a fan of blogs, be sure to read carefully. The information on blogs hasn't been critically reviewed in the way that traditional print sources edit their stories. But also remember that blogs have reported many instances of the mainstream media's failure to live up to their own standards.

Political blogs get plenty of attention, and you can easily join in on the conversation there, bringing your arguments to bear on issues they raise. If you do blog, or comment on blogs, remember to follow commonsense good manners: be respectful and think carefully about what you are saying and about the impression you want to leave with those who read you.

RESPOND●

Go to a blog that you admire or consult frequently. Then answer the following questions:

Why is a blog—a digital presentation—the best way to present this material?

What advantages over a print text or a live oral and multimedia presentation does the blog have?

How could you "translate" the argument(s) of this site into print or live oral format? What might be gained or lost in the process?

PART 4

RESEARCH AND
arguments

16
Academic Arguments

Much of the writing you will do in college (and some of what you may do later in your professional work) is called **academic discourse** or **academic argument**. Although this kind of writing has many distinctive features, in general it shares these characteristics:

- It is based on research and uses evidence that can be documented.
- It is written for a professional, academic, or school audience likely to know something about its topic.
- It makes a clear and compelling point in a formal, objective, and often technical style.
- It follows agreed-upon conventions of format, usage, and punctuation.
- It is documented, using some professional citation style.

Academic writing is serious work, the kind you are expected to do whenever you are assigned a term paper, research paper, or capstone project. Manasi Deshpande's proposal "A Call to Improve Campus Accessibility for the Mobility Impaired" in Chapter 12 is an example of an academic argument of the kind you may write in college. You will find other examples of such work throughout this book.

Understanding What Academic Argument Is

Academic argument covers a wide range of writing. But its hallmarks are an appeal to reason and a faith in research. As a consequence, such arguments cannot be composed quickly, casually, or off the top of one's head. They require careful reading, accurate reporting, and a conscientious commitment to truth. Academic pieces do not entirely tune out appeals to ethos or emotions: such arguments often convey power and authority through their impressive lists of sources and their formal style. But an academic argument simply crumbles if its facts are skewed or its content proves to be unreliable.

Look, for example, how systematically a communications scholar presents facts and evidence in an academic argument about privacy and social networking in the United States:

> According to three 2005 Pew Reports (Lenhart, 2005; Lenhart, et al., 2005; Lenhart and Madden, 2005), 87 percent of American teens aged 12–17 are using the Internet. Fifty-one percent of these teenagers state that they go online on a daily basis. Approximately four million teenagers or 19 percent say that they create their own weblogs (personal online journals) and 22 percent report that they maintain a personal Web page (Lenhart and Madden, 2005). In blogs and on personal Web sites, teenagers are providing so much personal information about themselves that it has become a concern. Today, content creation is not only sharing music and videos; it involves personal diaries.
>
> —Susan B. Barnes, "A Privacy Paradox:
> Social Networking in the United States"

Note, too, that this writer draws her material from reports produced by the Pew Research Center, a well-known and respected organization. Chances are you immediately recognize that this paragraph is an example of a researched academic argument.

You can also identify academic argument by the way it addresses its audiences. Some academic writing is clearly aimed at specialists in a field who are familiar with both the subject and the terminology that surrounds it. As a result, the researchers make few concessions to general readers unlikely to encounter or appreciate their work. You see that single-mindedness in this abstract of an article about migraine headaches in a scientific journal: it quickly becomes unreadable to nonspecialists.

Abstract

Migraine is a complex, disabling disorder of the brain that manifests itself as attacks of often severe, throbbing head pain with sensory sensitivity to light, sound and head movement. There is a clear familial tendency to migraine, which has been well defined in a rare autosomal dominant form of familial hemiplegic migraine (FHM). FHM mutations so far identified include those in CACNA1A (P/Q voltage-gated Ca(2+) channel), ATP1A2 (N(+)-K(+)-ATPase) and SCN1A (Na(+) channel) genes. Physiological studies in humans and studies of the experimental correlate — cortical spreading depression (CSD) — provide understanding of aura, and have explored in recent years the effect of migraine preventives in CSD. . . .

—Peter J. Goadsby, "Recent Advances in Understanding Migraine Mechanisms, Molecules, and Therapeutics," *Trends in Molecular Medicine*, Vol. 13, No. 1, pp. 39–44 (January 2007)

Yet this very article might later provide data for a more accessible argument in a magazine such as *Scientific American*, which addresses a broader (though no less serious) readership. Here's a selection from an article on migraine headaches from that more widely read journal (see also the infographic on p. 370):

At the moment, only a few drugs can prevent migraine. All of them were developed for other diseases, including hypertension, depression and epilepsy. Because they are not specific to migraine, it will come as no surprise that they work in only 50 percent of patients — and, in them, only 50 percent of the time — and induce a range of side effects, some potentially serious.

Recent research on the mechanism of these antihypertensive, antiepileptic and antidepressant drugs has demonstrated that one of their effects is to inhibit cortical spreading depression. The drugs' ability to prevent migraine with and without aura therefore supports the school of thought that cortical spreading depression contributes to both kinds of attacks. Using this observation as a starting point, investigators have come up with novel drugs that specifically inhibit cortical spreading depression. Those drugs are now being tested in migraine sufferers with and without aura. They work by preventing gap junctions, a form of ion channel, from opening, thereby halting the flow of calcium between brain cells.

—David W. Dodick and J. Jay Gargus, "Why Migraines Strike," *Scientific American* (August 2008)

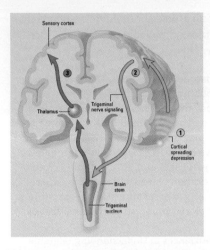

Infographic: the root of migraine pain

Such writing still requires attention, but it delivers important and comprehensible information to any reader seriously interested in the subject and the latest research on it.

Even when academic writing is less technical and demanding, its style will retain a noticeable formality—maybe even stiffness. To some extent in academic arguments, the authors seem to disappear, the tone is objective and dispassionate, the language avoids highly connotative expressions, and all the i's are dotted and t's crossed. Here's an abstract for an academic paper on the Burning Man phenomenon, demonstrating those qualities:

Every August for more than a decade, thousands of information technologists and other knowledge workers have trekked out into a barren stretch of alkali desert and built a temporary city devoted to art, technology, and communal living: Burning Man. Drawing on extensive archival research, participant observation, and interviews, this paper explores the ways that Burning Man's bohemian ethos supports new forms of production emerging in Silicon Valley and especially at Google. It shows how elements of the Burning Man world—including the building of a socio-technical commons, participation in project-based artistic labor, and the fusion of social and professional interaction—help shape and legitimate the collaborative manufacturing processes driving the growth of Google and other firms. The paper thus develops the notion that Burning Man serves as a key cultural infrastructure for the Bay Area's new media industries.
—Fred Turner, "Burning Man at Google: A Cultural Infrastructure for New Media Production"

A scene from Burning Man.

You might imagine a different and far livelier way to tell a story about the annual Burning Man gathering in Nevada, but this piece respects the conventions of its academic field.

Another way you likely identify academic writing—especially term papers—is by the way it draws upon sources and builds arguments from research done by experts and reported in journal articles and books. Using an evenhanded tone and dealing with all points of view fairly, such writing brings together multiple voices and intriguing ideas. You can see these moves in just one paragraph from a heavily documented student essay examining the comedy of Chris Rock:

> The breadth of passionate debate that [Chris] Rock's comedy elicits from intellectuals is evidence enough that he is advancing discussion of the foibles of black America, but Rock continually insists that he has no political aims: "Really, really at the end of the day, the only important thing is being funny. I don't go out of my way to be political" (qtd. in Bogosian 58). His unwillingness to view himself as a black leader triggers Justin Driver to say, "[Rock] wants to be caustic and he wants to be loved" (32). Even supporters wistfully sigh, "One wishes Rock would own up to the fact that he's a damned astute social critic" (Kamp 7).
>
> —Jack Chung, "The Burden of Laughter:
> Chris Rock Fights Ignorance His Way"

Readers can quickly tell that author Jack Chung has read widely and thought carefully about how to present his argument.

As you can see even from these brief examples, academic arguments cover a broad range of topics and appear through a variety of media—as a brief note in a journal like *Nature*, for example, a poster session at a conference on linguistics, a short paper in *Physical Review Letters*, a full research report in microbiology, or an undergraduate honors thesis in history. Moreover, scholars today are pushing the envelope of traditional academic writing in some fields. Physicians, for example, are using narrative more often in medicine to communicate effectively with other medical personnel.

What do all these projects have in common? One professor we know defines academic argument as "carefully structured research," and that seems to us to be a pretty good definition.

Developing an Academic Argument

In your first years of college, the academic arguments you make will probably include the features and qualities we've discussed above—and which you see demonstrated in the sample academic arguments at the end of this chapter. In addition, you can make a strong academic argument by following some time-tested techniques.

Choose a topic you want to explore in depth. Unless you are assigned a topic (and remember that even assigned topics can be tweaked to match your interests), look for a subject that intrigues you—one you *want* to learn more about. One of the hardest parts of producing an academic argument is finding a topic narrow enough to be manageable in the time you have to work on it but also rich enough to sustain your interest over the same period. Talk with friends about possible topics and explain to them why you'd like to pursue research on this issue. Browse through books and articles that interest you, make a list of potential subjects, and then zero in on one or two top choices.

Get to know the conversation surrounding your topic. Once you've chosen a topic, expect to do even more reading and browsing—a lot more. Familiarize yourself with what's been said about your subject and especially with the controversies that currently surround it. Where do scholars agree, and where do they disagree? What key issues seem to be at stake? You can start by exploring the Internet, using key terms that are associated with your topic. But you may be better off searching the more specialized databases at your library with the assistance of a librarian who can help you narrow your search and make it more efficient. Library databases will also give you access to materials not available via Google or other online search engines — including, for example, full-text versions of journal articles. For much more on identifying appropriate sources, see Chapter 17, "Finding Evidence."

Assess what you know and what you need to know. As you read about your topic and discuss it with others, keep notes on what you have learned, including what you already know about it. Such notes should soon reveal where the gaps are in your knowledge. For instance, you may discover a need to learn about legal issues and thus end up doing research in a law school library. Or perhaps talking with experts about your topic might be helpful. Instructors on your campus may have the knowledge you need, so explore your school's Web site to find faculty or staff to talk with. Make an appointment to visit them during office hours and bring the sorts of questions to your meeting that show you've done basic work on the subject.

Come up with a claim about your topic. The chapters in Part 2, "Writing Arguments," offer instruction in formulating thesis statements, which most academic arguments must have. Chapters 8–12, in particular, explain how to craft claims tailored to individual projects ranging from arguments of fact to proposals. Remember here, though, that good claims are controversial. After all, you don't want to debate something that everyone already agrees upon or accepts.

In addition, your claim needs to say something consequential about an important or controversial topic and be supported with strong evidence and good reasons (see Chapter 17). Here, for example, is the claim that Brian Riady defends in his research argument on problems writing centers face when helping international students (reprinted at the end of this chapter): "Non-directive tutoring fails non-native English speakers for the exact reason that it so effectively assists native English speakers: *culture*." Each piece of evidence that Brian presents after stating his thesis develops that claim and leads to the specific recommendations with which he ends his paper.

Consider your rhetorical stance and purpose. Once you have a claim, ask yourself where you stand with respect to your topic and how you want to represent yourself to those reading your argument.

- You may take the stance of a reporter: you review what has been said about the topic; analyze and evaluate contributions to the conversation surrounding it; synthesize the most important strands of that conversation; and finally draw conclusions based on them.

- You may see yourself primarily as a critic: you intend to point out the problems and mistakes associated with some view of your topic.

- You may prefer the role of an advocate: you present research that strongly supports a particular view on your topic.

Whatever your perspective, remember that in academic arguments you want to come across as fair and evenhanded, especially when you play the advocate. Your stance will always be closely tied to your purpose, which in most of your college writing will be at least twofold: to do the best job in fulfilling an assignment for a course and to support the claim you are making to the fullest extent possible. Luckily, these two purposes work well together.

Think about your audience(s). Here again, you will often find that you have at least two audiences—and maybe more. First, you will be writing to the instructor who gave you the project, so take careful notes when the assignment is given and, if possible, set up a conference to nail down your teacher's expectations: what will it take to convince this audience that you have done a terrific job of writing an academic argument? Beyond your instructor, you should also think of your classmates as an audience—informed, intelligent peers who will be interested in what you have to say. Again, what do you know about these readers, and what will they expect from your project?

Finally, consider yet another audience—people who are already discussing your topic. These will include the authors whose work you have read and the larger academic community of which they are now a part. If your work appears online or in some other medium, you could reach more people than you initially expect.

Concentrate on the material you are gathering. Any academic argument is only as good as the evidence it presents to support its claims. Give each major piece of evidence (a lengthy article, say, that addresses your subject directly) careful scrutiny:

- Summarize its main points.
- Analyze how those points are pertinent.
- Evaluate the quality of the supporting evidence.
- Synthesize the results of your analysis and evaluation.
- Summarize what you think about the article.

In other words, test each piece of evidence and then decide which to keep—and which to throw out. But do not gather only materials that favor your take on the topic. You want, instead, to look at all legitimate perspectives on your claim, and in doing so, you may even change your mind. That's what good research for an academic argument can do: remember the "conscientious commitment to truth" we mentioned earlier? Keep yourself open to discovery and change. (See Chapter 18, "Evaluating Sources," and Chapter 19, "Using Sources.")

Give visual and nonprint materials the same scrutiny you would to print sources since these days you will likely be gathering or creating such materials in many fields. Remember that the graphic representation of data always involves an interpretation of that material: numbers can lie and pictures distort. (For more information on evaluating visuals, see Chapter 14.)

Take special care with documentation. As you gather materials for your academic argument, record where you found each source so that you can cite it accurately. For print sources, develop a working bibliography either on your computer or in a notebook you can carry with you. For each book, write the name of the author, the title of the book, the city of publication, the publisher, the date of publication, and the place that you found it (the section of the library, for example, and the call number for the book). For each article, write the name of the author, the title of the article, the title of the periodical, and the volume, issue, and exact page numbers. Include any other information you may later need in preparing a works cited list or references list.

For electronic sources, keep a careful record of the information you'll need in a works cited list or references list. Write the author and title information, the name of the database or other online site where you found the source, the full electronic address (URL), the date the document was first produced, the date it was published on the Web or most recently updated, and the date you accessed and examined it. The simplest way to ensure that you have this information is to print a copy of the source, highlight source information, and write down any other pertinent information.

Remember, too, that different academic fields use different systems of documentation, so if your instructor has not recommended a style of documentation to you, ask in class about it. Scholars have developed these systems over long periods of time to make research in an area reliable and routine. Using documentation responsibly shows that you understand the conventions of your field or major and that you have paid your dues, thereby establishing your position as a member of the academic community. (For more detailed information, see Chapter 21, "Documenting Sources.")

Think about organization. As you review the research materials you have gathered, you are actually beginning the work of drafting and designing your project. Study the way those materials are organized, especially any from professional journals. You may need to include in your own argument some of the sections or features you find in professional research:

- Does the article open with an abstract, summarizing its content?
- Is there a formal introduction to the subject or a clear statement of a thesis or hypothesis?
- Does the article begin with a "review of literature," summarizing recent research on its topic?
- Does the piece describe its methods of research?
- How does the article report its results and findings?
- Does the article use charts and graphs to report data?
- Does the piece use headings and subheadings?
- How does the work summarize its findings or make recommendations?
- Does the essay offer a list of works cited or references?

Anticipate some variance in the way materials are presented from one academic field to another.

As you organize your own project, check with your instructor to see if there is a recommended pattern for you to follow. If not, create a scratch outline or storyboard to describe how your essay will proceed. In reviewing your evidence, decide which pieces support specific points in the argument. Then try to position your strongest pieces of evidence in key places — near the beginning of paragraphs, at the end of the introduction, or toward a powerful conclusion. In addition, strive to achieve a balance between, on the one hand, your own words and arguments, and on the other hand, the sources that you use or quote in support of the argument. The sources of evidence are important props in the design, but they shouldn't overpower the structure of your argument itself.

And remember that your organization needs to take into account the placement of visuals — charts, tables, photographs, and so on. (For specific advice on structuring arguments, review the "Thinking about Organization" sections in the "Guides to Writing" for Chapters 8–12.)

Consider style and tone. Most academic argument adopts the voice of a reasonable, fair-minded, and careful thinker who is interested in coming as close to the truth about a topic as possible. A style that achieves that tone may have some of the following features:

- It strives for clarity and directness, though it may tolerate jargon.
- It favors denotative rather than connotative language.
- It is usually impersonal, avoiding "I" and using the third person.
- In some fields, it may use the passive voice routinely.
- It uses technical language, symbols, and abbreviations for efficiency.
- It avoids colloquialisms, slang, and even contractions.

The examples at the end of this chapter demonstrate traditional academic style, though there is, as always, a range of possibilities in its manner of expression.

Consider design and visuals. Most college academic arguments look more like articles in professional journals than those one might find in a glossier periodical like *Scientific American*—that is, they are usually black on white, use a traditional font size and type (like 11-point Times New Roman), and lack any conscious design other than inserted tables or figures. But such conventions are changing as more students gain access to software that allows for more sophisticated design elements.

Indeed, student writers today may now go well beyond print, creating digital documents that can integrate a variety of media and array data in strikingly original ways. But always consider what kinds of design best suit your topic, purpose, and audience and then act accordingly. As you think about the design possibilities for your academic argument, you may want to consult your instructor—and to test your ideas and innovations on friends or classmates.

In choosing visuals to include for your argument, be sure each one makes a strong contribution to your message and is appropriate and fair to your topic and your audience. Treat visuals as you would any other sources and integrate them into your text. Like quotations, paraphrases, and summaries, visuals need to be introduced and commented on in some way. In addition, label and number ("Figure 1," "Table 2," and so on) all visuals, provide a caption that includes source information and describes the visual, and cite the source in your references page or works cited list. Even if you create a visual (such as a bar graph) by using information from a source (the results, say, of a Gallup poll), you must cite the source. If you use a photograph you took yourself, cite it as a personal photograph.

JSTOR is a database for journal articles in many disciplines. Such articles are important to academic arguments.

Reflect on your draft and get responses. As with any important piece of writing, an academic argument calls for careful reflection on your draft. You may want to do a "reverse outline" to test whether a reader can pull a logical and consistent pattern out of the paragraphs or sections you have written. In addition, you can also judge the effectiveness of your overall argument, assessing what each paragraph contributes and what may be missing. Turning a critical eye to your own work at the draft stage can save much grief in the long run. Be sure to get some response from classmates and friends too: come up with a set of questions to ask them about your draft and push them for honest responses. Find out what is confusing or unclear to others in your draft, what needs further evidence, and so on.

Edit and proofread your text. Proofread an academic argument at least three times. First review it for ideas, making sure that all your main points and supporting evidence make sense and fit nicely together. Give special attention to transitions and paragraph structure and the way you have arrayed information, positioned headings, and captioned graphic items. Make sure the big picture is in focus.

Then read the text word by word to check spelling, punctuation, quotation marks, apostrophes, abbreviations—in short, all the details that can go wrong simply because of a slip in attention. To keep their focus at this level, some readers will even read an entire text backwards. Notice too where your computer's spelling and grammar checkers may be underlining particular words and phrases. Don't ignore these clear signals.

Finally, check that every source mentioned in the academic argument appears in the references list and that every citation is correct. This is also the time to make any final touchups to your overall design. Remember that how the document looks is part of what establishes its credibility.

RESPOND●

1. Look closely at the following five passages, each of which is from an opening of a published work, and decide which ones provide examples of academic argument. How would you describe each one, and what are its key features? Which is the most formal and academic? Which is the least? How might you revise them to make them more—or less—academic?

During the Old Stone Age, between thirty-seven thousand and eleven thousand years ago, some of the most remarkable art ever conceived was etched or painted on the walls of caves in southern France and northern Spain. After a visit to Lascaux, in the Dordogne, which was discovered in 1940, Picasso reportedly said to his guide, "They've invented everything." What those first artists invented was a language of signs for which there will never be a Rosetta stone; perspective, a technique that was not rediscovered until the Athenian Golden Age; and a bestiary of such vitality and finesse that, by the flicker of torchlight, the animals seem to surge from the walls, and move across them like figures in a magic-lantern show (in that sense, the artists invented animation). They also thought up the grease lamp—a lump of fat, with a plant wick, placed in a hollow stone—to light their workplace; scaffolds to reach high places; the principles of stenciling and Pointillism; powdered colors, brushes, and stumping cloths; and, more to the point of Picasso's insight, the very concept of an image. A true artist reimagines that concept with every blank canvas—but not from a void.

—Judith Thurman, "First Impressions," *The New Yorker*

I stepped over the curb and into the street to hitchhike. At the age of ten I'd put some pretty serious mileage on my thumb. And I knew how it was done. Hold your thumb up, not down by your hip as though you didn't much give a damn whether you got a ride or not. Always hitch at a place where a driver could pull out of traffic and give you time to get in without risking somebody tailgating him.

—Harry Crews, "On Hitchhiking," *Harper's*

Coral reef ecosystems are essential marine environments around the world. Host to thousands (and perhaps millions) of diverse organisms, they are also vital to the economic well-being of an estimated 0.5 billion people, or 8% of the world's population who live on tropical coasts (Hoegh-Guldberg 1999). Income from tourism and fishing industries, for instance, is essential to the economic prosperity of many countries, and the various plant and animal species present in reef ecosystems are sources for different natural products and medicines. The degradation of coral reefs can therefore have a devastating impact on coastal populations, and it is estimated that between 50% and 70% of all reefs around the world are currently threatened (Hoegh-Guldberg). Anthropogenic influences are cited as the major cause of this degradation, including sewage, sedimentation, direct trampling of reefs, over-fishing of herbivorous fish, and even global warming (Umezawa et al. 2002; Jones et al. 2001; Smith et al. 2001).

—Elizabeth Derse, "Identifying the Sources of Nitrogen to Hanalei
Bay, Kauai, Utilizing the Nitrogen Isotope Signature
of Macroalgae," *Stanford Undergraduate Research Journal*

While there's a good deal known about invertebrate neurobiology, these facts alone haven't settled questions of their sentience. On the one hand, invertebrates lack a cortex, amygdala, as well as many of the other major brain structures routinely implicated in human emotion. And unsurprisingly, their nervous systems are quite minimalist compared to ours: we have roughly a hundred thousand bee brains worth of neurons in our heads. On the other hand, some invertebrates, including insects, do possess the rudiments of our stress response system. So the question is still on the table: do they experience emotion in a way that we would recognize, or just react to the world with a set of glorified reflexes?

—Jason Castro, "Do Bees Have Feelings?" *Scientific American*

From the richest high school to the poorest high school in America, students are being told that employment in the computer industry is nothing less than salvation from the indignities of the jobs those others have to do to survive. If you don't learn your computer skills well, if by some chance you're bored sitting in front of that screen, day after day under buzzing fluorescents, pecking at a vanilla keyboard, clicking a mouse, it's your problem, and there will be no excuse for your fate in this new economy: you will be doomed to menial, manual labor. That dirty, anybody-can-do-that work. Poor income, low prestige. *Pues, así va la vida, compa,* that's life if you don't get your stuff right.

—Dagoberto Gilb, "Work Union," *Gritos*

2. Working with another student in your class, find examples from two or three different fields of academic arguments that strike you as being well written and effective. Spend some time looking closely at them. Do they exemplify the key features of academic arguments discussed in this chapter? What other features do they use? How are they organized? What kind of tone do the writers use? What use do they make of visuals? Draw up a brief report on your findings (a list will do), and bring it to class for discussion.

3. Read the following three paragraphs, and then list changes that the writer might make to convert them into an academic argument:

The book—the physical paper book—is being circled by a shoal of sharks, with sales down 9 percent this year alone. It's being chewed by the e-book. It's being gored by the death of the bookshop and the library. And most importantly, the mental space it occupied is being eroded by the thousand Weapons of Mass Distraction that surround us all. It's hard to admit, but we all sense it: it is becoming almost physically harder to read books.

In his gorgeous little book *The Lost Art of Reading—Why Books Matter in a Distracted Time,* the critic David Ulin admits to a strange feeling. All his life, he had taken reading as for granted as eating—but then, a few years ago, he "became aware, in an apartment full of books, that I could no longer find within myself the quiet necessary to read." He would sit down to do it at night, as he always had, and read a few paragraphs, then find his mind was wandering, imploring him to check his email, or Twitter, or Facebook. "What I'm struggling with," he writes, "is the encroachment of the buzz, the sense that there's something out there that merits my attention."

I think most of us have this sense today, if we are honest. If you read a book with your laptop thrumming on the other side of the room, it can be like trying to read in the middle of a party, where everyone is shouting to each other. To read, you need to slow down. You need mental silence except for the words. That's getting harder to find.

—Johann Hari, "How to Survive the Age of Distraction"

4. Choose two pieces of your college writing, and examine them closely. Are they examples of strong academic writing? How do they use the key features that this chapter identifies as characteristic of academic arguments? How do they use and document sources? What kind of tone do you establish in each? After studying the examples in this chapter, what might you change about these pieces of writing, and why?

5. Go to a blog that you follow, or check out one like the *Huffington Post* or *Ricochet*. Spend some time reading the articles or postings on the blog, and look for ones that you think are the best written and the most interesting. What features or characteristics of academic argument do they use, and which ones do they avoid?

A Directive Approach toward ESL/EFL Writers

BRIAN RIADY

Opening paragraph explains the context for this academic argument.

Since its origin in Stephen North's "The Idea of a Writing Center" and Jeff Brooks's "Minimalist Tutoring," a non-directive approach has become firmly embedded in writing center methodology (Clark 33). The premise of the non-directive approach is that minimizing direct instruction at a writing center will simultaneously improve student learning, keep student writers accountable, and make students feel more comfortable about seeking writing help. At the same time, non-directive tutoring lets students retain ownership of their work, while circumventing potential problems with plagiarism. This approach, which was initially accepted precisely because its collaborative methods rejected the dominant top-down, current traditional pedagogy of its time, persists as a fundamental element of American writing center culture today.

But in recent years, a dramatic increase in ESL [English as a Second Language] consultations at writing centers, caused mainly by escalating admission rates for international students, has led writing center faculty to reevaluate the effectiveness of this non-directive pedagogy. In an attempt to adapt traditional conferencing strategies to the ESL writer, writing center faculty have found that the non-directive approach—which has been hailed as a writing center "bible" (Shamoon and Burns 135), writing

Brian Riady wrote this research argument for a course at the University of Texas at Austin that prepares undergraduates to work as tutors at the Undergraduate Writing Center. Brian's topic reflects his own status as an international student from Singapore majoring in Communication Studies, Rhetoric and Writing, and Economics. The paper uses MLA documentation.

center "dogma" (Clark 34), and a writing center "mantra" (Blau 1)—does not effectively assist ESL writers. Non-directive tutoring fails non-native English speakers for the exact reason that it so effectively assists native English speakers: culture.

Culture is at the heart of the ESL student's struggle with writing because culture informs writing. Every culture defines effective writing—and the means to achieving it—differently. Most ESL students understand what good writing looks and sounds like in their own culture, but because good writing is culturally constructed, these students have difficulty understanding what good writing is in standardized, academic American English. Hence, writing that appears to be effective to the non-native English speaker may seem illogical or nonsensical to the native speaker.

Take Arabic, for instance. In Arabic, good language is decorative, ornate, and intentionally pleasing (Zinsser). "It's all proverbs," writes William Zinsser. "Arabic is full of courtesy and deference, some of which is rooted in fear of the government." And because Arabic is a historically oral culture, Arabs emphasize a balanced sound and "prefer symmetry to variety" (Thonus 19). What constitutes effective Arabic, then, is a result of a combination of cultural, historical, and in some countries, political factors. But what Arabs consider good writing—ornate, proverbial, symmetrical prose—would be the ruin of someone trying to write good English.

The same is true of Japanese. Persuasive rhetoric in Japanese follows the *ki-shoo-ten-ketsu* form (Thonus 18). *Ki-shoo-ten-ketsu* form begins with *ki-shoo*, or the full development of an argument; then proceeds with *ten*, an indirectly related subtheme; before ending with *ketsu*, or the conclusion or thesis (Thonus 18). Transitions are rarely if ever present, because the Japanese believe that it is the reader's responsibility to connect the various parts of the essay. Thonus notes that this "deviates from western argumentation in that the *ten* subtheme departs

Second paragraph ends with a thesis sentence.

Explains how culture defines writing, quoting from experts.

Provides evidence that Arabic and Japanese cultures define "good writing" differently.

from the topic, while the thesis . . . is withheld until the final paragraph" (18). When the *ki-shoo-ten-ketsu* rhetorical form is used in English, writing often sounds foreign and is more descriptive than persuasive.

When ESL writers of Japanese or Arabic or any other foreign descent attempt to learn English, they are hampered not only by their "limited backgrounds in the rhetoric of written English but also by their learned patterns as educated writers of their own languages" (Powers 41). Such writers deal simultaneously with an unfamiliar culture and an unfamiliar language. For them, learning to write effectively in English is not merely transferring the rules of "good writing" from their native language and applying them to English; rather it is learning a new set of cultural assumptions of what "good writing" is altogether. Such writers often struggle to deviate from their instinctive cultural assumptions and fail to think about writing in a new way.

Consequently, when writing center tutors and ESL student writers collaborate for a writing consultation, the traditional non-directive model of writing center consultations falls short. Non-directive consulting works well with native English speakers precisely because consultant and writer share certain cultural notions of "good writing." By asking the right questions, an experienced consultant can unobtrusively lead a writer to discover ways to improve his own writing (Powers 41). In this sense, a writing consultant can actually direct "the conference through the use of questions, much as Socrates determined the direction of the Platonic dialogues" (Clark 35).

But when tutor and writer come into a consultation with different sets of cultural assumptions, the routine technique of Socratic, non-directive questioning often does not work. Leading questions can only lead a student writer to discover his own mistakes if he has a basic grasp of how his writing should be. Non-directively asking an ESL student to consider his audience is inherently problematic if the ESL student is unfamiliar with what his audience knows and expects. Similarly, a writer will fail to discover his own mechanical errors by reading his work out loud if he does not understand how "correct" writing should sound (Powers 41–42). As Powers puts it: "[to] merely take the [non-directive] techniques we use with native-speaking writers and apply them to ESL writers may fail to assist the writers we intend to help" (41).

Hence, Powers argues, "successful assistance to ESL writers may involve more intervention in their writing processes than we consider appropriate with native-speaking writers" (44). ESL writers struggle with an unfamiliar culture, audience, and rhetoric, and what they need from writing consultants is knowledge of how an American academic audience will respond to their work. To best assist the ESL writer, a consultant must be directive insofar as she becomes a "cultural informant about American academic expectations" (Powers 41). A writing consultant must in other words be directive in teaching an ESL student what constitutes "good writing" and how to accomplish "good writing" in the culture of American academia.

This is not to say that consultants should completely disregard the non-directive approach; consultants should still refrain from acting as a one-stop proofreading service. In "Tutors as Teachers: Assisting ESL/EFL Students in the Writing Center," Terese Thonus advises consultants to avoid the tendency to merely correct surface-level errors in ESL writing, even if such errors may seem overwhelming. Most ESL students demonstrate basic proficiency of English vocabulary and grammar by passing the TOEFL, and may be able to isolate mechanical problems and self-correct with a little guidance. But emphasizing correctness in a directive, current traditional manner, and demanding a correct product of ESL writers "will engender frustration and even the loss of confidence, just as does demanding perfect native-like English pronunciation" (Kobayashi 107). Rather,

Argues for using more directive tutoring of international students.

Qualifies his argument, citing several experts.

consultants must find a balance between directive teaching and non-directive tutoring that is most effective for ESL students.

Learning to be more directive with ESL students poses an especially tricky problem for writing tutors accustomed to non-directive consulting. Non-directive consulting is so firmly embedded in the culture of writing centers that it is "hard for practitioners to accept possible tutoring alternatives as useful or compelling" (Shamoon and Burns 135). Directive tutoring when measured against this predominant writing center culture is seen as a failure. Consequently, a consultant who does engage in directive tutoring may feel that she has betrayed the non-directive philosophy when in fact she has successfully met the needs of the ESL student writer.

Acknowledges difficulties in implementing his proposal.

What needs to occur is a significant paradigm shift in the culture of writing centers. The existing writing center culture assumes that there is one correct standard for writing, and a one-size-fits-all approach to assisting writers in consultations. Writing centers and their staff must first reassess their own cultural assumptions, and realize that their way is but a single option amongst myriad equally "correct" alternatives. They must in other words recognize that the non-directive methodology is not the right method in an absolute sense, but a helpful method that must be appropriately adapted to assist writers with different needs.

Such a paradigm shift will not be easy, but as writing centers move forward and prepare to meet the challenges of the future, it will be necessary. Improving the methods of writing instruction at writing centers is a continuous process: it began with the conception of the writing center, proceeded with a rejection of the current traditional pedagogy for the non-directive approach, and must continue on with an enhanced cultural sensitivity and awareness for ESL student writers.

Concludes by asserting the need for greater cultural awareness.

Works Cited

Blau, Susan. "Issues in Tutoring Writing: Stories from Our Center." *The Writing Lab Newsletter* 19.2 (1992): 1–4. Web. 10 Apr. 2011.

Clark, Irene L. "Perspectives on the Directive/Non-Directive Continuum in the Writing Center." *The Writing Center Journal* 22.1 (2001): 33–50. Web. 11 Apr. 2011.

Kobayashi, Toshihiko. "Native and Nonnative Reactions to ESL Compositions." *TESOL Quarterly* 26.1 (1992): 81–112. Web. 6 Apr. 2011.

Powers, Judith K. "Rethinking Writing Center Conferencing Strategies for the ESL Writer." *The Writing Center Journal* 13.2 (1993): 39–47. Web. 6 Apr. 2011.

Shamoon, Linda K., and Deborah H. Burns. "A Critique of Pure Tutoring." *The Writing Center Journal* 15.2 (1995): 134–151. Print.

Thonus, Terese. "Tutors as Teachers: Assisting ESL/EFL Students in the Writing Center." *The Writing Center Journal* 13.2 (1993): 13–22. Web. 10 Apr. 2011.

Zinsser, William. "Writing English as a Second Language." *The American Scholar* (2009): Web. 11 Apr. 2011.

China: The Prizes and Pitfalls of Progress

LAN XUE

ABSTRACT

Pushes to globalize science must not threaten local innovations in developing countries, argues Lan Xue.

Developing countries such as China and India have emerged both as significant players in the production of high-tech products and as important contributors to the production of ideas and global knowledge. China's rapid ascent as a broker rather than simply a consumer of ideas and innovation has made those in the "developed" world anxious. A 2007 report by UK think tank Demos says that "U.S. and European pre-eminence in science-based innovation cannot be taken for granted. The centre of gravity for innovation is starting to shift from west to east."[1]

But the rapid increase in research and development spending in China—of the order of 20% per year since 1999—does not guarantee a place as an innovation leader. Participation in global science in developing

This article was written by Lan Xue, a faculty member in the School of Public Policy and Management and the director of the China Institute for Science and Technology Policy, both at Tsinghua University in Beijing, China. It was published in the online edition of *Nature* in July 2008.

Illustrations by D. Parkins.

countries such as China is certainly good news for the global scientific community. It offers new opportunities for collaboration, fresh perspectives, and a new market for ideas. It also presents serious challenges for the management of innovation in those countries. A major discovery in the lab does not guarantee a star product in the market. And for a country in development, the application of knowledge in productive activities and the related social transformations are probably more important than the production of the knowledge itself. By gumming the works in information dissemination, by misplacing priorities, and by disavowing research that, although valuable, doesn't fit the tenets of modern Western science, developing countries may falter in their efforts to become innovation leaders.

VICIOUS CIRCLE

China's scientific publications (measured by articles recorded in the Web of Science) in 1994 were around 10,000, accounting for a little more than 1% of the world total. By 2006, the publications from China rose to more than 70,000, increasing sevenfold in 12 years and accounting for almost 6% of the world total (see graph, next page). In certain technical areas, the growth has been more dramatic. China has been among the leading countries in nanotechnology research, for example, producing a volume of publications second only to that of the United States.

The publish-or-perish mentality that has arisen in China, with its focus on Western journals, has unintended implications that threaten to obviate the roughly 8,000 national scientific journals published in Chinese. Scientists in developing countries such as China and India pride themselves on publishing articles in journals listed in the Science Citation Index (SCI) and the Social Science Citation Index (SSCI) lists. In some top-tier research institutions in China, SCI journals have become the required outlet for research.

A biologist who recently returned to China from the United States was told by her colleague at the research institute in the prestigious Chinese Academy of Sciences (CAS) that publications in Chinese journals don't really count toward tenure or promotion. Moreover, the institute values only those SCI journals with high impact factors. Unfortunately, the overwhelming majority of the journals in SCI and SSCI lists are published in developed countries in English or other European languages. The language requirement and the high costs of these journals mean that few researchers in China will have regular access to the content. Thus as China spends more and publishes more, the results will become harder to

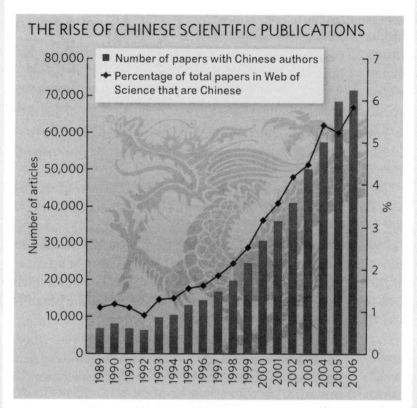

THE RISE OF CHINESE SCIENTIFIC PUBLICATIONS

find for Chinese users. This trend could have a devastating impact on the local scientific publications and hurt China's ability to apply newly developed knowledge in an economically useful way.

Several members of the CAS expressed their concerns on this issue recently at the 14th CAS conference in Beijing. According to Molin Ge, a theoretical physicist at the Chern Institute of Mathematics, Nankai University, Tianjin, as more high-quality submissions are sent to overseas journals, the quality of submissions to local Chinese journals declines, which lowers the impact of the local Chinese journals. This becomes a vicious circle because the lower the impact, the less likely these local journals are to get high-quality submissions.[2]

SETTING AGENDAS

Research priorities in developing countries may be very different from those in developed nations, but as science becomes more globalized, so too do priorities. At the national level, developing countries' research priorities increasingly resemble those of the developed nations, partly as a result of international competitive pressures. For example, after the United States announced its National Nanotechnology Initiative (NNI) in 2001, Japan and nations in Europe followed suit, as did South Korea, China, India, and Singapore. According to a 2004 report by the European Union,[3] public investment in nanotechnology had increased from €400 million (U.S. $630 million) in 1997 to more than €3 billion in 2004.

Part of the pressure to jump on the international bandwagon comes from researchers themselves. Scientists in the developing world maintain communications with those elsewhere. It is only natural that they want to share the attention that their colleagues in the developed Western world and Japan are receiving by pursuing the same hot topics. The research is exciting, fast-moving, and often easier to publish. At the same time, there are many other crucial challenges to be met in developing countries. For example, public health, water and food security, and environmental protection all beg for attention and resources. If people perceive these research areas as less intellectually challenging and rewarding, the issues will fail to receive the resources, support, and recognition they require. Without better agenda-setting practices, the scientific community will continue to face stinging criticism. It can send a satellite to Mars but not solve the most basic problems that threaten millions of lives in the developing world.

The introduction of Western scientific ideals to the developing world can generate an environment that is hostile to the indigenous research that prima facie does not fit those ideals. The confrontation between Western medicine and traditional Chinese medicine dates back to the early days of the twentieth century when Western medicine was first introduced in China. The debate reached a peak last year when a famous actress, Xiaoxu Chen, died from breast cancer. She allegedly insisted on treatment by Chinese traditional medicine, raising the hackles of some who claimed it to be worthless. Many Chinese still support traditional medicine and say that the dominance of Western medicine risks endangering China's scientific and cultural legacy.

A similar row erupted around earthquake prediction. In the 1960s and 1970s, China set up a network of popular earthquake-prediction stations, using simple instruments and local knowledge. For the most part, the network was decommissioned as China built the modern earthquake-monitoring system run by the China Earthquake Administration. When the system failed to predict the recent Sichuan earthquake, several people claimed that non-mainstream approaches had predicted its imminence. Scientists in the agency have tended to brush off such unofficial and individual predictions. To many this seems arrogant and bureaucratic.

It would be foolish and impossible to stop the globalization of science. There are tremendous benefits to science enterprises in different countries being integrated into a global whole. One should never think of turning back the clock. At the same time, it is possible to take some practical steps to minimize the harmful effects of this trend on local innovation.

PRIORITIZING FOR THE PEOPLE

First of all, there is a need to re-examine the governance of global science in recognition of the changing international geography of science. Many international norms and standards should be more open and accommodating to the changing environment in developing countries. For example, there is a need to re-evaluate the SCI and SSCI list of journals to include quality journals in the developing countries. In the long run, the relevant scientific community could also think about establishing an international panel to make decisions on the selection of journals for these indices, given their important influence. The recent move by Thomson Reuters, the parent company of ISI, to expand its coverage of the SCI list by adding 700 regional academic journals, is a step in the right direction.[4]

English has become the de facto global language of science. Developing countries should invest in public institutions to provide translation services so that global scientific progress can be disseminated quickly. Developing countries can learn from Japan, a world leader in collecting scientific information and making it available to the public in the local language. At the same time, there should also be international institutions to provide similar services to the global science community so that "results and the knowledge generated through research should be freely accessible to all," as advocated by Nobel Laureates John Sulston and Joseph Stiglitz.[5]

When setting agendas, governments in developing countries must be careful in allocating their resources for science to achieve a balance between following the science frontier globally and addressing crucial domestic needs. A balance should also be struck between generating knowledge and disseminating and using knowledge. In addition, the global science community has a responsibility to help those developing countries that do not have adequate resources to solve problems themselves.

Finally, special efforts should be made to differentiate between pseudoscience and genuine scientific research. For the latter, one should tolerate or even encourage such indigenous research efforts in developing countries even if they do not fit the recognized international science paradigm. After all, the real advantage of a globalized scientific enterprise is not just doing the same research at a global scale, but doing new and exciting research in an enriched fashion.

REFERENCES

1. Leadbeater, C. & Wilsdon, J. *The Atlas of Ideas: How Asian Innovation Can Benefit Us All* (Demos, 2007).
2. Xie, Y. et al. *Good submissions went overseas—Chinese S&T journals could not keep up with their overseas peers, Chinese Youth Daily*, 25 June 2008.
3. http://ec.europa.eu/nanotechnology/pdf/nano_com_en_new.pdf
4. http://scientific.thomsonreuters.com/press/2008/8455931/
5. Sulston, J. & Stiglitz, J. *Science is being held back by outdated laws, The Times* (5 July 2008).

17

Finding Evidence

In making and supporting claims for academic arguments, writers use all kinds of evidence — data from journal articles, scholarly books, records from archives, personal observations, fieldwork and surveys, and so on. But such evidence doesn't exist in a vacuum. Instead, the quality of evidence — how it was collected, by whom, and for what purposes — may become part of the argument itself. Evidence may be persuasive in one time and place but not in another; it may convince one kind of audience but not another; it may work with one type of argument but not the kind you are writing. The point is that finding "good" evidence for a research project is rarely a simple matter.

Considering the Rhetorical Situation

To be most persuasive, evidence should match the time and place in which you make your argument—that is to say, your rhetorical situation. For example, arguing that government officials in the twenty-first century should use the same policies to deal with economic troubles that were employed in the middle of the twentieth might not be convincing on its own. After all, almost every aspect of the world economy has changed in the past fifty years. In the same way, a writer may achieve excellent results by citing a detailed survey of local teenagers as evidence for education reform in her rural hometown, but she may have less success using the same evidence to argue for similar reforms in a large inner-city community.

College writers also need to consider the fields that they're working in. In disciplines such as experimental psychology or economics, **quantitative data**—the sort that can be observed and counted—may be the best evidence. In many historical, literary, or philosophical studies, however, the same kind of data may be less appropriate or persuasive, or even impossible to come by. As you become more familiar with a discipline, you'll gain a sense of what it takes to support a claim. The following questions will help you understand the rhetorical situation of a particular field:

- What kinds of data are preferred as evidence? How are such data gathered and presented?
- How are definitions, causal analyses, evaluations, analogies, and examples used as evidence?
- How does the field use firsthand and secondhand sources as evidence? What kinds of data are favored?
- How are statistics or other numerical information used and presented as evidence? Are tables, charts, or graphs commonly used? How much weight do they carry?
- What or who counts as an authority in this field? How are the credentials of authorities established?
- What weight do writers in the field give to **precedence**—that is, to examples of similar actions or decisions made in the past?
- Is personal experience allowed as evidence? When?
- How are quotations used as part of evidence?
- How are images used as part of evidence, and how closely are they related to the verbal parts of the argument being presented?

As these questions suggest, evidence may not always travel well from one field to another. Nor does it always travel easily from culture to culture. Differing notions of evidence can lead to arguments that go nowhere fast. For instance, when Italian journalist Oriana Fallaci interviewed Ayatollah Khomeini, Iran's supreme leader, in 1979, she argued in a way that's common in North American and Western European cultures: she presented claims that she considered to be adequately backed up with facts ("Iran denies freedom to people. . . . Many people have been put in prison and even executed, just for speaking out in opposition"). In response, Khomeini relied on very different kinds of evidence—analogies ("Just as a finger with gangrene should be cut off so that it will not destroy the whole body, so should people who corrupt others be pulled out like weeds so they will not infect the whole field") and, above all, the authority of the Qur'an. Partly because of these differing beliefs about what counts as evidence, the interview ended

The need for evidence depends a lot on the rhetorical situation.

unsuccessfully. In arguing across cultural divides, whether international or more local, you need to think carefully about how you're accustomed to using evidence—and about what counts as evidence to other people (without surrendering your own intellectual principles).

Using Data and Evidence from Research Sources

The evidence you will use in most academic arguments—books, articles, films, documents, photographs—will likely come from sources you locate in libraries, databases, or online. How well you can navigate these complex territories will determine the success of many of your academic and professional projects. Research suggests that most students overestimate their ability to manage these tools and, perhaps more important, don't seek the help they need to find the best materials for their projects. We can't cover all the nuances of doing academic research here, but we can at least point you in the right directions.

   Explore library resources: printed works and databases. Your college library has printed materials (books, periodicals, reference works) as well as terminals that provide access to its electronic catalogs, other libraries' catalogs via the Internet, and numerous proprietary databases (such as Academic Search Complete, Academic OneFile, JSTOR) not available publicly on the Web. Crucially, libraries also have librarians whose job it is to guide you through these resources, help you identify reputable materials, and show you how to search for materials efficiently. The best way to begin a serious academic argument then is often with a trip to the library or a discussion with your professor or librarian. Also be certain that you know your way around the library. If not, ask the staff there to help you locate the following tools: general and specialized encyclopedias; biographical resources; almanacs, yearbooks, and atlases; book and periodical indexes; specialized indexes and abstracts; the circulation computer or library catalog; special collections; audio, video, and art collections; and the interlibrary loan office.

   At the outset of a project, determine what kinds of sources you will need to support your project. (You might also review your assignment to see whether you're required to consult different kinds of sources.) If you'll use print sources, find out whether they're readily available in your library or whether you must make special arrangements (such as an interlibrary loan) to acquire them. For example, your argument for a senior thesis might benefit from material available mostly in old newspapers and magazines: access to them might require time and ingenuity. If you need to locate other nonprint sources (such as audiotapes, videotapes, artwork, or photos), find out where those are kept and whether you need special permission to examine them.

Most academic resources, however, will be on the shelves or available electronically through databases. Here's when it's important to understand the distinction between library databases and the Internet/Web. Your library's computers hold important resources that aren't on the Web or aren't available to you except through the library's system. The most important of these resources is the library's catalog of its holdings (mostly books), but college libraries also pay to subscribe to *scholarly databases*—guides to journal and magazine articles, the LexisNexis database of news stories and legal cases, and compilations of statistics, for example—that you can use for free.

You should consult these electronic sources through your college library, perhaps even before turning to the Web. But using these professional databases isn't always easy or intuitive, even when you can reach them on your own computer. You likely need to learn how to focus and narrow your searches (by date, field, types of material, and so on) so that you don't generate unmanageable lists of irrelevant items. That's when librarians or your instructor can help, so ask them for assistance. They expect your questions.

For example, librarians can draw your attention to the distinction between subject headings and keywords. The Library of Congress Subject Headings (LCSH) are standardized words and phrases that are used to classify the subject matter of books and articles. Library catalogs and databases usually use the LCSH headings to index their contents by author, title, publication date, and subject headings. When you do a subject search of the library's catalog, you're searching only one part of the electronic record of the library's books, and you need to use the exact wording of the LCSH. These subject headings are available in your library.

On the other hand, searches with *keywords* use the computer's ability to look for any term in any field of the electronic record. Keyword searching is less restrictive than searching by subject headings, but it requires you to think carefully about your search terms to get usable results. In addition, you need to learn techniques to limit (or expand) your search. These include combining keywords with *and, or, not,* parentheses, and quotation marks or using similar procedures that are built into the catalog's or database's search mechanism.

Determine, too, early on, how current your sources need to be. If you must investigate the latest findings about, say, a new treatment for HIV/AIDS, check very recent periodicals, medical journals, and the Web. If you want broader, more detailed coverage and background information, look for scholarly books. If your argument deals with a specific time period, newspapers, magazines, and books written during that period may be your best assets.

How many sources should you consult for an academic argument? Expect to look over many more sources than you'll end up using, and be sure to cover all major perspectives on your subject. Read enough sources to feel comfortable discussing it with someone with more knowledge than you. You don't have to be an expert, but your readers should sense that you are well informed.

Explore online resources. Chances are your first instinct when you need to find information is to do a quick keyword search on the Web. Even a smartphone app may suffice when you want simple data—like the names of the actors in a recent film. But if you intend to support a serious academic argument, you need to approach the Web more professionally. Like library catalogs and databases, the Internet offers two ways to search for sources related to an argument—one using subject categories and one using keywords.

A subject directory organized by categories (such as you might find at Yahoo! Directory) allows you to choose a broad category like "Entertainment" or "Science," and then click on increasingly narrow categories like "Movies" or "Astronomy," and then "Thrillers" or "The Solar System," until you reach a point where you're given a list of Web sites or the opportunity to do a keyword search.

With the second kind of Internet search option, a search engine, you start right off with a keyword search—filling in a blank, for example, on Google's opening screen. Because the Internet contains vastly more material than even the largest library catalog or database, exploring it with a search engine requires careful choices and combinations of keywords. For an argument about the fate of the antihero in contemporary films, for example, you might find that *film* and *hero* produce far too many possible matches, or hits. You might further narrow the search by adding a third keyword—say, *American* or *current*. In doing such searches, you'll need to observe the search logic that is followed by a particular database. Using *and* between keywords (*movies and heroes*) usually indicates that both terms must appear in a file for it to be called up. Using *or* between keywords usually instructs the computer to locate every file in which either one word or the other shows up, and using *not* tells the computer to exclude files containing a particular word from the search results (*movies not heroes*).

More crucially with a tool like Google is to discover how the resources of the site itself can refine your choice or direct you to works better suited to academic argument. When you search for any term, you can click "Advanced Search" at the bottom of the results page and bring up a full screen of options to narrow your search in important ways.

But that's not the end of your choices. With an *academic* argument, you might want to explore your topic in either Google Books or Google Scholar. Both resources send you to the level of materials you might need for a term paper or professional project. And Google offers other

Google offers many kinds of research tools like this "Advanced Search" page. Explore them from the "More" and "Even More" menus on search pages.

SEARCHING ONLINE OR IN DATABASES

- Don't rely on simple Web searches only.
- Find library databases targeted to your subject.
- Use advanced search techniques to focus your search.
- Learn the difference between *subject heading* and *keyword* searches.
- Understand the differences between academic and popular sources.
- Admit when you don't know how to find material.
- *Routinely* ask for help from librarians and instructors.

options as well: it can direct you to images, photographs, blogs, and so on. The lesson is simple. If your current Web searches typically involve no more than using the first box that a search engine offers, you aren't close to using all the power available to you. Explore that tool you use all the time and see what it can really do.

Collecting Data on Your Own

Not all your supporting materials for an academic argument must come from print or online sources. You can present research that you have carried out or been closely involved with; this kind of research usually requires that you collect and examine data. Here, we discuss the kinds of firsthand research that student writers do most often.

Perform experiments. Academic arguments can be supported by evidence you gather through experiments. In the sciences, data from experiments conducted under rigorously controlled conditions are highly valued. For other kinds of writing, more informal experiments may be acceptable, especially if they're intended to provide only part of the support for an argument.

If you want to argue, for instance, that the recipes in *Bon Appétit* magazine are impossibly tedious to follow and take far more time than the average person wishes to spend preparing food, you might ask five or six people to conduct an experiment—following two recipes from a recent issue and recording and timing every step. The evidence that you gather from this informal experiment could provide some concrete support—by way of specific examples—for your contention.

But such experiments should be taken with a grain of salt (maybe organic in this case). They may not be effective with certain audiences. And if your experiments can easily be attacked as skewed or sloppily done ("The people you asked to make these recipes couldn't cook a Pop-Tart"), then they may do more harm than good.

Make observations. "What," you may wonder, "could be easier than observing something?" You just choose a subject, look at it closely, and record what you see and hear. But trained observers say that recording an observation accurately requires intense concentration and mental agility. If observing were easy, all eyewitnesses would provide reliable accounts. Yet experience shows that when several people observe the same phenomenon, they generally offer different, sometimes even contradictory, accounts of those observations. For instance, when TWA Flight 800 exploded off the coast of New York in 1996, eyewitnesses gave various accounts, some even claiming that they saw a missile streaking toward the passenger jet. The official report found that an internal electrical short likely ignited vapors in a fuel tank.

Before you begin an observation yourself, decide exactly what you want to find out, and anticipate what you're likely to see. Do you want to observe an action that is repeated by many people—perhaps how people behave at the checkout line in a grocery store? Or maybe you want to study a sequence of actions—for instance, the stages involved in student registration, which you want to argue is far too complicated. Or maybe you are motivated to examine the interactions of a notoriously contentious campus group. Once you have a clear sense of what you'll analyze and what questions you'll try to answer through the observation, use the following guidelines to achieve the best results:

- Make sure that the observation relates directly to your claim.
- Brainstorm about what you're looking for, but don't be rigidly bound to your expectations.
- Develop an appropriate system for collecting data. Consider using a split notebook or page: on one side, record the minute details of your observations; on the other, record your thoughts or impressions.

- Be aware that the way you record data will affect the outcome, if only in respect to what you decide to include in your observational notes and what you leave out.
- Record the precise date, time, and place of the observation(s).

You may be asked to prepare systematic observations in various science courses, including anthropology or psychology, where you would follow a methodology and receive precise directions. But observation can play a role in other kinds of arguments and use various media: a photo essay, for example, might serve as an academic argument in some situations.

Conduct interviews. Some evidence is best obtained through direct interviews. If you can talk with an expert—in person, on the phone, or online—you might obtain information you couldn't have gotten through any other type of research. In addition to an expert opinion, you might ask for firsthand accounts, biographical information, or suggestions of other places to look or other people to consult. The following guidelines will help you conduct effective interviews:

- Determine the exact purpose of the interview, and be sure it's directly related to your claim.
- Set up the interview well in advance. Specify how long it'll take, and if you wish to record the session, ask permission to do so.
- Prepare a written list of both factual and open-ended questions. (Brainstorming with friends can help you come up with good questions.) Leave plenty of space for notes after each question. If the interview proceeds in a direction that you hadn't expected but that seems promising, don't feel that you have to cover every one of your questions.
- Record the subject's full name and title, as well as the date, time, and place of the interview.
- Be sure to thank those people whom you interview, either in person or with a follow-up letter or email message.

A serious interview can be eye-opening when the questions get a subject to reveal important experiences or demonstrate their knowledge or wisdom.

Use questionnaires to conduct surveys. Surveys usually require the use of questionnaires. Questions should be clear, easy to understand, and designed so that respondents' answers can be easily analyzed. Questions that ask respondents to say "yes" or "no" or to rank items on a scale (1 to 5, for example, or "most helpful" to "least helpful") are particularly easy to tabulate. Because tabulation can take time and effort, limit the number of questions you ask. Note also that people often resent being asked to answer more than about twenty questions, especially online.

A key requirement of survey questions is that they be easy to understand.

"Next question: I believe that life is a constant striving for balance, requiring frequent tradeoffs between morality and necessity, within a cyclic pattern of joy and sadness, forging a trail of bittersweet memories until one slips, inevitably, into the jaws of death. Agree or disagree?"

Here are some other guidelines to help you prepare for and carry out a survey:

- Write out your purpose in conducting the survey, and make sure that its results will be directly related to your purpose.
- Brainstorm potential questions to include in the survey, and ask how each relates to your purpose and claim.
- Figure out how many people you want to contact, what the demographics of your sample should be (for example, men in their twenties or an equal number of men and women), and how you plan to reach these people.
- Draft questions that are as free of bias as possible, making sure that each calls for a short, specific answer.
- Think about possible ways that respondents could misunderstand you or your questions, and revise with these points in mind.
- Test the questions on several people, and revise those questions that are ambiguous, hard to answer, or too time-consuming to answer.
- If your questionnaire is to be sent by mail or email or posted on the Web, draft a cover letter explaining your purpose and giving a clear deadline. For mail, provide an addressed, stamped return envelope.
- On the final draft of the questionnaire, leave plenty of space for answers.
- Proofread the final draft carefully. Typos will make a bad impression on those whose help you're seeking.
- After you've done your tabulations, set out your findings in clear and easily readable form, using a chart or spreadsheet if possible.

Draw upon personal experience. Personal experience can serve as powerful evidence when it's appropriate to the subject, to your purpose, and to the audience. If it's your only evidence, however, personal experience usually won't be sufficient to carry the argument. Your experiences may be regarded as merely "anecdotal," which is to say possibly exceptional, unrepresentative, or even unreliable. Nevertheless, personal experience can be effective for drawing in listeners or readers, as N'Gai Croal does in the following example arguing that the video games with the greatest potential are those that appeal to the nongeek:

> I still get questions every now and then from people looking for advice on how to get their hands on a Nintendo Wii. But more and more, I'm hearing stories from people who've already scored one and are still

Personal experience provides evidence for the popularity of Wii bowling (at least among humans).

rhapsodizing about it months after taking possession of the slim white console. The gushing comes from some of the most unexpected people. The grill man at my favorite New York burger joint told me last week that in his household, he mows down zombies in Resident Evil 4, his wife works out using Wii Fit, and he's introducing his son to the classic games of his youth via the Wii's download service. Similarly, a cardiologist friend of mine and his medical-resident girlfriend use Wii Golf to unwind; when they have friends over on the weekends, the same relaxing game turns into a fierce competition.

As someone who covers videogames for *Newsweek*, I've marveled at how quickly the tastes of nontraditional players have moved from the margins of the industry toward the center. This is happening at the same time that geek tastes have taken center stage in other areas of pop culture: witness the summer movie schedule, which looks like new-release Wednesdays at your local comic-book shop.

—N'Gai Croal, "You Don't Have to Be a Nerd"

RESPOND ●

1. The following is a list of general topic ideas from the Yahoo! Directory's "Issues and Causes" page. Narrow one or two of the items down to a more specific subject by using research tools in the library or online

such as scholarly books, journal articles, encyclopedias, magazine pieces, and/or informational Web sites. Be prepared to explain how the particular research resources influenced your choice of a more specific subject within the general subject area. Also consider what you might have to do to turn your specific subject into a full-blown topic proposal for a research paper assignment.

Age discrimination	Multiculturalism
Climate change	Pornography
Cloning	Poverty
Corporal punishment	Racial profiling
Drinking age	Social Security reform
Drugs and sports	Tax reform
Factory farming	Urban sprawl
Global warming	Video games
Immigration reform	Weight and nutrition
Media ethics and accountability	Zoos

2. Go to your library's online catalog page and locate its list of research databases. You may find them presented in various ways: by subject, by field, by academic major, by type—even alphabetically. Try to identify three or four databases that might be helpful to you either generally in college or when working on a specific project, perhaps one you identified in the previous exercise. Then explore the library catalog to see how much you can learn about each of these resources: What fields do they cover? What kinds of data do they offer? How do they present the content of their materials (by abstract, by full text)? What years do they cover? What search strategies do they support (keyword, advanced search)? To find such information, you might look for a help menu or an "About" link on the catalog or database homepages. Write a one-paragraph description of each database you explore and, if possible, share your findings via a class discussion board or wiki.

3. What counts as evidence depends in large part on the rhetorical situation. One audience might find personal testimony compelling in a given case, whereas another might require data that only experimental studies can provide. Imagine that you want to argue that advertisements should not include demeaning representations of chimpanzees and that the use of primates in advertising should be banned. You're encouraged to find out that a number of companies such as Honda and Puma have already agreed to such a ban, so you decide to present your argument to other companies' CEOs and advertising officials. What kind of evidence would be most compelling to this group? How

would you rethink your use of evidence if you were writing for the campus newspaper, for middle schoolers, or for animal-rights group members? What can you learn about what sort of evidence each of these groups might value—and why?

4. Finding evidence for an argument is often a discovery process. Sometimes you're concerned not only with digging up support for an already established claim but also with creating and revising tentative claims. Surveys and interviews can help you figure out what to argue, as well as provide evidence for a claim.

Interview a classmate with the goal of writing a brief proposal argument about the career that he or she should pursue. The claim should be something like *My classmate should be doing X five years from now.* Limit yourself to ten questions. Write them ahead of time, and don't deviate from them. Record the results of the interview (written notes are fine; you don't need to tape the interview). Then interview another classmate with the same goal in mind. Ask the same first question, but this time let the answer dictate the next nine questions. You still get only ten questions.

Which interview gave you more information? Which one helped you learn more about your classmate's goals? Which one better helped you develop claims about his or her future?

18
Evaluating Sources

As many examples in this text have shown, the effectiveness of an argument often depends on the quality of the sources that support or prove it. You'll need to carefully evaluate and assess all your sources, including those that you gather in libraries, from other print sources, in online searches, or in your own field research.

Remember that different sources can contribute in different ways to your work. In most cases, you'll be looking for reliable sources that provide accurate information or that clearly and persuasively express opinions that might serve as evidence for a case you're making. At other times, you may be seeking material that expresses ideas or attitudes—how people are thinking and feeling at a given time. You might need to use a graphic image, a sample of avant-garde music, or a controversial YouTube clip that doesn't fit neatly into categories such as "reliable" or "accurate" yet is central to your argument. With any and all such sources and evidence, your goals are to be as knowledgeable about them and as responsible in their use as you can be and to share honestly what you learn about them with readers.

When might a tattle-tale actually be a
reliable source—and how would you know?

"I'm *not* being a tattle-tale! —
I'm being a reliable source!"

© www.cartoonstock.com

You don't want to be naïve in your use of any source material. Most of
the evidence that is used in arguments on public issues—even material
from influential and well-known sources—comes with considerable
baggage. Scientists and humanists alike have axes to grind, corporations
have products to sell, politicians have issues to promote, journalists
have reputations to make, publishers and media companies have readers, listeners, viewers, and advertisers to attract and to avoid offend-
ing. All of these groups produce and use information to their own benefit,
and it's not (usually) a bad thing that they do so. You just have to be
aware that when you take information from a given source, it will often
carry with it at least some of the preferences, assumptions, and biases
(conscious or not) of the people who produce and disseminate it. Teachers and librarians are not exempted from this caution.

To correct for these biases, draw on as many reliable sources as you can
handle when you're preparing to write. You shouldn't assume that all arguments are equally good or that all the sides in a controversy can be supported by the same weight of evidence and good reasons. But you want to
avoid choosing sources so selectively that you miss essential issues and

CNN's Nancy Grace, a former prosecutor, has been accused of allowing her pro-prosecution bias to influence her commentary.

perspectives. That's easy to do when you read only sources that agree with you or when the sources that you read all seem to carry the same message.

Especially when writing on political subjects, be aware that the sources you're reading or citing almost always support particular beliefs and goals. That fact has been made apparent in recent years by bloggers—from all parts of the political spectrum—who put the traditional news media under daily scrutiny, exposing errors, biases, and omissions. Even so, these political bloggers (mostly amateur journalists, although many are professionals in their own fields) have their own agendas and so must be read with caution themselves.

Assessing Print Sources

Since you want information to be reliable and persuasive, it pays to evaluate each potential source thoroughly. The following principles can help you evaluate print sources:

- **Relevance.** Begin by asking what a particular source will add to your argument and how closely the source is related to your argumentative claim. For a book, the table of contents and the index may help you decide. For an article, look for an abstract that summarizes its content. If you can't think of a good reason for using the source, set it aside. You can almost certainly find something better.

- **Credentials of the author.** Sometimes the author's credentials are set forth in an article, in a book, or on a Web site, so be sure to look for them. Is the author an expert on the topic? To find out, you can gather information about the person on the Internet using a search engine like Yahoo! or Ask.com. Another way to learn about the credibility of an author is to search Google Groups for postings that mention the author or to check the Citation Index to find out how others refer to this author. If you see your source cited by other sources you're using, look at how they cite it and what they say about it that could provide clues to the author's credibility.

- **Stance of the author.** What's the author's position on the issue(s) involved, and how does this stance influence the information in the source? Does the author's stance support or challenge your own views?

- **Credentials of the publisher or sponsor.** If your source is from a newspaper, is it a major one (such as the *Wall Street Journal* or the *Washington Post*) that has historical credentials in reporting, or is it a tabloid? Is it a popular magazine like *O: The Oprah Magazine* or a journal sponsored by a professional group, such as the *Journal of the American Medical Association*? If your source is a book, is the publisher one you recognize or that has its own Web site? When you don't know the reputation of a source, ask several people with more expertise: a librarian, an instructor, or a professional in the field.

- **Stance of the publisher or sponsor.** Sometimes this stance will be obvious: a magazine called *Save the Planet!* will take a pro-environmental stance, whereas one called *America First!* will probably take a conservative stance. But other times, you need to read carefully between the lines to identify particular positions and see how the stance affects the message the source presents. Start by asking what the source's goals are: what does the publisher or sponsoring group want to make happen?

- **Currency.** Check the date of publication of every book and article. Recent sources are often more useful than older ones, particularly in the sciences. However, in some fields (such as history and literature), the most authoritative works are often the older ones.

- **Accuracy.** Check to see whether the author cites any sources for the information or opinions in the article and, if so, how credible and current they are.

- **Level of specialization.** General sources can be helpful as you begin your research, but later in the project you may need the authority or currency of more specialized sources. Keep in mind that highly specialized works on your topic may be difficult for your audience to understand.

Reprinted with permission from *American Journal of Physics*, vol. 6, no. 7, July 2008. American Association of Physics Teachers.

Note the differences between the cover of *Popular Science* and that of a physics journal.

- **Audience.** Was the source written for a general readership? For specialists? For advocates or opponents?
- **Length.** Is the source long enough to provide adequate details in support of your claim?
- **Availability.** Do you have access to the source? If it isn't readily accessible, your time might be better spent looking elsewhere.
- **Omissions.** What's missing or omitted from the source? Might such exclusions affect whether or how you can use the source as evidence?

Assessing Electronic Sources

You'll probably find working with new media both exciting and frustrating, for even though these tools (the Web, social networks, Twitter, and so on) are enormously useful, they offer information of widely varying quality. Because Web sources are mostly open and unregulated, careful researchers look for corroboration before accepting evidence they find online, especially if it comes from a site whose sponsor's identity is unclear.

In such an environment, you must be the judge of the accuracy and trustworthiness of particular electronic sources. In making these judgments, rely on the same criteria and careful thinking that you use to assess print sources. In addition, you may find the following questions helpful in evaluating online sources:

- Who has posted the document or message or created the site/medium? An individual? An interest group? A company? A government agency? For Web sites, does the URL offer any clues? Note especially the final suffix in a domain name—*.com* (commercial), *.org* (nonprofit organization), *.edu* (educational institution), *.gov* (government agency),

What are the kinds and levels of information available on these Web sites—a federal site on tornadoes and severe weather, a personal site about tornadoes and storm chasing, and a commercial site about the TV show *Storm Chasers*?

.mil (military), or *.net* (network). Also note the geographical domains that indicate country of origin—as in *.ca* (Canada) or *.ar* (Argentina). Click on some links of a Web site to see if they lead to legitimate and helpful sources or organizations.

- What can you determine about the credibility of the author or sponsor? Can the information in the document or site be verified in other sources? How accurate and complete is it? On a blog, for example, look for a link that identifies the creator of the site (some blogs are managed by multiple authors).

- Who can be held accountable for the information in the document or site? How well and thoroughly does it credit its own sources? On a wiki, for example, check its editorial policies: who can add to or edit its materials?

- How current is the document or site? Be especially cautious of undated materials. Most reliable sites are refreshed or edited regularly.

- What perspectives are represented? If only one perspective is represented, how can you balance or expand this point of view? Is it a straightforward presentation, or could it be a parody or satire?

Assessing Field Research

If you've conducted experiments, surveys, interviews, observations, or any other field research in developing and supporting an argument, make sure to review your results with a critical eye. The following questions can help you evaluate your own field research:

- Have you rechecked all data and all conclusions to make sure they're accurate and warranted?

- Have you identified the exact time, place, and participants in all your field research?

- Have you made clear what part you played in the research and how, if at all, your role could have influenced the results or findings?

- If your research involved other people, have you gotten their permission to use their words or other materials in your argument? Have you asked whether you can use their names or whether the names should be kept confidential?

RESPOND•

1. The chapter claims that "most of the evidence that is used in arguments on public issues . . . comes with considerable baggage" (p. 411). Find an article in a journal, newspaper, or magazine that uses evidence to support a claim of some public interest. It might be a piece about traffic safety, funding of public schools, dietary recommendations for school children, proposals for air-quality regulation, and so on. Identify several specific pieces of evidence, information, or data presented in the article and then evaluate the degree to which you would accept, trust, or believe those statements. Be prepared to explain specifically why you would be inclined to trust or mistrust any claims based on the data.

2. *The Chronicle of Higher Education* routinely publishes a list called "What They're Reading on College Campuses." Locate one such list either by consulting the journal itself in the library or searching the feature's title on the Web. Then choose one of the listed books, preferably a work of nonfiction, and analyze it by using as many of the principles of evaluation for printed books listed in this chapter as you can without actually reading the book: Who is the author and what are his/her credentials? Who is the publisher and what is its reputation? What can you find out about the book's relevance and popularity: why might the book be on the list? Who is the primary audience for the book? How lengthy is it? How difficult? Finally, consider how likely it is that the book you have selected would be used in an academic paper. If you do choose a work of fiction, might the work be studied in a literature course?

3. Choose a news or information Web site that you visit routinely. Then, using the guidelines discussed in this chapter, spend some time evaluating its credibility. You might begin by comparing it with Google News or Arts & Letters Daily, two sites that have a reputation for being reliable.

19
Using Sources

You may gather an impressive amount of evidence on your topic—from firsthand interviews, from careful observations, and from intensive library and online research. But until that evidence is woven into the fabric of your own argument, it's just a stack of details. You still have to turn that data into information that will be persuasive to your intended audiences.

Building a Critical Mass

Throughout the chapters in Part 4, "Research and Arguments," we've stressed the need to discover as much evidence as possible in support of your claim. If you can find only one or two pieces of evidence—only one or two reasons or illustrations to back up your thesis—then you may be on unsteady ground. Although there's no definite way of saying how much evidence is enough, you should build toward a critical mass by having several pieces of evidence all pulling in the direction of your claim.

Casey Anthony at trial

And remember that **circumstantial evidence** (that is, indirect evidence that *suggests* that something occurred but doesn't prove it directly) may not be enough if it is the only evidence that you have. Many Americans were outraged in July 2011 when a jury acquitted defendant Casey Anthony of the murder of her two-year-old daughter Caylee. But in its case the prosecution had presented no direct evidence for Anthony's guilt to the jury—no eyewitness, confession, or murder weapon; it could point only to highly suspicious situations and behavior. And, as Jennifer Dearborn, editor of the *Rutgers Law Record*, explains, citing Kevin Jon Heller:

> The problem with relying on mostly circumstantial evidence . . . is that it can "simultaneously [be] evidence of guilt and innocence." Thus, the evidence presented in the Anthony trial, when taking everything into account, did not particularly point in one direction or another.

If your evidence for a claim relies solely on circumstantial evidence, on personal experience, or on one major example, you should extend your search for additional sources and good reasons to back up your claim—or modify the argument. Your initial position may simply have been wrong.

Synthesizing Information

As you gather information, you must find a way to make all the facts, ideas, points of view, and quotations you have encountered work with and for you. The process involves not only reading information and recording data carefully, but also pondering and synthesizing it—that is, figuring out how what you've examined supports your specific claims.

You typically begin by paraphrasing or summarizing sources so that you understand exactly what they offer and which ideas are essential to your project. You also decide which, if any, sources offer materials you want to quote directly or reproduce (such as an important graph or table). Then you work to introduce or frame such borrowed materials so that readers grasp their significance and see important relationships. Throughout this review process, ask questions such as the following:

- Which sources help to set the context for your argument? In particular, which items present new information or give audiences an incentive for reading your work?

- Which items provide background information that is essential for anyone trying to understand your argument?

- Which items help to define, clarify, or explain key concepts of your case? How can these sources be presented or sequenced so that readers appreciate your claims as valid or, at a minimum, reasonable?

- Which of your sources might be used to illustrate technical or difficult aspects of your subject? Would it be best to summarize such technical information to make it more accessible, or would direct quotations be more authoritative and convincing?

- Which sources (or passages within sources) furnish the best support or evidence for the claims within your argument? How can these materials be presented or arranged most effectively?

- Which materials do the best job outlining conflicts or offering counterarguments to claims within a project? Which sources might help you to address any important objections or rebuttals?

Remember that yours should be the dominant and controlling voice in an argument. You are like the conductor of an orchestra, calling upon separate instruments to work together to create a rich and coherent sound. The worst kinds of academic papers are those that mechanically walk through a string of sources—often just one item per paragraph—without ever getting all these authorities to talk to each other or with the author. Such papers go through the motions, but don't get anywhere. You can do better.

Paraphrase sources you will use extensively. In a **paraphrase**, you put an author's ideas—including major and minor points—into your own words and sentence structures, following the order the author has given them in the original piece. You usually paraphrase sources that you expect to use

Backing up your claims with well-chosen sources makes almost any argument more credible.

"Who is the fairest one of all, and state your sources!"

heavily in a project. But if you compose your notes well, you may be able to use much of the paraphrased material directly in your paper (with proper citation) because all of the language is your own. A competent paraphrase proves you have read material or data carefully: you demonstrate not only that you know what a source contains, but that you also appreciate what it means. There's an important difference.

Here are guidelines to help you paraphrase accurately and effectively in an academic argument:

- Identify the source of the paraphrase, and comment on its significance or the authority of its author.

- Respect your sources. When paraphrasing an entire work or any lengthy section of it, cover all its main points and any essential details, following the same order the author uses. If you distort the shape of the material, your notes will be less valuable, especially if you return to them later.

- If you're paraphrasing material that extends over more than one page in the original source, note the placement of page breaks since it is highly likely that you will use only part of the paraphrase in your argument. You will need the page number to cite the specific page of material you want to cite.

- Make sure that the paraphrase is in your own words and sentence structures. If you want to include especially memorable or powerful language from the original source, enclose it in quotation marks.

- Keep your own comments, elaborations, or reactions separate from the paraphrase itself. Your report on the source should be clear, objective, and free of connotative language.

- Collect all the information necessary to create an in-text citation as well as an item in your works cited list or references list. For online materials, be sure you know how to recover the source later.

- Label the paraphrase with a note suggesting where and how you intend to use it in your argument.

- Recheck to make sure that the words and sentence structures are your own and that they express the author's meaning accurately.

Following is a paraphrase of "A Directive Approach toward ESL/EFL Writers," a research essay by Brian Riady reprinted in Chapter 16 on p. 383.

> In "A Directive Approach toward ESL/EFL Writers," Brian Riady argues that the tutoring method used most often in writing centers, called "non-directive," may not work for ESL students because it does not deal with the cultural differences of non-native students. Riady explains that Arabic and Japanese students, for example, think differently about style and argument than do American writers. Unfortunately, non-directive tutoring—which uses questions to get students to understand their writing problems—does not help when foreign students do not recognize what good writing in a culture is. So ESL students usually need more help and advice than writing center tutors trained in non-directive methods are comfortable giving. Riady cites research suggesting that writing centers need to adapt their methods to the needs of writers, understanding that no single approach to tutoring works for everyone.

> **Note:** This source gains credibility because Riady is himself an international student who works as a tutor in a writing center.

Summarize all sources that you examine. Unlike a paraphrase, a **summary** records just the gist of a source or a key idea—that is, only enough information to identify a point you want to emphasize. Once again, this much-shortened version of a source puts any borrowed ideas into your own words. At the research stage, summaries help you identify key points you want to make and, just as important, provide a record of what you have read. In a project itself, a summary helps readers understand the sources you are using.

Here are some guidelines to help you prepare accurate and helpful summaries:

- Identify the thesis or main point in a source and make it the heart of your summary. In a few detailed phrases or sentences, explain to yourself (and readers) what the source accomplishes.

- If your summary includes a comment on the source (as it might in the summaries used for annotated bibliographies), be sure that you won't later confuse your comments with what the source itself asserts.

- When using a summary in an argument, identify the source, state its point, and add your own comments about why the material is significant for the argument that you're making.

- Include just enough information to recount the main points you want to cite. A summary is usually much shorter than the original. When you need more information or specific details, you can return to the source itself or prepare a paraphrase.

- Use your own words in a summary and keep the language objective and denotative. If you include any language from the original source, enclose it in quotation marks.

- Collect all the information necessary to create an in-text citation as well as an item in your works cited list or references list. For online sources without page numbers, record the paragraph, screen, or other section number(s) if available.

- Label the summary with a note that suggests where and how you intend to use it in your argument.

- Recheck the summary to make sure that you've captured the author's meaning accurately and that the wording is entirely your own.

Following is a summary of "A Directive Approach toward ESL/EFL Writers," a research essay by Brian Riady. Notice how much shorter it is than the paraphrase of the same article on p. 422.

> In "A Directive Approach toward ESL/EFL Writers," Brian Riady argues that because the tutoring method used most often in writing centers, called "non-directive," may not work for non-native students, alternative and more straightforward forms of instruction need to be considered.

Use quotations selectively and strategically. To support your argumentative claims, you'll want to quote (that is, to reproduce an author's precise words) in at least three kinds of situations:

- when the wording expresses a point so well that you cannot improve it or shorten it without weakening it,
- when the author is a respected authority whose opinion supports your own ideas powerfully, and/or
- when an author or authority challenges or seriously disagrees with others in the field.

Consider, too, that charts, graphs, and images may also function like direct quotations, providing convincing evidence for your academic argument.

In an argument, quotations from respected authorities will establish your ethos as someone who has sought out experts in the field. Just as important sometimes, direct quotations (such as a memorable phrase in your introduction or a detailed eyewitness account) may capture your readers' attention. Finally, carefully chosen quotations can broaden the appeal of your argument by drawing on emotion as well as logic, appealing to the reader's mind and heart. A student who is writing on the ethical issues of bullfighting, for example, might introduce an argument that bullfighting is not a sport by quoting Ernest Hemingway's comment that "the formal bull-fight is a tragedy, not a sport, and the bull is certain to be killed" and then accompany the quotation with an image such as the one on the facing page.

The following guidelines can help you quote accurately and effectively:

- Quote or reproduce materials that readers will find especially convincing, purposeful, and interesting. You should have a specific reason for every quotation.
- Don't forget the double quotations marks [" "] that must surround a direct quotation in American usage. If there's a quote within a quote, it is surrounded by a pair of single quotation marks [' ']. British usage does just the opposite, and foreign languages often handle direct quotations much differently.
- When using a quotation in your argument, introduce its author(s) and follow the quotation with commentary of your own that points out its significance.
- Keep quoted material relatively brief. Quote only as much of a passage necessary to make your point while still accurately representing what the source actually said.

A tragedy, not a sport?

- If the quotation extends over more than one page in the original source, note the placement of page breaks in case you decide to use only part of the quotation in your argument.
- In your notes, label a quotation you intend to use with a note that tells you where you think you'll use it.
- Make sure you have all the information necessary to create an in-text citation as well as an item in your works cited list or references list.
- Copy quotations carefully, reproducing the punctuation, capitalization, and spelling exactly as they are in the original. If possible, copy the quotation from a reliable text and paste it directly into your project.
- Make sure that quoted phrases, sentences, or passages fit smoothly into your own language. Consider where to begin the quotation to

make it work effectively within its surroundings or modify the words you write to work with the quoted material.

- Use square brackets if you introduce words of your own into the quotation or make changes to it ("And [more] brain research isn't going to define further the matter of 'mind'").

- Use ellipsis marks if you omit material ("And brain research isn't going to define . . . the matter of 'mind'").

- If you're quoting a short passage (four lines or less in MLA style; forty words or less in APA style), it should be worked into your text, enclosed by quotation marks. Longer quotations should be set off from the regular text. Begin such a quotation on a new line, indenting every line one inch or ten spaces (MLA) or a half inch or five to seven spaces (APA). Set-off quotations do not need to be enclosed in quotation marks.

- Never distort your sources when you quote from them, or present them out of context. Misusing sources is a major offense in academic arguments.

Frame all materials you borrow with signal words and introductions. Because source materials are crucial to the success of arguments, you need to introduce borrowed words and ideas carefully to your readers. Doing so usually calls for using a signal phrase of some kind in the sentence to introduce or frame the source. Often, a signal phrase will precede a quotation. But you need such a marker whenever you introduce borrowed material, as in the following examples:

> According to noted primatologist Jane Goodall, the more we learn about the nature of nonhuman animals, the more ethical questions we face about their use in the service of humans.

> The more we learn about the nature of nonhuman animals, the more ethical questions we face about their use in the service of humans, according to noted primatologist Jane Goodall.

> The more we learn about the nature of nonhuman animals, according to noted primatologist Jane Goodall, the more ethical questions we face about their use in the service of humans.

In each of these sentences, the signal phrase tells readers that you're drawing on the work of a person named Jane Goodall and that this person is a "noted primatologist."

Now look at an example that uses a quotation from a source in more than one sentence:

> In *Job Shift*, consultant William Bridges worries about "dejobbing and about what a future shaped by it is going to be like." Even more worrisome, Bridges argues, is the possibility that "the sense of craft and of professional vocation . . . will break down under the need to earn a fee" (228).

The signal verbs *worries* and *argues* add a sense of urgency to the message Bridges offers. They also suggest that the writer either agrees with—or is neutral about—Bridges's points. Other signal verbs can have a more negative slant, indicating that the point being introduced by the quotation is open to debate and that others (including the writer) might disagree with it. If the writer of the passage above had said, for instance, that Bridges *unreasonably contends* or that he *fantasizes,* these signal verbs would carry quite different connotations from those associated with *argues.*

In some cases, a signal verb may require more complex phrasing to get the writer's full meaning across:

> Bridges recognizes the dangers of changes in work yet refuses to be overcome by them: "The real issue is not how to stop the change but how to provide the necessary knowledge and skills to equip people to operate successfully in this New World" (229).

As these examples illustrate, the signal verb is important because it allows you to characterize the author's or source's viewpoint as well as your own—so choose these verbs with care.

Some Frequently Used Signal Verbs

acknowledges	claims	emphasizes	remarks
admits	concludes	expresses	replies
advises	concurs	hypothesizes	reports
agrees	confirms	interprets	responds
allows	criticizes	lists	reveals
argues	declares	objects	states
asserts	disagrees	observes	suggests
believes	discusses	offers	thinks
charges	disputes	opposes	writes

Note that in APA style, these signal verbs should be in the past tense: *Blau (1992) claimed; Clark (2001) concluded.*

Connect the sources in a project with your own ideas. The best academic arguments often have the flavor of a hearty but focused intellectual conversation. Scholars and scientists create this impression by handling research materials strategically and selectively. Here's how some college writers use sources to achieve specific goals within an academic argument.

- **Establish a context.** Brian Riady, whose full essay appears in Chapter 16, sets the context for his thesis statement by offering it only after he first cites three scholars who take a contrary view. Even if you know nothing about methods of tutoring in a writing center, you immediately understand that Riady's thesis is controversial and potentially significant just from the individual words he selects from those sources to describe the kind of instruction he intends to challenge:

In an attempt to adapt traditional conferencing strategies to the ESL writer, writing center faculty have found that the non-directive approach—which has been hailed as a writing center "bible" (Shamoon and Burns 135), writing center "dogma" (Clark 34), and a writing center "mantra" (Blau 3)—does not effectively assist ESL writers. Non-directive tutoring fails non-native English speakers for the exact reason that it so effectively assists native English speakers: culture.

When using Web sources, take special care to check authors' backgrounds and credentials.

The brief quotations also have the interesting rhetorical effect of undermining the traditional view by making it seem hardened and doctrinaire.

- **Review the literature on a subject.** You will often need to tell readers what authorities have already written about your topic. So, in a paper on the effectiveness of peer editing, Susan Wilcox does a very brief "review of the literature" on her subject, pointing to three authorities who support using the method in writing courses. She quotes from the authors and also puts some of their ideas in her own words:

Bostock cites one advantage of peer review as "giving a sense of ownership of the assessment process" (1). Topping expands this view, stating that "peer assessment also involves increased time on task: thinking, comparing, contrasting, and communicating" (254). The extra time spent thinking over the assignment, especially in terms of helping someone else, can draw in the reviewer and add a greater importance to taking the process seriously, especially since the reviewer knows that the classmate is relying on his advice. This also adds an extra layer of accountability for the student; his hard work— or lack thereof—will be seen by peers, not just the instructor. Cassidy notes, "students work harder with the knowledge that they will be assessed by their peers" (509): perhaps the knowledge that peer review is coming leads to a better-quality draft to begin with.

The paragraph is straightforward and useful, giving readers an efficient overview of the subject. If they want more information, they can find it by consulting Wilcox's works cited page.

- **Introduce a term or define a concept.** Quite often in an academic argument, you may need to define a term or explain a concept. Relying on a source may make your job easier *and* enhance your credibility. That is what Laura Pena achieves in the following paragraph, drawing upon two authorities to explain what teachers mean by a "rubric" when it comes to grading student work.

To understand the controversy surrounding rubrics, it is best to know what a rubric is. According to Heidi Andrade, a professor at SUNY-Albany, a rubric can be defined as "a document that lists criteria and describes varying levels of quality, from excellent to poor, for a specific assignment" ("Self-Assessment" 61). Traditionally, rubrics have been used primarily as grading and evaluation tools (Kohn 12), meaning that a rubric was not used until after students handed their papers in to their teacher. The teacher would then use a rubric to evaluate the students' papers according to the criteria listed on the rubric.

Note that the first source provides the core definition while information from the second offers a detail important to understanding when and how rubrics are used — a major issue in Pena's paper. Her selection of sources here serves her thesis while also providing readers with necessary information.

- **Present technical material.** Sources can be especially helpful, too, when material becomes technical or difficult to understand. Writing on your own, you might lack the confidence to handle the complexities of some subjects. While you should challenge yourself to learn a subject well enough to explain it in your own words, there will be times when a quotation from an expert serves both you and your readers. Here is Natalie San Luis dealing with some of the technical differences between mainstream and Black English:

> The grammatical rules of mainstream English are more concrete than those of Black English; high school students can't check out an MLA handbook on Ebonics from their school library. As with all dialects, though, there are certain characteristics of the language that most Black English scholars agree upon. According to Samy Alim, author of *Roc the Mic Right,* these characteristics are the "[h]abitual *be* [which] indicates actions that are continuing or ongoing. . . . Copula absence. . . . Stressed *been.* . . . *Gon* [indicating] the future tense. . . . *They* for possessive. . . . Postvocalic –*r.* . . . [and] *And* and *ang* for 'ink' and 'ing'" (115). Other scholars have identified "[a]bsence of third-person singular present-tense *s.* . . . Absence of possessive '*s*," repetition of pronouns, and double negatives (Rickford 111–24).

Note that using ellipses enables San Luis to cover a great deal of ground. Readers not familiar with linguistic terms may have trouble following the quotation, but remember that academic arguments often address audiences comfortable with some degree of complexity.

- **Develop or support a claim.** Even academic audiences expect to be convinced and one of the most important strategies for a writer is to use sources to amplify or support a claim. Here's Brian Riady again, combining his voice (as an international student himself) with that of two scholars to warn against making writing centers seem like editing services for international students for whom English is a second or foreign language (ESL/EFL):

> This is not to say that consultants should completely disregard the non-directive approach; consultants should still refrain from acting as a one-stop proofreading service. In "Tutors as Teachers: Assisting ESL/EFL Students in the

Writing Center," Terese Thonus advises consultants to avoid the tendency to merely correct surface-level errors in ESL writing, even if such errors may seem overwhelming. Most ESL students demonstrate basic proficiency of English vocabulary and grammar by passing the TOEFL, and may be able to isolate mechanical problems and self-correct with a little guidance. But emphasizing correctness in a directive, current traditional manner, and demanding a correct product of ESL writers "will engender frustration and even the loss of confidence, just as does demanding perfect native-like English pronunciation" (Kobayashi 107). Rather, consultants must find a balance between directive teaching and non-directive tutoring that is most effective for ESL students.

- **Highlight differences or counterarguments.** The sources you encounter in developing a project won't always agree with each other or you. In academic arguments, you don't want to hide such differences, but instead point them out honestly and let readers make judgments based upon actual claims. Here is a paragraph in which Laura Pena again presents two views on the use of rubrics as grading tools:

> Some naysayers, such as Alfie Kohn, assert that "any form of assessment that encourages students to keep asking, 'How am I doing?' is likely to change how they look at themselves and what they're learning, usually for the worse." Kohn cites a study that found that students who pay too much attention to the quality of their performance are more likely to chalk up the outcome of an assignment to factors beyond their control, such as innate ability, and are also more likely to give up quickly in the face of a difficult task (14). However, Ross and Rolheiser have found that when students are taught how to properly implement self-assessment tools in the writing process, they are more likely to put more effort and persistence into completing a difficult assignment and may develop higher self-confidence in their writing ability (sec. 2). Building self-confidence in elementary-age writers can be extremely helpful for when they tackle more complicated writing endeavors in the future.

In describing Kohn as a "naysayer," Pena may tip her hand and lose some degree of objectivity. But her thesis has already signaled her support for rubrics as a grading tool, so academic readers will probably not find the connotations of the term inappropriate.

These examples suggest only a few of the ways that sources, either summarized or quoted directly, can be incorporated into an academic argument to support or enhance a writer's goals. Like these writers, you should think of sources as your copartners in developing and expressing ideas. But you are still in charge.

- **Avoid "patchwriting."** When using sources in an argument, someone accustomed to working online may be tempted to do what Professor Rebecca Moore Howard termed "patchwriting." **Patchwriting** is the process of stitching a paper together from Web or online materials that have been copied or only lightly reworked; in addition, these materials are usually presented with little or no documentation. Here, for example, is a patchwork paragraph about the dangers wind turbines pose to wildlife:

Scientists are discovering that technology with low carbon impact does not mean low environmental or social impacts. That is the case especially with wind turbines, whose long massive fiberglass blades have been chopping up tens of thousands of birds that fly into them, including golden eagles, red-tailed hawks, burrowing owls and other raptors in California. Turbines are also killing bats in great numbers. The 420 wind turbines now in use across Pennsylvania killed more than 10,000 bats last year—mostly in the late summer months, according to the State Game Commission. That's an average of 25 bats per turbine per year, and the Nature Conservancy predicts as many as 2,900 turbines will be set up across the state by 2030. It's not the spinning blades that kill the bats; instead, their lungs effectively blow up from the rapid pressure drop that occurs as air flows over the turbine blades. But there's hope we may figure out solutions to these problems because, since we haven't had too many wind turbines heretofore in the country, we are learning how to manage this new technology as we go.

The paragraph reads well and is full of details. But it would be considered plagiarized (see Chapter 20) because it fails to identify its sources and because most of the material has simply been lifted directly from the Web. How much is actually copied? We've highlighted the borrowed material:

Scientists are discovering that technology with low carbon impact does not mean low environmental or social impacts. That is the case especially with wind turbines, whose long massive fiberglass blades have been chopping up tens of thousands of birds that fly into them, including golden eagles, red-tailed hawks, burrowing owls and other raptors in California. Turbines are also killing bats in great numbers. The 420 wind turbines now in use across Pennsylvania killed more than 10,000 bats last year—mostly in the late summer months, according to the State Game Commission. That's an average of 25 bats per turbine per year, and the Nature Conservancy predicts as many as 2,900 turbines will be set up across the state by 2030. It's not the spinning blades that kill the bats; instead, their lungs effectively blow up from the rapid pressure drop that occurs as air flows over the turbine blades. But there's hope we may figure out solutions to these problems because, since we haven't had too many wind turbines heretofore in the country, we are learning how to manage this new technology as we go.

But here's the point. An academic writer who has gone to the trouble of finding so much information will gain more credit and credibility just by properly identifying, paraphrasing, and quoting the sources used. The resulting paragraph is actually more impressive because it demonstrates how much reading and synthesizing the writer has actually done:

Scientists like George Ledec of the World Bank are discovering that technology with low carbon impact "does not mean low environmental or social impacts" (Tracy). That is the case especially with wind turbines. Their massive blades spinning to create pollution-free electricity are also killing thousands of valuable birds of prey, including eagles, hawks, and owls in California (Rittier). Turbines are also killing bats in great numbers (Thibodeaux). The *Pittsburgh Post-Gazette* reports that 10,000 bats a year are killed by the 420 turbines currently in Pennsylvania. According to the state game commissioner, "That's an average of 25 bats per turbine per year, and the Nature Conservancy predicts as many as 2,900 turbines will be set up across the state by 2030" (Schwartzel). It's not the spinning blades that kill the animals; instead, *DiscoveryNews* explains, "the bats' lungs effectively blow up from the rapid pressure drop that occurs as air flows over the turbine blades" (Marshall). But there's hope that scientists can develop turbines less dangerous to animals of all kinds. "We haven't had too many wind turbines heretofore in the country," David Cottingham of the Fish and Wildlife Service points out, "so we are learning about it as we go" (Tracy).

Works Cited

Marshall, Jessica. "Wind Turbines Kill Bats without Impact." *DiscoveryNews.com*. Discovery Communications, 25 Aug. 2008. Web. 11 Dec. 2011.

Rittier, John. "Wind Turbines Taking Toll on Birds of Prey." *USA Today*. Gannett, 4 Jan. 2005. Web. 10 Dec. 2011.

Schwartzel, Erich. "Pa. Wind Turbines Deadly to Bats, Costly to Farmers." *Post-Gazette.com*. PG Publishing, 17 July 2011. Web. 12 Dec. 2011.

Thibodeaux, Julie. "Bats Getting Caught in Texas Wind Turbines." *PegasusNews*.com. PanLocal Media, 9 Nov. 2011. Web. 10 Dec. 2011.

Tracy, Ryan. "Wildlife Slows Wind Power." *WallStreetJournal.com*. Dow Jones, 10 Dec. 2011. Web. 10 Dec. 2011.

RESPOND•

1. Select one of the essays from Chapters 8–12 or 16. Following the guidelines in this chapter, write a paraphrase of the essay that you might use subsequently in an academic argument. Be careful to describe the essay accurately and to note on what pages specific ideas or claims are located. The language of the paraphrase should be entirely your own—though you may include direct quotations of phrases, sentences, or longer passages you would likely use in a paper. Be sure these quotations are introduced and cited in your paraphrase: *Pearson claims that nuclear power is safe, even asserting that "your toaster is far more likely to kill you than any nuclear power plant" (175).* When you are done, trade your paraphrase with a partner to get feedback on its clarity and accuracy.

2. Summarize three readings or fairly lengthy passages from Parts 1–3 of this book, following the guidelines in this chapter. Open the item with a correct MLA or APA citation for the piece (see Chapter 21). Then provide the summary itself. Follow up with a one- or two-sentence evaluation of the work describing its potential value as a source in an academic argument. In effect, you will be preparing three items that might appear in an annotated bibliography. Here's an example:

   > Pearson, Taylor. "Why You Should Fear Your Toaster More Than Nuclear Power." In *Everything's an Argument* by Andrea A. Lunsford and John J. Ruszkiewicz. Boston: Bedford, 2013. 174–79. Print. Argues that since the dangers of nuclear power (death, radiation, waste) are actually less than those of energy sources we rely on today, nuclear plants represent the only practical way to generate the power we need and still reduce greenhouse gases. The journalistic piece provides many interesting facts about nuclear energy, but is informally documented and so does not identify its sources in detail or include a bibliography.

3. Working with a partner, agree upon an essay that you will both read from Chapters 8–12 or 16, examining it as a potential source for a research argument. As you read it, choose about a half-dozen words, phrases, or short passages that you would likely quote if you used the essay in a paper and attach a frame or signal phrase to each quotation. Then compare the passages you selected to quote with those your partner culled from the same essay. How do your choices of quoted material create an image or ethos for the original author that differs from the one your partner has created? How do the signal phrases shape a reader's sense of the author's position? Which set of quotations best represents the author's argument? Why?

4. Select one of the essays from Chapters 8–12 or 16 to examine the different ways an author uses source materials to support claims. Begin by highlighting the signal phrases you find attached to borrowed ideas or direct quotations. How well do they introduce or frame this material? Then categorize the various ways the author actually uses particular sources. For example, look for sources that provide context for the topic, review the scholarly literature, define key concepts or terms, explain technical details, furnish evidence, or lay out contrary opinions. When you are done, write a paragraph assessing the author's handling of sources in the piece. Are the borrowed materials integrated well with the author's own thoughts? Do the sources represent an effective synthesis of ideas?

20
Plagiarism and Academic Integrity

In many ways, "nothing new under the sun" is more than just a cliché. Most of what you think or write is built on what you've previously read or experienced. Luckily, you'll seldom be called on to list every influence on your life. But you do have responsibilities in school and professional situations to acknowledge any intellectual property you've borrowed when you create arguments of your own. If you don't, you may be accused of **plagiarism**—claiming as your own the words, research, or creative work of others.

What is intellectual property? It's complicated. But, for academic arguments in Western culture, it is the *expression* of ideas you find in works produced by others that you then use to advance and support your own claims. You have to document not only when you use or reproduce someone's exact words, images, music, or other creations (in whole or in part), but also when you borrow the framework others use to put ideas together in original or creative ways. Needless to say, intellectual property rights have always been contentious, but never more so than

The FBI has warned consumers for decades about the penalties for violating copyright. Your school no doubt has its own policies for handling violations such as plagiarism.

today, when new media make it remarkably easy to duplicate and share all sorts of materials. Accustomed to uploading and downloading files, cutting and pasting passages, you may be comfortable working with texts day-to-day in ways that are considered dishonest in school.

So it is essential that you read and understand any policies on academic integrity that your school has set down. In particular, pay attention to how those policies define, prosecute, and punish cheating, plagiarism, and collusion. Some institutions recognize a difference between intentional and unintentional plagiarism, but you don't want the honesty of anything you write to be questioned. You need to learn the rules and understand that the penalties for plagiarism are severe not only for students but for professional writers as well.

Fortunately there's an upside to handling borrowed materials responsibly. When you give full credit to your sources, you enhance your ethos in academic arguments—which is why "Academic Integrity" appears in this chapter's title. Audiences will applaud you for saying thanks to those who've helped you. Crediting your sources also proves that you have shown "due diligence": you demonstrate that you understand what others have written about the topic and encourage others to join the intellectual conversation. Finally, citing sources reminds you to think critically about how to use the evidence you've collected. Is it timely and reliable? Have you referenced authorities in a biased or overly selective way? Have you double-checked all quotations and paraphrases? Thinking through such questions helps to guarantee the integrity of your academic work.

In the nineteenth century, before patents applied to living organisms, beautiful lithographs like this hand-colored illustration of the Red Astrachan apple were published to establish the claims that breeders of new fruit species had to their intellectual property.

RED ASTRACHAN APPLE.

Acknowledging Your Sources Accurately and Appropriately

The basic principles for documenting materials are relatively simple. Give credit to all source materials you borrow by following these three steps: (1) placing quotation marks around any words you quote directly, (2) citing your sources according to the documentation style you're using, and (3) identifying all the sources you have cited in a list of references or works cited. Materials to be cited in an academic argument include all of the following:

- direct quotations
- facts that are not widely known
- arguable statements
- judgments, opinions, and claims that have been made by others

- images, statistics, charts, tables, graphs, or other illustrations that appear in any source
- collaboration — that is, the help provided by friends, colleagues, instructors, supervisors, or others

However, three important types of evidence or source material do not need to be acknowledged or documented. They are the following:

- common knowledge, which is a specific piece of information most readers in your intended audience will know (that Barack Obama won the 2008 presidential election, for instance)
- facts available from a wide variety of sources (that the Japanese bombed Pearl Harbor on December 7, 1941, for example)
- your own findings from field research (observations, interviews, experiments, or surveys you have conducted), which should be clearly presented as your own

For the actual forms to use when documenting sources, see Chapter 21.

Of course, the devil is in the details. For instance, you may be accused of plagiarism in situations like the following:

- if you don't indicate clearly the source of an idea you obviously didn't come up with on your own
- if you use a paraphrase that's too close to the original wording or sentence structure of your source material (*even* if you cite the source)
- if you leave out the parenthetical in-text reference for a quotation (*even* if you include the quotation marks themselves)

And the accusation can be made even if you didn't intend to plagiarize.

Online, you will encounter materials that obviously remix or parody images and ideas that belong to others. But intellectual property is treated much differently in school: clear guidelines apply whenever you use source materials. So you must learn to document sources accurately and fully and not be careless about this very important procedure.

Here, for example, is the first paragraph from an essay by Russell Platt published in the *Nation*:

> Classical music in America, we are frequently told, is in its death throes: its orchestras bled dry by expensive guest soloists and greedy musicians unions, its media presence shrinking, its prestige diminished, its educational role ignored, its big record labels dying out or merging into faceless corporate entities. We seem to have too many

well-trained musicians in need of work, too many good composers going without commissions, too many concerts to offer an already satiated public.

—Russell Platt, "New World Symphony"

To cite this passage correctly in MLA documentation style, you could quote directly from it, using both quotation marks and some form of note identifying the author or source. Either of the following versions would be acceptable:

> Russell Platt has doubts about claims that classical music is "in its death throes: its orchestras bled dry by expensive guest soloists and greedy musicians unions" ("New World").

> But is classical music in the United States really "in its death throes," as some critics of the music scene suggest (Platt)?

You might also paraphrase Platt's paragraph, putting his ideas entirely in your own words but still giving him due credit by ending your remarks with a simple in-text note:

> A familiar story told by critics is that classical music faces a bleak future in the United States, with grasping soloists and unions bankrupting orchestras and classical works vanishing from radio and television, school curricula, and the labels of recording conglomerates. The public may not be willing to support all the talented musicians and composers we have today (Platt).

All of these sentences with citations would be keyed to a works cited entry at the end of the paper that would look like the following in MLA style:

> Platt, Russell. "New World Symphony." *The Nation*. The Nation, 3 Oct. 2005.
> Web. 15 Oct. 2009.

How might a citation go wrong? As we indicated, omitting either the quotation marks around a borrowed passage or an acknowledgment of the source is grounds for complaint. Neither of the following sentences provides enough information for a correct citation:

> But is classical music in the United States really in its death throes, as some critics of the music scene suggest, with its prestige diminished, its educational role ignored, and its big record labels dying (Platt)?

> But is classical music in the United States really in "its death throes," as some critics of the music scene suggest, with "its prestige diminished, its educational role ignored, [and] its big record labels dying"?

Just as faulty is a paraphrase such as the following, which borrows the words or ideas of the source too closely. It represents plagiarism, despite the fact that it identifies the source from which almost all the ideas—and a good many words—are borrowed:

> In "New World Symphony," Russell Platt observes that classical music is thought by many to be in bad shape in America. Its orchestras are being sucked dry by costly guest artists and insatiable unionized musicians, while its place on TV and radio is shrinking. The problem may be that we have too many well-trained

A *Doonesbury* cartoon on intellectual property pokes fun at best-selling historian and presidential biographer Stephen Ambrose, who was found to have plagiarized passages from at least twelve authors in at least six of his books—and in his doctoral dissertation.

DOONESBURY   BY GARRY TRUDEAU

musicians who need employment, too many good composers going without jobs, too many concerts for a public that prefers *Desperate Housewives*.

Even the fresh idea not taken from Platt at the end of the paragraph doesn't alter the fact that the paraphrase is mostly a mash-up of Platt's original words, lightly stirred.

Using Copyrighted Internet Sources

If you've done any surfing on the Internet, you know that it opens the door to worldwide collaborations: you can contact individuals and groups around the globe and have access to whole libraries of information. As a result, writing (especially online writing) often is made up of materials woven from many sources. But when you gather information from Internet sources and use it in your own work, it's subject to the same rules that govern information gathered from other types of sources.

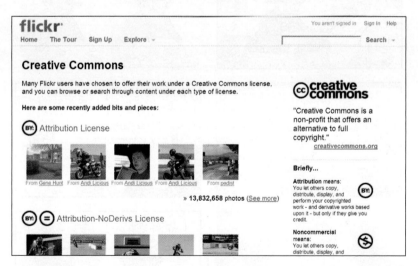

A growing number of works, such as photographs, music, and video, are published online under the so-called Creative Commons license, which often eliminates the need to request permission. These works—marked with a Creative Commons license at Flickr, for example—are made available to the public under this alternative to copyright, which grants blanket permission to reuse or remix work under certain terms if credit is given to the work's creator.

Even if the material does not include a copyright notice or symbol ("© 2013 by Andrea A. Lunsford and John J. Ruszkiewicz," for example), it's likely to be protected by copyright laws, and you may need to request permission to use part or all of it. Although they're currently in flux, "fair-use" legal precedents still allow writers to quote brief passages from published works without permission from the copyright holder if the use is for educational or personal, noncommercial reasons and if full credit is given to the source. For blog postings or any serious professional uses (especially online), however, you should ask permission of the writer before you include any of his or her material in your own argument. For graphics, photos, or other images that you wish to reproduce in your text, you should also request permission from the creator or owner if the text is going to be disseminated beyond your classroom—again, especially if it's going to appear on the Web.

If you do need to make a request for permission, here are some examples:

From: sanchez.32@stanford.edu
To: litman@mindspring.com
CC: lunsford.2@stanford.edu
Subject: Request for permission

Dear Professor Litman:

I am writing to request permission to quote from your essay "Copyright, Owners' Rights and Users' Privileges on the Internet: Implied Licenses, Caching, Linking, Fair Use, and Sign-on Licenses." I want to quote some of your work as part of an article I am writing for the *Stanford Daily* to explain the complex debates over ownership on the Internet and to argue that students at my school should be participating in these debates. I will give full credit to you and will cite the URL where I first found your work (msen.com/~litman/dayton/htm).

Thank you very much for considering my request.

Raul Sanchez

From: fox.360@stanford.edu
To: fridanet@aol.com
CC: lunsford.2@stanford.edu
Subject: Request for permission

Dear Kimberley Masters:

I am a student at Stanford University writing to request your permission to download and use a photograph of Frida Kahlo in a three-piece suit (fridanet/suit.htm#top) as an illustration in a project about Kahlo that I and two other students are working on in our composition class. This project will be posted on a school Web site. In the report on our project, we will cite members.aol.com/fridanet/kahlo.htm as the URL, unless you wish for us to use a different source.

Thank you very much for considering our request.

Jennifer Fox

Acknowledging Collaboration

Writers generally acknowledge all participants in collaborative projects at the beginning of the presentation, report, or essay. In print texts, the acknowledgment is often placed in a footnote or brief prefatory note.

The seventh edition of the *MLA Handbook for Writers of Research Papers* (2009) calls attention to the growing importance of collaborative work and gives the following advice on how to deal with issues of assigning fair credit all around:

> Joint participation in research and writing is common and, in fact, encouraged in many courses and in many professions. It does not constitute plagiarism provided that credit is given for all contributions. One way to give credit, if roles were clearly demarcated or were unequal, is to state exactly who did what. Another way, especially if roles and contributions were merged and shared, is to acknowledge all concerned equally. Ask your instructor for advice if you are not certain how to acknowledge collaboration.

RESPOND●

1. Not everyone agrees that intellectual material is property that should be protected. The slogan "information wants to be free" has been showing up in popular magazines and on the Internet, often with a call to readers to take action against protection such as data encryption and further extension of copyright.

   Using a Web search engine, look for pages where the phrase "free information" appears. Find several sites that make arguments in favor of free information, and analyze them in terms of their rhetorical appeals. What claims do the authors make? How do they appeal to their audience? What's the site's ethos, and how is it created? After you've read some arguments in favor of free information, return to this chapter's arguments about intellectual property. Which arguments do you find most persuasive? Why?

2. Although this book is concerned principally with ideas and their written expression, other forms of intellectual property are also legally protected. For example, scientific and technological developments are protectable under patent law, which differs in some significant ways from copyright law.

   Find the standards for protection under U.S. copyright law and U.S. patent law. You might begin by visiting the U.S. copyright Web site (http://copyright.gov). Then imagine that you're the president of a small high-tech corporation and are trying to inform your employees of the legal protections available to them and their work. Write a paragraph or two explaining the differences between copyright and patent, and suggest a policy that balances employees' rights to intellectual property with the business's needs to develop new products.

3. Define *plagiarism* in your own terms, making your definition as clear and explicit as possible. Then compare your definition with those of two or three other classmates, and write a brief report on the similarities and differences you noted in the definitions. You might research terms such as *plagiarism, academic honesty*, and *academic integrity* on the Web. Also be certain to check how your own school defines the words.

4. Spend fifteen or twenty minutes jotting down your ideas about intellectual property and plagiarism. Where do you stand, for example, on the issue of music file sharing? On downloading movies free of charge? Do you think these forms of intellectual property should be protected under copyright law? How do you define your own intellectual property, and in what ways and under what conditions are you willing to share it? Finally, come up with your own definition of *academic integrity*.

21
Documenting Sources

What does documenting sources have to do with argument? First, the sources that a writer chooses form part of any argument, showing that he or she has done some research, knows what others have said about the topic, and understands how to use these items as support for a claim. Similarly, the list of works cited or references makes a statement, saying, "Look at how thoroughly this essay has been researched" or "Note how up-to-date I am!"

Even the choice of documentation style makes an argument in a subtle way. You'll note in the instructions that follow, for example, that the Modern Language Association (MLA) style requires putting the date of publication of a print source at or near the end of a works cited list entry, whereas the American Psychological Association (APA) style places that date near the beginning of a reference list citation. Pay attention to such fine points of documentation style, always asking what these choices suggest about the values of scholars and researchers who use a particular system of documentation.

MLA Style

Documentation styles vary from discipline to discipline, with one format favored in the social sciences and another in the natural sciences, for example. Widely used in the humanities, MLA style is fully described in the *MLA Handbook for Writers of Research Papers* (7th edition, 2009). In this discussion, we provide guidelines drawn from the *MLA Handbook* for in-text citations, notes, and entries in the list of works cited.

In-Text Citations

MLA style calls for in-text citations in the body of an argument to document sources of quotations, paraphrases, summaries, and so on. For in-text citations, use a signal phrase to introduce the material, often with the author's name (*As LaDoris Cordell explains, . . .*). Keep an in-text citation short, but include enough information for readers to locate the source in the list of works cited. Place the parenthetical citation as near to the relevant material as possible without disrupting the flow of the sentence, as in the following examples.

1. Author Named in a Signal Phrase

Ordinarily, use the author's name in a signal phrase to introduce the material, and cite the page number(s) in parentheses.

Loomba argues that Caliban's "political colour" is black, given his stage representations, which have varied from animalistic to a kind of missing link (143).

2. Author Named in Parentheses

When you don't mention the author in a signal phrase, include the author's last name before the page number(s) in the parentheses.

Oil from shale in the western states, if it could be extracted, would be equivalent to six hundred billion barrels, more than all the crude so far produced in the world (McPhee 413).

3. Two or Three Authors

Use all authors' last names.

Gortner, Hebrun, and Nicolson maintain that "opinion leaders" influence other people in an organization because they are respected, not because they hold high positions (175).

4. Four or More Authors

The MLA allows you to use all authors' last names or to use only the first author's name with *et al.* (in regular type, not italicized). Although either format is acceptable when applied consistently throughout a paper, in an argument it is better to name all authors who contributed to the work.

Similarly, as Goldberger, Tarule, Clinchy, and Belenky note, their new book builds on their collaborative experiences (xii).

5. Organization as Author

Give the full name of a corporate author if it's brief or a shortened form if it's long.

In fact, one of the leading foundations in the field of higher education supports the recent proposals for community-run public schools (Carnegie Corporation 45).

6. Unknown Author

Use the full title of the work if it's brief or a shortened form if it's long.

"Hype," by one analysis, is "an artificially engendered atmosphere of hysteria" ("Today's Marketplace" 51).

7. Author of Two or More Works

When you use two or more works by the same author, include the title of the work or a shortened version of it in the citation.

Gardner presents readers with their own silliness through his description of a "pointless, ridiculous monster, crouched in the shadows, stinking of dead men, murdered children, and martyred cows" (*Grendel* 2).

8. Authors with the Same Last Name

When you use works by two or more authors with the same last name, include each author's first initial in the in-text citation.

Father Divine's teachings focused on eternal life, salvation, and socioeconomic progress (R. Washington 17).

9. Multivolume Work

Note the volume number first and then the page number(s), with a colon and one space between them.

Aristotle's "On Plants" is now available in a new translation edited by Barnes (2: 1252).

10. Literary Work

Because literary works are often available in many different editions, you need to include enough information for readers to locate the passage in any edition. For a prose work such as a novel or play, first cite the page number from the edition you used, followed by a semicolon; then indicate the part or chapter number (114; ch. 3) or act or scene in a play (42; sc. 2).

> In *The Madonnas of Leningrad*, Marina says, "she could see into the future" (7; ch. 1).

For a poem, cite the stanza and line numbers. If the poem has only line numbers, use the word *line(s)* in the first reference (lines 33–34) and the number(s) alone in subsequent references.

> On dying, Whitman speculates, "All that goes onward and outward, nothing collapses, / And to die is different from what any one supposed, and luckier" (6.129-30).

For a verse play, omit the page number, and give only the act, scene, and line numbers, separated by periods.

> Before he takes his own life, Othello says he is "one that loved not wisely but too well" (5.2.348).

> As *Macbeth* begins, the witches greet Banquo as "Lesser than Macbeth, and greater" (1.3.65).

11. Works in an Anthology

For an essay, short story, or other short work within an anthology, use the name of the author of the work, not the editor of the anthology; but use the page number(s) from the anthology.

> In the end, if the black artist accepts any duties at all, that duty is to express the beauty of blackness (Hughes 1271).

12. Sacred Text

To cite a sacred text, such as the Qur'an or the Bible, give the title of the edition you used, the book, and the chapter and verse (or their equivalent), separated by a period. In your text, spell out the names of books. In a parenthetical reference, use an abbreviation for books with names of five or more letters (for example, *Gen.* for Genesis).

> He ignored the admonition "Pride goes before destruction, and a haughty spirit before a fall" (*New Oxford Annotated Bible*, Prov. 16.18).

13. Indirect Source

Use the abbreviation *qtd. in* to indicate that what you're quoting or paraphrasing is quoted (as part of a conversation, interview, letter, or excerpt) in the source you're using.

> As Catherine Belsey states, "to speak is to have access to the language which defines, delimits and locates power" (qtd. in Bartels 453).

14. Two or More Sources in the Same Citation

Separate the information for each source with a semicolon.

> Adefunmi was able to patch up the subsequent holes left in worship by substituting various Yoruba, Dahomean, or Fon customs made available to him through research (Brandon 115-17; Hunt 27).

15. Entire Work or One-Page Article

Include the citation in the text without any page numbers or parentheses.

> The relationship between revolutionary innocence and the preservation of an oppressive postrevolutionary regime is one theme Milan Kundera explores in *The Book of Laughter and Forgetting*.

16. Work without Page Numbers

If the work isn't numbered by page but has numbered sections, parts, or paragraphs, include the name and number(s) of the section(s) you're citing. (For paragraphs, use the abbreviation *par.* or *pars.*; for section, use *sec.*; for part, use *pt.*)

> Zora Neale Hurston is one of the great anthropologists of the twentieth century, according to Kip Hinton (par. 2).

> Describing children's language acquisition, Pinker explains that "what's innate about language is just a way of paying attention to parental speech" (Johnson, sec. 1).

17. Electronic or Nonprint Source

Give enough information in a signal phrase or parenthetical citation for readers to locate the source in the list of works cited. Usually give the author or title under which you list the source.

> In his film version of *Hamlet*, Zeffirelli highlights the sexual tension between the prince and his mother.

Explanatory and Bibliographic Notes

The MLA recommends using explanatory notes for information or commentary that doesn't readily fit into your text but is needed for clarification, further explanation, or justification. In addition, the MLA allows bibliographic notes for citing several sources for one point and for offering thanks to, information about, or evaluation of a source. Use a superscript number in your text at the end of a sentence to refer readers to the notes, which usually appear as endnotes (with the heading *Notes*, not underlined or italicized) on a separate page before the list of works cited. Indent the first line of each note five spaces, and double-space all entries.

TEXT WITH SUPERSCRIPT INDICATING A NOTE

Stewart emphasizes the existence of social contacts in Hawthorne's life so that the audience will accept a different Hawthorne, one more attuned to modern times than the figure in Woodberry.[3]

NOTE

[3] Woodberry does, however, show that Hawthorne was often unsociable. He emphasizes the seclusion of Hawthorne's mother, who separated herself from her family after the death of her husband, often even taking meals alone (28). Woodberry seems to imply that Mrs. Hawthorne's isolation rubbed off on her son.

List of Works Cited

A list of works cited is an alphabetical listing of the sources you cite in your essay. The list appears on a separate page at the end of your argument, after any notes, with the heading *Works Cited* centered an inch from the top of the page; don't underline or italicize it or enclose it in quotation marks. Double-space between the heading and the first entry, and double-space the entire list. (If you're asked to list everything you've read as background—not just the sources you cite—call the list *Works Consulted*.) The first line of each entry should align on the left; subsequent lines indent one-half inch or five spaces. See p. 464 for a sample works cited page.

BOOKS

The basic information for a book includes four elements, each followed by a period:

- the author's name, last name first (for a book with multiple authors, only the first author's name is inverted)
- the title and subtitle, italicized
- the publication information, including the city followed by a colon, a shortened form of the publisher's name (such as Harvard UP) followed by a comma, and the publication date
- the medium of publication (*Print*)

1. One Author

Skloot, Rebecca. *The Immortal Life of Henrietta Lacks*. Waterville: Thorndike, 2010. Print.

2. Two or More Authors

Jacobson, Sid, and Ernie Colón. *The 9/11 Report: A Graphic Adaptation*. New York: Hill, 2006. Print.

3. Organization as Author

American Horticultural Society. *The Fully Illustrated Plant-by-Plant Manual of Practical Techniques*. New York: American Horticultural Society and DK, 1999. Print.

4. Unknown Author

National Geographic Atlas of the World. New York: Natl. Geographic, 2004. Print.

5. Two or More Books by the Same Author

List the works alphabetically by title. Use three hyphens for the author's name for the second and subsequent works by that author.

Lorde, Audre. *A Burst of Light*. Ithaca: Firebrand, 1988. Print.

---. *Sister Outsider*. Trumansburg: Crossing, 1984. Print.

6. Editor

Rorty, Amelie Oksenberg, ed. *Essays on Aristotle's Poetics*. Princeton: Princeton UP, 1992. Print.

7. Author and Editor

Shakespeare, William. *The Tempest*. Ed. Frank Kermode. London: Routledge, 1994. Print.

8. Selection in an Anthology or Chapter in an Edited Book

List the author(s) of the selection or chapter; its title; the title of the book in which the selection or chapter appears; *Ed.* and the name(s) of the editor(s); the publication information; and the inclusive page numbers of the selection or chapter.

Brown, Paul. "'This thing of darkness I acknowledge mine': *The Tempest* and the Discourse of Colonialism." *Political Shakespeare: Essays in Cultural Materialism.* Ed. Jonathan Dillimore and Alan Sinfield. Ithaca: Cornell UP, 1985. 48-71. Print.

9. Two or More Works from the Same Anthology

Include the anthology itself in the list of works cited.

Gates, Henry Louis, Jr., and Nellie McKay, eds. *The Norton Anthology of African American Literature.* New York: Norton, 1997. Print.

Then list each selection separately by its author and title, followed by a cross-reference to the anthology.

Karenga, Maulana. "Black Art: Mute Matter Given Force and Function." Gates and McKay 1973-77.

Neal, Larry. "The Black Arts Movement." Gates and McKay 1960-72.

10. Translation

Hietamies, Laila. *Red Moon over White Sea.* Trans. Borje Vahamaki. Beaverton: Aspasia, 2000. Print.

11. Edition Other Than the First

Lunsford, Andrea A., John J. Ruszkiewicz, and Keith Walters. *Everything's an Argument with Readings.* 6th ed. Boston: Bedford, 2013. Print.

12. One Volume of a Multivolume Work

Byron, Lord George. *Byron's Letters and Journals.* Ed. Leslie A. Marchand. Vol. 2. London: Murray, 1973-82. Print. 12 vols.

13. Two or More Volumes of a Multivolume Work

Byron, Lord George. *Byron's Letters and Journals.* Ed. Leslie A. Marchand. 12 vols. London: Murray, 1973-82. Print.

14. Preface, Foreword, Introduction, or Afterword

Kean, Thomas H., and Lee H. Hamilton. Foreword. *The 9/11 Report: A Graphic Adaptation.* By Sid Jacobson and Ernie Colón. New York: Hill, 2006. ix-x. Print.

15. Article in a Reference Work

Kettering, Alison McNeil. "Art Nouveau." *World Book Encyclopedia*. 2002 ed.
   Print.

16. Book That Is Part of a Series

Include the series title and number after the publication information.

Moss, Beverly J. *A Community Text Arises*. Cresskill: Hampton, 2003. Print.
   Language and Social Processes Ser. 8.

17. Republication

Scott, Walter. *Kenilworth*. 1821. New York: Dodd, 1996. Print.

18. Government Document

United States. Cong. House Committee on the Judiciary. *Impeachment of the
   President*. 40th Cong., 1st sess. H. Rept. 7. Washington: GPO, 1867. Print.

19. Pamphlet

An Answer to the President's Message to the Fiftieth Congress. Philadelphia:
   Manufacturer's Club of Philadelphia, 1887. Print.

20. Published Proceedings of a Conference

Edwards, Ron, ed. *Proceedings of the Third National Folklore Conference*. 26-27
   Nov. 1988. Canberra, Austral.: Australian Folk Trust, 1988. Print.

21. Title within a Title

Tauernier-Courbin, Jacqueline. *Ernest Hemingway's* A Moveable Feast: *The
   Making of a Myth*. Boston: Northeastern UP, 1991. Print.

PERIODICALS

The basic entry for a periodical includes four elements, each followed by
a period:

- the author's name, last name first
- the article title, in quotation marks
- the publication information, including the periodical title (italicized),
  the volume and issue numbers (if any, not italicized), the date of publication, and the page number(s)
- the medium of publication (*Print*)

For works with multiple authors, only the first author's name is inverted. Note that the period following the article title goes inside the closing quotation mark. Finally, note that the MLA omits *the* in titles such as *The New Yorker*.

22. Article in a Journal

Give the issue number, if available.

Anderson, Virginia. "'The Perfect Enemy': Clinton, the Contradictions of Capitalism, and Slaying the Sin Within." *Rhetoric Review* 21 (2002): 384-400. Print.

Radavich, David. "Man among Men: David Mamet's Homosocial Order." *American Drama* 1.1 (1991): 46-66. Print.

23. Article That Skips Pages

Seabrook, John. "Renaissance Pears." *New Yorker* 5 Sept. 2005: 102+. Print.

24. Article in a Monthly Magazine

Lelyveld, Joseph. "What 9/11 Wrought." *Smithsonian* Sept. 2011: 58-64. Print.

25. Article in a Weekly Magazine

Reed, Julia. "Hope in the Ruins." *Newsweek* 12 Sept. 2005: 58-59. Print.

26. Article in a Newspaper

Friend, Tim. "Scientists Map the Mouse Genome." *USA Today* 2 Dec. 2002: A1. Print.

27. Editorial or Letter to the Editor

Posner, Alan. "Colin Powell's Regret." Editorial. *New York Times* 9 Sept. 2005: A20. Print.

28. Unsigned Article

"Court Rejects the Sale of Medical Marijuana." *New York Times* 26 Feb. 1998, late ed.: A21. Print.

29. Review

Wildavsky, Ben. "Bad Educations." Rev. of *Academically Adrift: Limited Learning on College Campuses*, by Richard Arum and Joseph Roksa. *Wilson Quarterly* 35.2 (2011): 98-99. Print.

ELECTRONIC SOURCES

Most of the following models are based on the MLA's guidelines for citing electronic sources in the *MLA Handbook* (7th edition, 2009), as well as on up-to-date information available at its Web site (http://mla.org). The MLA no longer requires the use of URLs but assumes that readers can locate a source by searching the author, title, and other publication information given in the citation. The basic MLA entry for most electronic sources should include the following elements:

- name of the author, editor, or compiler
- title of the work, document, or posting
- information for print publication, if any
- information for electronic publication
- medium of publication (e.g., *Web*, CD-ROM, etc.)
- date of access

30. Document from a Professional Web Site

When possible, include the author's name; the title of the document, in quotations; the name of the Web site, italicized; the sponsor or publisher; the date of publication; the medium consulted (*Web*); and the date you accessed the site.

> "Fair Use and Short Form Media." *Critical Commons: For Fair & Critical Participation in Media Culture.* USC Institute for Multimedia Literacy, 23 Nov. 2010. Web. 3 Sept. 2011.

31. Entire Web Site

Include the name of the person or group who created the site, if relevant; the title of the site, italicized, or (if there is no title) a description such as *Home page*, not italicized; the publisher or sponsor of the site; the date of publication or last update; the medium consulted (*Web*); and the date of access.

> *Kotaku.* Gawker Media, 12 Jan. 2011. Web. 30 Aug. 2011.

> Mitten, Lisa. *Native American Sites.* Lisa A. Mitten, 16 Sept. 2008. Web. 3 Dec. 2008.

32. Course, Department, or Personal Web Site

For a course Web site, include the instructor's name; the title of the site, italicized; a description of the site (such as *Course home page, Dept. home page,* or *Home page* — not italicized); the sponsor of the site (academic department and institution); dates of the course or last update to the page; the medium; and date of access. For an academic department, list the name of the department; a description; the academic institution; the date the page was last updated (use *n.d.* for no date, not italicized); the medium (*Web*); and the date of access.

> Dept. of English. Home page. Amherst Coll., n.d. Web. 5 Apr. 2007.

> Lunsford, Andrea A. Home page. Stanford U, 27 Mar. 2003. Web. 10 Sept. 2011.

> Lunsford, Andrea A. *Memory and Media*. Course home page. Dept. of English, Stanford U, Sept.-Dec. 2002. Web. 13 Mar. 2006.

33. Online Book

Cite an online book as you would a print book. After the print publication information (if any), give the title of the Web site or database in which the book appears, italicized; the medium (*Web*); and the date of access.

> Riis, Jacob A. *How the Other Half Lives: Studies among the Tenements of New York*. Ed. David Phillips. New York: Scribner's, 1890. *The Authentic History Center*. Web. 26 Mar. 2009.

Treat a poem, essay, or other short work within an online book as you would a part of a print book. After the print publication information (if any), give the title of the Web site or database, italicized; the medium (*Web*); and the date of access.

> Dickinson, Emily. "The Grass." *Poems: Emily Dickinson*. Boston: Roberts Brothers, 1891. *Humanities Text Initiative American Verse Project*. Web. 6 Jan. 2008.

34. Article in an Online Journal

For an article in an online journal, cite the same information that you would for a print journal. If the online article does not have page numbers, use *n. pag.* (not italicized). Then add the medium consulted (*Web*) and the date of access.

> Edwards, Chris. "A Wealth of Opportunity: An Undergraduate Consultant's Look into the Benefits of Working at a Writing Center." *Praxis: A Writing Center Journal* 7.2 (2010): n. pag. Web. 28 May 2011.

35. Article in an Online Magazine or Newspaper

For an article in an online magazine or newspaper, cite the author; the title of the article, in quotation marks; the name of the magazine or newspaper, italicized; the sponsor of the Web site; the date of publication; the medium (*Web*); and the date you accessed the article.

> Broad, William J. "In Ancient Fossils, Seeds of a New Debate on Warming." *New York Times*. New York Times, 7 Nov. 2006. Web. 12 Jan. 2009.

> McIntosh, Jill. "First Drive: 2013 Audi Q5 Hybrid." *Canadian Driver*. CanadianDriver Communications, 20 June 2011. Web. 15 Aug. 2011.

36. Posting to a Discussion Group

Begin with the author's name; the title of the posting, in quotation marks (if there is no title, use the description *Online posting*, not italicized); the name of the Web site, italicized; the sponsor or publisher of the site (use *N.p.*, not italicized, if there is no sponsor); the date of the posting; the medium; and the date of access.

> Kent, Robert. "Computers Legalized, Net Still Banned for Cubans." *Freenet Chat*. The Free Network Project, 5 May 2008. Web. 15 Nov. 2008.

37. Work from an Online Database or a Subscription Service

For a work from an online database, list the author's name; the title of the work, in quotation marks; any print publication information; the name of the database, italicized; the medium consulted (*Web*); and the date of access.

> "Bolivia: Elecciones Presidenciales de 2002." *Political Database of the Americas*. Web. 12 Nov. 2006.

> Penn, Sean, and Jon Krakauer. "*Into the Wild* Script." *Internet Movie Script Database*. Web. 12 June 2011.

For a work from an online service to which your library subscribes, include the same information as for an online database. After the information about the work, give the name of the database, italicized; the medium; and the date you accessed the work.

> "Breaking the Dieting Habit: Drug Therapy for Eating Disorders." *Psychology Today* Mar. 1995: 12+. *ProQuest*. Web. 30 Nov. 2010.

If you're citing an article from a subscription service to which you subscribe (such as AOL), use the following model:

> Weeks, W. William. "Beyond the Ark." *Nature Conservancy* Mar.-Apr. 1999. *America Online*. Web. 30 Nov. 2008.

38. Email Message

Include the writer's name; the subject line, in quotation marks; *Message to [recipient's name]* (not italicized); the date of the message; and the medium of delivery (*E-mail*). (Note that MLA style is to hyphenate *e-mail*.)

Moller, Marilyn. "Seeing Crowns." Message to Beverly Moss. 3 Jan. 2003. E-mail.

39. Computer Software or Video Game

Include the title, italicized; the version number (if given); publication information; and the medium. If you are citing material downloaded from a Web site, include the title and version number (if given), but instead of publication information, add the publisher or sponsor of the Web site; the date; the medium (*Web*); and the date of access.

The Sims 3. Vers. 1.24. Redwood City: Electronic Arts, 2009. CD-ROM.

Web Cache Illuminator. Vers. 4.02. NorthStar Solutions, n.d. Web. 12 Nov. 2007.

40. CD-ROM, Diskette, or Magnetic Tape, Single Issue

McPherson, James M., ed. *The American Heritage New History of the Civil War*. New York: Viking, 1996. CD-ROM.

41. Periodically Revised CD-ROM

Include the author's name; publication information for the print version of the text (including its title and date of publication); the medium (*CD-ROM*); the title of the database (italicized); the name of the company producing it; and the publication date of the database (month and year, if possible).

Heyman, Steven. "The Dangerously Exciting Client." *Psychotherapy Patient* 9.1 (1994): 37-46. CD-ROM. *PsycLIT*. SilverPlatter. Nov. 2006.

42. Multidisc CD-ROM

The 1998 Grolier Multimedia Encyclopedia. Danbury: Grolier Interactive, 1998. CD-ROM. 2 discs.

OTHER SOURCES (INCLUDING ONLINE VERSIONS)

43. Unpublished Dissertation

Fishman, Jenn. "'The Active Republic of Literature': Performance and Literary Culture in Britain, 1656–1790." Diss. Stanford U, 2003. Print.

44. Published Dissertation

Baum, Bernard. *Decentralization of Authority in a Bureaucracy*. Diss. U of
   Chicago, 1959. Englewood Cliffs: Prentice, 1961. Print.

45. Article from a Microform

Sharpe, Lora. "A Quilter's Tribute." *Boston Globe* 25 Mar. 1989: 13. Microform.
   NewsBank: Social Relations 12 (1989): fiche 6, grids B4-6.

46. Personal, Published, or Broadcast Interview

For a personal interview, list the name of the person interviewed, the
label *Personal interview* (not italicized), and the date of the interview.

Mullin, Joan. Personal interview. 2 Sept. 2010.

For a published interview, list the name of the person interviewed and
the title (if any), or if there is no title, use the label *Interview by [inter-
viewer's name]* (not italicized); then add the publication information, including the medium.

Marshall, Andrew. "The Marshall Plan." Interview by Douglas McGray. *Wired*.
   CondéNet, Feb. 2003. Web. 17 Mar. 2010.

Taylor, Max. "Max Taylor on Winning." *Time* 13 Nov. 2000: 66. Print.

For a broadcast interview, list the name of the person interviewed, and
the label *Interview* (not italicized), and the name of the interviewer (if
relevant); then list information about the program, the date of the interview, and the medium.

Fairey, Shepard. "Spreading the Hope: Street Artist Shepard Fairey." Interview
   by Terry Gross. *Fresh Air*. Natl. Public Radio. WBUR, Boston. 20 Jan. 2009.
   Radio.

If you listened to an archived version online, after the site's sponsor (if
known), add the interview date, medium (*Web*), and date of access.

Fairey, Shepard. "Spreading the Hope: Street Artist Shepard Fairey." Interview by
   Terry Gross. *Fresh Air*. Natl. Public Radio. 20 Jan. 2009. Web. 13 Feb. 2009.

47. Letter

Treat a published letter like a work in an anthology, but include the
date of the letter.

Jacobs, Harriet. "To Amy Post." 4 Apr. 1853. *Incidents in the Life of a Slave Girl*.
   Ed. Jean Fagan Yellin. Cambridge: Harvard UP, 1987. 234-35. Print.

48. Film

Jenkins, Tamara, dir. *The Savages*. Perf. Laura Linney and Philip Seymour
    Hoffman. 2007. Fox Searchlight. Web. 4 Mar. 2008.

The Lord of the Rings: The Return of the King. Dir. Peter Jackson. Perf. Elijah
    Wood, Ian McKellen. New Line Cinema, 2003. Film.

49. Television or Radio Program

"Baelor." *Game of Thrones*. Dir. Alan Taylor. Writ. David Benioff and D. B. Weiss.
    Perf. Sean Bean, Emilia Clarke, and Kit Harington. HBO. 9 June 2011.
    Television.

Schorr, Daniel. "Week in Review with Daniel Schorr." *Weekend Edition*. Natl.
    Public Radio. KQED, San Francisco. 20 Dec. 2008. Radio.

50. Sound Recording

Black Rebel Motorcycle Club. "Howl." *Howl*. RCA Records, 2005. CD.

Brandon Flowers. "Crossfire." *Flamingo*. Island, 2010. MP3.

51. Work of Art or Photograph

List the artist or photographer; the work's title, italicized; the date of
composition (if unknown, use *n.d.*); and the medium of composition (*Oil
on canvas, Bronze, Photograph*, etc.). Then cite the name of the museum or
other location and the city.

Ulmann, Doris. *Man Leaning against a Wall*. 1930. Photograph. Smithsonian
    American Art Museum, Washington, DC.

To cite a reproduction in a book, add the publication information.

General William Palmer in Old Age. 1810. Oil on canvas. National Army Museum,
    London. *White Mughals: Love and Betrayal in Eighteenth-Century India*.
    William Dalrymple. New York: Penguin, 2002. 270. Print.

To cite artwork found online, omit the medium of composition, and after
the location add the title of the database or Web site, italicized; the medium consulted (*Web*); and the date of access.

Chagall, Marc. *The Poet with the Birds*. 1911. Minneapolis Inst. of Arts. *Artsmia
    .org*. Web. 6 Oct. 2003.

52. Lecture or Speech

Jobs, Steve. Baccalaureate Address. Stanford University, Stanford, CA. 18 June
    2005. Address.

53. Performance

Anything Goes. By Cole Porter. Perf. Klea Blackhurst. Shubert Theatre, New Haven. 7 Oct. 2003. Performance.

54. Map or Chart

World Political Map (Classic). Washington: Natl. Geographic, 2007. Print.

55. Cartoon

Ramirez, Michael. "The Phoenix." Cartoon. *Investors.com*. Investor's Business Daily. 10 Sept. 2011. Web. 11 Sept. 2011.

56. Advertisement

Banana Republic. Advertisement. *Wired* Sept. 2009: 13. Print.

On p. 463, note the formatting of the first page of a sample essay written in MLA style. On p. 464, you'll find a sample works cited page written for the same student essay.

Sample First Page for an Essay in MLA Style

Lesk 1

Emily Lesk

Professor Arraéz

Electric Rhetoric

15 November 2008

Red, White, and Everywhere

America, I have a confession to make: I don't drink Coke. But don't call me a hypocrite just because I am still the proud owner of a bright red shirt that advertises it. Just call me an American. Even before setting foot in Israel three years ago, I knew exactly where I could find one. The tiny T-shirt shop in the central block of Jerusalem's Ben Yehuda Street did offer other designs, but the one with a bright white "Drink Coca-Cola Classic" written in Hebrew cursive across the chest was what drew in most of the dollar-carrying tourists. While waiting almost twenty minutes for my shirt (depicted in Fig. 1), I watched nearly every customer ahead of me ask for "the Coke shirt, *todah rabah* [thank you very much]."

Fig. 1. *Hebrew Coca-Cola T-shirt*. Personal photograph. Despite my dislike for the beverage, I bought this Coca-Cola T-shirt in Israel.

At the time, I never thought it strange that I wanted one, too. After having absorbed sixteen years of Coca-Cola propaganda through everything from NBC's Saturday morning cartoon lineup to the concession stand at Camden Yards (the Baltimore Orioles' ballpark), I associated the shirt with singing along to the "Just for the Taste of It" jingle and with America's favorite pastime, not with a brown fizzy beverage I refused to consume.

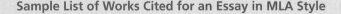
Sample List of Works Cited for an Essay in MLA Style

Works Cited

Coca-Cola Santa pin. Personal photograph by the author. 9 Nov. 2008.

"The Fabulous Fifties." *Beverage Industry* 87.6 (1996): 16. *General OneFile*. Web. 2 Nov. 2008.

"Fifty Years of Coca-Cola Television Advertisements." *American Memory*. Motion Picture, Broadcasting and Recorded Sound Division, Lib. of Cong. 29 Nov. 2000. Web. 5 Nov. 2008.

"Haddon Sundblom and Coca-Cola." *Thehistoryofchristmas.com*. 10 Holidays, 2004. Web. 2 Nov. 2008.

Hebrew Coca-Cola T-shirt. Personal photograph by the author. 8 Nov. 2008.

Ikuta, Yasutoshi, ed. *'50s American Magazine Ads*. Tokyo: Graphic-Sha, 1987. Print.

Pendergrast, Mark. *For God, Country, and Coca-Cola: The Definitive History of the Great American Soft Drink and the Company That Makes It*. 2nd ed. New York: Basic, 2000. Print.

APA Style

The *Publication Manual of the American Psychological Association* (6th edition, 2010) provides comprehensive advice to student and professional writers in the social sciences. Here we draw on the *Publication Manual*'s guidelines to provide an overview of APA style for in-text citations, content notes, and entries in the list of references.

In-Text Citations

APA style calls for in-text citations in the body of an argument to document sources of quotations, paraphrases, summaries, and so on. These in-text citations correspond to full bibliographic entries in the list of references at the end of the text.

1. Author Named in a Signal Phrase

Generally, use the author's name in a signal phrase to introduce the cited material, and place the date, in parentheses, immediately after the author's name. For a quotation, the page number, preceded by *p.* (neither underlined nor italicized), appears in parentheses after the quotation. For electronic texts or other works without page numbers, paragraph numbers may be used instead, preceded by the abbreviation *para.* For a long, set-off quotation, position the page reference in parentheses one space after the punctuation at the end of the quotation.

> According to Brandon (1993), Adefunmi opposed all forms of racism and believed that black nationalism should not be a destructive force.

> As Johnson (2005) demonstrated, contemporary television dramas such as *ER* and *Lost* are not only more complex than earlier programs but "possess a quality that can only be described as subtlety and discretion" (p. 83).

2. Author Named in Parentheses

When you don't mention the author in a signal phrase, give the name and the date, separated by a comma, in parentheses at the end of the cited material.

> *The Sopranos* has achieved a much wider viewing audience than ever expected, spawning a cookbook and several serious scholarly studies (Franklin, 2002).

3. Two Authors

Use both names in all citations. Use *and* in a signal phrase, but use an ampersand (&) in parentheses.

Associated with purity and wisdom, Obatala is the creator of human beings, whom he is said to have formed out of clay (Edwards & Mason, 1985).

4. Three to Five Authors

List all the authors' names for the first reference. In subsequent references, use just the first author's name followed by *et al.* (in regular type, not underlined or italicized).

Lenhoff, Wang, Greenberg, and Bellugi (1997) cited tests that indicate that segments of the left brain hemisphere are not affected by Williams syndrome whereas the right hemisphere is significantly affected.

Shackelford (1999) drew on the study by Lenhoff et al. (1997).

5. Six or More Authors

Use only the first author's name and *et al.* (in regular type, not underlined or italicized) in every citation, including the first.

As Flower et al. (2003) demonstrated, reading and writing involve both cognitive and social processes.

6. Organization as Author

If the name of an organization or a corporation is long, spell it out the first time, followed by an abbreviation in brackets. In later citations, use the abbreviation only.

First Citation   (Federal Bureau of Investigation [FBI], 2002)

Subsequent Citations (FBI, 2002)

7. Unknown Author

Use the title or its first few words in a signal phrase or in parentheses (in the example below, a book's title is italicized).

The school profiles for the county substantiate this trend (*Guide to secondary schools*, 2003).

8. Authors with the Same Last Name

If your list of references includes works by different authors with the same last name, include the authors' initials in each citation.

G. Jones (1998) conducted the groundbreaking study of retroviruses, whereas P. Jones (2000) replicated the initial trials two years later.

9. Two or More Sources in the Same Citation

List sources by the same author chronologically by publication year. List sources by different authors in alphabetical order by the authors' last names, separated by semicolons.

While traditional forms of argument are warlike and agonistic, alternative models do exist (Foss & Foss, 1997; Makau, 1999).

10. Specific Parts of a Source

Use abbreviations (*p.*, *pt.*, and so on) in a parenthetical citation to name the part of a work you're citing. However, *chapter* is not abbreviated.

Pinker (2003, p. 6) argued that his research yielded the opposite results.

Pinker (2003, Chapter 6) argued that his research yielded the opposite results.

11. Online Document

To cite a source found on the Internet, use the author's name and date as you would for a print source, and indicate the chapter or figure of the document, as appropriate. If the source's publication date is unknown, use *n.d.* ("no date"). To document a quotation, include paragraph numbers if page numbers are unavailable. If an online document has no page or paragraph numbers, provide the heading of the section and the number of the paragraph that follows.

Werbach argued convincingly that "despite the best efforts of legislators, lawyers, and computer programmers, spam has won. Spam is killing email" (2002, p. 1).

12. Email and Other Personal Communication

Cite any personal letters, email messages, electronic postings, telephone conversations, or personal interviews by giving the person's initial(s) and last name, the identification, and the date. Do not list email in the references list, and note that APA style uses a hyphen in the word *e-mail*.

E. Ashdown (personal communication, March 9, 2003) supported these claims.

Content Notes

The APA recommends using content notes for material that will expand or supplement your argument but otherwise would interrupt the text. Indicate such notes in your text by inserting superscript numerals. Type the notes themselves on a separate page headed *Footnotes* (not underlined, italicized, or in quotation marks), centered at the top of the page. Double-space all entries. Indent the first line of each note five to seven spaces, and begin subsequent lines at the left margin.

TEXT WITH SUPERSCRIPT INDICATING A NOTE

Data related to children's preferences in books were instrumental in designing the questionnaire.[1]

NOTE

[1]Rudine Sims Bishop and members of the Reading Readiness Research Group provided helpful data.

List of References

The alphabetical list of sources cited in your text is called *References*. (If your instructor asks you to list everything you've read as background — not just the sources you cite — call the list *Bibliography*.) The list of references appears on a separate page or pages at the end of your paper, with the heading *References* (not underlined, italicized, or in quotation marks) centered one inch from the top of the page. Double-space after the heading, and begin your first entry. Double-space the entire list. For print sources, APA style specifies the treatment and placement of four basic elements — author, publication date, title, and publication information. Each element is followed by a period.

- **Author:** List all authors with last name first, and use only initials for first and middle names. Separate the names of multiple authors with commas, and use an ampersand (&) before the last author's name.

- **Publication date:** Enclose the publication date in parentheses. Use only the year for books and journals; use the year, a comma, and the month or month and day for magazines and newspapers. Do not abbreviate the month. If a date is not given, put *n.d.* ("no date," not italicized) in the parentheses. Put a period after the parentheses.

- **Title:** Italicize titles and subtitles of books and periodicals. Do not enclose titles of articles in quotation marks. For books and articles, capitalize only the first word of the title and subtitle and any proper nouns or proper adjectives; also capitalize the first word following a colon. Capitalize all major words in the title of a periodical.

- **Publication information:** For a book published in the United States, list the city of publication and state abbreviation. For books published outside the United States, identify city and country. Provide the publisher's name, dropping *Inc.*, *Co.*, or *Publishers*. If the state is already included within the publisher's name, do not include the postal abbreviation for the state. For a periodical, follow the periodical title with a comma, the volume number (italicized), the issue number (if provided) in parentheses and followed by a comma, and the inclusive page numbers of the article. For newspaper articles and for articles or chapters in books, include the abbreviation *p.* ("page") or *pp.* ("pages").

The following APA style examples appear in a "hanging indent" format, in which the first line aligns on the left and the subsequent lines indent one-half inch or five spaces.

BOOKS

1. One Author

Jones, L. H. (2004). *William Clark and the shaping of the West.* New York, NY: Hill and Wang.

2. Two or More Authors

Steininger, M., Newell, J. D., & Garcia, L. (1984). *Ethical issues in psychology.* Homewood, IL: Dow Jones-Irwin.

3. Organization as Author

Use the word *Author* (neither underlined nor italicized) as the publisher when the organization is both the author and the publisher.

Linguistics Society of America. (2002). *Guidelines for using sign language interpreters.* Washington, DC: Author.

4. Unknown Author

National Geographic atlas of the world. (2004). Washington, DC: National Geographic Society.

5. Book Prepared by an Editor

Hardy, H. H. (Ed.). (1998). *The proper study of mankind*. New York, NY: Farrar, Straus.

6. Selection in a Book with an Editor

Villanueva, V. (1999). An introduction to social scientific discussions on class. In A. Shepard, J. McMillan, & G. Tate (Eds.), *Coming to class: Pedagogy and the social class of teachers* (pp. 262-277). Portsmouth, NH: Heinemann.

7. Translation

Perez-Reverte, A. (2002). *The nautical chart* (M. S. Peaden, Trans.). New York, NY: Harvest. (Original work published 2000)

8. Edition Other Than the First

Wrightsman, L. (1998). *Psychology and the legal system* (3rd ed.). Newbury Park, CA: Sage.

9. One Volume of a Multivolume Work

Will, J. S. (1921). *Protestantism in France* (Vol. 2). Toronto, Canada: University of Toronto Press.

10. Article in a Reference Work

Chernow, B., & Vattasi, G. (Eds.). (1993). Psychomimetic drug. In *The Columbia encyclopedia* (5th ed., p. 2238). New York, NY: Columbia University Press.

If no author is listed, begin with the title.

11. Republication

Sharp, C. (1978). *History of Hartlepool*. Hartlepool, United Kingdom: Hartlepool Borough Council. (Original work published 1816)

12. Government Document

U.S. Bureau of the Census. (2001). *Survey of women-owned business enterprises*. Washington, DC: Government Printing Office.

13. Two or More Works by the Same Author

List the works in chronological order of publication. Repeat the author's name in each entry.

Rose, M. (1984). *Writer's block: The cognitive dimension*. Carbondale: Southern Illinois University Press.

Rose, M. (1995). *Possible lives: The promise of public education in America*. Boston, MA: Houghton Mifflin.

PERIODICALS

14. Article in a Journal Paginated by Volume

Bowen, L. M. (2011). Resisting age bias in digital literacy research. *College Composition and Communication, 62*, 586-607.

15. Article in a Journal Paginated by Issue

Carr, S. (2002). The circulation of Blair's Lectures. *Rhetoric Society Quarterly, 32*(4), 75-104.

16. Article in a Monthly Magazine

Baker, C. (2008, September). Master of the universe. *Wired, 16*(9), 134-141.

17. Article in a Newspaper

Nagourney, A. (2002, December 16). Gore rules out running in '04. *The New York Times*, pp. A1, A8.

18. Letter to the Editor or Editorial

Erbeta, R. (2008, December). Swiftboating George [Letter to the editor]. *Smithsonian, 39*(9), 10.

19. Unsigned Article

Guidelines issued on assisted suicide. (1998, March 4). *The New York Times*, p. A15.

20. Review

Avalona, A. (2008, August). [Review of the book *Weaving women's lives: Three generations in a Navajo family*, by L. Lamphere]. *New Mexico, 86*(8), 40.

21. Published Interview

Shor, I. (1997). [Interview with A. Greenbaum]. *Writing on the Edge, 8*(2), 7-20.

22. Two or More Works by the Same Author in the Same Year

List two or more works by the same author published in the same year alphabetically by title (excluding *A*, *An*, or *The*), and place lowercase letters (*a*, *b*, etc.) after the dates.

Murray, F. B. (1983a). Equilibration as cognitive conflict. *Developmental Review, 3*, 54-61.

Murray, F. B. (1983b). Learning and development through social interaction. In L. Liben (Ed.), *Piaget and the foundations of knowledge* (pp. 176-201). Hillsdale, NJ: Erlbaum.

ELECTRONIC SOURCES

The following models are based on the *APA's Publication Manual* (6th edition). A change for handling electronic sources involves the use of a digital object identifier (DOI) when available (instead of a URL) to locate an electronic source. The DOI is a unique number assigned to an electronic text (article, book, or other item) and intended to give reliable access to it. A second change is that a date of retrieval is no longer necessary unless a source changes very frequently. The basic APA entry for most electronic sources should include the following elements:

- name of the author, editor, or compiler
- date of electronic publication or most recent update
- title of the work, document, or posting
- publication information, including the title, volume or issue number, and page numbers
- the DOI (digital object identifier) of the document, if one is available
- a URL, only if a DOI is not available, with no angle brackets and no closing punctuation.

23. World Wide Web Site

To cite a whole site, give the address in a parenthetical reference. To cite a document from a Web site, include information as you would for a print document, followed by a note on its retrieval. Provide a date of retrieval only if the information is likely to change frequently.

American Psychological Association. (2000). DotComSense: Commonsense ways
to protect your privacy and assess online mental health information.
Retrieved from http://helping.apa.org/dotcomsense

Mullins, B. (1995). Introduction to Robert Hass. Readings in contemporary
poetry at Dia Center for the Arts. Retrieved from http://www.diacenter
.org/prg/poetry/95_96/intrhass.html

24. Article from an Online Periodical

For an article you read online, provide either a DOI or the URL of the periodical's home page preceded by *Retrieved from*.

Lambert, N. M., Graham, S. M., & Fincham, F. D. (2009). A prototype analysis of
gratitude: Varieties of gratitude experiences. *Personality and Social
Psychology Bulletin, 35*, 1193-1207. doi:10.1177/0146167209338071

Palmer, K. S. (2000, September 12). In academia, males under a microscope. *The Washington Post.* Retrieved from http://www.washingtonpost.com

25. Article or Abstract from a Database

For an article you find on a database, provide a DOI if one is available. If the online article does not have a DOI, locate the homepage for the journal in which the article appears and provide that URL. You need not identify the database you have used.

Kennedy, C., & Covell, K. (2009). Violating the rights of the child through inadequate sexual health education. *International Journal of Children's Rights, 17*(1), 143-154. doi:10.1163/092755608X278939

Hayhoe, G. (2001). The long and winding road: Technology's future. *Technical Communication, 48*(2), 133-145. Retrieved from http://www.stc.org/pubs/ techcommGeneral01.asp

26. Software or Computer Program

OSX Lion (Version 10.7) [Computer operating system]. (2011). Cupertino, CA: Apple, Inc.

27. Online Government Document

Cite an online government document as you would a printed government work, adding the date of access and the URL. If you don't find a date, use *n. d.*

Finn, J. D. (1998, April). *Class size and students at risk: What is known? What is next?* Retrieved from United States Department of Education website http://www.ed.gov/pubs/ClassSize/title.html

28. Posting to a Discussion Group

Include an online posting in the references list only if you're able to retrieve the message from a mailing list's archive. Provide the author's name; the date of posting, in parentheses; and the subject line from the posting. Include any information that further identifies the message in square brackets. For a listserv message, end with the retrieval statement, including the name of the list and the URL of the archived message.

Troike, R. C. (2001, June 21). Buttercups and primroses [Msg 8]. Message posted to the American Dialect Society's ADS-L electronic mailing list, archived at http://listserv.linguistlist.org/archives/ads-1.html

29. Newsgroup Posting

Include the author's name, the date and subject line of the posting, the access date, and the name of the newsgroup.

Wittenberg, E. (2001, July 11). Gender and the Internet [Msg 4]. Retrieved
from news://comp.edu.composition

30. Email Message or Synchronous Communication

Because the APA stresses that any sources cited in your list of references must be retrievable by your readers, you shouldn't include entries for email messages or synchronous communications (MOOs, MUDs); instead, cite these sources in your text as forms of personal communication (see p. 167). And remember that you shouldn't quote from other people's email without asking their permission to do so.

OTHER SOURCES

31. Technical or Research Reports and Working Papers

Kinley-Horn and Associates. (2011). *ADOT bicycle safety action plan* (Working
Paper No. 3). Phoenix: Arizona Department of Transportation.

32. Unpublished Paper Presented at a Meeting or Symposium

Welch, K. (2002, March). *Electric rhetoric and screen literacy*. Paper presented at
the meeting of the Conference on College Composition and
Communication, Chicago.

33. Unpublished Dissertation

Seward, D. E. (2008). *Civil voice in Elizabethan parliamentary oratory: The
rhetoric and composition of speeches delivered at Westminster in 1566*
(Unpublished doctoral dissertation). University of Texas at Austin,
Austin, TX.

34. Poster Session

Mensching, G. (2002, May). *A simple, effective one-shot for disinterested
students*. Poster session presented at the National LOEX Library Instruction
Conference, Ann Arbor, MI.

35. Motion Picture, Video, or DVD

Bigelow, K. (Director). (2009). *The hurt locker*. [Motion picture]. United States:
Summit Entertainment.

36. Television Program, Single Episode

Imperioli, M. (Writer), & Buscemi, S. (Director). (2002, October 20). Everybody hurts [Television series episode]. In D. Chase (Executive producer), *The Sopranos*. New York, NY: Home Box Office.

37. Sound Recording

Begin with the writer's name, followed by the date of copyright. Give the recording date at the end of the entry (in parentheses, after the period) if it's different from the copyright date.

Ivey, A., Jr., & Sall, R. (1995). Rollin' with my homies [Recorded by Coolio]. On *Clueless* [CD]. Hollywood, CA: Capitol Records.

RESPOND.

1. The MLA and APA styles differ in several important ways, both for in-text citations and for lists of sources. You've probably noticed a few: the APA lowercases most words in titles and lists the publication date right after the author's name, whereas the MLA capitalizes most words and puts the publication date at the end of the works cited entry. More interesting than the details, though, is the reasoning behind the differences. Placing the publication date near the front of a citation, for instance, reveals a special concern for that information in the APA style. Similarly, the MLA's decision to capitalize titles isn't arbitrary: that style is preferred in the humanities for a reason. Working in a group, find as many consistent differences between the MLA and APA styles as you can. Then, for each difference, speculate about the reasons these groups organize or present information in that way. The MLA and APA style manuals themselves may be of help. You might also begin by determining which academic disciplines subscribe to the APA style and which to the MLA.

2. Working with another person in your class, look for examples of the following sources: an article in a journal, a book, a film, a song, and a TV show. Then make a references page or works cited entry for each one, using either MLA or APA style.

GLOSSARY

academic argument writing that is addressed to an audience well informed about the topic, that aims to convey a clear and compelling point in a somewhat formal style, and that follows agreed-upon conventions of usage, punctuation, and formats.

accidental condition in a definition, an element that helps to explain what's being defined but isn't essential to it. An accidental condition in defining a bird might be "ability to fly" because most, but not all, birds can fly. (See also *essential condition* and *sufficient condition*.)

ad hominem **argument** a fallacy of argument in which a writer's claim is answered by irrelevant attacks on his or her character.

analogy an extended comparison between something unfamiliar and something more familiar for the purpose of illuminating or dramatizing the unfamiliar. An analogy might, say, compare nuclear fission (less familiar) to a pool player's opening break (more familiar).

anaphora a figure of speech involving repetition, particularly of the same word at the beginning of several clauses.

antithesis the use of parallel structures to call attention to contrasts or opposites, as in *Some like it hot; some like it cold.*

antonomasia use of a title, epithet, or description in place of a name, as in *Your Honor* for *Judge.*

argument (1) a spoken, written, or visual text that expresses a point of view; (2) the use of evidence and reason to discover some version of the truth, as distinct from *persuasion*, the attempt to change someone else's point of view.

artistic appeal support for an argument that a writer creates based on principles of reason and shared knowledge rather than on facts and evidence. (See also *inartistic appeal*.)

assumption a belief regarded as true, upon which other claims are based.

assumption, cultural a belief regarded as true or commonsensical within a particular culture, such as the belief in individual freedom in American culture.

audience the person or persons to whom an argument is directed.

authority the quality conveyed by a writer who is knowledgeable about his or her subject and confident in that knowledge.

background the information a writer provides to create the context for an argument.

backing in Toulmin argument, the evidence provided to support a *warrant*.

bandwagon appeal a fallacy of argument in which a course of action is recommended on the grounds that everyone else is following it.

begging the question a fallacy of argument in which a claim is based on the very grounds that are in doubt or dispute: *Rita can't be the bicycle thief; she's never stolen anything.*

causal argument an argument that seeks to explain the effect(s) of a cause, the cause(s) of an effect, or a causal chain in which A causes B, B causes C, C causes D, and so on.

ceremonial argument an argument that deals with current values and addresses questions of praise and blame. Also called *epideictic*, ceremonial arguments include eulogies and graduation speeches.

character, appeal based on a strategy in which a writer presents an authoritative or credible self-image to convince an audience to accept a claim.

circumstantial evidence in legal cases, evidence from which conclusions cannot be drawn directly but have to be inferred.

claim a statement that asserts a belief or truth. In arguments, most claims require supporting evidence. The claim is a key component in *Toulmin argument.*

classical oration a highly structured form of an argument developed in ancient Greece and Rome to defend or refute a thesis. The oration evolved to include six parts—*exordium, narratio, partitio, confirmatio, refutatio,* and *peroratio.*

confirmatio the fourth part of a classical oration, in which a speaker or writer offers evidence for the claim.

connotation the suggestions or associations that surround most words and extend beyond their literal meaning, creating associational effects.

Slender and *skinny* have similar meanings, for example, but carry different connotations, the former more positive than the latter.

context the entire situation in which a piece of writing takes place, including the writer's purpose(s) for writing; the intended audience; the time and place of writing; the institutional, social, personal, and other influences on the piece of writing; the material conditions of writing (whether it's, for instance, online or on paper, in handwriting or print); and the writer's attitude toward the subject and the audience.

conviction the belief that a claim or course of action is true or reasonable. In a proposal argument, a writer must move an audience beyond conviction to action.

credibility an impression of integrity, honesty, and trustworthiness conveyed by a writer in an argument.

criterion in evaluative arguments, the standard by which something is measured to determine its quality or value.

deductive reasoning a process of thought in which general principles are applied to particular cases.

definition, argument of an argument in which the claim specifies that something does or doesn't meet the conditions or features set forth in a definition: *Pluto is not a major planet.*

deliberative argument an argument that deals with action to be taken in the future, focusing on matters of policy. Deliberative arguments include parliamentary debates and campaign platforms.

delivery the presentation of a spoken argument.

dogmatism a fallacy of argument in which a claim is supported on the grounds that it's the only conclusion acceptable within a given community.

either-or **choice** a fallacy of argument in which a complicated issue is misrepresented as offering only two possible alternatives, one of which is often made to seem vastly preferable to the other.

emotional appeal a strategy in which a writer tries to generate specific emotions (such as fear, envy, anger, or pity) in an audience to dispose it to accept a claim.

enthymeme in Toulmin argument, a statement that links a claim to a supporting reason: *The bank will fail* (claim) *because it has lost the support of its largest investors* (reason). In classical rhetoric, an enthymeme is a *syllogism* with one term understood but not stated: *Socrates is mortal because he is a human being.* (The understood term is: *All human beings are mortal.*)

epideictic argument see *ceremonial argument.*

equivocation a fallacy of argument in which a lie is given the appearance of truth, or in which the truth is misrepresented in deceptive language.

essential condition in a definition, an element that must be part of the definition but, by itself, isn't enough to define the term. An essential condition in defining a bird might be "winged": all birds have wings, yet wings alone don't define a bird since some insects and mammals also have wings. (See also *accidental condition* and *sufficient condition.*)

ethical appeal see *character, appeal based on,* and *ethos.*

ethnographic observation a form of field research involving close and extended observation of a group, event, or phenomenon; careful and detailed note-taking during the observation; analysis of the notes; and interpretation of that analysis.

ethos the self-image a writer creates to define a relationship with readers. In arguments, most writers try to establish an ethos that suggests authority and credibility.

evaluation, argument of an argument in which the claim specifies that something does or doesn't meet established criteria: *The Nikon D3X is the most sophisticated digital SLR camera currently available.*

evidence material offered to support an argument. See *artistic appeal* and *inartistic appeal.*

example, definition by a definition that operates by identifying individual examples of what's being defined: *sports car—Corvette, Viper, Miata, Boxster.*

exordium the first part of a classical oration, in which a speaker or writer tries to win the attention and goodwill of an audience while introducing a subject.

experimental evidence evidence gathered through experimentation; often evidence that can be quantified (for example, a survey of students before and after an election might yield statistical evidence about changes in their attitudes toward the candidates). Experimental evidence is frequently crucial to scientific arguments.

fact, argument of an argument in which the claim can be proved or disproved with specific evidence or testimony: *The winter of 1998 was the warmest on record for the United States.*

fallacy of argument a flaw in the structure of an argument that renders its conclusion invalid or suspect. See ad hominem *argument*, *bandwagon appeal*, *begging the question*, *dogmatism*, either-or *choice*, *equivocation*, *false authority*, *faulty analogy*, *faulty causality*, *hasty generalization*, *non sequitur*, *scare tactic*, *sentimental appeal*, *slippery slope*, and *straw man*.

false authority a fallacy of argument in which a claim is based on the expertise of someone who lacks appropriate credentials.

faulty analogy a fallacy of argument in which a comparison between two objects or concepts is inaccurate or inconsequential.

faulty causality a fallacy of argument making the unwarranted assumption that because one event follows another, the first event causes the second. Also called *post hoc, ergo propter hoc*, faulty causality forms the basis of many superstitions.

firsthand evidence data—including surveys, observations, personal interviews, etc.—collected and personally examined by the writer. (See also *secondhand evidence*.)

flashpoint see *fallacy of argument*.

forensic argument an argument that deals with actions that have occurred in the past. Sometimes called judicial arguments, forensic arguments include legal cases involving judgments of guilt or innocence.

formal definition a definition that identifies something first by the general class to which it belongs (*genus*) and then by the characteristics that distinguish it from other members of that class (*species*): *Baseball is a game* (genus) *played on a diamond by opposing teams of nine players who score runs by circling bases after striking a ball with a bat* (species).

genus in a definition, the general class to which an object or concept belongs: *baseball is a* sport; *green is a* color.

grounds in Toulmin argument, the evidence provided to support a claim and reason—that is, an *enthymeme*.

hard evidence support for an argument using facts, statistics, testimony, or other evidence the writer finds.

hasty generalization a fallacy of argument in which an inference is drawn from insufficient data.

hyperbole use of overstatement for special effect.

hypothesis an expectation for the findings of one's research or the conclusion to one's argument. Hypotheses must be tested against evidence, opposing arguments, and so on.

immediate reason the cause that leads directly to an effect, such as an automobile accident that results in an injury to the driver. (See also *necessary reason* and *sufficient reason*.)

inartistic appeal support for an argument using facts, statistics, eyewitness testimony, or other evidence the writer finds rather than creates. (See also *artistic appeal*.)

inductive reasoning a process of thought in which particular cases lead to general principles.

intended readers the actual, real-life people whom a writer consciously wants to address in a piece of writing.

invention the process of finding and creating arguments to support a claim.

inverted word order moving grammatical elements of a sentence out of their usual order (subject-verb-object/complement) for special effect, as in *Tired I was; sleepy I was not.*

invitational argument a term used by Sonja Foss to describe arguments that are aimed not at vanquishing an opponent but at inviting others to collaborate in exploring mutually satisfying ways to solve problems.

invoked readers the readers directly addressed or implied in a text, which may include some that the writer didn't consciously intend to reach. An argument that refers to *those who have experienced a major trauma*, for example, invokes all readers who have undergone this experience.

irony use of language that suggests a meaning in contrast to the literal meaning of the words.

kairos the opportune moment; in arguments, the timeliness of an argument and the most opportune ways to make it.

line of argument a strategy or approach used in an argument. Argumentative strategies include appeals to the heart (emotional appeals), to character (ethical appeals), and to facts and reason (logical appeals).

logical appeal a strategy in which a writer uses facts, evidence, and reason to make audience members accept a claim.

metaphor a figure of speech that makes a comparison, as in *The ship was a beacon of hope.*

narratio the second part of a classical oration, in which a speaker or writer presents the facts of a case.

necessary reason a cause that must be present for an effect to occur; for example, infection with a particular virus is a necessary reason for the development of AIDS. (See also *immediate reason* and *sufficient reason*.)

non sequitur a fallacy of argument in which claims, reasons, or warrants fail to connect logically; one point doesn't follow from another: *If you're really my friend, you'll lend me five hundred dollars.*

operational definition a definition that identifies an object by what it does or by the conditions that create it: *A line is the shortest distance between two points.*

parallelism use of similar grammatical structures or forms for pleasing effect: *in the classroom, on the playground, and at the mall.*

paraphrase a restatement of the meaning of a piece of writing using different words from the original.

partitio the third part of a classical oration, in which a speaker or writer divides up the subject and explains what the claim will be.

patchwriting a misuse of sources in which a writer's phrase, clause, or sentence stays too close to the original language or syntax of the source.

pathos, appeal to see *emotional appeal*.

peroratio the sixth and final part of a classical oration, in which a speaker or writer summarizes the case and moves the audience to action.

persuasion the act of seeking to change someone else's point of view.

plagiarism the act of using the words, phrases, and expressions of others without proper citation or acknowledgment.

precedents actions or decisions in the past that have established a pattern or model for subsequent actions. Precedents are particularly important in legal cases.

premise a statement or position regarded as true and upon which other claims are based.

propaganda an argument advancing a point of view without regard to reason, fairness, or truth.

proposal argument an argument in which a claim is made in favor of or opposing a specific course of action: *Sport-utility vehicles should have to meet the same fuel economy standards as passenger cars.*

purpose the goal of an argument. Purposes include entertaining, informing, convincing, exploring, and deciding, among others.

qualifiers words or phrases that limit the scope of a claim: *usually; in a few cases; under these circumstances.*

qualitative argument an argument of evaluation that relies on nonnumerical criteria supported by reason, tradition, precedent, or logic.

quantitative argument an argument of evaluation that relies on criteria that can be measured, counted, or demonstrated objectively.

reason in writing, a statement that expands a claim by offering evidence to support it. The reason may be a statement of fact or another claim. In *Toulmin argument*, a *reason* is attached to a *claim* by a *warrant*, a statement that establishes the logical connection between claim and supporting reason.

rebuttal an answer that challenges or refutes a specific claim or charge. Rebuttals may also be offered by writers who anticipate objections to the claims or evidence they offer.

rebuttal, conditions of in Toulmin argument, potential objections to an argument. Writers need to anticipate such conditions in shaping their arguments.

red herring a fallacy of argument in which a writer abruptly changes the topic in order to distract readers from potentially objectionable claims.

refutatio the fifth part of a classical oration, in which a speaker or writer acknowledges and refutes opposing claims or evidence.

reversed structures a figure of speech that involves the inversion of clauses: *What is good in your writing is not original; what is original is not good.*

rhetoric the art of persuasion. Western rhetoric originated in ancient Greece as a discipline to prepare citizens for arguing cases in court.

rhetorical analysis an examination of how well the components of an argument work together to persuade or move an audience.

rhetorical questions questions posed to raise an issue or create an effect rather than to get a response: *You may well wonder, "What's in a name?"*

rhetorical situation the relationship between topic, author, audience, and other contexts (social, cultural, political) that determine or evoke an appropriate spoken or written response.

Rogerian argument an approach to argumentation based on the principle, articulated by psychotherapist Carl Rogers, that audiences respond best when they don't feel threatened. Rogerian argument stresses trust and urges those who disagree to find common ground.

scare tactic a fallacy of argument presenting an issue in terms of exaggerated threats or dangers.

scheme a figure of speech that involves a special arrangement of words, such as inversion.

secondhand evidence any information taken from outside sources, including library research and online sources. (See also *firsthand evidence*.)

sentimental appeal a fallacy of argument in which an appeal is based on excessive emotion.

simile a comparison that uses *like* or *as*: *My love is like a red, red rose* or *I wandered lonely as a cloud*.

slippery slope a fallacy of argument exaggerating the possibility that a relatively inconsequential action or choice today will have serious adverse consequences in the future.

species in a definition, the particular features that distinguish one member of a *genus* from another: *Baseball is a sport* (genus) *played on a diamond by teams of nine players* (species).

spin a kind of political advocacy that makes any fact or event, however unfavorable, serve a political purpose.

stacking the deck a fallacy of argument in which the writer shows only one side of an argument.

stance the writer's attitude toward the topic and the audience.

stasis theory in classical rhetoric, a method for coming up with appropriate arguments by determining the nature of a given situation: *a question of fact; of definition; of quality;* or *of policy*.

straw man a fallacy of argument in which an opponent's position is misrepresented as being more extreme than it actually is, so that it's easier to refute.

sufficient condition in a definition, an element or set of elements adequate to define a term. A sufficient condition in defining God, for example, might be "supreme being" or "first cause." No other conditions are necessary, though many might be made. (See also *accidental condition* and *essential condition*.)

sufficient reason a cause that alone is enough to produce a particular effect; for example, a particular level of smoke in the air will set off a smoke alarm. (See also *immediate reason* and *necessary reason*.)

summary a presentation of the substance and main points of a piece of writing in very condensed form.

syllogism in formal logic, a structure of deductive logic in which correctly formed major and minor premises lead to a necessary conclusion:

Major premise	All human beings are mortal.
Minor premise	Socrates is a human being.
Conclusion	Socrates is mortal.

testimony a personal experience or observation used to support an argument.

thesis a sentence that succinctly states a writer's main point.

Toulmin argument a method of informal logic first described by Stephen Toulmin in *The Uses of Argument* (1958). Toulmin argument describes the key components of an argument as the *claim, reason, warrant, backing,* and *grounds.*

trope a figure of speech that involves a change in the usual meaning or signification of words, such as *metaphor, simile,* and *analogy.*

understatement a figure of speech that makes a weaker statement than a situation seems to call for. It can lead to powerful or to humorous effects.

values, appeal to a strategy in which a writer invokes shared principles and traditions of a society as a reason for accepting a claim.

warrant in *Toulmin argument,* the statement (expressed or implied) that establishes the logical connection between a claim and its supporting reason.

Claim	Don't eat that mushroom;
Reason	it's poisonous.
Warrant	What is poisonous should not be eaten.

ACKNOWLEDGMENTS

Text

Daniel Ben-Ami. "Why People Hate Fat Americans." From *Spiked*, September 9, 2005. Copyright © 2005. Reprinted by permission of the author.

David Brooks. "It's Not about You." From the *New York Times*, July 26, 2011. Copyright © 2011 The New York Times. All rights reserved. Used by permission and protected by the Copyright Laws of the United States. The printing, copying, redistribution, or retransmission of this Content without express written permission is prohibited.

N'Gai Croal. "You Don't Have to Be a Nerd." From *Newsweek*, August 8, 2008. Copyright © 2008 The Newsweek/DailyBeast Company LLC. All rights reserved. Used by permission and protected by the Copyright Laws of the United States. The printing, copying, redistribution, or retransmission of the Material without express written permission is prohibited.

Rod Dreher. "Poll's Shocking SOS for Texas GOP." From Dallasnews.com, December 3, 2008. Reprinted with permission of The Dallas Morning News.

Daniel S. Hamermesh. "Ugly? You May Have a Case." From the *New York Times*, August 27, 2011. Copyright © 2011 by The New York Times. All rights reserved. Used by permission and protected by the Copyright Laws of the United States. The printing, copying, redistribution, or retransmission of this Content without express written permission is prohibited.

Lia Hardin. "Cultural Stress Linked to Suicide." From the *Stanford Daily*, May 31, 2007. Copyright © 2007 The Stanford Daily, Inc. All rights reserved. Reprinted with permission of the publisher.

Molly Ivins. Excerpt from "Eloquent Barbara Jordan: A Great Spirit Has Left Us." From the *Seattle Times*, January 22, 1996. Reprinted by permission of Pom, Inc.

Brooks Jackson. "Democrats Deny Social Security's Red Ink." Posted February 25, 2011, on FactCheck.org, a project of the Annenberg Public Policy Center of the University of Pennsylvania. Reprinted by permission.

Martin Luther King Jr. Excerpt from "I Have a Dream." Reprinted by arrangement with The Heirs to the Estate of Martin Luther King Jr. c/o Writers House as agent for the proprietor, New York, NY.

Paul Krugman. Excerpt from "The Cult That Is Destroying America." From the *New York Times*, July 26, 2011. Copyright © 2011 The New York Times. All rights reserved. Used by permission and protected by the Copyright Laws of the United States. The printing, copying, redistribution, or retransmission of this Content without express written permission is prohibited.

Adam Kuban. Excerpt from "Martha, Martha, Martha." From *Serious Eats*, April 10, 2007. Copyright © 2007. Reprinted by permission of the author.

Michael Lassell. "How to Watch Your Brother Die." Copyright © 1985 by Michael Lassell. Reprinted by permission of the author.

Andi Miller. Review of *The Invention of Hugo Cabret*, by Brian Selznick. Reprinted by permission of Andi Miller.

Moonlight Social. Web posting from February 8, 2011. Reprinted by permission of Moonlight Social LLC.

New York Times. Excerpt from "Beijing's Bad Faith Olympics" (editorial). From the *New York Times*, August 23, 2008. Copyright © 2008 by The New York Times. All rights reserved. Used by permission and protected by the Copyright Laws of the

United States. The printing, copying, redistribution, or retransmission of this Content without express written permission is prohibited.

Omar Offendum. Excerpt from the lyrics to "#Jan25" by Omar Offendum, Freeway, The Narcicyst, Amri Sulaiman, and Ayah. Reprinted by permission of Advent Media Productions and Omar Offendum.

Onion. Excerpt from "First-Ever Gay 'Dear John' Letters Begin Reaching U.S. Troops Overseas." Reprinted with permission of THE ONION. Copyright © 2011 by Onion, Inc., www.theonion.com.

Alex Pattakos. "The Meaning of Friendship in a Social-Networked World." Posted October 16, 2010, HUFFPOST Healthy Living. Reprinted by permission of the author.

Virginia Postrel. "Why We Prize That Magical Mystery Pad." From the *Wall Street Journal*, March 12, 2011. Copyright © 2011 Dow Jones & Company. Used by permission.

Alan Salzberg. Excerpt from his blog "What Are the Chances? Musings on Everyday Probability." http://what-are-the-chances.blogspot.com/2008/08/atlantic-monthly-indicted-for-criminal.html. Reprinted by permission of Alan Salzberg.

Seth Stevenson. Excerpt from "Tangled Up in Boobs." From *Slate*, April 12, 2004. Copyright © 2004 by Seth Stevenson. Reprinted by permission of the author.

Margaret Talbot. Excerpt from "Men Behaving Badly." Originally published in the *New York Times Magazine*. Copyright © 2002 by Margaret Talbot. Used by permission of The Wylie Agency LLC.

Deborah Tannen. "Why Is Compromise Now a Dirty Word?" From *Politico*, June 15, 2011. Reprinted by permission of the author.

Stuart Taylor Jr. and K.C. Johnson. Excerpt from "Guilty in the Duke Case." Published in the *Washington Post*, September 7, 2007. Reprinted by permission of the authors.

John Tierney. "Can a Playground Be Too Safe?" From the *New York Times*, July 18, 2011. Copyright © 2011 by The New York Times. All rights reserved. Used by permission and protected by the Copyright Laws of the United States. The printing, copying, redistribution, or retransmission of this Content without express written permission is prohibited.

Neil Warner. Excerpt from "The Anatomy of a Spring." From teaandtoast.ie, May 12, 2011. Reprinted by permission of Neil Warner.

Sean Wilsey. "The Things They Buried." From the *New York Times* Book Review Section, June 18, 2006. Copyright © 2006 New York Times. All rights reserved. Used by permission and protected by the Copyright Laws of the United States. The printing, copying, redistribution, or retransmission of this Content without express written permission is prohibited.

Lan Xue. "China: The Prizes and Pitfalls of Progress." Reprinted by permission from Macmillan Publishers Ltd. from *Nature* magazine, vol. 454, July 24, 2008. Copyright © 2008 by the Nature Publishing Group.

Byron York. Excerpt from "White House: Libya Fight Is Not War, It's 'Kinetic Military Action.'" From the *Washington Examiner*, March 23, 2011. Reprinted by permission of the author and publisher.

Illustrations

p. iv: (left to right) Jamie Sabau/Getty Images; Jonathan Oiley/Getty Images; Michael N. Todaro/FilmMagic/Getty Images; Justin Sullivan/Getty Images; AP/Wide World Photos; NBC/Photofest; Robert Galbraith/Reuters/Landov; p. 3: (left to right) STR/Reuters/Landov; © Chappatte in *International Herald Tribune*, www.globe cartoon.com; p. 4: AP/Wide World Photos; p. 7: © David Sipress/The New Yorker Collection/www.cartoonbank.com; p. 8: © Benjamin Hummel; p. 9: Justin Sullivan/ Getty Images; p. 10: Kelly Woen/Zuma/Corbis; p. 12: (top) © Tribune Media Services, Inc. All rights reserved. Reprinted with permission; (bottom) Peter Macdiarmid/ Getty Images; p. 14: AP Photo/Office de Tourisme de Chartres; p. 17: Michael N. Todaro/FilmMagic/Getty Images; p. 19: Robert Galbraith/Reuters/Landov; p. 21: Bettmann/Corbis; p. 23: (t + b) Courtesy of Mellcom.com; pp. 26–27: © Doctors Without Borders/Medecins Sans Frontieres; p. 29: www.bumperart.com; p. 30: (l-r) AP/Wide World Photos; © Tribune Media Services, Inc. All Rights Reserved. Reprinted with permission; p. 31: Pete Souza/The White House/Getty Images; p. 33: Chip Somodevilla/Getty Images; p. 35: © Robert Mankoff/The New Yorker Collection/www.cartoonbank.com; p. 37: Sara D. Davis/Getty Images; p. 40: (l) www.bumperart.com; (r) Courtesy of www.cafepress.com; p. 42: (l-r) John Arnold Images Ltd/Alamy; Andy Kropa/Getty Images; Tony Avelar/Bloomberg via Getty Images; p. 43: Ezra Shaw/Getty Images; p. 44: Jim Spellman/WireImage/Getty Images; p. 46: Martin H. Simon/Pool via Bloomberg/Getty Images; p. 48: Used with permission of Volkswagen Group of America, Inc.; p. 49: Kim Ludbrook/epa/Corbis; p. 55: (l-r) CBS/Photofest; NBC/Photofest; Frank Cotham/www.cartoonbank.com; p. 57: AP/Wide World Photos; p. 58: Jake Fuller/Artizans.com; p. 59: (l + r) © Sepah News/Handout/Document Iran/Corbis; p. 63: www.CartoonStock.com; p. 64: From *USA Today* (Academic Permission), 2/1/2012 Issue, © 2012 Gannett. All rights reserved. Used by permission and protected by the Copyright Laws of the United States. The printing, copying, redistribution, or retransmission of this Content without express written permission is prohibited; p. 68: © Randy Glasbergen; p. 71: AP/Wide World Photos; p. 74: (l) Illustration by Rob Corley in "The Fallacy Detective"; (m) Scott Olson/Getty Images; p. 77: Tim Boyle/Getty Images; p. 78: © Roz Chast/ The New Yorker Collection/www.cartoonbank.com; p. 82: (t-b) Courtesy of Google, Inc. Reprinted with permission; p. 84: Al Messerschmidt/Getty Images; p. 85: V.J. Lovero/Sports Illustrated/Getty Images; p. 87: William Warren, Americans for Limited Government, 2009; p. 90: (l-r) Robert Galbraith/Reuters/Landov; David Becker/Getty Images; Junko Kimura/Getty Images; p. 94: Chris Maddaloni/CQ Roll Call/Getty Images; p. 95: Designed by Sean Geng (www.designspasm.net); p. 97: Beth Hall/Bloomberg News via Getty Images; p. 99: The Ad Council; p. 103: AP/Wide World Photos; p. 107: City of Munster, Germany; p. 108: David Levene/eyevine/ Redux; p. 129: World History Archive/Alamy; p. 130: AP/Wide World Photos; p. 135: © Charles Barsotti/The New Yorker Collection/www.cartoonbank.com; p. 137: PhotoLink/Getty Images; p. 141: Design copyright © 2010 Steven Barrymore; p. 144: NEA; p. 147: Photo © Stephen Voss; p. 152: (l-r) mediablitzimages (UK) Limited/ Alamy; Alfred Eisenstaedt/Pix Inc./Time & Life Pictures/Getty Images; David R. Frazier Photolibrary, Inc./Alamy; p. 154: Pat Bagley/CagleCartoons.com; p. 157: PolitiFact.com; p. 159: The Arthritis Foundation and the Ad Council. Young and Rubicam, NY; p. 187: (l-r) Eightfish/Alamy; Frederick M. Brown/Getty Images; Bill

Wight/Getty Images; p. 189: Nate Beeler, politicalcartoons.com; p. 191: Jonathan Alcorn/Bloomberg via Getty Images; p. 193: www.cartoonstock.com; p. 194: © Discovr Music 2012; p. 199: Design by Shane Snow. Originally appeared on SixRevisions.com via Wix; p. 214: (l-r) Mario Tama/Getty Images; AP/Wide World Photos; Hulton Archive/Getty Images; p. 215: Jamie Sabau/Getty Images; p. 217: The Ad Council, Discovering Nature Campaign in partnership with the USDA Forest Service; p. 220: Gareth Cattermole/Getty Images for Netflix; p. 223: © Cho Taussig/Courtesy Everett Collection; p. 224: Chiaki Nozu/Wire Images/Getty Images; p. 226: Cover of *Fun Home: A Family Tragicomic* by Alison Bechdel. Jacket art copyright © 2006 by Alison Bechdel. Reprinted by permission of Houghton-Mifflin Harcourt Publishing Company. All rights reserved; p. 228: NHTSA; p. 242: (l-r) U.S. Fish and Wildlife Service via Bloomberg/Getty Images; Robyn Beck/AFP/Getty Images; Mario Tama/Getty Images; p. 243: Karen Kasmauski/National Geographic/ Getty Images; p. 246: Paresh Nath, www.politicalcartoons.com; p. 249: Ed Arno/The New Yorker Collection/www.cartoonbank.com; p. 258: Image Courtesy of PETA, www.peta2.com; p. 269: Dith Pran/The New York Times/Redux; p. 273: (l-r) Martin Bernetti/AFP/Getty Images; AP/Wide World Photos; Spencer Platt/Getty Images; p. 274: Dave Granlund, www.politicalcartoons.com; p. 277: Michael Williamson/The Washington Post/Getty Images; p. 278: Joshua Roberts/Bloomberg/Getty Images; p. 279: Ron Sanford/Photo Researchers; p. 281: Mike Keefe, www.politicalcartoons .com; p. 283: Andy Singer, www.politicalcartoons.com; p. 285: (l) Chris Goodney/ Bloomberg News/Getty Images; (r) Lucy Nicholson/Reuters/Landov; p. 289: AP/ Wide World Photos; p. 296: Courtesy of Manasi Deshpande; p. 309: (l-r) Andrew D. Bernstein/NBAE via Getty Images; Lynda Barry/*Drawn & Quarterly*; Justin Sullivan/ Getty Images; p. 310: *Sir Isaac Newton (1642–1723)* (oil on canvas) (detail) by Sir Godfrey Kneller (1646–1723), Academie des Sciences, Paris, France/Giraudon/The Bridgeman Art Library; p. 313: Photofest; p. 318: Miluckovich Atlanta Journal-Constitution; p. 320: © 1999 Aaron McGruder. Reprinted by permission of Universal Press Syndicate. All rights reserved; p. 321: www.cartoonstock.com; p. 326: (l-r) AP/ Wide World Photos; National Institute of Mental Health, National Institutes of Health, Department of Health and Human Services; AP/Wide World Photos; p. 328: Bernard Gotfryd/Getty Images; p. 329: Poster Design: Woody Pirtle; p. 330: Khaled Desoaki/AFP/Getty Images; p. 331: © 2012 Paul Davis; p. 332: © Carlos Barria/ Reuters/Corbis; p. 333: Creative Commons/Wikipedia; p. 335: NASA; p. 336: (l-r) Used with permission of the American Red Cross; U.S. Deparment of Homeland Security; TM/MC © Used under license from the Canadian Olympic Committee, 2012; p. 338: Dave Granlund/politicalcartoons.com; p. 340: Ron Kimball Stock; p. 342: Bureau of Labor Statistics; p. 344: (l-r) AP/Wide World Photos; Phoebe Yu/ Cornell University; AP/Wide World Photos; p. 349: AP/Wide World Photos; p. 351: Fox Broadcasting/Photofest, © and ™ Fox; p. 352: AP/Wide World Photos; p. 356: (t + b) © Frank Miller; p. 360: © Moonlight Social LLC, 2012. Photography by Mark Rocha; p. 362: Courtesy of Max Cougar Oswald; p. 364: (clockwise from top l) Wonkette.com; Courtesy of Talking Points Memo; Courtesy of HotAir.com; p. 367: (l-r) Jonathan Oiley/Getty Images; Ryan Collerd/The NY Times/Redux; Juan Castillo/ AFP/Getty Images; p. 370: © 2008 Tolpa Studios, Inc.; p. 371: Jonathan Oiley/Getty Images; p. 378: © 2012 ITHAKA. Reprinted courtesy of JSTOR. All rights reserved; pp. 389, 391: Nature Publishing Group; p. 397: John Ditchburn/INKCINCT Cartoons;

p. 401: Courtesy of Google, Inc. Reprinted with permission; p. 405: © George Price/ The New Yorker Collection/www.cartoonbank.com; p. 407: Ryan Collerd/The NY Times/Redux; p. 411: www.cartoonstock.com; p. 412: AP/Wide World Photos; p. 414: (l) Printed with permission from *Popular Science* ® Bonnier Corporation. Copyright 2009. All rights reserved; (r) Reprinted with permission from *American Journal of Physics*, vol. 6, no. 7, July 2008. American Association of Physics Teachers; p. 415: (clockwise from top l) NOAA; Discovery Channel; Courtesy of http://tornado chaser.net; p. 419: Joe Burbank/Orlando Sentinel/MCT via Getty Images; p. 421: Ed Fisher/The New Yorker Collection/www.cartoonbank.com; p. 425: Juan Castillo/ AFP/Getty Images; p. 428: Roz Chast/The New Yorker Collection/www.cartoon bank.com; p. 437: FBI; p. 438: Courtesy of the Massachusetts Horticultural Society; p. 441: Doonesbury Copyright © 2002 G. B. Trudeau. Reprinted with permission of Universal Press Syndicate. All rights reserved; p. 442: Creative Commons/ Wikipedia.

e-Pages

Gist. "Rise of the Mobile Workstyle." Courtesy of Gist.

Paula Lavigne. "What's Lurking in Your Stadium Food?" Courtesy of Outside the Lines/ESPN.com.

Jennifer Siebel Newsom. "Trailer for *Miss Representation*." Courtesy of Missrepresentation.org.

***New York Times* (with photos by Ruth Fremson).** "After Iraq, a New Chapter at College." From the *New York Times*, January 9, 2010. Copyright © 2010 The New York Times. All rights reserved. Used by permission and protected by the Copyright Laws of the United States. The printing, copying, redistribution, or retransmission of this Content without express written permission is prohibited.

***New York Times* (with photos by Jim Wilson).** "An Education, Over the Border and Under the Radar." From the *New York Times*, January 12, 2012. Copyright © 2012 The New York Times. All rights reserved. Used by permission and protected by the Copyright Laws of the United States. The printing, copying, redistribution, or retransmission of this Content without express written permission is prohibited.

Max Cougar Oswald. "Progress." Courtesy of Max Cougar Oswald.

Landon Thomas Jr. "Young and Unemployed." From the *New York Times*, February 15, 2012. Copyright © 2012 The New York Times. All rights reserved. Used by permission and protected by the Copyright Laws of the United States. The printing, copying, redistribution, or retransmission of this Content without express written permission is prohibited.

INDEX

Entries followed by a 🄴 symbol may be found online at
bedfordstmartins.com/everythingsanargument/epages.

Missing something? To access the e-Pages that accompany this text, visit **bedfordstmartins.com /everythingsanargument/epages**. Students who do not buy a new print book can purchase access to e-Pages at this site.

Inside the e-Pages for
Everything's an Argument

Barack Obama, *President Obama on the Death of Osama bin Laden* [speech]

Max Cougar Oswald, *Progress* [multimedia presentation]

Jennifer Siebel Newsom, *Trailer for* Miss Representation [documentary film trailer]

New York Times (with photos by Jim Wilson), *An Education, Over the Border and Under the Radar* [slide show]

Paula Lavigne, ESPN, *What's Lurking in Your Stadium Food?* [Web article]

Landon Thomas Jr., *Young and Unemployed* [video]

Gist, *Rise of the Mobile Workstyle* [infographic]

The White House, *The Buffett Rule* [video]

... and more!